CONTESTED STATES IN WAR AND LAW

Edited by
Janis Grzybowski, Giulia Prelz Oltramonti,
and Agatha Verdebout

BRISTOL
UNIVERSITY
PRESS

First published in Great Britain in 2025 by

Bristol University Press
University of Bristol
1–9 Old Park Hill
Bristol
BS2 8BB
UK
t: +44 (0)117 374 6645
e: bup-info@bristol.ac.uk

Details of international sales and distribution partners are available at bristoluniversitypress.co.uk

Editorial selection and matter © the editors; individual chapters © their respective authors 2025

The digital PDF and ePub versions of this title are available open access and distributed under the terms of the Creative Commons Attribution-NonCommercial-NoDerivatives 4.0 International licence (https://creativecommons.org/licenses/by-nc-nd/4.0/) which permits reproduction and distribution for non-commercial use without further permission provided the original work is attributed.

British Library Cataloguing in Publication Data
A catalogue record for this book is available from the British Library

ISBN 978-1-5292-4689-6 paperback
ISBN 978-1-5292-4690-2 ePub
ISBN 978-1-5292-4691-9 OA PDF

The right of Janis Grzybowski, Giulia Prelz Oltramonti, and Agatha Verdebout to be identified as editors of this work has been asserted by them in accordance with the Copyright, Designs and Patents Act 1988.

All rights reserved: no part of this publication may be reproduced, stored in a retrieval system, or transmitted in any form or by any means, electronic, mechanical, photocopying, recording, or otherwise without the prior permission of Bristol University Press.

Every reasonable effort has been made to obtain permission to reproduce copyrighted material. If, however, anyone knows of an oversight, please contact the publisher.

The statements and opinions contained within this publication are solely those of the editors and contributors and not of the University of Bristol or Bristol University Press. The University of Bristol and Bristol University Press disclaim responsibility for any injury to persons or property resulting from any material published in this publication.

Bristol University Press works to counter discrimination on grounds of gender, race, disability, age and sexuality.

Cover design: Qube Design
Front cover image: 123RF/alexkich

Contents

Notes on Contributors v
Acknowledgements x

Introduction: Contested States in War and Law 1
Janis Grzybowski, Giulia Prelz Oltramonti, and Agatha Verdebout

PART I   Ambiguous Status and the (Il)legal Use of Force
1 The *Ratione Personae* Element of the *Jus ad Bellum* and Taiwan   25
   Christian Henderson
2 The Use of Force Against Taiwan as a Contested State: 42
   An Analysis of Legality and Great-Power Politics
   Ming-chin Monique Chu
3 International Law and the Legitimation of State Violence   63
   in the Fourth Eelam War (2006–2009)
   Megan Price
4 Russia-Manufactured 'Secessions' in Ukraine: The Attempted   83
   Ambiguity of Status, Kosovo, and International Law
   Júlia Miklasová
5 Legitimization of Violence and State Dissolution in   105
   Nagorno-Karabakh: A Critical Legal Analysis
   Sheila Paylan

**PART II   Vulnerability and Agency on the Ground: People
and Institutions Navigating War and Law**
6 Contested Statehood, Ambiguities and Volatility: 129
   The Effects of Lawfare and Warfare in the Western
   Sahara Conflict
   Irene Fernández-Molina
7 Hardening Ceasefire Lines in Protracted Secessionist   151
   Conflicts: From the Negotiating Table and International
   Law to Realities on the Ground in the Case of the
   Abkhaz-Georgian War
   Giulia Prelz Oltramonti and Gaëlle Le Pavic

| 8 | Sovereign Experimentation by Separatist Insurgencies: A Performative Perspective
Bart Klem | 172 |

PART III Contesting and Constructing States at International Courts

| 9 | Contested States Framed by the European Court of Human Rights
Anne Lagerwall | 195 |
| 10 | Hide and Seek: Bracketing and Projecting the States of Kosovo and Palestine at International Courts
Janis Grzybowski | 212 |

PART IV Conclusions

11	Four Normative Positions on the Contestation of Statehood in War and Law *Bruno Coppieters*	235
12	Speculative Legalities and the Ambiguities of Contested States *Rebecca Bryant*	249
13	The Melancholy Statehood *Martti Koskenniemi*	258

| Index | | 265 |

Notes on Contributors

Rebecca Bryant is Professor and holder of the Chair in Cultural Anthropology at Utrecht University. Bryant is an anthropologist of politics and law focusing on the ethnography of the state, particularly ethnic conflict and displacement, border practices, post-conflict reconciliation, and contested sovereignty on both sides of the Cyprus Green Line and in Turkey. She has long-term research interests in temporality, memory, and historical reconciliation, and has investigated these topics through research in Cyprus and Turkey. For the past decade, she has researched everyday life in unrecognized states, adding to her Cyprus research preliminary investigations in Abkhazia. Her most recent works include *The Anthropology of the Future* (Cambridge, 2019) with Daniel M. Knight; *Sovereignty Suspended: Building the So-Called State* (Pennsylvania, 2020) with Mete Hatay, and *The Everyday Lives of Sovereignty: Political Imagination Beyond the State* (Cornell, 2021), co-edited with Madeleine Reeves. Her latest work, *Lives in Limbo: Syrian Youth in Turkey* (with Amal Abdalla, Maissam Nimer, and Ayşen Üstübici), was published in 2023 with Berghahn Books.

Ming-chin Monique Chu is a lecturer in Chinese Politics in the Department of Politics and International Relations at the University of Southampton. Her research interests include the impact of globalization on security with reference to semiconductors, the concept and practice of sovereignty, emerging technologies and great power rivalry, and Cross-Strait relations. Her first monograph, *The East Asian Computer Chip War* (Routledge, 2013), has been widely cited as the authoritative work on the geopolitics of semiconductors. Her other scholarly research has been published in *The China Quarterly*, *The Journal of Strategic Studies*, and *China Perspectives*. She is currently working on her second monograph on the fragmented sovereignty on China's peripheries, including Taiwan, Hong Kong, and Tibet. She obtained MPhil and PhD degrees in international relations from the University of Cambridge.

Bruno Coppieters is Emeritus Professor at the Department of Political Science at the Vrije Universiteit Brussel (Free University of Brussels). His published works deal with federalism, the ethics of war and secession, and conflicts over sovereignty in the Caucasus and the Balkans. He co-edited the book *Contextualizing Secession: Normative Studies in Comparative Perspective* (Oxford University Press, 2003) and *Moral Constraints on War: Principles and Cases* (3rd edn) (Lexington Books, 2020).

Irene Fernández-Molina is a senior lecturer in international relations at the University of Exeter. Her research deals with international relations of the Global South, foreign policy, conflicts, and constructivist IR theory, with a regional focus on North Africa as well as EU foreign policy and Euro-Mediterranean relations. Her recent projects address the diplomatic practices of contested states and the international politics of recognition in the context of frozen conflicts and civil wars. Her research has been published in journals such as *International Affairs*, *International Studies Review*, *Review of International Studies*, *International Political Sociology*, *Global Studies Quarterly*, *Journal of Intervention and Statebuilding*, *Nationalities Papers*, and *Mediterranean Politics*. She is also the author of *Moroccan Foreign Policy under Mohammed VI, 1999–2014* (Routledge, 2016).

Janis Grzybowski is currently Jean Monnet Fellow at the Robert Schuman Center for Advanced Studies at the European University Institute (EUI) in Florence and Associate Professor of Political Science/International Relations at ESPOL at the Université Catholique de Lille, France. He holds a PhD from the Geneva Graduate Institute (IHEID). His research focuses on state creation, international theory, and the politics of international law. He is co-editor, with Hannes Černy, of *Variations on Sovereignty: Contestations and Transformations from around the World* (Routledge, 2023) and his articles have appeared in the *Review of International Studies*, *International Theory*, *International Relations*, *Geopolitics*, and the *European Journal of International Law*, among others.

Christian Henderson is currently Professor of International Law at the University of Sussex, a position he has held since 2015. Prior to this he was a senior lecturer in law at the University of Liverpool and obtained his PhD from the University of Nottingham. His research and teaching interests are in public international law, in particular international law governing the use of force, collective security, and international humanitarian law. He is the former co-editor-in-chief of the *Journal on the Use of Force and International Law*, a general editor of the *Journal of International Humanitarian Legal Studies*, a member of the International Law Association Committee on the Use of Force, and on the Advisory Council for the Institute for International Peace and Security Law (University of Cologne, Germany).

Bart Klem is Associate Professor in Peace and Development Research at the School of Global Studies, Gothenburg University. He does fieldwork-based research on civil war, post-war transition, contested sovereignty, separatist politics, and *de facto* states. He mainly writes about Sri Lanka and Cyprus. In 2024, he published *Performing Sovereign Aspirations: Tamil Insurgency and Postwar Transition in Sri Lanka* (Cambridge University Press, 2024). This monograph adopts a performative perspective on the frictions and contradictions around the Tamil nationalist movement in Sri Lanka. He has also edited special issues on legal identity and citizenship in unrecognized states (*Citizenship Studies*, 2024) and on public authority and violent conflict (*Modern Asian Studies*, 2018).

Martti Koskenniemi is a leading critical scholar in the theory and history of international law. His works notably include *From Apology to Utopia: the Structure of International Legal Argument* (Cambridge University Press, 2005), *The Gentle Civilizer of Nations: the Rise and Fall of International Law, 1870–1960* (Cambridge University Press, 2001) and *To the Uttermost Parts of the Earth: Legal Imagination and Political Power 1300–1870* (Cambridge University Press, 2021). He has held visiting professorships at many of the world's leading universities, including Cambridge University, the LSE, NYU and Harvard University. He is a corresponding fellow of the British Academy and a member of American Academy of Arts and Sciences.

Anne Lagerwall is Professor of International Law at the Université libre de Bruxelles. She pursues her research on issues relating to international peace and security, including questions of interpretation of norms such as the prohibition to use force, the duty not to recognize unlawful situations, the protection of human rights in occupied territories or the prosecution of crimes committed by States agents entitled to immunities. She is the author of *Le principe ex injuria jus non oritur en droit international* (2016) and co-author of *A Critical Introduction to International Law* (2024, 2nd ed, with Olivier Corten, François Dubuisson and Vaios Koutroulis). She is the editor-in-chief of the *Belgian Review of International Law* (with Olivier Corten) and the editor of the book reviews for the *European Journal of International Law* (with Doreen Lustig).

Gaëlle Le Pavic is an associate researcher at the United Nations University (CRIS) and at Ghent University, where she completed her PhD with a thesis titled 'Social Services within and across Contested Border: Insights from Transnistria, Abkhazia and Samegrelo'. Her research interests include contested borders, knowledge production, and civil society organizations. Currently, Gaëlle holds a fellowship at the Leibniz Institute for Regional Geography (IfL) in Leipzig, where she works on the production of space in the context of the Georgian–Abkhazian case. Before that, Gaëlle worked for the College of Europe in Belgium, the French diplomatic services in Russia and Croatia and interned in the EU delegations to Ukraine and Moldova.

Júlia Miklasová is a postdoctoral researcher at the Academy for European Human Rights Protection at the University of Cologne, Germany. She obtained her PhD degree (summa cum laude avec les félicitations du jury) from the Graduate Institute Geneva (IHEID). Her monograph, *Secession in International Law with a Special Reference to the Post-Soviet Space*, was published by Brill in 2024. Júlia was previously a visiting researcher at the Lauterpacht Centre for International Law, University of Cambridge, a junior visiting fellow at the Institute for Human Sciences (IWM) in Vienna, a research assistant at the Global Migration Centre in Geneva and a legal assistant to a member of the UN International Law Commission (ILC) in Geneva.

Sheila Paylan is a human rights lawyer and war crimes investigator with more than 15 years of experience advising the United Nations on international legal issues across countries and regions. Now based in Yerevan, she frequently consults for various international organizations, NGOs, think tanks, and governments. She holds a BSc in Psychology and a BCL/JD from McGill University, along with an LLM specializing in public international law from the University of London.

Giulia Prelz Oltramonti is a research fellow for the Centre for Security and Defense Studies (CSDS), within the Royal Higher Institute for Defence, in Brussels, and a research fellow at the REPI, Université libre de Bruxelles (ULB). Before joining the CSDS in February 2025, she was Associate Professor in International Relations at ESPOL, Université Catholique de Lille, and a lecturer at the ULB and Université Catholique de Louvain. Her research focuses on security issues in the post-Soviet area, and she has published on issues related to political economies of conflict in the Caucasus, processes of border and boundary formation in the European neighbourhood, the viability of contested states, and secessionist entities' alternative diplomatic practices.

Megan Price is a lecturer in international relations at the University of Western Australia. Her research interests include international legitimacy, civil war, IHL, and the politics of recognition. She explores many of these themes in her monograph, *International Legitimacy and the Domestic Use of Force: a New Theoretical Framework* (Routledge, 2022). Prior to joining the University of Western Australia in 2025, Megan was a postdoctoral research associate at the University of Sheffield. She completed her PhD at the University of Queensland, Australia.

Agatha Verdebout is a senior researcher at the Groupe de recherche et d'information sur la paix et la sécurité (GRIP) and associate member of the Center for International Law (CDI) of the Université Libre de Bruxelles

(ULB). She studied law as well as international relations and holds a PhD in public international law from the ULB (2017). The monograph based on her thesis, 'Rewriting Histories of the Use of Force', was published with Cambridge University Press in 2021. Before joining GRIP in May 2022, she was Associate Professor of Public International Law at ESPOL, Université Catholique de Lille. Her research focuses on the law on the prohibition of the use of force, critical theories of international law, and the politics of international law.

Acknowledgements

This book is the product of a collaboration that started when the three of us were colleagues at the European School of Political and Social Sciences (ESPOL) at Lille Catholic University. Although we are steeped in different fields and disciplines, we shared a concern with the challenge and precarity of 'contested states' and a wish to illuminate the thorny dilemmas that conflicts over their status pose. We came to regularly discuss contested states from our different vantage points, drawing on international relations (IR) and theory, area studies and field research, and international law and history. The discussions led to a project on 'contested states in war and law' for which we obtained a small budget, to workshops with researchers who shared our interest, and eventually to this book. We are most grateful for this collaboration and, in addition to the amazing scholars assembled in the volume, we wish to thank several others who helped us bring the project to this conclusion.

We would like to thank the Commission de recherche de l'Université Catholique de Lille (Fonds fédératifs) and ESPOL-Lab for financial support through the Ambroise and Inès funding schemes that allowed us to organize an initial workshop in Lille and to publish the book in Open Access. Our thanks go, in particular, to Nicolas Vaillant, Aurélie Seiler, and Sabine Weiland for endorsing and selecting our project for support. We are also grateful to Axel Gougelet and Zixuan Gou for their logistical assistance, as well as Natalia Tejero Rivas for her eager participation as research assistant. Our discussions over the years also involved many colleagues who did not contribute chapters to the edited volume, but nevertheless shaped it indirectly through inspirations along the way. These notably include Michelle Burgis-Kasthala, Anita Khachaturova, Aude Merlin, Marika Sosnowski, and Cindy Wittke. We also thank the anonymous reviewers for their insightful comments and suggestions. Finally, we truly appreciate the enthusiasm and guidance by Stephen Wenham and Zoë Forbes at Bristol University Press; it was a pleasure to work with them on this volume.

Janis, Giulia, and Agatha

Introduction: Contested States in War and Law

Janis Grzybowski, Giulia Prelz Oltramonti, and Agatha Verdebout

On the morning of 27 September 2020, shelling by Azerbaijani armed forces at the line of contact with the breakaway region of Nagorno-Karabakh heralded the beginning of an offensive to take control of the region that had enjoyed – with Armenian support – *de facto* autonomy since the early 1990s. Foreign governments and the United Nations condemned the violence and called for a peaceful resolution, without contesting that Nagorno-Karabakh was part of Azerbaijan's territory and, therefore, under its sovereignty (GA Res. 62/243, 25 April 2008). Three years later, a renewed offensive led, on 19 September 2023, to the surrender of the self-proclaimed Republic of Artsakh, which declared its dissolution for 1 January 2024, and its absorption into Azerbaijan. Former officials of Nagorno-Karabakh were arrested and prosecuted on charges of separatism and terrorism, among others. Three decades into its existence, the republic is no more. Depending on one's perspective, the war ended a long-standing rebellion and occupation, or it ushered in a 'state death' (Fazal 2011) of a state unrecognized as such.

The war over Nagorno-Karabakh is not the only conflict in which contested claims to sovereignty and territory have recently turned, or were turned, into manifest violence. Other notable cases include the 2021 skirmishes between Algeria and Morocco over Western Sahara, the 2022 Russian invasion of Ukraine in support of the so-called 'People's Republics' of Donetsk and Luhansk in eastern Ukraine, and the Israeli military campaign against the Palestinian Hamas in Gaza in response to the group's attack on Israel on 7 October 2023. In other simmering conflicts over statehood around the world, from Taiwan to Kosovo to Somaliland, the use of force has been threatened, sometimes drawing in third states as well. Meanwhile, where state claims clash and overlap, populations are caught up in-between, excluded, and exposed.

Despite their differences, for instance between peoples with a right to self-determination, local rebel governors, and externally created entities, all contested states are characterized by a particular ambiguity, vulnerability, and – constrained – agency due to their contested status.[1] From a majority viewpoint in international law and diplomacy, most contested states do not constitute proper states, but they often display key 'elements of statehood', enjoy a right to become a state, or are regarded as states by particular third parties. Foreign governments sometimes establish tacit relations with them, fostering 'engagement without recognition' (Berg and Ker Lindsay 2020), even while denying them formal diplomatic relations (Ker-Lindsay 2012). As such, '*de facto*' (Pegg 1998; Bahcheli et al 2004), 'unrecognized' (Caspersen 2012), partially recognized, or, most generally, 'contested states' (Geldenhuys 2009; Kursani 2021) straddle the line between international and non-international status in ways that allow third parties to hold diverging views on whether or not they should be regarded as states, generally or for specific purposes, practically or formally. Whatever position one takes towards them, contested states probe and blur the conventional distinctions between state and non-state, international and domestic, and war and peace, with important consequences.

The contestation of state status is not just political rhetoric. It reflects actual conflicts over the rule and representation of particular territories, often backed up by force and varying degrees of institutionalization on the ground; and it also shows that international law can be used, if with varying degrees of success, to justify or reject conflicting claims. Rather than being a mere tool of either substantive regulation or superficial rhetoric, international law is inherently intertwined with assumptions and challenges of statehood and sovereignty. Indeed, as David French (2013: 1) puts it, '[i]t is in statehood that one seeks to find a seamless amalgam of legal doctrine and social reality'. If so, then cases of overlapping claims raise thorny questions that point beyond both determinist legal interpretations and dismissive realist views focused on power politics alone. Rights and rules matter for the constitution of states, from self-determination and self-defence to deep-seated assumptions about exclusive sovereignty, people, and territory. But they must be applied and interpreted, which allows opposed arguments to vie for acceptance (Kennedy 1987; Koskenniemi 2005). Where claims to sovereignty clash, the law does not retreat; some claims are often more plausible or find wider acceptance than others. But the law becomes evidently political when interpretations vary and collide. To grasp these moments and their repercussions, including for the authorization and

---

[1] There is no consensus, among actors on the ground, on terminology; on the contrary, the use of 'state', together with the qualifiers of '*de facto*', 'contested', or 'parent', 'patron', or 'occupying' is a matter of fierce debate that is mostly seen as indissolubly linked to the existence and security of those same actors, in line with the *ambiguity* that characterizes them.

regulation of violence, it is helpful to go beyond trying to settle whether certain entities 'really' are states, legally or sociologically, and to instead explore the *effects* of claiming and contesting states, in international law, politics, and everyday life alike.

Three dimensions play a particularly important role for understanding contested states in war and law and guide the analysis in this volume. First, to appreciate the extent to which statehood can be inherently *ambiguous* when contested, it is important to revisit the basic assumptions and strategies of attributing statehood, bypassing the clichés of statehood as either a matter of objective law or brute fact. Neither recognition doctrines, nor rights to self-determination, nor the prohibition of the use of force in facilitating state creation are as determinate as it might seem, and it is in the intricate contradictions that conflicting views on statehood are usually grounded. Moreover, due to the central role that statehood and sovereignty still play in international law and diplomacy, the ambiguity of contested states reverberates across various legal regimes, from the law of the use of force to international humanitarian and human rights law. It therefore cannot be easily shunned, and it is across different sites of international law that status claims play out, and in which they are rejected, circumvented, or adapted.

Second, where claims to statehood are contested, the entities and populations thus affected are rendered particularly *vulnerable*. The attribution of statehood matters because the 'law of sharp distinctions' (Kennedy 2007) operates with dichotomies that determine applicable rights and rules, in theory and practice, including for the legality of the use of force, classification of armed conflicts, status of combatants and migrants, and access to international courts, among others. Contested states and their populations are therefore often *made* vulnerable by the comparison to, and placement *within*, those uncontested states that they have challenged. Ceasefire lines lack the international guarantees of recognized borders, internal armed conflicts are less regulated than international ones, and entities other than states have, *a priori*, no right to self-defence, territorial integrity, or non-interference, as recently illustrated by the fate of Nagorno-Karabakh. Focusing on vulnerabilities helps to reflect on how international law not only limits but also enables war and violence, and how it is used and experienced in different contexts in practice, from ceasefire lines to international courts. This vulnerability is not a function of legal assumptions and assessments alone, but emerges in interaction with diplomatic strategies, geopolitical constellations, domestic politics, etc.

Finally, the conditions of ambiguity and vulnerability not only foreclose but also engender new spaces for *agency*, whether by contested state authorities, ordinary people, or – for that matter – parent states and third parties. Depending on their positions, perspectives, and access, these actors navigate this environment in ways that help them cope with, challenge, or exploit the blurring of conventional distinctions and legal regimes. What is already in flux can also be more easily moved. From trade across the porous ceasefire line between Abkhazia and Georgia to the performance of Tamil Tiger sovereignty in Sri Lankan court rooms and at the United Nations, and from Russia's self-determination claims in Ukraine to Palestine's case at the International Criminal Court (ICC), conflicts involving contested states are characterized by creative strategies to operate in the grey zone of international law, politics, and war. International courts, too, are then confronted with situations involving contested states and must respond to, or circumvent, tricky status questions for their own purposes of adjudication.

In focusing on contested states at the intersections of war, law, and politics, the volume's contributions investigate their predicament from different angles, drawing on perspectives from international law, international relations (IR), area studies, and anthropology. The remainder of this introduction outlines the general ambiguity, vulnerability, and constrained agency of contested states in more detail. While in practice all these dimensions are intertwined, different chapters engage with and combine them in function of their own specific analyses. At the end, we briefly introduce the individual chapters that, each in their own way, explore various contested states in war and law, thereby shedding light on some of the most intricate conflicts around the world today.

Ambiguous status: claiming and contesting states in international law and politics

In both international law and IR scholarship, the proliferation of secessionist entities in the 1990s, especially but not exclusively in the wake of the Soviet and Yugoslav dissolutions and subsequent conflicts, prompted interest in old and new questions of state creation. While in IR the predicament of contested states was highlighted as an anomaly of international politics that resulted from a mismatch between dominant norms and realities on the ground (Pegg 1998; Lynch 2004; Geldenhuys 2009; Caspersen 2012), most studies in international law sought to determine the conditions under which these entities would have a claim to statehood and formal independence, or not, precipitating debates over self-determination beyond decolonization, the criteria of territory, population, government, and the capacity to enter into relations with other states, as stipulated in the Montevideo Convention on the Rights and Duties of States (1933), and questions of secession, third party intervention, and recognition more generally (Degan 1999; Kohen 1997; Tancredi 1998; Grant 1999; Crawford 2006; Wilson 2009; Farley 2010).

Debates over state creation, secession, and recognized status not only concern cases of contested states but are relevant for the international – legal – order more generally. Despite changes in international law, states and sovereignty have remained crucial for attributing fundamental rights, obligations, responsibility, and jurisdiction. State status is in turn central for entities to become members of an international organization, act before international courts and tribunals, accede to treaties, enjoy the guarantees of the principles of non-intervention and of the prohibition of the use of force (*jus ad bellum*), or yet to determine the rules that will apply in case of armed conflict (*jus in bello*). International law is still deeply tied up with the 'state vs non-state' distinction (Cutler 2001; Bianchi 2011), although debates about the attribution of legal obligations to non-state actors reveal apparent 'cracks' (Vidmar 2021) in the international legal order.

Yet while the determination of states under international law is therefore held to be of utmost importance, it remains fraught with difficulties and controversies that still echo the age-old debate between so-called 'declaratory' and 'constitutive' theories of recognition (Institut de Droit International 1936; Grant 1999; Talmon 2004; Crawford 2006). According to the first, the existence of a state is a matter of fact, not recognition (Chen 1951). An entity is a state under international law as soon as its government exercises effective authority over a specific territory and a permanent population. Thus, if contested states are thought to fulfil the criteria laid down in the Montevideo Convention (Pegg 1998; Casperson 2012), the lack of recognition by other states should not *per se* exclude them from state status (Chen 1951). By contrast, the constitutive theory argues that an entity becomes a state for purposes of international law only upon its recognition as such (Oppenheim 1905).

Both approaches suffer from important inconsistencies (Koskenniemi 2005: 272–282; Crawford 2006; Vidmar 2013; Wyler 2013; Grzybowski 2017). Problems with the 'declaratory theory' include that the observation of facts on the ground is neither straightforward nor sufficient for the legal establishment of statehood, that it says nothing about who has the right to assess these facts and other criteria of state creation, and that, without recognition, new states would be severely hampered in practice, and thus perhaps not functional states after all (Kelsen 1941; Lauterpacht 1947; Crawford 2006). The 'constitutive theory', for its part, has been criticized because it abstracts from facts on the ground, because it is unclear how many states would need to recognize an entity for it to reach a particular threshold of statehood, and because the notion that recognition alone determines statehood essentially leaves assessments of state creation to the discretion of third states. It has consequently been rejected as both overtly political (Crawford 2006) and ineffective on the ground (Kunz 1950).

Different attempts to reconcile the two views (for example, Kelsen 1941; Lauterpacht 1947; Schoiswohl 2004; Crawford 2006) have accentuated rather than resolved their contradictions (Grzybowski 2017). At least in theory, then, it is unclear whether or when entities that claim to be states but remain widely unrecognized should be treated as states. Although formal recognition is widely used in diplomatic and legal practice to identify states, its basis in international law is questionable. As such, international law provides argumentative space for contesting and promoting claims to statehood, even against prevailing reductions to recognition (Koskenniemi 2005; Grzybowski 2017; 2019).

Today, the evolution of international law has arguably somewhat eclipsed the role of both recognition and effectiveness, in favour of rights and regulations of state creation held to be genuinely legal (Crawford 2006). Since the 1960s, self-determination, in particular, has become an important vehicle for granting and restricting rights to independence, and thereby regulating state creation. According to Article 7 of UN General Assembly (UNGA) Resolution 3314 – adopted in 1974 in the wake of the 1960 UNGA Resolutions 1514 and 1541, both hallmarks of decolonization – only peoples living under colonial domination, foreign occupation, or under a racist regime are granted the right to external self-determination and, thus, independence. Some contested states today, notably Palestine and Western Sahara, meet these formal criteria in the traditional interpretation, but most do not. Yet even a certified right to independence, as enjoyed by Palestine and Western Sahara, does not translate into automatic state status (Crawford 2006). Furthermore, the criteria and their application have also been challenged. From the 1971 secession of Bangladesh from Pakistan to the dissolutions of the USSR and Yugoslavia in 1990s to the later recognition of Kosovo, the question which community constituted a 'people' with a right to independent statehood has been contested time and again (Emerson 1971; Berman 1988; Koskenniemi 1994b; Milanović and Wood 2015). The so-called 'saltwater test', which restricts decolonization to overseas territories, does not account for other forms of colonization and oppression, leading some to suggest that the law of self-determination might be outdated (Simpson 1996; Knop 2002). Some scholars have also argued that populations submitted to widespread and systematic violations of their human rights should be granted an exceptional right to so-called 'remedial secession' (Fisher 2016; Summers 2010; Laurinavičiūtė and Biekša 2015). Although this proposition has been widely rejected, debates about extraordinary rights to self-determination, from Bangladesh to Kosovo, haunt the discourse of state creation and add further to its ambiguity. Not only states, but the status of 'peoples' with a right to self-determination, too, is contestable (Berman 1988; Koskenniemi 1994b).

Another important dimension of the regulation of state creation under international law is the prohibition of the illegal use of force by third states. Ever since the rejection of the State of Manchukuo set up by Japan in north-eastern China in 1932, the establishment of 'puppet states' has widely been deemed illegal and invalid (Crawford 2006: 78–83; Lagerwall 2016). However, since the denial of self-determination to a people with a designated right to independence also constitutes a violation of international law, third states might use force to assist a people or national movement in its struggle for self-determination (UNGA Resolution 2625). This exception can beget further ambiguity. As cases such as Indian military assistance to East Pakistan and Turkish intervention on behalf of Turkish Cypriots in the 1970s illustrate, differences of opinion about the status and rights of particular peoples or communities, and 'exceptional' circumstances, can lead to different notions of whether the use of force by a third state to support them is justified or illegal. How such conflicts turn out also depends on which interpretation becomes eventually accepted (Crawford 2006: 131–134). While Indian assistance to Bangladesh was construed as justified, mainly in view of the mass atrocities committed by Pakistani forces, Turkish intervention was condemned, as reflected in the recognition of Bangladesh and the lack of recognition for the Turkish Republic of Northern Cyprus (TRNC), respectively.[2] More recently, from South Ossetia to Nagorno-Karabakh and the Donbass Republics, the presence of foreign troops has been presented as either a fundamental violation of the parent state's sovereignty or – if only by the patron states of the contested regions and authorities – as justified assistance to self-determination.

Questions of the legality of state creation, self-determination, and the use of force have complicated assessments of statehood, but they have not arrested the controversies. The inherent contradictions of the concept of statehood in international law show that the ambiguity runs deep, and for good reasons. A state is not merely a legal fiction, nor can it be reduced to the recognition of third states; but it is also 'not a fact in the sense that a chair is a fact' (Crawford 2006: 5). Sovereignty and statehood are 'social constructs' (Koskenniemi 1994a; Biersteker and Weber 1996) co-constituted by claims and control on the ground, in diplomatic engagements, and in applications of international law (Weber 1998; Aalberts 2012; Grzybowski and Koskenniemi 2015; Černy and Grzybowski 2023). Clearly, recognitions by third states are powerful, and often all too political (Sterio 2012; Coggins 2014). Yet it is equally clear that there is more to statehood. Therefore, instead of simply and circularly reaffirming the dominant position that contested states are no states, it is worth taking the ambiguity of statehood in fact and in law seriously, and to engage with the politics of claiming and contesting states in practice.

---

[2] On the TRNC, see also Leigh 1990; Bryant and Hatay 2011; 2020.

Vulnerability in law and war: contested states and populations in the crossfire

Because statehood has a central position in international law and across different legal regimes, its attribution to some entities and contestation of others can have far-reaching consequences, including for the prohibition, limitation, and authorization of violence.

As per the wording of the UN Charter (1945), the rules on the right to use armed force apply in 'international relations', understood as the relations between states (Art. 2 (4) UN Charter). Based on these premises, most international lawyers argue that the use of armed force by the parent state to re-establish its sovereignty over *de facto* independent territories is not forbidden under international law (Gray 2018; Corten 2021). Because these territories are generally considered to be within the internationally recognized border of their parent state, they consider it to be an internal affair and one that *jus ad bellum* does not govern. While exceptions are sometimes suggested – for instance, Crawford (2006: 221) maintains that, in the case of Taiwan, there is 'a cross-Strait boundary for the purposes of the use of force' (2006: 221) and the use of force by China would thus be illegal (see also Ediger 2018) – the general assumption under international law is that contested states do not enjoy the guarantee of existence and other rights of formal states (see also Chan 2009).

Consequently, the principle of self-defence, which includes the right to seek outside help to resist an armed attack, does not apply either. The contested state facing violent crackdown from the government of the internationally recognized parent state cannot call on its patron, or more generally third parties, for assistance. Providing such assistance, whether by direct or indirect intervention (for example, by providing weapons) constitutes a violation of the parent state's sovereignty and territorial integrity and, therefore, of the prohibition of the use of force. If the third state exercises 'effective control' over the secessionist entity, it can even be considered as having committed an act of aggression that could warrant the use of force by the parent state (Resolution 3314, Art. 3 (g)) and others supporting it in its self-defence. For instance, Azerbaijan's offensive against Nagorno-Karabakh in 2020 did not only target the *de facto* authorities of Stepanakert but also Armenia, whom the government of Azerbaijan accused of occupying the region and surrounding districts since 1994.[3] The majority view has been that Baku's use of force could be regarded as an exercise of

---

[3] Before 2008, a few Security Council resolutions confirmed this position, setting forth that Armenia had troops around Nagorno-Karabakh on Azerbaijani territory; all the while, Nagorno-Karabakh professed its independence from Armenia, denying Armenian military involvement.

self-defence against Yerevan's occupation and was, therefore, legal (Akande and Tzanakopoulos 2021).

Due to this exposure to armed violence, others argue that the dominant position is too extreme (Ruys and Rodriguez Silvestre 2021a; 2021b) and contend that occupation, when it lasted for a certain period of time, cannot be regarded as a continuous act of aggression warranting the use of force in self-defence. In this perspective, the offensive by Azerbaijan to claim the Armenian-supported territory of Nagorno-Karabakh was illegal. Yet this position comes with its own drawbacks. Beyond the cases of Nagorno-Karabakh, one may wonder to what extent these purported exceptions would not bar states like Cyprus, Georgia, and Ukraine from re-establishing their sovereignty over Northern Cyprus, Abkhazia and South Ossetia, or the Donbass Republics and Crimea respectively, whose creation and/or persistence was made possible by what most deem illegal uses of force by a patron state, in these cases Turkey and Russia.[4] In other words, while they surely alleviate some of the vulnerabilities that contested states at war face, exceptions also risk consecrating the politics of force. They create new vulnerabilities, not only for sovereign and recognized states but also for a legal system that was established for the purpose of guaranteeing the rule of law and peace among states (Verdebout 2021).

Since the application of the prohibition of the use of force is rarely extended to any contested states in practice, international law tends to put them in a precarious position that can be politically exploited, especially by their parent state. Most notoriously, renewed 'war', if unrecognized as such, can have fatal consequences for the contested states themselves, as illustrated by the destruction of the Chechen Republic of Ichkeria in Russia in the early 2000s (Politkovskaya 2007), the Serbian Republic in the Croatian Krajina in 1995 (Kolstø and Paukovic 2014), the Tamil Eelam statelet in Sri Lanka in 2009 (Klem and Maunaguru 2017) and, most recently, Nagorno-Karabakh. Precisely because they are threatened by extinction, secessionists often argue their case legally and show a willingness to respect various rules of international law voluntarily (Fazal 2018). At the same time, many contested states prepare for the worst and remain ready for war. In fact, many exist and persist only thanks to their military success on the ground (Dembinska and Campana 2017; Florea 2017). This typically leads to significant military expenditures, mostly on grey and black markets, the militarization of society,

---

[4] On contested states and *jus ad bellum*, see Henderson 2013. On aggression against them as a potential international crime, see Wills 2012. On the legal regulation of violence and the ambiguous status of *de facto* regimes, emergent states, and non-state actors striving for self-determination more generally, see also Frowein 1968, van Essen 2012, and Hadden 2021.

and opportunities for external actors to step in as seeming security providers (Kolstø 2006; Berg and Mölder 2012; Beacháin et al 2016). The dilemma is that, by restricting status to widely accepted states, violence against their breakaway 'states' is legally justified, but extending the protection to contested states would authorize *their* use of force for 'self-defence', and perhaps that of third states 'assisting' them. Either way, the law is not simply opposed to violence, but also enables it (Kennedy 2007).

Vulnerability concerns not only the contested states as entities, but also the individuals – fighters and civilians – who become caught up in wars. The lack of state status has notably an impact on the application of *jus in bello* – that is, international humanitarian law (IHL), which makes a distinction between international armed conflicts (IACs) and non-international armed conflicts (NIACs) (see Moir 2002; Cullen 2010). The former are understood as conflicts opposing at least two sovereign states, while the latter are defined as armed clashes between a state and one or more non-state armed groups, or between non-state armed groups. The rules that apply in IACs and NIACs are different and wars opposing *de facto* independent entities to their parent states, when no third party is involved, are generally considered as falling in the latter category (Akande 2012), which offers less protection. One major difference lies in the right of combatants to be granted a prisoner of war status when captured by the enemy. Indeed, the 1949 Geneva Convention (III) relative to the Treatment of Prisoners of War only applies in IACs (Art. 2). This status comes with safeguards and guarantees; in particular, prisoners of war cannot be prosecuted for participating in hostilities and for the lawful acts of war that they may have carried out – such as attacking and killing soldiers of enemy forces. By contrast, fighters from non-state armed groups in NIACs are considered unlawful combatants and, as a result, can be prosecuted for these same acts as common-law criminals. As a matter of illustration, the leaders of Nagorno-Karabakh, who were forced to surrender following the 2023 crackdown, are now facing charges of separatism, terrorism, and creating an illegal armed organization.

Moreover, in conflicts involving contested states, civilians are often caught in the crossfire, expelled from their homes, and forced to struggle for their rights. State status matters when civilians are displaced: if they cross an international border, they can claim the status of refugees, which gives them protection in international law under the 1951 Geneva Convention and the 1967 Protocol Relating to the Status of Refugees. However, when civilians are displaced within their country of origin, they fall under the responsibility of the state that they are in, which is more loosely regulated by a set of Guiding Principles on Internal Displacement (OCHA 1998). War and violence have affected the demographic composition of most contested, parent, and (often) patron states, with mass displacement taking place in the majority of cases. These displacements have created winners and losers within and outside the contested states. The lack of conflict resolution has also shaped the economies of both parent states and contested states, as well as the strategies of the inhabitants of the areas affected by war and separatism and resource allocation in situations of legal uncertainty (King 2001; Korf 2004; Baumann et al. 2015; Prelz Oltramonti 2015; Phillips 2020; Merlin 2021).

In contrast to most of the separatist *de facto* states discussed, some contested states and their populations are in a different legal situation and benefit from limited standing because they have a widely agreed right to external self-determination. This concerns most prominently Palestine and Western Sahara. They enjoy protections that do not extend to unrecognized or otherwise contested states that are construed as secessionist movements. Not only is the use of force against these entities forbidden when they seek to exercise their right to self-determination, but third states can (and to some extent should) help them to achieve independence (GA Resolution 1514, para. 4; GA Resolution 2625, Principle 1, para. 8). Likewise, the individuals who fight on their behalf are to be considered as lawful combatants and granted all associated protections (Additional Protocol (I) to the Geneva Conventions, Art. 1 (4)) that apply in IACs generally.

In these cases, the denial of self-determination occurs largely *against* prevailing views of international law, enabled by stark local power disparities, but also by international dynamics of geopolitics and diplomacy. If this shows how power politics matter, not only for bending but also for breaking rules, it again does not mean that the law simply retreats. Both Palestine and Western Sahara are widely considered to be under lasting foreign occupations that prevent them from realizing their right to self-determination. The application of the laws of occupation under IHL place their populations under a permanent state of exception, whereby the occupying power can take the measures that it deems necessary to ensure public order and security. Restrictions, walls, and checkpoints sometimes bar individuals from accessing their property or force them to travel for hours before being able to reach their workplace, the source of their livelihood. In the case of Israel's occupation, third states sometimes justify these measures as necessary for the provision of security. However, IHL imposes limits on the conduct of occupying powers, the breach of some of which can constitute international crimes. Moreover, the right to self-determination remains a claim to wield in the international arena; legally it does not disappear by being ignored. International politics and law interact even where contested states with a right to self-determination remain occupied and violence is justified in various ways.

There are many other legal regimes in which the attribution or lack of statehood matter, some of which are introduced and elaborated in the chapters of this volume. When it comes to war and violence, the legal dichotomies between states and non-states and international and non-international conflicts clearly both protect and render vulnerable, in ways that are more contingent, political, and tragic than strictly legalist views would allow for, and yet with more consequence than political realists would readily admit. These normative and political concepts, structures, and dilemmas play out differently in different situations and contexts and must be analyzed across cases to appreciate the predicament of contested states and other actors caught up in conflicts over secession and self-determination. It would be misleading to suggest that everything is already determined in these conceptual oppositions and structural contradictions. The grey zones of international law and politics only set the stage for various actors to creatively navigate them in a range of constellations, whether they are contesting, exploiting, or circumventing them.

Constrained agency: navigating the grey zones of contested statehood

Agency is a concept of social theory that comes with considerable baggage and has been construed in different ways for different purposes. For our purposes, invoking agency helps emphasize three important dimensions of contested statehood. To begin with, as we speak habitually of sovereign states, we are implicitly attributing collective agency by imagining 'macro-actors' (Callon and Latour 1981: 279) that are not natural persons but that are construed, in international relations and law alike, *as if* they were (Schiff 2008; Bartelson 2015). Indeed, states are routinely held to 'decide', 'agree', 'object', and act in various other ways as quasi-persons, not to mention further attributions of rationality, identity, and feelings in IR scholarship specifically.[5] By claiming statehood, those who come to speak for and act on behalf of projected states help bring about an image of collective agency that invokes and enables, in line with the modern state form, authority within and outside of their claimed territories. In contrast to widely recognized states, the presumed agency of contested states is in doubt and potentially fleeting. Yet to the extent that the claims to statehood are picked up, they project a collective agency that empowers its representatives, undermines parent states, and challenges international borders. Making and breaking state agency is part and parcel of claiming and contesting states.

---

[5] Debates on state personhood reappear periodically in IR, but see, for instance, Wendt 2004; Mitzen 2005; Schiff 2008; Bartelson 2015.

Second, agency also lies with the people who act in the broader landscape of contested statehood, including the authorities of contested states, the governments of parent states and third states, or the ordinary people affected by and seeking to cope with their situation of in-between, as contested citizens, refugees, combatants, merchants, and others. Whether by (para-)diplomacy to promote or dispute the claims of contested states (Ker-Lindsay 2012; Berg and Ker-Lindsay 2020; Prelz Oltramonti 2023), the crafting, authorization, and rejection of everyday lifecycle documents (Navaro-Yashin 2007; Ganohariti 2024; Immanuel 2024; Sosnowski and Klem 2024), or economic activities beyond international boundaries and controls (Prelz Oltramonti 2020), actors in the grey zone creatively use, emphasize, or work around contested statehood. That is, they are not simply or only victims of ambiguity and vulnerability, but also agents in their own right, although always in circumstances that constrain their 'aporetic agency' (Bryant and Hatay 2020), including by the categories of international law and politics that shape the liminal predicament of contested states.

Finally, another kind of agency is at play where the ambiguities of contested states are interpreted in explicit arguments and formal opinions and judgments in international law (Besson 2019). This dimension of interpretation is entangled with the other two, but the recourse to the legal idiom invokes the authority of international law specifically as the arbiter of claims to statehood. Because the rights and rules require interpretation, there is always agency involved, specifically the professional agency of legal experts – or other experts with some knowledge of law – in various positions (Koskenniemi 2005; 2011; Kennedy 2007; Bianchi et al 2015). Governments, of course, employ lawyers and diplomacy too is deeply intertwined with international law, giving public officials the opportunity to privilege formal-legal registers over openly political ones when opportune. Yet invoking the authority of international law by making legal arguments also invites others to weigh in, from attorneys and rights groups to international organizations and courts. They, too, engage in 'lawfare' (Werner 2010). Opinions and decisions of international courts specifically showcase the agency of legal interpretation, including when claims of statehood are contested and come to occupy, directly or indirectly, the judges, whose rulings in turn affect people and states caught up in contested territory.

The three dimensions of agency are not opposed but, depending on the circumstances, entangled to one degree or another. Claiming and contesting any particular states as collective agents occurs similarly in ordinary practices, political rationalizations, and legal discourse, just as practical ways to circumvent tricky questions of contested status are cultivated at ceasefire lines and in courtrooms alike. And in each case, a focus on agency adds to perspectives on ambiguity and vulnerability by bringing actors to the fore.

The chapters of this volume explore these manoeuvres in their variety and complexity.

The contributions of this volume

The contributions are organized into three parts that highlight different aspects, actors, and perspectives in approaching contested states in war and law. In investigating claims and counterclaims of state status, the first part of the volume zooms in on three very different cases of Taiwan, Sri Lanka, and Ukraine. Christian Henderson ('The *Ratione Personae* Element of the *Jus ad Bellum* and Taiwan') sets the stage with exploring the difficulty to legally determine the status of Taiwan, while Monique Chu's chapter ('The Use of Force against Taiwan as a Contested State') focuses on the implications of this ambiguity for the risk of conflict escalation over Taiwan. Megan Price's chapter ('International Law and the Legitimation of State Violence in the Fourth Eelam War (2006–2009)') considers how the Sri Lankan government drew on international law arguments related to the war on terror in its ruthless campaign against the separatist group of the Liberation Tigers of Tamil Eelam (LTTE), 2006–2009, as it opted to contest the meaning of its legal obligations. Júlia Miklasová's chapter ('Russia-Manufactured "Secessions" in Ukraine: The Attempted Ambiguity of Status, Kosovo and International Law') highlights how Russia as a *mala fide* actor has bent international law in order to justify its intervention on behalf of pro-Russian separatists and eventual annexation of Ukrainian territories. Finally, Sheila Paylan scrutinizes Azerbaijan's use of law to justify the violent destruction of Nagorno-Karabakh ('Legitimization of Violence and State Dissolution in Nagorno-Karabakh: A Critical Legal Analysis').

Part 2 draws attention to vulnerability on the ground as local authorities, rebel leaders, fighters, and ordinary people navigate the implications of contested territories, whether by working around the law, ignoring it as best possible, or instrumentalizing it to advance their position. Irene Fernández-Molina identifies key legal grey areas in her chapter on Western Sahara ('Contested Statehood, Ambiguities and Volatility'), discussing their implications for the strategies of lawfare and warfare that the Polisario Front and Sahrawi Arab Democratic Republic have pursued since the mid-2000s and 2020, respectively. Giulia Prelz Oltramonti and Gaëlle Le Pavic's chapter ('Hardening Ceasefire Lines in Protracted Secessionist Conflicts') focuses on the changes and evolutions in the management of the ceasefire line along the Inguri River that divides Georgian- and Abkhaz-controlled territories, and on their divergences with the different legal arrangements governing it since 1994. This results in the development of an array of formal and informal practices by various actors, including local authorities and residents, to navigate the ambiguity of the situation and reduce their own vulnerability. Bart Klem's contribution ('Sovereign Experimentation by Separatist Insurgencies') mobilizes fieldwork, interviews, and document analysis to engage with legal claims by Tamil nationalists and the LTTE, showing how they performed an alternative sovereignty in various fora and by different means, thereby challenging the sovereignty of the Sri Lankan state.

Part 3 turns to how international courts become involved in adjudicating situations and cases that are directly or – more often – indirectly linked to contested states. More specifically, Anne Lagerwall's chapter ('Contested States Framed by the European Court of Human Rights') explores cases at the European Court of Human Rights (ECtHR) involving the Turkish Republic of Northern Cyprus, the Moldovan Republic of Transnistria, the Republic of Nagorno-Karabakh and the Republics of Donetsk and Luhansk. Through an analysis of case-law, the chapter seeks to determine if, or to what extent, the ECtHR legitimizes the official apparatus of these contested states. Finally, Janis Grzybowski discusses how international courts have sought to remain agnostic about the state status of Kosovo and Palestine when considering their statehood 'functionally' – and yet became entangled in state attributions that cut across functional regimes of legality, thus co-producing them as states ('Hide and Seek: Bracketing and Projecting the States of Kosovo and Palestine at International Courts').

In the Conclusions, three authors reflect on the volume's contributions. Bruno Coppieters revisits in his chapter ('Four Normative Positions on the Contestation of Statehood in War and Law') the different cases and arguments made by the authors to rethink them through the lens of four distinct normative positions on the justification of claims to statehood. Differentiating between the 'continuity', 'remedial', 'choice', and 'effectivist' views allows him to illustrate dilemmas and diverging positions across the cases and perspectives presented in the book. Rebecca Bryant's chapter ('Speculative Legalities and the Ambiguities of Contested States') first zooms in on the case of the Turkish Republic of Northern Cyprus to introduce the notion of 'speculative legalities', that is, wagers on the normative force of facts on the ground that might become normalized over time. She then shows how many chapters in the volume provide ample examples of such bets on the future, and their transformative potential. Martti Koskenniemi's conclusion ('The Melancholy Statehood') instead highlights the entrapment that the vocabulary of statehood entails beyond all its promises, provocations, and permutations. Arguments over statehood in various legal and geopolitical constellations invariably hold our political imagination hostage. The 'melancholy statehood' that comes to the fore in the dreams and frustrations of contested states warns us not to pin all hopes for liberation and security blindly on the state, that is, one's own against that of others. Instead, it calls for rethinking these state-bound limits of our imagination.

References

Aalberts, T. (2012). *Constructing Sovereignty between Politics and Law*. London: Routledge.

Akande, D. (2012). Classification of Armed Conflicts: Relevant Legal Concepts. In: E. Wilmshurst (ed.), *International Law and the Classification of Conflicts*. Oxford: Oxford University Press, 32–79.

Akande, D. and Tzanakopoulos, A. (2021). Legal: Use of Force in Self-Defence to Recover Occupied Territory. *European Journal of International Law*, 32(4), 1299–1307.

Bahcheli, T., Bartmann, B., and Srebnik, H. (2004). *De Facto States: the Quest for Sovereignty*. London: Routledge.

Bartelson, J. (2015). Sovereignty and the Personality of the State. In: R. Schuett and P.M.R. Stirk (eds), *The Concept of the State in International Relations: Philosophy, Sovereignty and Cosmopolitanism*. Edinburgh: Edinburgh University Press, 81–107.

Baumann, M., Radeloff, V.C., and Avedian, V. (2015) Land-use Change in the Caucasus during and after the Nagorno-Karabakh Conflict. *Regional Environmental Change,* 15, 1703–1716.

Berg, E. and Ker-Lindsay, J. (2020) *The Politics of International Interaction with De Facto States. Conceptualising Engagement without Recognition*. London: Routledge.

Berg, E. and Mölder, M. (2012). Who is Entitled to 'Earn Sovereignty'? Legitimacy and Regime Support in Abkhazia and Nagorno-Karabakh. *Nations and Nationalism*, 18(3), 527–545.

Berman, N. (1988) Sovereignty in Abeyance: Self-determination and International Law. *Wisconsin International Law Journal*, 7, 51–105.

Besson, S. (2019). International Courts and the Jurisprudence of Statehood. *Transnational Legal Theory*, 10(1), 30–64.

Bianchi, A. (2011). The Fight for Inclusion: Non-State Actors and International Law. In: U. Fastenrath, R. Geiger, D.-E. Khan, A. Paulus, S. von Schorlem, and C. Vedder (eds), *From Bilateralism to Community Interest*. Oxford: Oxford University Press, 39–57.

Bianchi, A., Peat, D., and Windsor, M. (eds) (2015). *Interpretation in International Law*. Oxford: Oxford University Press.

Biersteker, T.J. and Weber, C. (eds) (1996). *State Sovereignty as Social Construct*. Cambridge: Cambridge University Press.

Bryant, R. and Hatay, M. (2011). Guns and Guitars: Simulating Sovereignty in a State of Siege. *American Ethnologist*, 38(4), 631–649.

Bryant, R. and Hatay, M. (2020). *Sovereignty Suspended: Building the So-Called State*. Philadelphia: University of Pennsylvania Press.

Callon, M. and Latour, B. (1981). Unscrewing the Big Leviathan: How Actors Macrostructure Reality and How Sociologists Help Them to Do so. In: K. Knorr-Cetina and A.V. Cicourel (eds), *Advances in Social Theory and Methodology: Toward an Integration of Micro- and Macro-Sociologies*. London: Routledge, 277–303.

Caspersen, N. (2012). *Unrecognized States: the Struggle for Sovereignty in the Modern International System*. Cambridge: Polity Press.

Černy, H. and Grzybowski, J. (eds) (2023). *Variations on Sovereignty: Contestations and Transformations from around the World*. London: Routledge.

Chan, P.C.W. (2009). The Legal Status of Taiwan and the Legality of the Use of Force in a Cross-Taiwan Strait Conflict. *Chinese Journal of International Law*, 8(2), 455–492.

Chen, T. (1951). *The International Law of Recognition*. New York: Frederick A. Praeger.

Coggins, B. (2014). *Power Politics and State Formation in the Twentieth Century: the Dynamics of Recognition*. Cambridge: Cambridge University Press.

Corten, O. (2021). *The Law Against War: the Prohibition on the Use of Force in Contemporary International Law*. London: Bloomsbury Publishing.

Crawford, J. (2006). *The Creation of States in International Law*. 2nd edn. Oxford: Oxford University Press.

Cullen, A. (2010). *The Concept of Non-International Armed Conflict in International Humanitarian Law*. Cambridge: Cambridge University Press.

Cutler, A.C. (2001). Critical Reflections on the Westphalian Assumptions of International Law and Organization: a Crisis of Legitimacy. *International Studies Association*, 27, 133–150.

Degan, V.-D. (1999). Création et disparition de l'État (à la lumière du démembrement des trois fédérations multiethnique en Europe). *Recueil des cours de l'Académie de droit international*, 279, 195–376.

Dembinska, M., and Campana, A. (2017). Frozen Conflicts and Internal Dynamics of De Facto States: Perspectives and Directions for Research, *International Studies Review*, 19(2), 254–278.

Ediger, M.L. (2018). International Law and the Use of Force against Contested States: the Case of Taiwan. *New York University Law Review*, 93, 1668–1706.

Emerson, R. (1971). Self-Determination. *American Journal of International Law*, 65(3), 459–475.

Farley, B.R. (2010). Calling a State a State: Somaliland and International Recognition. *Emory International Law Review*, 24(2), 777–820.

Fazal, T.M. (2011). *State Death: the Politics and Geography of Conquest, Occupation, and Annexation*. Princeton: Princeton University Press.

Fazal, T.M. (2018). *Wars of Law: Unintended Consequences in the Regulation of Armed Conflict*. Ithaca: Cornell University Press.

Fisher, S. (2016). Towards Never Again: Searching for a Right to Remedial Secession under Extant International Law. *Buffalo Human Rights Law Review*, 22, 261–296.

Florea, A. (2017). De Facto States: Survival and Disappearance (1945–2011). *International Studies Quarterly*, 61(2), 337–351.

French, D. (2013). Introduction. In: D. French (ed.), *Statehood and Self-Determination: Reconciling Tradition and Modernity in International Law*. Cambridge: Cambridge University Press, 1–20.

Frowein, J.A. (1968). *Das de facto-Regime im Völkerrecht: Eine Untersuchung zur Rechtsstellung' nichtanerkannter Staaten' und ähnlicher Gebilde*. Köln: C. Heymanns.

Ganohariti, R. (2024). (Non)recognition of Legal Identity in Aspirant States: Evidence from Abkhazia, South Ossetia and Transnistria. *Citizenship Studies*, 1–18.

Geneva Convention (III) on Prisoners of War, adopted in Geneva on 12 August 1949, entry into force: 21 October 1950.

Geldenhuys, D. (2009) *Contested States in World Politics*. London: Palgrave MacMillan.

Grant, T.D. (1999). Defining Statehood: the Montevideo Convention and Its Discontents. *Columbia Journal of Transnational Law*, 37, 403–457.

Gray, C. (2018). *International Law and the Use of Force*. Oxford: Oxford University Press.

Grzybowski, J. (2017). To Be or Not to Be: the Ontological Predicament of State Creation in International Law. *European Journal of International Law*, 28(2), 409–432.

Grzybowski, J. (2019). The Paradox of State Identification: *De Facto* States, Recognition, and the (Re-)production of the International. *International Theory*, 11(3), 241–263.

Grzybowski, J. and Koskenniemi, M. (2015). International Law and Statehood: a Performative View. In: R. Schuett and P.M.R. Stirk (eds), *The Concept of the State in International Relations: Philosophy, Sovereignty and Cosmopolitanism*. Edinburgh: Edinburgh University Press, 23–47.

Hadden, T. (2021). Armed Groups and Emergent States: Legal and Pragmatic Approaches to Filling the Gaps in International Law. *Hague Yearbook of International Law/Annuaire de La Haye de Droit International*, 32, 209–238.

Henderson, C. (2013). Contested States and the Rights and Obligations of the *Jus Ad Bellum*. *Cardozo Journal of International and Comparative Law*, 21, 367–407.

Institut de Droit International (1936). *La reconnaissance des nouveaux Etats et des nouveaux gouvernements*. Résolution, Session de Bruxelles.

Immanuel, A.M.P. (2024). The Right to Nationality of the Saharawis and their Legal Identity Documents. *Citizenship Studies*, 1–19.

Kelsen, H. (1941). Recognition in International Law: Theoretical Observations. *American Journal of International Law*, 35(4), 605–617.
Kennedy, D. (1987). *International Legal Structures*. Baden-Baden: Nomos.
Kennedy, D. (2007). *Of War and Law*. Princeton: Princeton University Press.
Ker-Lindsay, J. (2012). *The Foreign Policy of Counter-Secession: Preventing the Recognition of Contested States*. Oxford: Oxford University Press.
King, C. (2001). The Benefits of Ethnic War: Understanding Eurasia's Unrecognized States. *World Politics*, 53(4), 524–552.
Klem, B. and Maunaguru, S. (2017). Insurgent Rule as Sovereign Mimicry and Mutation: Governance, Kingship, and Violence in Civil Wars. *Comparative Studies in Society and History*, 59(3), 629–656.
Knop, K. (2002). *Diversity and Self-Determination in International Law*, Cambridge: Cambridge University Press.
Korf, B. (2004). War, Livelihoods and Vulnerability in Sri Lanka. *Development and Change*, 35, 275–295.
Kohen, M.G. (1997). *Possession contestée et souveraineté territoriale*. Geneva, Switzerland: Graduate Institute Publications.
Kolstø, P. (2006). The Sustainability and Future of Unrecognized Quasi-States. *Journal of Peace Research*, 43(6), 723–740.
Kolstø, P. and Paukovic, D. (2014). The Short and Brutish Life of Republika Srpska Krajina: Failure of a De Facto State. *Ethnopolitics*, 13(4), 309–327.
Koskenniemi, M. (1994a). The Wonderful Artificiality of States. In *Proceedings of the ASIL Annual Meeting*, 88, 22–29.
Koskenniemi, M. (1994b). National Self-Determination Today: Problems of Legal Theory and Practice. *International & Comparative Law Quarterly*, 43(2), 241–269.
Koskenniemi, M. (2005). *From Apology to Utopia: the Structure of International Legal Argument*. 2nd edn. Cambridge: Cambridge University Press.
Koskenniemi, M. (2011). *The Politics of International Law*. Oxford: Hart.
Kunz, J.L. (1950). Critical Remarks on Lauterpacht's 'Recognition in International Law'. *American Journal of International Law*, 44(4), 713–719.
Kursani, S. (2021). Reconsidering the Contested State in Post-1945 International Relations: an Ontological Approach. *International Studies Review*, 23(3), 752–778.
Lagerwall, A. (2016), *Le principe ex injuria ius non oritur en droit international*. Bruxelles: Larcier.
Laurinavičiūtė, L. and Biekša, L. (2015). The Relevance of Remedial Secession in the Post-Soviet 'Frozen Conflicts'. *International Comparative Jurisprudence*, 1(1), 66–75.
Lauterpacht, H. (1947). *Recognition in International Law*. Cambridge: Cambridge University Press.

Leigh, M. (1990). The Legal Status in International Law of the Turkish Cypriot and the Greek Cypriot Communities in Cyprus (20 July 1990). *Republic of Turkey, Ministry of Foreign Affairs*, www.mfa.gov.tr/chapter5.en.mfa (accessed 1 October 2019).

Lynch, D. (2004). *Engaging Eurasia's Separatist States: Unresolved Conflicts and De Facto States*. Washington D.C.: US Institute of Peace Press.

Merlin, A. (2021). Au cœur ou à la marge: Les combattants et l'État abkhaze: de l'engagement armé à la légitimation symbolique. *Revue d'études comparatives Est- Ouest*, 1, 63–102.

Milanovic, M. and Wood, M. (eds) 2015. *The Law and Politics of the Kosovo Advisory Opinion*. Oxford: Oxford University Press.

Mitzen, J. (2005). Ontological Security in World Politics: State Identity and the Security Dilemma. *European Journal of International Relations*, 12(3), 341–370.

Moir, L. (2002). *The Law of Internal Armed Conflict*. Cambridge: Cambridge University Press.

Montevideo Convention on the Rights and Duties of States, adopted in Montevideo on 26 December 1933, entered into force: 26 December 1934.

Navaro-Yashin, Y. (2007). Make-Believe Papers, Legal Forms and the Counterfeit: Affective Interactions Between Documents and People in Britain and Cyprus. *Anthropological Theory*, 7(1), 79–98.

O Beacháin, D., Comai, G., and Tsurtsumia-Zurabashvili, A. (2016). The Secret Lives of Unrecognized States: Internal Dynamics, External Relations, and Counter-Recognition Strategies. *Small Wars and Insurgencies*, 27(3), 440–466.

OCHA (1998). The guiding principles on internal displacement. E/CN.4/1998/53/Add.l, 11 February. New York, NY: United Nations. New York: United Nations.

Oppenheim, L. (1905). *International Law: A Treatise*. London: Longman Greens.

Pegg, S. (1998). *International Society and the De Facto State*. Aldershot: Ashgate.

Phillips, S.G. (2020) *When There Was No Aid: War and Peace in Somaliland*, Ithaca and London: Cornell University Press.

Politkovskaya, A. (2007). *A Small Corner of Hell: Dispatches from Chechnya*. Chicago: Chicago University Press.

Prelz Oltramonti, G. (2015). The Political Economy of a De Facto State: the Importance of Local Stakeholders in the Case of Abkhazia. *Caucasus Survey*, 3(3), 291–308.

Prelz Oltramonti, G. (2020) Viability as a Strategy of Secession: Enshrining De Facto Statehood in Abkhazia and Somaliland. In R.D. Griffiths and D. Muro (eds), *Strategies of Secession and Counter-Secession*. Colchester: ECPR Press, 180–199.

Prelz Oltramonti, G. (2023). Practicing and Performing Sovereignty Abroad: Alternative Diplomacy. In: H. Černy and J. Grzybowski (eds), *Variations on Sovereignty: Contestations and Transformations from around the World*. London: Routledge, 153–173.

Protocol Additional (I) to the Geneva Conventions of 12 August 1949, and relating to the Protection of Victims of International Armed Conflicts, adopted in Geneva on 8 June 1977, entry into force: 7 December 1978.

Ruys, T. and Rodriguez Silvestre, F. (2021a). Military Action to Recover Occupied Land: Lawful Self-defense or Prohibited Use of Force? The 2020 Nagorno-Karabakh Conflict Revisited. *International Law Studies*, 97(1), 665–738.

Ruys, T. and Rodriguez Silvestre, F. (2021b). Illegal: the Recourse to Force to Recover Occupied Territory and the Second Nagorno-Karabakh War. *European Journal of International Law*, 32(4), 1287–1297.

Schiff, J. (2008). 'Real'? *As If!* Critical Reflections on State Personhood. *Review of International Studies*, 34(2), 363–377.

Schoiswohl, M. (2004). *Status and (Human Rights) Obligations of Non-Recognized De Facto Regimes in International Law: the Case of Somaliland*. Leiden and Boston: Martinus Nijhoff Publishers.

Simpson, G.J. (1996). The Diffusion of Sovereignty: Self-Determination in the Post- Colonial Age. *Stanford Journal of International Law*, 32, 255.

Sosnowski, M. and Klem, B. (2024). Legal Identity in a Looking-Glass World: Documenting Citizens of Aspirant States. *Citizenship Studies*, 1–18.

Sterio, M. (2012) *The Right to Self-determination under International Law: 'Selfistans,' Secession, and the Rule of the Great Powers*. London: Routledge.

Summers, J. (2010). Relativizing Sovereignty: Remedial Secession and Humanitarian Intervention in International Law. *St Antony's International Review*, 6(1), 16–36.

Tancredi, A. (1998). Secessione e diritto internazionale. *Rivista di diritto internazionale*, 673–768.

Talmon, S. (2004). The Constitutive and the Declaratory Theory of Recognition: *Tertium non datur?*. *British Yearbook of International Law*, 75(1), 101–181.

UN Charter (1945). Adopted in San Francisco on 26 June 1945, entry into force: 24 October 1945.

UNGA (1960). Resolution 1514, adopted on 14 December 1960.

UNGA (1960). Resolution 1541, adopted on 15 December 1960.

UNGA (1970). Resolution 2625, adopted on 24 October 1970.

UNGA (1974). Resolution 3314, adopted on 14 December 1974.

UNGA (1974). Resolution 62/243, adopted on 25 April 2008.

van Essen, J. (2012). De Facto Regimes in International Law. *Merkourios-Utrecht Journal of International and European Law*, 28(74), 31–49.

Verdebout, A. (2021). *Rewriting Histories of the Use of Force. The Narrative of 'Indifference'*. Cambridge: Cambridge University Press.

Vidmar, J. (2013). Palestine and the Conceptual Problem of Implicit Statehood. *Chinese Journal of International Law*, 12(1), 19–41.

Vidmar, J. (2021). The Structural Crack of the International Legal System: What Happens with Unattributed Conduct? *Hague Yearbook of International Law/Annuaire de La Haye de Droit International*, 32, 1–29.

Weber, C. (1998). Performative States. *Millennium*, 27(1), 77–95.

Wendt, A. (2004). The State as Person in International Theory. *Review of International Studies*, 30(2), 289–316.

Werner, W.G. (2010). The Curious Career of Lawfare. *Case Western Reserve Journal of International Law*, 43(1), 61–72.

Wills, A.G. (2012). The Crime of Aggression and the Resort to Force Against Entities in Statu Nascendi. *Journal of International Criminal Justice*, 10(1), 83–110.

Wilson, G. (2009). Self-Determination, Recognition and the Problem of Kosovo. *Netherlands International Law Review*, 56(3), 455–481.

Wyler, E. (2013). *Théorie et pratique de la reconnaissance d'État: Une approche épistémologique du droit international*. Bruxelles: Bruylant.

PART I

Ambiguous Status and the (Il)legal Use of Force

1

The *Ratione Personae* Element of the *Jus ad Bellum* and Taiwan

Christian Henderson

Introduction

Contested states – also known as 'state-like entities' or 'entities short of statehood' – are entities that, while having many of the characteristics of a fully-fledged state, have failed, for one reason or another, to attract widespread recognition as one. Examples of entities that fall within this general description might include Abkhazia, South Ossetia, Taiwan, Kosovo, Palestine, and Somaliland. Such entities are sometimes not recognized at all, while others are recognized only by other contested states. However, many have received a limited or partial amount of recognition from existing states. Some have only received recognition from the state that brought about their claim to statehood, for example Turkey in the context of Northern Cyprus[1] or, most recently, Russia in the context of the Donetsk and Luhansk People's Republics.[2] From this list alone, one can see that the concept of 'contested states' is not a monolithic one and incorporates entities exhibiting a spectrum of differences. As the introduction to this volume discusses, this creates an ambiguity in status that is of both legal and political significance.

However, regardless of the level of recognition that they possess, these entities do share some similar state-like characteristics.

---

[1] See 'Victorious Erdogan demands recognition of northern Cyprus', *France 24*, 12 June 2023, www.france24.com/en/live-news/20230612-victorious-erdogan-demands-reco gnition-of-northern-cyprus

[2] 'Ukraine: Putin announces Donetsk and Luhansk recognition', *BBC News*, 21 February 2022, www.bbc.co.uk/news/av/world-europe-60470900

Indeed, many satisfy or come close to satisfying the Montevideo Convention criteria for statehood in that they have a territory, a population, a form of governmental authority and government institutions, and have, or at least the potential to have, relations with other states (Art. 1, Montevideo Convention on the Rights and Duties of States [1933]), including diplomatic and trade links with other states, occasionally including *de facto* embassies. Additionally, many contested states have constitutions, or have pledged to draft one; working political systems; individual currencies; membership in, or observer status within, international organizations; postal systems; flags, national anthems; coats of arms; and formal declarations of independence (or at least consider themselves to be sovereign entities). However, it is important to note that claims of statehood may be contested by many, or even the majority, of existing states, and especially by the original states of which they still officially constitute a part. Consequently, this means that they have an ambiguous status, and are in this respect in international legal limbo, in connection with the application of many international legal rights and obligations which are traditionally accorded to states.

In particular, the rights and obligations governing the use or threat of force in international law have traditionally been accorded exclusively to those entities with established statehood due mainly to the states-only conception of international legal personality dominating the 19th and much of the 20th century as well as, for all practical purposes, states being the only entities capable of using large-scale force and defending themselves internationally. This has meant that the question of whether other entities are currently subject to the prohibition of the use of force and/or possess the right of self-defence is a largely unexplored and, especially in terms of the right of self-defence, controversial issue. Given that such entities often possess many of the characteristics of a state, with many also possessing at least some form of armed forces, the question arises as to the legal, moral, ethical, and practical realities and consequences of denying the applicability of certain fundamental rights and obligations within international law due to a general lack of recognition, for whatever reason, by other international persons. Indeed, the state-like yet ambiguous status of these entities leads to an uncertainty in regards to the applicability of these fundamental norms and, with that, contributes to their vulnerability, another theme that was discussed and developed in the introduction to this volume.

This chapter[3] has as its focus Taiwan. This particular 'contested state' is arguably the *least* contested in terms of its factual attributes, in that it

---

[3] This chapter is based upon a previous article of the author: Henderson 2013.

possesses a clearly defined territory that is geographically separated from its parent state, it has a permanent population that, for the most part, sees itself as distinct from citizens in the People's Republic of China (PRC), the general election that took place in January 2024 demonstrating that it continues to possess a distinct, effective, and democratic government, but it is also an entity that clearly has economic and diplomatic relations with other states. Yet, the paradoxical nature of this particular contested state is seen in the fact that it is also arguably one of the *most* contested in terms of the extent to which states are willing to recognize it as a state. Yet, the ambiguity regarding its status is also multifaceted, with it being premised on the fact that for some time following the Chinese Civil War in 1949 the governing authorities in Taiwan did not see – or wish to see – themselves as governing Taiwan as an independent state, but rather as the government of the whole of China. It was only in 1971 when delegates from the Republic of Chaina (ROC) were replaced at the United Nations by those from the PRC. There is some ambiguity in this respect regarding the extent to which the 11 states that continue to recognize Taiwan today do so in its capacity as an independent state or as hosting the legitimate government of China.[4]

However, the chapter seeks to explore the specific question of the possible or potential *ratione personae* applicability of the international legal framework governing the resort to armed force in international law to Taiwan, that is, the extent to which it applies to it given its contested statehood, most notably the prohibition of the threat or use of force and the right of self-defence.[5] This is an issue that has received a certain amount of attention over recent years,[6] particularly due to the various military drills undertaken by the PRC in the Taiwan Strait (Lee and Wu 2022), with the additional and ominous backdrop of express statements by its president regarding the inevitability of the reunification of Taiwan (or the 'Republic of China') and the PRC, which will be realized by force if necessary (Tian and Blanchard 2022). Indeed, it is a question not just of academic interest, but also one that potentially has real implications in terms of international peace and security. The central claim made in this chapter is that, while it is difficult to draw any concrete conclusions regarding the *lex lata* (or the actual) application of the *jus ad bellum* to Taiwan, there are strong *lex ferenda* arguments for potentially doing so.

---

[4] See, further, the chapter in this volume by Monique Chu on 'The Use of Force against Taiwan as a Contested State'.
[5] On this framework of international law see, in general, Henderson 2023.
[6] See also, for example, Chan 2009; Ediger 2018; Fisher 2020; Helmersen 2021; Bultrini 2022; Dumont 2023; Gazzini 2023; Kuo 2023.

The prohibition of the threat or use of force

Is Taiwan bound by the prohibition of the threat or use of force as found in Article 2(4) of the UN Charter?

Article 2(4) of the UN Charter provides that '[a]ll Members shall refrain in their international relations from the threat or use of force against the territorial integrity or political independence of any state, or in any other manner inconsistent with the Purposes of the United Nations'. This provision as such expressly applies to '[a]ll *members*' of the United Nations.[7] Certain entities that we might describe as 'contested states' have attempted without success to obtain full-blown membership of the United Nations, thus leading one to conclude on this very basis that the prohibition as contained within the Charter does not apply to their actions. It might be contended that the provision applies to 'non-member observer states' of the United Nations (currently the Holy See and the State of Palestine), although the wording of this particular title would seem to rule out the applicability of the provision, given that its applicability is clearly restricted to – presumably full-blown – 'members' of the United Nations. Indeed, despite 14 attempts, Taiwan has not succeeded in becoming a member, and neither has it received 'observer' status.[8]

There are, however, ways by which the provisions of a treaty can apply to Taiwan as a non-party. Indeed, Article 35 of the Vienna Convention on the Law of Treaties (1969) provides that '[a]n obligation arises for a third State from a provision of a treaty if the parties to the treaty intend the provision to be the means of establishing the obligation and the third State expressly accepts that obligation in writing'. Again, it might be argued that Taiwan has attempted to expressly accept 'in writing' the obligation through its formal attempts at joining the United Nations,[9] although, of course, this is only a possibility if one is to accept that it is indeed a *state* for the purposes of the Convention.

Yet, while Taiwan may presumably be open to accepting this obligation – and those that have attempted to join the United Nations have indeed done so expressly and in writing – discerning the intention of the parties to the

---

[7] Membership is open to 'all other peace-loving states which accept the obligations contained in the ... Charter and, in the judgment of the Organization, are able and willing to carry out these obligations'. Art. 4(1), UN Charter (1945).

[8] 'UN rejects Taiwan membership bid', *BBC News*, 24 July 2007, http://news.bbc.co.uk/1/hi/world/asia-pacific/6913020.stm. In rejecting Taiwan's membership bid, UN Secretary-General, Ban Ki-moon, cited UN General Assembly Resolution 2758 (1971), which acknowledged that Taiwan is a part of China.

[9] It might also be argued that they have implicitly accepted this obligation through generally refraining from using or threating to use force in practice.

treaty, that is, the broader membership of the United Nations, is arguably more complicated. On the one hand states, in general, might be said to have an interest in ensuring that as many entities with the capacity to launch large-scale force as possible are prohibited, or at least feel that they are prohibited, from resorting to such force or the threat thereof. Yet, on the other hand, there is nothing to suggest that there was an intention by the drafters of the Charter at the time of its adoption that this norm should specifically apply to non-member contested states. Indeed, this might be clear from the fact that member states agree/d that '[t]he Organization shall ensure that states which are not Members of the United Nations act in accordance with [its] Principles so far as may be necessary for the maintenance of international peace and security' (Art. 2(6), UN Charter [1945]). In any case, the obligation in this provision would appear to be on the member states and the United Nations in general, as opposed to the non-member states referred to. On the basis of this, while member states of the United Nations may attempt to ensure that states of a contested nature such as Taiwan act in accordance with Article 2(4), there is no specific obligation upon for such contested states to act in this way.

However, there is also nothing in subsequent practice to specifically suggest that the applicability of Article 2(4) has broadened, and, in any case, while states may have a general interest in ensuring that as many entities as possible act in a way that the maintenance of international peace and security is not jeopardized, we also run into the fact that any acceptance that this norm applies to states which are *contested* imbues these entities with a certain legitimacy in their claims to statehood,[10] something which many states, not least of all the PRC in this case, would wish to seek to avoid.

The applicability of the prohibition of the threat or use of force as found in Article 2(4) of the UN Charter to China in respect to its relationship with Taiwan

Article 2(4) explicitly prohibits the use of force by members in their '*international* relations'. In this respect, while the 'one China' policy may mean that the relations between the PRC and Taiwan are officially internal,[11]

---

[10] A similar problem can be seen in the case of the application of International Humanitarian Law to non-state armed groups.

[11] Article 2 of China's 2005 Anti-Secession Law clearly states that '[t]here is only one China in the world. Both the mainland and Taiwan belong to one China. China's sovereignty and territorial integrity brook no division. Safeguarding China's sovereignty and territorial integrity is the common obligation of all Chinese people, the Taiwan compatriots included', http://www.china.org.cn/english/2005lh/122724.htm. However, this policy is also something that many states adhere to, the US. included. See Joint Communique

the question arises whether the PRC might be prohibited from using force against Taiwan to the extent that this would be seen in the context of the PRC's 'international relations'. The notion that a situation is 'international' in nature has broadened in other contexts to refer to more than simply situations involving two or more states. For example, the UN Security Council now regularly deems situations that for all intents and purposes are domestic in nature as constituting a threat to *'international* peace and security'.[12] In addition, the 1977 Additional Protocol I to the Geneva Conventions which applies specifically to *international* armed conflicts nonetheless extends to peoples fighting in the exercise of their right of self-determination.[13] In this respect, it might be possible to argue that Article 2(4)'s limited applicability to the 'international relations' of the members of the United Nations does not mean that it is limited to applying on a purely inter-state basis.

However, the prohibition of force might seem to be of relevance in situations where there is at least a geographical separation between the parent state and the contested element, with the PRC and Taiwan being separated by the Strait of Taiwan and/or where the contested element is exercising a form of sustained and effective governance of a people within a particular territory, again something that would seem to be applicable in the case of Taiwan. In this respect, while Roth has observed that forcible action by China against Taiwan would, at least, be 'seen as a matter of serious international concern' (Roth 2009: 100), Corten has more specifically speculated:

> If mainland China were to undertake military action against [Taiwan], it would probably claim to be acting in its own territory, in the context of its internal affairs. One might suppose, however, that such action would prompt criticism on the basis of article 2(4), with the criticism probably being backed by military aid from the United States to Taiwan by way of 'self-defence'. In this case, it may be supposed that Taiwan would either be characterised as a State, or at least assimilated to a State, because of its sustained effective government of a given territory. (Corten 2021, 164)

Between the People's Republic of China and the United States of America, 17 August 1982, 21 ILM 1147, 19 1, 3–5, 8.

[12] For example, the preamble of Security Council Resolution 940 talks of the 'desperate plight of Haitian refugees' as one of the factors that led to the situation being determined as a threat to peace and security and which opened the door to force being authorized by the Security Council. UNSC Resolution 940, UN Doc. S/RES/940 (31 July 1994).

[13] Protocol Additional to the Geneva Conventions of 12 August 1949, and Relating to the Protection of Victims of International Armed Conflicts (Protocol I), Art. 1(4), 8 June 1977, 1125 UNTS 3.

One might also question whether the population within the contested state are a 'people' for the purposes of the right of self-determination. Antonio Cassese has gone as far as to argue that the principle of self-determination 'has extended the general ban on force (previously existing for States in their relations with other States)' (Cassese 2005: 63). Indeed, the 1970 Declaration of Friendly Relations provides that '[e]very State has the duty to refrain from any forcible action which deprives peoples referred to in the elaboration of the principle of equal rights and self-determination of their right to self-determination and freedom and independence'.[14] Of course, while the result may be the same, one may question whether any prohibition of forcible action through the application of the principle of self-determination is – and indeed should be seen to be – the same as that which is a result of the application of Article 2(4).

Of course, Article 2(4) prohibits not just the use of force but also the threat of force and, as proclaimed by the ICJ in the *Nuclear Weapons* advisory opinion, '[the] notions of "threat" and "use" of force under Article 2, paragraph 4, of the Charter stand together in the sense that if the use of force itself in a given case is illegal – for whatever reason – the threat to use such force will likewise be illegal'.[15] As such, China's Anti-Secession Law and its threat of force if Taiwan is to declare independence is potentially caught by this norm. Article 8 of the Anti-Secession Law states:

> In the event that the 'Taiwan independence' secessionist forces should act under any name or by any means to cause the fact of Taiwan's secession from China, or that major incidents entailing Taiwan's secession from China should occur, or that possibilities for a peaceful reunification should be completely exhausted, the state shall employ non-peaceful means and other necessary measures to protect China's sovereignty and territorial integrity. (Anti-Secession Law, Art. 8)

Providing that the 'acts' and 'incidents' of Taiwan causing secession are peaceful, the threat or use of force is consequently unlawful.

---

[14] Declaration on Principles of International Law Concerning Friendly Relations and Co-operation Among States in Accordance with the Charter of the United Nations, G.A.Res. 2625 (XXV), U.N. GAOR, 25th Sess., Supp. No. 18, U.N. Doc. A/8018 (24 October 1970).

[15] See *Legality of the Threat or Use of Nuclear Weapons*, Advisory Opinion, (1996) *ICJ Reports* 226, at para. 47.

The applicability of the prohibition of the threat or use of force as found in Article 2(4) of the UN Charter to third states in their actions in regards to Taiwan

While the subjects of the obligation contained in Article 2(4) are 'members' of the United Nations, the objects of protection are instead 'any state'. If we are to assume that Taiwan is simply a part of their original state in the form of the PRC, third states would be prohibited from resorting to military force against it on the basis of this association. However, the pertinent question is whether third states are prohibited from resorting to force against Taiwan independent of this association.

The norm contained within Article 2(4) is specifically aimed at protecting the 'territorial integrity' and 'political independence' of other states, two attributes which, as noted above, Taiwan possesses. It might also be said that, during the sustained *de facto* independence that Taiwan has enjoyed, there has come to be what could be described as acquiescence in its existence as a functional international entity, including in the fact that it has a 'territorial integrity' and 'political independence' to protect.[16]

Yet, Article 2(4) also seeks to prohibit force which is 'in any other manner inconsistent with the purposes of the United Nations'. It could, in this respect, be argued that any forcible action outside of the territory, airspace, or waters of China which is not employed in self-defence or under the authorization of the UN Security Council is inconsistent with the purposes of the United Nations, regardless of the identity of the entity – in this case Taiwan – against which it is targeted.[17] Indeed, the broadening of the concept of 'international relations' in other contexts, as discussed above, arguably supports this. It might, however, also be argued that *any* force by a state outside of its territory that potentially disturbs the maintenance of international peace and security or is not a settlement of a dispute through peaceful means also infringes this aspect of Article 2(4).

A relevant consideration here is that member states are under an obligation '[t]o develop friendly relations among *nations*', and not specifically *states*, 'based on respect for the principle of equal rights and self-determination of peoples' (Art. 1(2), UN Charter [1945]). While the nature of a 'people' for the purposes of this right and the applicability of the right itself to modern-day

---

[16] If we are to conclude that the possession of these attributes is sufficient to describe contested states as unrecognized non-member states, then '[e]ven states that are not members of the UN are protected, though not bound, by Art. 2(4), owing to the provision's broad wording ("any state")' (Randelzhofer 1994: 115).

[17] Indeed, it has been observed that '[i]t is almost generally accepted that de facto regimes exercising their authority in a stabilized manner are also … protected by Art.2(4)' (Randelzhofer 1994: 115).

situations, including Taiwan, is far from clear, the right nonetheless carries with it an *erga omnes* obligation meaning that all states are under an obligation not to suppress or support the suppression of the right of self-determination through forcible means.[18]

The applicability of the prohibition of the threat or use of force as found in customary international law to Taiwan

Article 38 of the Vienna Convention of the Law of Treaties (1969) states that the provisions regarding third parties (as discussed above) do not 'preclude ... a rule set forth in a treaty from becoming binding upon a third State as a customary rule of international law, recognized as such'. The prohibition of the threat or use of force is widely regarded as a rule of customary international law and,[19] unlike in the context of the treaty form of the prohibition, the subjects of the customary form of the norm have not been expressly and categorically recognized.

Nicholas Tsagourias has gone as far as to argue that customary international law is 'the *a la carte law* of the international order that *binds all international actors*' (Tsagourias 2011: 327). Furthermore, the norm prohibiting force is widely – if not universally – considered to be *jus cogens*.[20] Norms of such a nature are concerned more with prohibiting a particular type of conduct (*ratione materiae*) as opposed to nature of the entity perpetrating it (*ratione personae*). As such it might be tempting to conclude that the prohibition of the use of force norm today prohibits *all* entities from using force. Yet, this is clearly not the case. Indeed, the very fact that states have applied the norm to the acts of individuals through the medium of the crime of aggression, for example, is arguably evidence that the norm *in and of itself* does not apply to *all* entities. Indeed, the norm prohibiting the international use of force is about *state*, rather than individual, conduct. But this raises the question as to whether it is restricted to confirmed states, or whether contested states

---

[18] See *Legal Consequences of the Construction of a Wall in the Occupied Palestinian Territory*, Advisory Opinion, (2004) *ICJ Reports* 136, para. 155.

[19] *Military and Paramilitary Activities in and Against Nicaragua (Nicaragua v. United States)*, (1986) *ICJ Reports* 14, para. 34.

[20] The International Law Commission expressed the view that 'the law of the Charter concerning the prohibition of the use of force in itself constitutes a conspicuous example of a rule in international law having the character of *jus cogens*'. Report of the International Law Commission to the General Assembly [1996] 2 *YB Int'l L. Comm'n* 247. Furthermore, the ICJ in the Nicaragua case noted that the prohibition of the use of force 'is frequently referred to in statements by State representatives as being not only a principle of customary international law but also a fundamental or cardinal principle of such law' *Nicaragua* Case, n.19, para. 190 (emphasis added). Cf. Green (2011).

are also covered. In this respect, Corten has noted that '[t]he peremptory character of the non-use of force … does not readily square with a condition for application of the rule of official recognition by each State of an entity that otherwise meets all the conditions for statehood' (Corten 2021: 152).[21]

However, we might in addition ask if an entity, and in this case contested states, fits what might be described as the 'paradigm of compliance' that exists in connection with the prohibition of the threat or use of force. That is, the set of assumptions and expectations that inform the implementation and enforcement of the legal norm. In the case of the prohibition of the threat or use of force this would seem to primarily take the form of the existence of a certain level of reciprocity between its subjects.[22] If this is the case then it is perhaps logical to conclude that 'an element of equality or approximate symmetry between its subjects is required' (Henderson 2013: 390). This can be seen in the potential for Taiwan to use force, the possibilities that exist to hold it accountable, and its susceptibility to incentives for compliance.

In this respect, both the PRC and Taiwan has 'a territory to protect, a population to defend, and some political independence to maintain, leading to the conclusion that the privileges and mutual benefits of being subject to the norm in its customary form are applicable to both entities in equal measure' (Henderson 2013: 391). Indeed, 'the reciprocal benefits to be gained from having one's territory, sovereignty, political independence, and population protected through other entities that are in possession of these attributes similarly being prohibited from using force against them are of clear mutual interest, thus leading to the possibility for voluntary mutual compliance' (Henderson 2013: 390).

Furthermore, however, Taiwan, given its characteristics and capabilities, can be held accountable for its actions using the ad hoc means of enforcement that exist in connection with such a norm. For example, if it was to be found to be in violation of the prohibition of force, it could then be subject to the severance of diplomatic and/or economic relations, sanctions, embargoes, blockades, expulsion from international organizations, the loss of rights and privileges, and so on. The possibility

---

[21] The Definition of Aggression is applicable in the relations between 'states' but that '[i]n this Definition the term "State" … [i]s used without prejudice to questions of recognition or to whether a State is a member of the United Nations'. In addition, Art. 3 of the Montevideo Convention (1933) states that '[t]he political existence of the state is independent of recognition by the other states. Even before recognition the state has the right to defend its integrity and independence…'.

[22] As Shaw notes, '[t]here is the element of reciprocity at work and a powerful weapon it can be. . . .This constitutes an inducement to states to act reasonably and moderate demands in the expectation that this will similarly encourage other states to act reasonably and so avoid confrontations' (Shaw 2021: 6).

for such measures to be taken against Taiwan, as well as the ability to use many of these measures to hold others to account, are not only a means of enforcement, but also an incentive for compliance that are simply not applicable to other non-state entities (Henderson 2013: 391–392). In addition to – or arguably a result of – the possibility of these measures being taken against Taiwan, another incentive for compliance exists in respect to Taiwan in the form of 'perception and the interest in positive public opinion' (Henderson 2013: 392), particularly if its goal is securing generally recognized statehood.

Given that Taiwan possesses such state-like attributes, there would seem to be little rationale in excluding it from the applicability of such a fundamental norm as the prohibition of force (Henderson 2013: 392). Indeed, '[n]ot to accept some form of qualified personality in this area might be to free [it] from having to comply with such rules and that clearly would affect community requirements' (Henderson 2013: 393). Martin Shaw has noted that '[i]n the case of non-state territorial entities that are not totally dominated by a state, there would appear to be a community need to ensure that at least the rules relating to the resort to force and the laws of war operate' as '[n]ot to accept some form of qualified personality in this area might be to free such entities from having to comply with such rules and that clearly would affect community requirements' (Shaw 2008: 262).

The right of self-defence

Taiwan and the personal scope of Article 51 of the United Nations Charter

Article 51 of the UN Charter provides that '[n]othing in the present Charter shall impair the inherent right of individual or collective self-defence if an armed attack occurs against a Member of the United Nations'. As with the obligation to refrain from force norm contained in Article 2(4), Article 51's reference to 'members' of the United Nations again leads one to conclude that it does not directly provide Taiwan with a right of self-defence and the attempts by it to seek membership of the United Nations only highlights this.

Yet, Article 36(1) of the Vienna Convention on the Law of Treaties (1969) provides that the right of self-defence as contained in Article 51 may be accorded to a particular contested state or to contested states in general 'if the parties to the treaty intend the provision to' accord them with such a right and 'the third State assents thereto'. In regards to whether Taiwan has assented to such a right, its 'assent shall be presumed so long as the contrary is not indicated'. It is perhaps arguable that its consent to the provision of such a right can be presumed given the fact that it possesses armed forces presumably for the very purpose of defending itself, and mostly likely from the PRC. Such a presumption can also be gleaned from its attempts to join the United Nations.

More difficult, however, is ascertaining any intention on behalf of the parties to the UN Charter that the right of self-defence as contained therein should apply to Taiwan. The key distinction with respect to Article 2(4) is that while states will in general have an interest in Taiwan being expressly prohibited from using force,[23] they will not so readily accept or have an interest in it possessing an express right to use force. Article 36 of the Vienna Convention does not require any express intent, or for this to be in written form. In this respect, while it is arguable that we might be able to identify a degree of implicit intent through states' general acquiescence in Taiwan possessing weapons and armed forces,[24] and the publication of documents such as Taiwan's national security policy in May 2006,[25] such intent cannot be generally and safely presumed.

The applicability of the right of self-defence as found in Article 51 of the UN Charter to third states in their actions in regards to Taiwan

While Article 51 provides states with a right of self-defence, it does not specify from which type of entity an 'armed attack' must emanate. Given that there has been a significant degree of acceptance that terrorist groups may be the perpetrators of armed attacks, it might seem reasonable to assume that Taiwan as a contested state may also be the perpetrator of such attacks, thus providing in principle a third state with a right of self-defence against its actions.

Yet a potentially significant problem with the applicability of the right of self-defence in this context is that the PRC may take issue with a third state using force in self-defence against the actions of its contested element, Taiwan, seeing as it would for all intents and purposes be taking place on *its* territory. In this respect, any use of force in self-defence by a third state against Taiwan would put China's 'one China' policy to the test, particularly given that they both operate for all intents and purposes as entirely separate political and territorial entities.

Depending upon the degree of estrangement between the parent state and its contested element, however, the third state may attempt to claim that the parent state was fully responsible for the attacks due to its effective control of the actions of its contested limb or, alternatively, that it was either 'unable or unwilling' to take the necessary actions to suppress the attack

---

[23] This is aside, of course, from any concerns that providing them with such an obligation may confer them with legitimacy in their claims to statehood.

[24] There has been, for example, normal concern expressed when Taiwan has carried out missile tests. See 'Taiwan in Live-Fire Missile Tests', *BBC News*, 18 January 2011, www.bbc.co.uk/news/world-asia-pacific-12213185.

[25] See Cody 2006.

and/or continuing threat, both possibilities potentially opening up the parent state to a forcible response, neither of which would apply, of course, in the context of Taiwan and its relationship with the PRC.

The applicability of the right of self-defence as found in Article 51 of the UN Charter to the PRC in its actions in regards to Taiwan

If an attack by the PRC against Taiwan would be seen in the context of its 'international relations' and the PRC is indeed prohibited from using force under customary international law, both of which were discussed above, then any attack upon the PRC by Taiwan would arguably give rise to the right of self-defence.

But does the availability of the right to a parent state depend upon the degree of estrangement between it and its contested counterpart and, in particular, the degree of effective control maintained by the contested state within its territorial confines? This certainly seemed to be the view of the International Court of Justice in the *Wall* advisory opinion when it denied that the establishment by Israel of a security wall in the West Bank could be justified on the basis of the right of self-defence, in that the appropriate legal regime was in fact that of occupation rather than self-defence which, it infamously held, was only available by one state against another state.[26] This requirement for a level of estrangement is arguably supported by the UN Secretary General's Palmer Report on the Israeli flotilla raid, in which it was declared that the international law of blockade applied as Gaza and Israel were both distinct territorial and political areas.[27] Whether one agrees with the ICJ's approach to this issue, it nonetheless provides support for the proposition that, where an entity can be assimilated to a state, an armed attack from such a contested territorial entity gives rise to the right of the original state to respond proportionately in self-defence.

The personal scope of the right under customary international law and its applicability to Taiwan

The right of self-defence as found in Article 51 is an 'inherent right', something that has been recognized by the International Court of Justice as referring to the existence of the right in customary international law.[28]

---

[26] *Wall* Advisory Opinion, n. 18, para. 139.
[27] The Palmer Report on the Israeli flotilla raid in 2010 found the international law of blockade applicable based upon the fact that 'Gaza and Israel are both distinct territorial and political areas'. UN Secretary-General, *Report of the Secretary-General's Panel of Inquiry on the 31 May 2010 Flotilla Incident*, 2 September 2011, 1 73.
[28] *Nicaragua* Case, n. 19, para. 34.

But the question remains as to whether this applies only to confirmed recognized states. Some scholars have assumed that the customary form of the right applies to contested states but without providing any real explanation as to why and how.[29]

Contested states have a territory to defend, a population to protect, and political independence to sustain, and the principle of effectiveness might lead us to believe that contested states, as with confirmed states, should be in the possession of a right of self-defence to protect these. Indeed, if a contested state has enjoyed a period of sustained effective governance over a particular territory, its population would likely look solely to its governmental institutions and military forces to protect and defend it if subject to an armed attack, regardless of the identity of the entity from which the attack emanated. Furthermore, it could be argued that self-defence is a just and necessary counterpart to contested states being prohibited from using force, if one is to accept that they are so prohibited.

One might also discern a level of acquiescence in the possession of this right by contested states, or at least certain contested states. For example, Taiwan engages in transactions with other states, most notably the United States, for the procurement of military weapons. It might follow, then, that 'if contested states possess sufficient legal personality to engage in the sorts of transactions that lead to the procurement of such weapons then, by implication, this personality is sufficient for such states to be subject to the most fundamental legal rights and obligations that govern the use of those weapons' (Henderson 2013: 401). Furthermore, there has been a virtual absence of dissent to the idea that Taiwan would be permitted to defend itself should it come under attack from China.

In addition, the prospect of whether third states are permitted to act in *collective* self-defence of a contested state is a real one, particularly in the context of the tensions between China and Taiwan. Indeed, while since repealed and adopted at the time when the United States still recognized the ROC on Taiwan as a sovereign state, the United States committed itself to such action in the 1955 US Formosan Resolution, which authorized the use of US armed forces by the president 'as he deems necessary for the specific purpose of securing and protecting Formosa, and the Pescadores against armed attack'.[30] Today, while the United States has committed to supplying arms to Taiwan by which to defend itself under the Taiwan Relations Act, which became a US domestic law in 1979 after the derecognition of Taipei

---

[29] For example, Charney and Prescott talk of 'Taiwan's right of self-defence' without offering any real substantive discussion of the contours of this right or how Taiwan has come to possess it (Charney and Prescott 2000, 475).

[30] The island of Taiwan was formally known as Formosa.

by Washington, it has also committed itself to the 'one China policy', thereby making any supply of arms potentially a violation of the principle of non-intervention and the prohibition of the use of force.

Charney and Prescott have asserted that 'an attack by China would justify the exercise of self-defense by Taiwan, including by seeking outside support through collective self-defense' (Charney and Prescott 2000: 477, emphasis added). Yet, there has been some notable hesitancy in regards to the prospect of third states possessing the right to act in collective self-defence of contested states (Fisher 2020). There might indeed be problems with a right of collective self-defence for contested states in practice, given the inherently subjective nature of recognition. Furthermore, the Independent International Fact-Finding Mission on the Conflict in Georgia found in 2009 that, while an entity short of statehood may have a right of self-defence, they did not have the right to invite foreign support due to the fear of escalating the conflict.[31] Of course, this reasoning might be countered with the fact that contested states would most likely require such assistance to a greater degree than confirmed states given that they would likely be at an increased military disadvantage.

Finally, one might conceive of the use of force in this context as a response to an attempted prevention of the exercise of the right of self-determination. Peoples accorded with this right are entitled to seek and to receive support in accordance with the purposes and principles of the Charter,[32] although any support also has to be in accordance with the principles of the Charter (Fisher 2020), thereby arguably precluding the use of force, unless one accepts that contested states have the right of collective self-defence then it is arguable that a forcible response may well be permitted if the suppression of the right of self-determination amounts to an armed attack.

Conclusion

This chapter has not sought to firmly establish or discredit Taiwan as a 'contested state' or draw any firm conclusions as to applicability of the rights and obligations of the *jus ad bellum* to it. Indeed, as things stand, it is arguably not possible to draw such conclusions. The chapter has, however, attempted to adopt a contemporary approach in contending that in assessing its legal personality in connection with this branch of international law what it actually *is* and what it is *capable of* should be addressed, rather than

---

[31] CEIIG, Independent International Fact-Finding Mission on the Conflict in Georgia, Vol. II, at 241–242 and 282 (30 September 2009), www.ceiig.ch/pdf/IIFFMCGVolume-ll.pdf.
[32] *Declaration on Principles of International Law Concerning Friendly Relations and Co-operation Among States in Accordance with the Charter of the United Nations*, UNGA Res. 2625 (XXV), UN Doc. A/8018 (24 October 1970), at 124 (emphasis added).

simply focusing on what *is not*, that is, a fully recognized and confirmed state. Indeed, given the characteristics, capabilities and attributes of contested states, it is the case that '[t]he peremptory character of the non-use of force … does not readily square with a condition for application of the rule of official recognition by each State of an entity that otherwise meets all the conditions for statehood' (Corten 2021: 159).

However, the result of denying the applicability of the *jus ad bellum* to Taiwan, and in particular in the relations between it and the PRC, would seem to be to acknowledge that it is either able to use force freely, including for defensive or aggressive purposes or, alternatively, if viewed as part of the PRC, that it is not permitted to use force independently at all, including for defensive purposes should it be the subject of an armed attack. Neither of these is satisfactory nor do they provide a logical outcome given contemporary realities.

However, the legal and political ambiguity of Taiwan as an entity has potential implications not only for the legality of use of force by and against Taiwan, but also for the legality of the use of force of third states assisting it in self-defence should the need arise. In this respect, diverging assessments regarding whether or not Taiwan is a *de facto* independent state (or should be regarded as the equivalent to one for purposes of the law of the use of force) could ultimately light the spark of a China–US military confrontation, resulting in a very real and heightened vulnerability beyond the shores of the island of Taiwan and its 23 million inhabitants.

References

Bultrini, A. (2022). The Cross-Strait Relationship between China and Taiwan in Light of International Law: Not Quite a Mere Domestic Affair.… *Journal on the Use of Force and International Law*, 9, 391.

Cassese, A. (2005). *International Law*. 2nd edn. Oxford: Oxford University Press.

Chan, P.C.W. (2009). The Legal Status of Taiwan and the Legality of the Use of Force in a Cross-Taiwan Strait Conflict. *Chicago Journal of International Law*, 8, 455.

Charney, J.I. and Prescott, J.R.V. (2000). Resolving Cross-Strait Relations Between China and Taiwan. *American Journal of International Law*, 94, 453.

Cody, E. (2006). Taiwan Announces First National Security Policy / Plan Calls on China to Help Create Buffer Zone in the Strait. *Washington Post*, 21 May, www.sfgate.com/news/article/Taiwan-announces-first-national-security-policy-2496527.php.

Corten, O. (2021). *The Law against War: the Prohibition on the Use of Force in Contemporary International Law*. 2nd edn. Oxford: Hart.

Dumont, A. (2023). Just Like Ukraine, But Worse? Some Thoughts on the China-Taiwan Situation. *völkerrechtsblog*, 11 April, https://voelkerrechtsblog.org/just-like-ukraine-but-worse/.

Ediger, M.L. (2018). International Law and the Use of Force against Contested States: the Case of Taiwan. *New York University Law Review*, 93, 1688.

Fisher, R.M. (2020). Defending Taiwan: Collective Self-Defense of a Contested State. *Florida Journal of International Law*, 32, 101.

Gazzini, T. (2023). Statehood in Troubled Waters: the International Status of the Republic of China and the Rules on the Use of Force. *Questions of International Law*, 31 January, www.qil-qdi.org/statehood-in-troubled-waters-the-international-status-of-the-republic-of-china-and-the-rules-on-the-use-of-force/.

Green, J.A. (2011). Questioning the Preemptory Status of the Prohibition of the Use of Force. *Michigan Journal of International Law*, 32, 215.

Helmersen, S.T. (2021). China-Taiwan Threats of Force and the Paradox of the '*Nuclear Weapons* Principle'. *International Community Law Review*, 23, 403.

Henderson, C. (2013). Contested States and the Rights and Obligations of the *Jus ad Bellum*. *Cardozo Journal of International and Comparative Law*, 21, 367.

Henderson, C. (2023). *The Use of Force and International Law,*. 2nd edn. Cambridge: Cambridge University Press.

Kuo, M-S. (2023). Having Taiwan in Mind? Use of Force and the 'Peacefully Established Status of Territories. *EJIL Talk!*, 9 June, www.ejiltalk.org/having-taiwan-in-mind-the-principe-of-non-use-of-force-and-peacefully-established-status-of-territories/.

Lee, Y. and Wu, S. (2022). Furious China Fires Missiles Near Taiwan in Drills after Pelosi Visit. *Reuters*, 5 August, www.reuters.com/world/asia-pacific/suspected-drones-over-taiwan-cyber-attacks-after-pelosi-visit-2022-08-04/.

Randelzhofer, A. (1994). Article 2(4). In B. Simma (ed.), *The Charter of the United Nations: a Commentary*. Oxford: Oxford University Press, 112.

Roth, B.R. (2009). The Entity That Dare Not Speak its Name: Unrecognized Taiwan as a Right-Bearer in the International Legal Order. *East Asia Law Review*, 4, 92.

Shaw, M.N. (2008). *International Law*. 6th edn. Cambridge: Cambridge University Press.

Shaw, M.N. (2021). *International Law*. 9th edn. Cambridge: Cambridge University Press.

Tian, Y.L. and Blanchard, B. (2022). China Will Never Renounce Right to Use Force over Taiwan, Xi Says. *Reuters*, 16 October, www.reuters.com/world/china/xi-china-will-never-renounce-right-use-force-over-taiwan-2022-10-16/.

Tsagourias, N. (2011). Non-State Actors and the Use of Force. In: J. d'Aspremont (ed.), *Participants in the International Legal System: Multiple Perspectives on Non-State Actors in International Law*. Abingdon: Routledge, 326.

2

The Use of Force Against Taiwan as a Contested State: An Analysis of Legality and Great-Power Politics

Ming-chin Monique Chu

Introduction

The Russian invasion of Ukraine has heightened concerns about China's intentions toward Taiwan, which it considers a 'renegade province'. Beijing views Taiwan as an 'internal affair', aligning with the Westphalian principle of sovereignty and the conventional interpretation of the non-intervention tenet of Article 2(7) of the UN Charter. However, to what extent is the aforementioned perspective convincing? How does Taiwan's status as a contested state complicate the legality of China's use of force against the island? Considering Taiwan's unique assets and the evolving threat perception of China by the United States, the island's *de facto* security guarantor through the Taiwan Relations Act (TRA),[1] what insights can realist IR theory provide about potential third-party intervention during a Chinese military attack? This chapter addresses these questions from a multidisciplinary standpoint, combining a revisionist perspective in international law with realist great-power politics in IR. Despite existing literature on China's use of force against Taiwan in both disciplines (Hsiao 1998; Ross 2000; Whiting 2001; Chan 2009; Ediger 2018; Fisher 2020; Helmersen 2021), there has been a lack of synergy between them. This chapter fills that gap.

---

[1] For an excellent study of the importance of the TRA to relations between the United States and Taiwan, see Goldstein and Schriver (2001).

Following the introductory section, the first two sections of the chapter provide context for analyzing the issue from international law and IR perspectives. The second of these explores how Taiwan shares the distinctive features of ambiguity and vulnerability, common to contested states facing the threat of force, as outlined in the introductory chapter of the edited volume. In the third section, we delve deeper into the ambiguity of Taiwan's status by tracing its evolving sovereign features. This section also highlights how Taiwan's material assets and geostrategic importance set it apart from other contested states, potentially benefiting Taiwan in a conflict initiated by China. The following section argues from a revisionist perspective in international law that Taiwan can assume the status of rights holders regarding China's use of force. This is based on principles of self-determination, Taiwan's status as a *de facto* regime (as analyzed in the third section), and China's obligations to peacefully resolve disputes to prevent destabilizing international security. The fifth section explores the issue through the realist prism of IR, following the logic of great-power politics while considering Taiwan's material agency vis-à-vis China. It asserts that, with Washington's evolving perception of China as a peer competitor, the logic of great-power politics will shape its actions in a Cross-Strait contingency, though nuclear deterrence will likely limit US intervention. The final section examines the implications of a Chinese takeover of Taiwan for power redistribution in Asia and its impact on the liberal international order.

Two features of contested states under the threat of war in the case of Taiwan

The case of Taiwan, under the looming threat of a Chinese military takeover, exhibits the distinctive features of ambiguity and vulnerability commonly associated with contested states facing the potential use of force.

Firstly, Taiwan's status is marked by ambiguity, a legacy of the unresolved Chinese civil war since 1949. It is the only territory within the self-defined Chinese state where Beijing does not exert control. However, China considers itself Taiwan's parent state while rejecting Taiwan's claim to sovereignty,[2]

---

[2] In spite of the sovereignty disputes between Beijing and Taipei since 1949, the Cross-Strait relationship was characterized by a puzzling dichotomy of high tensions and the danger of military conflict on the one hand, and rapid economic integration into broader globalizing trends on the other. Economic and social ties grew rapidly even as tensions increased after the early 1990s. By the early 2000s, China had become Taiwan's largest trading partner, more than a million Taiwanese were living in mainland China, and both countries became deeply embedded in global production chains. The literature on the relationship between economic interdependence and conflict has not been discussed in this chapter due to space constraints, although it can shed light on the probability of China's use of force against Taiwan. See, for instance, Kastner (2022).

despite Taiwan developing and maintaining its sovereign features over time, as elaborated in the third section. The ambiguity surrounding Taiwan's status has ensnared Taipei and Beijing in a dangerously volatile relationship. Beijing has not ruled out the use of military force to reclaim Taiwan, aiming to prevent any perceived costs associated with further devolution of China's sovereignty claim over the island.

Recent tensions across the Taiwan Strait have intensified due to China's persistent emphasis on Taiwan within its military modernization programme. This focus serves a dual purpose: deploying coercive capabilities to deter perceived threats of Taiwan's formal independence and enhancing its anti-access/area-denial (A2/AD) capabilities. The latter aims to deter, delay, or deny any military intervention by third parties, such as the United States, on behalf of Taiwan during a Cross-Strait contingency (Chu 2017). Furthermore, conflicts between Taipei and Beijing are susceptible to escalation because Washington opposes Beijing's notion of a military invasion of Taiwan and might intervene in a Taiwan contingency due to its role as Taiwan's quasi-security guarantor since the late 1970s.[3]

Despite the absence of official recognition, recent efforts by Washington to enhance relations with Taipei – exemplified by US House Speaker Nancy Pelosi's visit to Taipei in August 2022, the highest-ranking American official to visit Taiwan in a quarter of a century – have heightened Beijing's insecurity concerning Taiwan. In response to Pelosi's visit, Beijing initiated large-scale military exercises and encirclement tactics in the seas around Taiwan, intensifying tensions across the Taiwan Strait.

Furthermore, Cross-Strait volatility escalated in 2024 when Beijing conducted its largest-ever military exercises around Taiwan to express displeasure with the election of William Lai, a pro-independence president in the eyes of Beijing. Simultaneously, Washington dispatched naval carriers through the Taiwan Strait to signal its commitment to defending Taiwan's democracy. As such, Taiwan significantly increases the risk of a direct military confrontation between China and the United States, both nuclear powers, thereby heightening the potential threat to regional security. Secondly, China's use of force against Taiwan could leave the island's 24 million inhabitants vulnerable, either caught in the crossfire or forced to flee as refugees. Given Taiwan's small size, an influx of refugees to neighboring countries is anticipated to trigger an unprecedented humanitarian crisis. Furthermore, the looming threat of a nuclear war between the two major

---

[3] The United States assumes this role under its commitment to safeguarding the island's national security, based on the TRA enacted in 1979 in place of the US–Taiwan Mutual Defense Treaty terminated the same year.

powers in a Taiwan contingency and the resulting human devastation would be catastrophic.

Taiwan as a unique case of contested states

To further illuminate the ambiguity of Taiwan's status in the international system, we can explore its characteristics as a contested state – a case of problematic sovereignty. This often stems from either the violation of conventional rules of sovereignty or the inability of such rules to offer actors the best means to achieve their objectives (Krasner 2001: viii). Drawing on a revised version of Krasner's four-component sovereignty typology (2001),[4] which will be elucidated later, and an analysis of original data comprising 63 interviews with elite actors engaged in Taiwan's alternative sovereignty practices, I present my findings summarizing Taiwan's evolving sovereign features below.

For analytical clarity, the concept of sovereignty has been disaggregated into various constituent parts in this chapter's nuanced typology, including *de jure* and *de facto* international legal sovereignty, Westphalian sovereignty, and domestic sovereignty. This revision stems from a two-step modification of Krasner's (1999) original model of four-component sovereignty. The first modification involves distinguishing between *de jure* and *de facto* recognition of state practices. This allows for the assessment of both forms of recognition, addressing a limitation in Krasner's original conceptualization that focused predominantly on *de jure* recognition. Informed by Geldenhuys' work on contested states (2009), which emphasizes varied degrees of *de jure* vs *de facto* recognition for disputed polities, this adjustment enables the analysis of non-state or quasi-state diplomatic practices that constitute *de facto* international legal sovereignty. The second modification I made incorporates Krasner's interdependence sovereignty into domestic sovereignty. His notion of interdependence sovereignty concerns control, not authority. Since this component involves the capacity to regulate trans-border flows and their domestic impact, a capacity often undermined by globalization, it differs from sovereignty. Domestic sovereignty is thus redefined in the nuanced typology as the ability of authorities to effectively control their authority structures and legitimacy and to regulate activities within and across territorial boundaries.

---

[4] They include: (1) international legal sovereignty, or recognition of territorial entities with formal juridical independence; (2) Westphalian sovereignty, defined as the exclusion of external actors from a territory's structures of authority; (3) interdependence sovereignty, meaning the ability of public authorities to regulate transborder flows; and (4) domestic sovereignty, defined as the organization of public authority in a territory and the authorities' ability to effectively control affairs within their polity (Krasner 1999: 3–4).

Constrained de jure *recognition vs consolidated* de facto *recognition*

De jure international legal sovereignty pertains to the formal juridical recognition of territorial entities as independent, while *de facto* international legal sovereignty involves the acknowledgment of these entities in practice. In the case of Taiwan, its *de jure* recognition has been constrained since the 1971 UN Resolution 2758, which ousted the Republic of China (ROC) and admitted the People's Republic of China (PRC) to the United Nations. Nonetheless, Taiwan has managed to consolidate its *de facto* recognition.

Since 1971, the bilateral *de jure* recognition of Taiwan has diminished. As of 2022, only 13 out of the 193 UN member states, along with the Holy See, extend *de jure* recognition to Taiwan, constituting just 7 per cent of UN member states that formally acknowledge Taipei. Similarly, Taiwan's multilateral *de jure* recognition has been restricted since 1971, evident in its constrained participation in inter-governmental organizations (IGOs). This limitation often manifests in compromised nomenclature, capacity, and rights, despite a finite growth in membership numbers. As of 2020, Taiwan holds full membership in 39 IGOs and their affiliated organizations (MOFA nd), the majority of which are either not limited to states or have a regional rather than global scope (Crawford 2006: 203), with the notable exception of the World Trade Organization.

Despite its constrained *de jure* international legal sovereignty, Taiwan has expanded its *de facto* recognition both multilaterally and bilaterally. Multilaterally, Taiwan's expanded *de facto* recognition stems from its participation in IGOs alongside states that officially derecognize Taipei. These states, while not offering *de jure* recognition, acknowledge Taiwan *de facto* through concurrent attendance at these international gatherings. Taipei's engagement with these confirmed states within IGOs has advanced its national interests on both non-political and political fronts, albeit with associated costs arising from compromises in its modalities of participation. Non-political benefits include substantive gains in international rulemaking and the governance of transnational issues. Politically, Taiwan's interests lie in maintaining a separate presence from Beijing and increasing visibility in multilateral fora. The former foreign minister, Joseph Wu, stresses that 'our participation is independent from other member states … If we continue taking part in international organizations as an independent participant, we repeatedly highlight the fact that Taiwan is different from China'.[5]

On a bilateral level, Taiwan has bolstered *de facto* recognition by creating a robust network of semi-official representations, replacing conventional diplomatic ties in major capitals of states that officially do not recognize Taiwan *de jure*. Despite the absence of *de jure* recognition, these countries

---

[5] Interview, Taipei, 25 March 2015.

have reciprocated by establishing semi-official offices in Taipei. Notably, institutions like the American Institute in Taiwan (AIT)[6] have become institutionalized due to strategic interest calculations.[7] An American diplomat describes the AIT as 'an embassy in all but in name'.[8]

As of 2022, Taipei operates 96 representative offices or trade missions in 59 non-diplomatic allied states, comprising 31 per cent of UN members. Notably, some Taiwanese diplomats enjoy diplomatic immunity despite the lack of formal recognition. Simultaneously, Taiwan maintains embassies in 14 allied countries, indicating that 38 per cent of UN member states either grant Taiwan *de jure* or *de facto* recognition.

Several foreign diplomats perceive countries with semi-official representative offices in Taipei as treating Taiwan as a *de facto* state. One diplomat acknowledges that his government recognizes Taiwan's *de facto* independence, even though it does not officially recognize its *de jure* sovereignty.[9] Another argues that 'we have an interest in working with the authorities that are in charge of this patch of land. If that amounts to *de facto* recognition of sovereignty, yes maybe'.[10]

The mentioned interest calculation stems from Taiwan's significance in economic, strategic, and normative terms. As a high-level European diplomat puts it: 'We need to have interactions with Taiwan because of economic and security interests. Diplomacy in a sense is recognition of facts on the ground. We need to have some form of communication with Taiwan- whatever name you call it- ROC, Taiwan, Taipei, an island, a country'. Normative interests are also important, as many liberal democracies have regarded Taiwan as a 'like-minded partner' due to shared values of democracy and freedom.[11]

Nevertheless, *de facto* recognition through semi-official ties is inherently limited. Representative offices operated by Taiwan's non-diplomatic allied states fall short of *de jure* recognition due to the overarching framework of the 'one-China policy'. As a Taipei-based senior European diplomat admits, 'Everybody here functions within the context of the one-China policy'.[12] Moreover, there are doubts among practitioners about the adequacy of *de facto* recognition to safeguard Taiwan's most critical foreign interests.

Taiwan's *de facto* sovereignty has been further solidified through the signing of a broader range of bilateral agreements with numerous

---

[6] Interview with former AIT director Bill Stanton, Taipei, 14 August 2018.
[7] Interview with Liu Chih-kung, Taiwanese representative to the United Kingdom, London, 5 February 2016.
[8] Interview with an American diplomat, Taipei, 24 August 2018.
[9] ibid.
[10] Interview with ambassador-level Western diplomat, Taipei, 23 August 2018.
[11] Interview with high-level European diplomat, Taipei, 22 August 2018.
[12] ibid.

countries, despite facing derecognition. This consolidation is driven by functional needs and interest calculations of the parties involved. As the world's 21st largest economy in 2021, Taiwan has entered into numerous pacts to address functional challenges arising from its deep integration into the global economy. For instance, in 2013 alone, Taiwan concluded 49 pacts with 24 non-diplomatic allies, covering areas such as judicial affairs, immigration and consulate matters, trade and investment promotion, and anti-money laundering (MOFA 2014). Additionally, from 1981 to 2020, Taiwan and 32 countries signed and implemented 45 double-taxation agreements (MOF 2020). The enhancement of Taipei's *de facto* recognition is further evidenced by visa-free arrangements for Taiwanese passport holders. As of 2019, Taiwan passport holders enjoy visa waivers, landing visas, or other preferential visa treatments from 167 countries and territories (MOFA 2019). Notably, a majority of these countries that extend such privileges do not officially recognize Taiwan *de jure*. According to the former foreign minister, David Lin, 'visa-free arrangements mean that these countries have recognized Taiwan's passports, although they do not recognize our statehood'.[13]

Sustained Westphalian and domestic sovereignty

Additionally, Taipei has maintained its Westphalian sovereignty, with its government retaining the ability to define the characteristics of its authoritative institutions, while Beijing has never exerted control over the island. From the judiciary and military to foreign affairs, the authority structures within Taiwanese territory[14] have operated independently, free from interference by external actors, with relevant government institutions remaining intact despite internal restructuring. An ambassador-level Western diplomat concurs: 'Taiwan has full control of the island, its army, its currency, etc. It has full control of the island'.[15]

Furthermore, Taiwan has fortified its domestic sovereignty through intensified cross-border cooperation with other nations and advancement in democratization. Taipei has collaborated with various countries to enhance its capacity to address challenges arising from globalization. A notable example is the increased cooperation with Taiwan, despite non-recognition, following the 9/11 attacks. Many countries have intensified collaboration with Taiwan to exchange information on transnational crimes and facilitate

---

[13] Interview with former foreign minister David Lin, Taipei, 29 July 2014.
[14] The 1990s constitutional amendment led to admission that the ROC government only controls Taiwan and outlying islands of Kinmen, Matsu, and Penghu.
[15] Footnote 10.

the repatriation of criminals.[16] Between 2004 and 2019, 47 pacts about the exchange of intelligence on money laundering and/or terrorist financing were signed or came into force between Taiwan and its counterparts.[17] Even in the Cross-Strait context, both parties signed a pact in 2009 for mutual legal assistance in crime matters. This can be interpreted as Taipei's intention to enhance its domestic sovereignty regarding trans-border controls by facilitating the repatriation of Taiwanese fugitives fleeing to the mainland.

Moreover, Taiwan has maintained the internal attributes of a typical statehood, as its authority effectively controls events within its borders. Taipei has actively determined the character of its institutions, ensured their operations, and enacted laws of its choice while overseeing their implementation. This is exemplified most recently by its decision to legalize same-sex marriage in 2019, as well as its successful management in fending off the COVID-19 pandemic since 2020.

According to a senior European diplomat, 'Taiwan is being squeezed formally, but it has an informal space which cannot be squeezed, and that informal space consists of Taiwan's own actions and decisions at home'.[18] As an American diplomat notes, 'China's sovereignty claim over Taiwan is at best aspirational. It has no basis in reality. The PRC, established in 1949, has never exerted control over Taiwan'.[19]

Furthermore, Taiwan's transition to democracy has bolstered the legitimacy of its domestic sovereignty. In January 2024, Taiwan successfully completed its eighth presidential election in accordance with conventional rules of international suffrage, marking a further deepening of its democratic consolidation. As Taiwan's democratization has enhanced its domestic sovereignty, the process of democratic consolidation further solidifies it.[20] As asserted by Bartelson (2016: 314), a political entity's domestic sovereignty does not necessarily require recognition by other states, unlike its external sovereignty, which requires such acknowledgment to be complete. Taiwan serves as a prominent example in this regard.

---

[16] Interview with Perry Shen, director-general of the Department of Treaty and Legal Affairs of MOFA, Taipei, 4 August 2014.

[17] MOFA Database on Treaties and Agreements (nd), https://no06.mofa.gov.tw/mofa treatys/ResultE.aspx?tysubject_c=Money+Laundering&tysubject_e=Money+Launder ing&tysubject_o=Money+Laundering&tycountry_c=&tycountry_e=&tyeffectivedate= 2001%2f09%2f11&tyeffectivedateE=2020%2f01%2f01&tysigneddate=&tysigneddateE= &start=Y&tykeyword=&Order=Signing&amp%3btyclass=.

[18] Footnote 11.

[19] Footnote 8.

[20] Although Taiwan's democratic transition has challenged the effectiveness of internal controls by the government, these challenges are governance hurdles, not hinderance to its domestic sovereignty.

However, despite the strengthening of its domestic sovereignty through democratization, Taipei's solidified internal autonomy has not led to an improvement in its *de jure* recognition. The progression of democratic practices in Taiwan, culminating in the establishment of a stable democracy (Wong 2003), has not altered the constrained acknowledgment of its statehood.

Considering the analysis presented in the preceding section, it is evident that Taiwan's status remains ambiguous within the inter-state system[21] – a characteristic it shares with other contested states.

One of its kind

However, Taipei's status as a contested state is unique, as compared to its counterparts, because its accumulated material power and importance in economic and strategic terms have helped mitigate its international isolation, as illustrated by the aforementioned bolstered *de facto* recognition that Taipei has received from international society. Taiwan's uniqueness can potentially become useful to the island in times of war initiated by China by influencing any third-party's calculations of intervention, as shall be analyzed in a later section ('Great-power politics and the use of force against Taiwan').

Economically, Taiwan, ranked as the world's 21st largest economy, has emerged as a global silicon powerhouse, renowned for its exceptional semiconductor manufacturing capabilities led by Taiwan Semiconductor Manufacturing Company (TSMC), the world's leading chip maker. In 2019, Taiwan dominated cutting-edge logic semiconductor production, commanding a remarkable 92 per cent of the global market share. Moreover, its chip fabrication technology, spanning both silicon and compound semiconductors,[22] has been in high demand in the defence microelectronics markets of the United States, China, and other regions (Chu 2013: 18; 2025; Lee and Kleinhans 2020; Shattuck 2021; Damjanovski 2022: 17–18; Shivakumar and Wessner 2022). For instance, the top three compound foundry players in Taiwan – namely WIN Semiconductors, AWSC, and

---

[21] The ambiguity of Taiwan's status has also been manifested in the US longstanding policy of 'strategic ambiguity' towards the mainland and Taiwan. Under this policy, the United States deliberately creates uncertainty with regard to the circumstances and the extent of its potential intervention in a conflict between the PRC and Taiwan. As a tool of dual deterrence, it aims to deter Chinese military attacks against Taiwan as well as Taiwan formal independence. However, this policy has been under scrutiny in recent years. See, for instance, Boon and Sworn (2020).

[22] Compound semiconductors, such as Gallium arsenide and gallium nitride, are often used in military-specific devices with superior electrical features such as high electron mobility and direct bandgap compared to silicon-based semiconductors.

Wavetek – control over 90 per cent of the global foundry market for GaAs devices, extensively utilized in military systems (Damjanovski 2022: 17–18).

More importantly, Taiwan's significance in the global semiconductor supply chain underscores its strategic importance at the global level. The dual-use nature of semiconductors, benefiting both the military and civilian sectors, coupled with the premise that information technology and the Internet of Things, wherein semiconductors are fundamental building blocks, play a defining role in inter-state relations.[23] Thus, as Taiwanese semiconductor firms become dominant players in a strategically vital sector that inherently influences another country's military buildup capabilities, such as the United States, it not only grants Taiwan a strategic advantage but also represents a security vulnerability for that country.

Beyond its material power accumulation, Taiwan holds a unique geostrategic importance due to its central position in the first island chain in the western Pacific. On the one hand, this arguably elevates Taiwan's strategic relevance to the United States, especially as Washington aims to secure long-term interests in balancing Beijing's expanding military presence in the region. If Taiwan demonstrates its capabilities to provide the United States with access and situational awareness regarding Chinese military operations across all domains, it will aid Washington and its formal allies in countering China's military control of the seas in the Taiwan Strait and beyond. On the other hand, Taiwan's pivotal location suggests that China has significant strategic interests in controlling Taiwan, as it would grant the Chinese navy direct access to the Pacific Ocean, enhancing its maritime power (Chu 2017).

The legality of the use of force against Taiwan

Against the backdrop of Taiwan being a unique case of contested states, how would we proceed to analyze the legality of China's use of force against Taiwan? The conventional perspective has centered on the states-only conception of international legal personality, which has dominated the nineteenth and much of the twentieth centuries, as Henderson asserts in this edited volume. This traditional standpoint has based the legality of China's use of force against Taiwan on the latter's legal status (Butterton 1997). Since Taiwan is not recognized as a full state in international law, it cannot

---

[23] The US military superiority has long been underpinned by its technological leadership in areas such as semiconductors, for instance. Hence when the United States starts to lose dominance in the global semiconductor race in terms of manufacturing capability, while the Taiwanese and the South Korean firms begin to lead instead, it results in potential security risks for the United States arising from foreign dependency.

be considered a subject in international legal matters. Additionally, the use of force by China against Taiwan is not deemed illegal because the Taiwan issue is viewed as part of the PRC's domestic affairs. This argument relies on a literal interpretation of Article 2(4) of the UN Charter, which states, '[a]ll Members [of the United Nations] shall refrain in their international relations from the threat or use of force against the territorial integrity or political independence of any state, or in any other manner inconsistent with the Purposes of the United Nations'.[24] Moreover, China has the right to resist secessionist breakaway attempts by Taiwan, while Taiwan, as a non-state actor, has no right to collective self-defence under Article 51.[25]

This conventional perspective is compounded by the non-intervention principle, which forbids states from interfering in each other's domestic affairs and supports states' right to use force within their borders. The international community has often acquiesced to the use of force by states to quell secession attempts, despite its overarching support for the self-determination of peoples (Crawford 2006: 389–390). One telling example pertains to the United Nations's aloofness to Russia's forceful suppression of Chechnya's breakaway efforts in the 1990s (Lapidus 1998). Concerning the Taiwan case, Fisher (2020) contends that third-party states cannot legally exercise collective defence of Taiwan unless they are willing to be perceived as intruding upon Beijing's territorial integrity, which requires them to grant Taiwan diplomatic recognition before such an exercise. However, a revisionist perspective (Ediger 2018) has highlighted three ways in which non-state entities can be rights-holders in international law regarding the use of force.

First, an emerging body of UN precedents has emphasized the primacy of the human right of self-determination by distinctive peoples.

Secondly, *de facto* independent regimes that exercise their authority in a stabilized manner have rights and obligations under international law, providing them with a certain degree of international legal personality (Van Essen 2012), and there are precedents of the applicability of Article 2(4) irrespective of recognition to all *de facto* regimes (Frowein 1987: 73).[26] Ediger (2018: 1691) contends that '[s]tates practice suggests that states respect the borders of *de facto* regimes and that states consider it illegal to change the status of a *de facto* regime by force'. Frowein (1987) and Dörr and Randelzhofer (2012: 29) concur. In their view, state practice demonstrates that the prohibition of the use of force applies to *de facto* regimes, prohibiting

---

[24] https://legal.un.org/repertory/art2.shtml.
[25] For an additional nuanced discussion of whether Taiwan has the right to self-defence, see Henderson, Chapter 1 in this volume.
[26] These examples include Taiwan, the German Democratic Republic before 1972, North Vietnam before the reunification of Vietnam, North Korea, the Confederation in the American Civil War, and the national government in the Spanish Civil War.

any military action that would violate international lines of demarcation, including the borders of *de facto* regimes.[27]

Thirdly, the revisionist standpoint highlights the relevance of UN Charter Article 33, which emphasizes states' obligations to peacefully resolve disputes to avoid undermining international security. Hence, a claim to a contested territory does not license the use of force against that territory if such action results in international insecurity and instability, even if the state in question believes it has sovereignty over the contested territory. A telling example pertains to the Korean War (Ediger 2018: 1694). The UN Security Council authorized intervention after North Korea attacked South Korea because it regarded the attack as a breach of international peace. This was despite the fact that North Korea was not widely recognized as a state while the conflict could have been characterized as a Korean civil war. Since then, the Security Council viewed conflicts in Haiti, Somalia, the former Yugoslavia, and Rwanda, despite being internal to those states, as threats to international peace and security (Charney and Prescott 2000).

Applying these three concepts to Taiwan suggests that its state-like characteristics should grant it specific rights under international law. Firstly, the Taiwanese qualify as a distinctive 'people' for self-determination, which shields them from the use of force under international law (Ediger 2018: 1696; Charney and Prescott 2000: 472–473). Any unprovoked attack by China aiming to bring Taiwan, now a fully-fledged democracy, under its autocratic control would infringe on Taiwan's right to self-determination. Taiwan's democratic regime reflects the political will of its people, with public opinion consistently favoring maintaining the *status quo* rather than unification under an autocracy (Election Study Center 2022).[28]

Secondly, Taiwan is a stable *de facto* regime, as discussed earlier, and the Taiwan Strait has become a *de facto* border between Beijing and Taipei. Therefore, the combination of UN declarations and state practice protecting

---

[27] To support his argument, Frowein refers to two related UN resolutions. The first, known as the Friendly Relations Resolution of 25 October 1970 (UN General Assembly Resolution 2625 [XXV]), states that 'Every State likewise has the duty to refrain from the threat or use of force to violate international lines of demarcation, such as armistice lines, established by or pursuant to an international agreement to which it is a party or which it is otherwise bound to respect'. He further explains that such international lines of demarcation include the borders of *de facto* regimes. The second resolution is Art. 1 of the definition of aggression adopted by the UN General Assembly in Resolution 3314(XXIX) of 14 December 1974. This resolution contains an explanatory note clarifying that the term '"State" is used "without prejudice to questions of recognition or to whether a State is a member of" the UN'.

[28] For instance, the poll by the Election Study Center released on 20 July 2021 shows that over 87 per cent of the respondents supported maintaining the *status quo*, with 5.6 per cent preferring to declare independence and 1.5 per cent supporting unification.

the borders and legal status of *de facto* regimes supports an argument that China, as a UN member state, is prohibited from using force against Taiwan under Article 2(4) (Ediger 2018: 1699).

Thirdly, a preemptive attack by China would significantly disrupt international peace and security, potentially involving other regional powers. According to the TRA, Washington regards 'any effort to determine the future of Taiwan by other than peaceful means, including by boycotts or embargoes, a threat to the peace and security of the Western Pacific area and of grave concern to the United States'.[29] Therefore, Washington does not view Chinese military actions against Taiwan as a purely domestic matter of the PRC due to its explicit regional implications. Consequently, such attacks undermine international peace and security, thus violating Article 33.

In sum, the conventional perspective fails to grasp Taiwan's reality because the polity is not merely a non-state actor, as demonstrated in the previous section, and it further creates 'perverse incentives' for China to take Taiwan by force. In contrast, the revisionist standpoint offers a more satisfactory resolution regarding the use of force. As argued by Ediger (2018: 1705), if contested states like Taiwan 'could enjoy some of those protections' outlined in the revisionist perspective, 'it may give claimant states and third parties pause before resorting to force during a crisis'.

Great-power politics and the use of force against Taiwan

Against the background of Taiwan's legally contested status, it is crucial to further investigate China's use of force against Taiwan by assessing pertinent geopolitical factors through the realist prism of IR,[30] following the logic of great-power politics while considering Taiwan's material agency vis-à-vis China. Given Washington's changing perception of China as a peer competitor, the logic of great-power politics will arguably dictate its actions to intervene in a Cross-Strait contingency, despite its lack of formal military alliance with Taipei. although the logic of nuclear deterrence will constrain the depth of its intervention.

Offensive realism, a useful perspective to analyze China's foreign policy behaviours because its actions have been broadly consistent with what offensive realists have to say about rising powers (Mearsheimer 2014; 2021),[31]

---

[29] For the original text of TRA, see: www.congress.gov/bill/96th-congress/house-bill/2479.
[30] Needless to say, various IR theories have been applied to the study of the prospect of war across the Taiwan Strait. For an excellent review of these theories, see Kastner (2018).
[31] Needless to say, for a committed offensive realist, Taiwan's legal status does not matter, and the law is merely the playing field on which both China and the United States will pursue their respective geopolitical ambitions, as detailed below.

posits that given the anarchic structure of the international system, countries concerned about their security are compelled to compete with each other in pursuit of power. Additionally, any major state actor aims to maximize its share of global power to dominate the system by establishing regional hegemony and excluding its rivals from domination. If China acts like all other great powers in the past,[32] it will try to dominate Asia and reduce the American military presence, while the United States, as the existing hegemonic actor, will seek to contain China's aspiration to rise.

Mearsheimer's theory about China and its intentions has been supported by Doshi's study (2021) of China's grand strategy, which outlines Beijing's move, after 2017, to shift to an even more aggressive scheme for undermining US hegemony and building a Chinese order in Asia. Beijing regarded the global US retreat following Donald Trump's election victory in 2016 as a golden opportunity to 'expand its strategic focus from Asia to the wider globe and its governance systems' (Doshi 2021: 262).

The incorporation of Taiwan into China, driven by what Mearsheimer (2014) describes as nationalism and security considerations, is crucial to China's strategy to dominate Asia. This is evident in the continuous centrality of Taiwan to the PLA posture, with its missions focused on increasing coercive capabilities to deter perceived threats of formal Taiwan independence and strengthening its A2/AD capabilities. The latter aims to deter, delay, or deny any third-party military intervention during a Cross-Strait contingency, including preventing American and allied military forces from operating freely in the A2/AD airspace and maritime bubble around China's coastline. The PLA's modernization, aiming to become a 'world-class' military by the end of 2049 (Department of Defense 2020), has enhanced its capabilities in both qualitative and quantitative terms. For instance, Doshi (2021: 91–92) documents that the PLA's accelerating development of anti-ship ballistic missiles, since the US aircraft carrier operations in the Taiwan Strait to deter Chinese military actions during the 1995–1996 missile crisis, aims to use these missiles to deter or respond to US carrier-based intervention. Another telling example is China's hypersonic missiles, which, if air-launched, may credibly threaten land-based US assets (for example, Guam Naval Base) and aircraft carrier groups (Episkopos 2020). Consequently, decades of PLA modernization have tilted the military balance across the Taiwan Strait in Beijing's favour, increasing the nontrivial chance of a Chinese invasion of the island.

Although Taiwan, as a contested state, has limited capacity to form any formal military alliance, over time the TRA has provided a legal basis for US military assistance to Taiwan through the sale of defensive arms. Additionally,

---

[32] For a counter-argument that emphasizes Chinese exceptionalism, see Zheng (2005).

the Taiwan Policy Act of 2022, which passed through the US Senate in September 2022, stipulates that Washington will provide around US$4.5 billion over four years to accelerate the modernization of Taiwan's military (Wu 2022). In July 2023, the Biden administration approved its first-ever transfer of military equipment to Taiwan under a programme normally reserved for helping sovereign states (Zengerle 2023). Furthermore, the current US policy towards Taiwan is partly based on the logic of deterrence by punishment. The 'AirSea Battle' concept, a key component of the US military strategy that became official in 2010 and was in 2015 renamed the Joint Concept for Access and Maneuver in the Global Commons, envisions extensive US strikes on the Chinese mainland in the event of a Chinese attack against Taiwan. This means US action against China in times of war will not be limited to the Taiwan Strait. Moreover, to counter the PLA's increasing A2/AD capabilities, the United States has intensified efforts in alliance building, such as the re-established QUAD[33] since 2017, the first-ever trilateral summits among the United States, Japan, and South Korea in 2023, the effective use of precision strikes, C4ISR,[34] and net-centric warfare.

Crucially, since the first Trump administration, the United States has abandoned its past policy of engagement and embraced a containment policy towards China, following the logic of great-power politics. In the US National Defense Strategy Fact Sheet released in March 2022, the Biden administration identified China as its most consequential strategic competitor. The logic of great-power politics has thus dictated Washington's actions to contain China's ambition to dominate Asia. It further justifies future US actions to keep Taiwan's assets on its side of the strategic balance (Mearsheimer 2014), as opposed to allowing them to be taken by China. Taiwan's assets in the field of semiconductors as detailed earlier may reinforce Washington's resolve to deter any Chinese military takeover of Taiwan, as the island's status as a top-notch semiconductor powerhouse has enabled it to become a trusted chip supply chain partner for Washington, meeting the US defence needs for semiconductors (Lee and Kleinhans 2020; Shattuck 2021; Wong and Plummer 2023: 56–60; Chu 2025). Similarly, Taiwan's dominant position in the global semiconductor supply chain has potentially increased its material agency vis-à-vis China because it – at least partially – 'enhances

---

[33] QUAD stands for the Quadrilateral Security Dialogue, a strategic security dialogue between the United States, Australia, Japan, India, and Australia. It was originally established in 2007 and then re-established in 2007 through negotiations, a move widely viewed as the US-led effort to contain China's rise to become a regional hegemon.

[34] C4ISR stands for Command, Control, Communications, Computers (C4) Intelligence, Surveillance and Reconnaissance (ISR). Advanced C4ISR capabilities form a critical part of modern warfare; it provides an advantage through situational awareness, knowledge of the enemy and environment, and shortening the time between sensing and response.

the availability of partners that cannot sit idly while Taiwan falls into China's hands' (Kim 2022: 11). Moreover, Taiwan's material power in this regard implies that a Chinese takeover of Taiwan would enable the PLA to utilize the world's top-notch semiconductor manufacturing infrastructure on the island to further its modernization and ultimately deny the United States access to such technology (Chu 2025). To prevent this, McKinley and Harris (2021) of the US Army War College suggest that, in times of war, the United States should adopt a targeted scorched-earth strategy to destroy semiconductor factories on the island in a Taiwan contingency, thereby denying China the chipmaking infrastructure.

Furthermore, Taiwan's geostrategic importance implies that, if China gains full control of Taiwan, which occupies the central position in the first island chain, Chinese naval power will gain direct access to the Pacific Ocean. This could potentially challenge the existing advantage of the United States as a major maritime power.

If this realist logic is correct, it follows that the United States will not stand by if China launches an unprovoked attack against Taiwan for unification. It is highly likely that its formal allies, such as Japan, will assist Washington with logistical support, including fuel and ammunition (Japan Times 2021). In particular, given Tokyo's perception of Beijing as 'the greatest strategic challenge' for Japan, as outlined in its National Security Strategy in 2022 (Liu and He 2023: 26), Japanese logistical support for US forces in a Taiwan contingency is extremely probable. Additionally, these countries' calculations of interests concerning their involvement in a Cross-Strait conflict may also factor in Taiwan's assets in the area of semiconductors. After all, any Chinese military action against the island would severely disrupt the highly concentrated chip production activities in both Taiwan and mainland China (Martin et al 2023). This disruption would negatively affect chip supplies to a wide range of downstream industries, including artificial intelligence, 5G, self-driving vehicles, and the military, causing significant adverse effects on output in these industries and ripple effects within the broader world economy. Any Chinese military action against Taiwan could result in a tremendous economic loss estimated at US$2.6 trillion (Nikkei Asia 2022). Furthermore, the United States and its allies may impose economic sanctions against China as punitive measures, similar to those imposed on Russia after it invaded Ukraine. Moreover, the United States may consider its credibility when determining whether to intervene in a Cross-Strait contingency. Inaction by Washington, allowing China to take over Taiwan, a quasi-ally, could undermine its reputation as a reliable partner in the region in the eyes of formal military allies such as Japan and South Korea.

In 2014, China might have been reluctant to engage in a conflict with US military power over a Taiwan contingency due to constraints stemming from the prevailing global balance of power, which favoured the United States

(Mearsheimer 2014). Additionally, China's hesitancy to launch an attack against Taiwan could be compounded by the tremendous difficulties the PLA would face in completing a full occupation of Taiwan, located more than 100 kilometres away across the Strait. This would involve establishing a new government and maintaining control for an extended period (Matsuda 2022).

By 2020, however, China had already surpassed the United States in several key military areas including shipbuilding, land-based conventional ballistic and cruise missiles, and integrated air defence systems (Department of Defense 2020). In 2021, China successfully conducted new tests of DF-17 nuclear-capable hypersonic missiles, designed to evade ballistic missile defence systems deployed by the United States and its regional allies, as there is currently no antimissile technology that can intercept such fast-moving, manoeuvrable vehicles (Episkopos 2020; Ross 2021). China's advancements in this critical area of military technology have outpaced those of the United States, which lacks comparable capabilities.

If China's economic power continues to grow, its military might will increase accordingly. The PLA is focusing on enhancing its capability to neutralize US forces, including those stationed in Japan, South Korea, Hawaii, and Guam, during a conflict, thereby extending the duration required for the occupation of Taiwan. Additionally, China is expanding its nuclear capabilities, such as intercontinental ballistic missiles (Matsuda 2022). Following the historical patterns of emerging great powers, Beijing may be inclined to use its growing military strength to establish regional dominance as a hegemon. The reunification of Taiwan is viewed as a significant step toward realizing the rejuvenation of the Chinese nation, as envisioned by Chinese President Xi Jinping. Over time, the temptation for a more powerful China to use force to retake Taiwan could increase. Mearsheimer (2014: 35) suggests that, at some point in the next decade or so, the United States may lack sufficient power to effectively intervene in a Cross-Strait contingency: 'It will become impossible for the United States to help Taiwan defend itself against a Chinese attack'. But even if the United States intervenes, it is unlikely that it would 'escalate to the nuclear level if Taiwan is being overrun by China' (Mearsheimer 2014: 36) due to the significant risk of triggering a widespread thermonuclear conflict between Washington and Beijing. The nuclear deterrence factor predominantly explains the United States's reluctance to directly engage in the conflict in Ukraine, fearing the possibility of escalating into an unclear war with Russia. A similar rationale could influence the extent of US military intervention in a Cross-Strait contingency.

Conclusion

This chapter's multidisciplinary approach draws on international law and IR to provide a nuanced analysis of China's possible use of force against

Taiwan, a contested state. If China succeeds in militarily taking over Taiwan, it would undermine one of the world's most vibrant economies, dismantle the only democracy with an ethnic Chinese population, and integrate the island into Chinese autocratic control. This action would also grant the PLA direct access to the Pacific Ocean, enhancing China's status as a major maritime superpower. Moreover, it would allow China to assimilate Taiwan's economic and technological assets, including its world-class semiconductor manufacturing capabilities, furthering its ambition to establish a regional Chinese order. While the legality of the Chinese use of force against Taiwan as a contested state is a critical issue, it is crucial to consider the implications of such a border change. If we view the Taiwan Strait as a *de facto* border between the island and the mainland, this absorption by China would significantly redistribute power in the region. China's absorption of Taiwan would strengthen its position as a regional hegemon, diminishing the US interests and further eroding Washington's regional influence, potentially signalling US hegemonic decline. This scenario would also challenge the existing liberal international order, as regional powers may be inclined to align with the new autocratic regional hegemon rather than balancing against it.

References

Bartelson, J. (2016). Recognition: A Short History. *Ethics and International Affairs*, 30 (3), 303–321.

Boon, H.T. and Sworn, H.E. (2020). Strategic Ambiguity and the Trumpian Approach to China–Taiwan Relations. *International Affairs*, 96 (6), 1487–1508.

Butterton, G.R. (1997). Signals, Threats, and Deterrence: Alive and Well in the Taiwan Strait. *Catholic University Law Review*, 47 (1), 52–111.

Chan, P.C.W. (2009). The Legal Status of Taiwan and the Legality of the Use of Force in a Cross-Taiwan Strait Conflict. *Chinese Journal of International Law*, 8 (2), 482–485.

Charney, J.I. and Prescott, J.R.V. (2000). Resolving Cross-Strait Relations between China and Taiwan. *American Journal of International Law*, 94 (3), 453–477.

Chu, M.M. (2013). *The East Asian Computer Chip War*. London and New York: Routledge.

Chu, M.M. (2017). Taiwan's Traditional Security Challenges as a Contested State. In: S. Ganguly, A. Scobell, and J. Chinyong Liow (eds), *The Routledge Handbook of Asian Security Studies*. New York and London: Routledge, 88–99.

Chu, M.M. (2025). Taiwan's Strategic Imperatives in Safeguarding National Security through Semiconductor Dominance amid Sino-US rivalry. In: P.C.Y. Chow (ed.), *Technology Rivalry Between the Two Great Powers*, London: Palgrave Macmillan.

Crawford, J.R. (2006). *The Creation of States in International Law.* Oxford: Oxford University Press.

Damjanovski, A. (2022). *'Buffering' The US-China Tech Rivalry: the EU Strategy in The Era of Technological Competition.* Torino: Centro Einaudi.

Department of Defense (2020). *Military and Security Developments involving the People's Republic of China 2020.* Washington, DC: Department of Defense.

Dörr, O. and Randelzhofer, A. (2012). Article 2 (4). In: B. Simma, D.-E. Khan, G. Nolte, A. Paulus, and N. Wessendorf (eds), *The Charter of the United Nations: A Commentary, Volume I.* Oxford: Oxford University Press, 200–274.

Doshi, R. (2021). *The Long Game: China's Grand Strategy to Displace American Order.* Oxford: Oxford University Press.

Ediger, M.L. (2018). International Law and the Use of Force against Contested States: The Case of Taiwan. *New York University Law Review*, 93 (6), 1668–1706.

Election Study Center, National Chengchi University (2022). Taiwan Independence Vs. Unification with the Mainland (1994/12~2021/12). 10 January, https://esc.nccu.edu.tw/PageDoc/Detail?fid=7801&id=6963#accesskey-1.

Episkopos, M. (2020). Why China's Df-17 Hypersonic Missile Is So Dangerous. *The National Interest*, 17 November, https://nationalinterest.org/blog/buzz/why-china%E2%80%99s-df-17-hypersonic-missile-so-dangerous-172721.

Fisher, R.M. (2020). Defending Taiwan: Collective Self-Defense of Contested State. *Florida Journal of International Law*, 32 (1), 101–111.

Frowein, J.A. (1987). De Facto Regime. *Encyclopedia of Disputes Installment*, 10, 73–75.

Geldenhuys, D. (2009). *Contested States in World Politics.* Houndmills: Palgrave Macmillan.

Goldstein, S.M. and Schriver, R. (2001). An Uncertain Relationship: the United States, Taiwan and the Taiwan Relations Act. *The China Quarterly*, 165, 147–172.

Helmersen, S.T. (2021). China–Taiwan Threats of Force and the Paradox of the 'Nuclear Weapons Principle'. *International Community Law Review*, 23 (4), 403–426.

Hsiao, A.H. (1998). Is China's Policy to Use Force against Taiwan a Violation of the Principle of Non-Use of Force under International Law? *New England Law Review*, 32 (3), 730–732.

Japan Times (2021). Japan and U.S. Draft Operation Plan for Taiwan Contingency. *Japan Times*, 2 February, www.japantimes.co.jp/news/2021/12/23/national/taiwan-contingency/.

Kastner, S.L. (2018). International Relations Theory and the Relationship across the Taiwan Strait. *International Journal of Taiwan Studies*, 1 (1), 161–183.

Kastner, S.L. (2022). *War and Peace in the Taiwan Strait*. New York: Columbia University Press.

Kim, J. (2022). The Agency of Secondary States in Order Transition in the Indo-Pacific. *The Pacific Review*, DOI: 10.1080/09512748.2022.2125049.

Krasner, S.D. (1999). *Sovereignty: Organized Hypocrisy*. Princeton, NJ: Princeton University Press.

Krasner, S.D. (ed.) (2001). *Problematic Sovereignty: Contested Rules and Political Possibilities*. New York: Columbia University Press.

Lapidus, G.W. (1998). Contested Sovereignty: the Tragedy of Chechnya. *International Security*, 23 (1), 5–49.

Lee, J. and Kleinhans, J.-P. (2020). Taiwan, Chips, and Geopolitics: Part 1. *The Diplomat*, 10 December, https://thediplomat.com/2020/12/taiwan-chips-and-geopolitics-part-1/.

Liu, F. and He, K. (2023). China's Bilateral Relations, Order Transition, and the Indo-Pacific Dynamics. *China Review*, 23 (1), 11–43.

Martin, B., Baldwin, L.H., DeLuca, P., Sanchez, N.H., Hvizda, M., Smith, C.D., and Whitehead, N.P. (2023). *Supply Chain Interdependence and Geopolitical Vulnerability: The Case of Taiwan and High-End Semiconductors*. Santa Monica: RAND.

Matsuda, Y. (2022). Will a Taiwan Emergency Happen? Analyzing the Challenges Facing China. *Japan SPOTLIGHT*, January/February, 18–20.

McKinney, J.M. and Harris, P. (2021). Broken Nest: Deterring China from Invading Taiwan. *Parameters*, 51 (4), 23–36.

Mearsheimer, J.J. (2014). Taiwan's Dire Straits. *The National Interest*, 130, 29–39.

Mearsheimer, J.J. (2021). The Inevitable Rivalry: America, China, and the Tragedy of Great-Power Politics. *Foreign Affairs*, 100 (6), 48–59.

MOFA (nd). IGOs in Which We Participate: Full Member. Taipei: Ministry of Foreign Affairs, ROC, www.mofa.gov.tw/enigo/Link3enigo.aspx?n=58BD38F4400A7167&sms=A72EC821FB103DD9.

MOFA (2014). The Foreign Relations Yearbook 2013. Taipei: Ministry of Foreign Affairs, ROC, http://multilingual.mofa.gov.tw/web/web_UTF-8/almanac/almanac2013/almanac2013.htm.

MOFA (2019). Taiwan at a Glance. Taipei: Ministry of Foreign Affairs, ROC, http://multilingual.mofa.gov.tw/web/web_UTF-8/MOFA/glance2019-2020/English.pdf.

MOFA (2020). List of ROC Double Taxation Agreements. Taipei: Ministry of Finance, ROC, www.mof.gov.tw/singlehtml/191?cntId=63930.

Nikkei Asia (2022). $2.6tn Could Evaporate from Global Economy in Taiwan Emergency. *Nikkei Asia*, 22 August, https://asia.nikkei.com/Spotlight/The-age-of-Great-China/2.6tn-could-evaporate-from-global-economy-in-Taiwan-emergency2.

Ross, P.E. (2021). Sure, China's Hypersonic Weapons May Have Incited a 'Sputnik Moment' but Why Is the Pentagon Surprised? *IEEE Spectrum*, 28 October, https://spectrum.ieee.org/china-hypersonic-weapons-sputnik-moment.

Ross, R.S. (2000). The 1995–96 Taiwan Strait Confrontation: Coercion, Credibility, and the Use of Force. *International Security*, 25 (2), 87–123.

Shattuck, T.J. (2021). Stuck in the Middle: Taiwan's Semiconductor Industry, the U.S.-China Tech Fight, and Cross-Strait Stability. *Orbis*, 65(1), 101–117.

Shivakumar, S. and Wessner, C. (2022). *Semiconductors and National Defense: What Are the Stakes?* Washington, DC: Centre for Strategic and International Studies, www.csis.org/analysis/semiconductors-and-national-defense-what-are-stakes.

Van Essen, J. (2012). De Facto Regimes in International Law. *Utrecht Journal of International and European Law*, 28 (4), 31–49.

Whiting, A.S. (2001). China's Use of Force, 1950–96, and Taiwan. *International Security*, 26 (2), 103–131.

Wong, H.-S.P. and Plummer, J. (2023). Implications of Technology Trends in the Semiconductor Industry. In: L. Diamond, J.O. Ellis JR., and O. Schell (eds), *Silicon Triangle: the United States, Taiwan, China, and Global Semiconductor Security*. Stanford: Hoover Institution Press, 51–86.

Wong, J. (2003). Deepening Democracy in Taiwan. *Pacific Affairs*, 76 (2), 235–256.

Wu, C.C.-H. (2022). The Taiwan Policy Act and the Future of U.S.–Taiwan Relations. 13 December, commentary, the Stimson Center, www.stimson.org/2022/the-taiwan-policy-act-and-the-future-of-u-s-taiwan-relations/.

Zengerle, P. (2023). Biden Approves Military Aid to Taiwan Under Program Normally Used for Sovereign States. *Reuters*, 31 August, www.reuters.com/world/asia-pacific/biden-approves-military-aid-taiwan-under-program-normally-used-sovereign-states-2023-08-30/.

Zheng, B. (2005). China's 'Peaceful Rise' to Great-Power Status. *Foreign Affairs*, 84 (5), 18–24.

3

International Law and the Legitimation of State Violence in the Fourth Eelam War (2006–2009)

Megan Price

Introduction

In early 2009, Sri Lankan government forces were closing in on an unprecedented military victory over the armed separatist group, the Liberation Tigers of Tamil Eelam (LTTE). The LTTE had been a formidable opponent. In 20 years of conflict with the government, the separatist group had established and operated its own state-like entity in north-east Sri Lanka. Yet in January 2009, the LTTE lost control of its administrative capital of Kilinochchi. With hundreds of thousands of civilians in tow, they were on the retreat. What followed was a brutal final standoff with government forces in the coastal area of Mullaitivu in the Northern Province or Wanni region. Here, the government took an 'any means necessary' approach to the fight. They shelled LTTE positions with no regard for trapped civilians, causing the majority of the estimated 40,000 civilian casualties (McMahan 2009).

Since the events of early 2009, there has been a considerable volume of work investigating the extent to which government forces and/or the LTTE violated the laws of armed conflict and international human rights law (UN POE 2011; Petrie 2012; Ratner 2012). Such work has formed part of an ongoing battle for accountability. This chapter takes a different approach to analyzing law's influence upon the conflict. Where the preceding accounts view the laws of war primarily as a potential constraint upon the conduct of armed action, in keeping with the central themes of this book, this chapter examines how law may have enabled the violence. It explores this theme through a focus on the Sri Lankan government's justifications for military action.

In the politics of legitimacy and military action, the law strengthened the government's hand in important respects. In contrast to cases where there is more ambiguity surrounding the status of the contested territory, few international actors viewed Tamil Eelam as a legitimate candidate for external self-determination. As such, the Sri Lankan government could readily claim a legal basis for their armed action and situate the fighting in the remit of the less restrictive paradigm of the Laws of Non-International Armed Conflict (NIAC). Legally speaking, the rebel group was acutely vulnerable.

Where we might have hoped the laws of war would exert a restraining effect on the conduct of hostilities, the Sri Lankan government opted to contest the meaning of its legal obligations. This contestation shows that, while the law can exert a constraining effect, it also provides the language through which actors can resist taking responsibility for their harms.

This chapter commences by drawing on insights from critical legalism and the constructivist tradition of IR to establish the conceptual premises of the analysis. In this chapter, I treat law as a medium through which actors contest the legitimacy of military action. The remaining sections of the chapter explore how the Sri Lankan government wielded the medium of law. The sections are divided into an account of Sri Lanka's justification for pursuing a military victory – the *jus ad bellum* dimension – and an account of how it described its conduct – the *jus in bello* dimension.

International law as a medium of political contestation: insights from critical legalism and constructivist IR

Recognizing that much of global politics is conducted in the language of international law, constructivist IR scholars have sought to grapple with law's precise nature and influence. Shirley Scott described international law as an *ideology* that underpins the contemporary states system. The ideology consists of a collectively held belief that legal principles are superior to non-legal ones and that, by wielding the language of international law, actors gain prestige (Scott 1994: 318). Chris Reus-Smit has described contractual international law as a *fundamental institution* that conditions the negotiation of more specific agreements such as the 1966 International Covenants (Reus-Smit 2014: 66). More recently, Ian Hurd argued that, because all actors recognize an imperative to explain their policies in the register of international law, it can be understood as a form of international *empire* (Hurd 2018: 265–278). These scholars alight upon a common theme – that much of contemporary international politics is mediated by and reconstituted through international law.

By virtue of its standing, international law affects the exercise of power. Here, power is conceptualized in a particular way. In traditional realpolitik terms, power means material resources. At most, material resources might be augmented by non-material things like symbols, ideas, and rules. Yet for constructivists, law plays a more significant role than one of augmentation (Bukovansky 2002: 19). If we accept that international law is an empire, an ideology, or a fundamental institution, then it does not stand separately from material resources but instead produces them. Critical legal theorist David Kennedy provides examples of this constitutive dynamic when he points to law's myriad of 'war generative' functions. Law serves as the 'background rules and institutions' for 'buying and selling weaponry, recruiting soldiers, managing armed forces, encouraging technological innovation, making the spoils of war profitable, channelling funds to and from belligerents or organizing public support' (Kennedy 2009: 32). We make sense of these practices through the language of law and when actors can show their preferred measures are legal, they find themselves empowered. This point has an important implication for our understanding of law and violence. We tend to think of international law as a constraint on conflict, yet it also significantly determines who wins and who loses, who is empowered, and who is stigmatized.

While international law might be constitutive of international politics, critical legal scholars have been at pains to point out that international law is indeterminate in nature (Kennedy 2009: 38; Koskenniemi 2011: 40). In any given circumstance, more than one law might apply, and actors might interpret a single law in very different ways (Kennedy 2009: 38). Law has an ever-present elastic quality. This view of law can be contrasted with the legal positivist notion that we can identify the difference between compliance and non-compliance (Scott 1994: 315). For critical legal scholars, when we form a judgment about whether something is legal, we invariably do so by smuggling in principles from the realm of politics. Law's indeterminacy is one of the reasons Scott described it as an ideology. International politics plays host to an intersubjective belief that law is a coherent body of rules which states are bound to follow (in other words, legal positivism) (Scott 1994: 316). This belief does not square with the practice of international law, but it nonetheless legitimizes institutions such as the rules of war and it puts a premium on the skill of legal argument.

At most, legal interpretations become more or less dominant. For instance, in the realm of international armed conflict, it is commonplace to insist on a strict separation between *jus ad bellum* and *jus in bello*. Such separation provides for the legal symmetry of combatants. A soldier might fight on the side of the 'unjust' party, but that does not preclude them from possessing the right to use lethal force (Walzer 2006: 127). It is also commonly accepted that this legal symmetry does not exist in the context of non-international armed conflicts. Should they be captured, non-state combatants in a civil war can be punished for their participation (Meisels 2014: 305). Importantly, these dominant interpretations are not fixed. They have evolved over time, and they continue to be contested.[1]

Because law is constitutive of power but indeterminate, we should think of it as a medium of political contestation and not a set of fixed standards for assessing the legality or illegality of measures. Actors use law to portray their preferred measures as legitimate and to shape possibilities for future action. When their preferred measures are in keeping with dominant interpretations of the law, then their task is often a straightforward one. Yet actors sometimes contest dominant interpretations. For instance, the Bush administration coined the term 'unlawful combatants' in a bid to place captured al Qaeda members in a lacuna between the Third and Fourth Geneva Conventions (Glazier 2010: 10). The legal strategist is cognizant of dominant interpretations of the law, but sometimes their strategy involves revising those interpretations (Kennedy 2009: 36). When they engage in such innovation, they illustrate the ideological heft of international law combined with its indeterminate nature.

For the purposes of examining how international law influenced the politics of armed action in Sri Lanka, there are a couple of important takeaways from the preceding discussion of constructivism and critical legalism. First, while the chapter identifies where Sri Lanka's claims depart from dominant interpretations of the law, it sides with Ian Hurd's argument that 'international law is often much more successful at constituting and legitimating government policies than at positively distinguishing between compliance and noncompliance' (Hurd 2020: 3). Second, and as a corollary of the preceding point, where many accounts identify law of war violations, this chapter situates such work within an ongoing contest to define the legitimacy of Sri Lanka's actions.

International law and the (un)contested state of Tamil Eelam:
Jus ad bellum

Between 2002 and 2008, the Sri Lankan government and the LTTE were party to a Norwegian-brokered ceasefire agreement. By 2007, however, the agreement was all but history. Tellingly, both parties had stopped bothering

---

[1] For instance, in his revisionist contribution to Just War theory, Jeff McMahan (2009) argues that unjust warriors should not have moral permission to harm people in conflicts. McMahan's book is an example of the continually contested nature of the Just War tradition. Debates in the Just War tradition then help reconstitute the law of war and thereby the practice of warfare itself.

to report ceasefire violations and the monitoring mission characterized the situation as one of all-out war (Sørbø et al 2011: 19). In the context of this resumption in full-scale hostilities, the Sri Lankan government set to work on a new narrative about the purpose of their military action. Before, they were responding to ceasefire violations and forcing an intransigent LTTE back to the negotiating table. Increasingly, they emphasized the benefits of their territorial gains. As Foreign Minister Rohitha Bogollogama told his audience at Johns Hopkins University in late 2007, 'the Eastern Province of Sri Lanka, which was until recently been terrorized by the LTTE, has been rid of that menace' (Bogollagama 2007). The theme of liberation was on full display by the following year when President Mahinda Rajapaksa spoke about the government's operations in the Northern Province:

> [W]hat the Government of Sri Lanka would not and could not do is to let an illegal and armed terrorist group, the LTTE, hold a fraction of our population, a part of the Tamil community, hostage to such terror in the Northern part of Sri Lanka and deny those people their democratic rights of dissent and free elections. (Rajapaksa 2008)

With this claim, the president set out a humanitarian rationale for military action. This notion of military action as 'hostage rescue' would resurface later in the conflict.

In Sri Lankan government accounts, there was no question that LTTE-held territory belonged to Sri Lanka. Responding to calls to return to the negotiating table, Rajapaksa asserted that he would only do so if the LTTE dismantled its military capability and recognized the Sri Lankan government's jurisdiction: 'the elected Government cannot and will not permit undermining of the territorial integrity of the sovereign UN Member State of Sri Lanka and the division of its territory' (Rajapaksa 2008). While in principle open to new talks, for the Rajapaksa government, Sri Lanka's borders were not up for negotiation.

References to territorial integrity were buttressed by claims about the LTTE's terrorist credentials. Speaking at the Japan Institute of International Affairs, Mangala Samaraweera provided a typical government account of the secessionist group: '[T]he LTTE are not freedom fighters fighting on behalf of an oppressed minority. They are a ruthless terrorist organization that rules the Tamil people through fear and intimidation' (Samaraweera 2006). Samaraweera's comments were part of a persistent government effort to situate the conflict within the parameters of the US-led global war on terror (Sørbø et al 2011: 78; Price 2022: 61–65). In fighting the LTTE, Sri Lanka was doing its bit for the international community.

When it came to squaring its resort to force with international law, the Sri Lankan government was in a far stronger position than the United States.

If anything, this position grew more commanding as a result of the US government's efforts to justify military action in the name of the war on terror. The US government used the terror discourse to advance a radical interpretation of 'the Caroline Criteria'. By the terms of the Caroline Criteria, states can engage in pre-emptive military intervention where threats are 'overwhelming' and 'leaving no choice of means and no moment of deliberation' (Byers 2005: 52). Yet for the Bush administration, this definition was not permissive enough. According to the administration, the US's adversaries were modern-day terrorists and 'rogue' regimes who were conspiring to attack the United States with nuclear weapons. The United States supposedly could not wait for such a threat to reach the thresholds of the Caroline Criteria. Yet, for the Bush administration, the difficulty in legitimising this claim lay in the fact that the original Caroline Criteria was already regarded as *too* permissive. Other states had all but ceased invoking it at all (Byers 2005: 52).

In the controversy surrounding the Bush doctrine and the global war on terror more generally, the Sri Lankan government was empowered from two directions. First, they had a compelling means of reducing the credibility of any criticism from the likes of the United States. If the Bush administration had cited the threat of terrorism to advance a permissive new conception of pre-emption, the Bush administration could hardly quibble with Sri Lanka for fighting terrorists at home. Yet, criticism of the Bush doctrine also helped reinforce the Sri Lankan government's position from a second direction because much of this criticism centred on the importance of the non-interference principle. By implication, domestic military action immediately appeared less transgressive, more legitimate. Unlike the United States and their controversial arguments about pre-emption, Sri Lanka's armed action transgressed no widely recognized international boundaries. The terror discourse and legal debates about *jus ad bellum* afforded Sri Lanka an advantageous position from which to legitimize their own military action.

The relative lack of *legal* controversy surrounding Sri Lanka's decision to escalate its military action is evident in international responses. As the ceasefire deteriorated, foreign governments confined their opposition to the question of how the Sri Lankan government would win the peace. The US Deputy Assistant Secretary for South and Central Asian Affairs, Evan Feigenbaum, offered such an argument in response to a question on the then escalating hostilities:

> I would repeat what the Ambassador and others have said many times, which is we continue to believe, fundamentally, that it ultimately will be a political solution that is required to give all communities, including the Tamil community and the Muslim community, a sense

of investment in the future of the island, a sense of being stakeholders in the future of this country, including the politics and governance of this country. (Feigenbaum 2008)

While Feigenbaum stressed the importance of finding a political solution to the issue of ethnic and religious grievances, he did not dispute the notion that Sri Lanka was entitled to engage in military action. It is also notable that the conflict never reached the UN Security Council agenda. While geopolitical factors undoubtedly facilitated this outcome, keeping the conflict away from the auspices of the council was likely made easier by the perception that the matter was internal.

To further show how the LTTE were made vulnerable by the law, debates about Sri Lanka's military action can be contrasted with those in other cases of contested statehood. Elsewhere, international law arguably does yield a more restraining effect on the prospect of full-scale hostilities. Consider Western Sahara. In a 1974 advisory opinion, the International Court of Justice found that Morocco did not have sovereignty over the territory and that Western Sahara was entitled to external self-determination. The Trump administration's 2020 decision to recognize Moroccan sovereignty over Western Sahara challenges the ICJ's ruling. Nonetheless, the original 1974 ruling presents a complication to the Moroccan government should it attempt to legitimize further military incursions into Polisaro-held territory (Fernandez-Molina, Chapter 6 in this volume). The Rajapaksa government in Sri Lanka faced no such adverse ruling.

The contested state of Taiwan provides another revealing comparison with the Sri Lankan case. Here, the possibility of superpower conflict complicates the surrounding legal dynamics. China maintains that Taiwan is part of its territory and that they therefore have the right to reincorporate it, forcefully or otherwise. Yet, the threat of great power conflict also potentially affects the case's legal terrain. Under Article 33 of the UN Charter, parties are required to resolve disputes peacefully if those disputes impinge upon international security. Citing the risk of superpower conflict, proponents of the revisionist doctrine argue that Taiwan should effectively be entitled to the protection of the non-interference principle (Chu, Chapter 2 in this volume).

In the Sri Lankan case, there was comparatively little risk of outside intervention on the LTTE's behalf. India had collaborated with the LTTE in the 1980s, but the rebels had long since burned their bridges with New Delhi. The group turned on Indian peacekeeping forces following the 1987 Indo-Sri Lanka Accords and then sealed their position of ignominy by assassinating former Indian Prime Minister Rajiv Gandhi (Keethaponcalan 2011: 41). Other powers were no more enthusiastic about helping the LTTE. Rajapaksa cultivated ties with Beijing and thereby made India wary of alienating Sri Lanka (Sørbø et al 2011: 76). The United States proscribed the LTTE as a terrorist organization in 1997 and were implementing an increasing array of measures to crack down on the LTTE's international funding networks (Lunstead 2011: 62). Like India, there is evidence that US foreign policy elites viewed growing Chinese influence in Sri Lanka as a reason to moderate their humanitarian stance (Committee on Foreign Relations 2009: 16). For our purposes, the cases of Taiwan and Western Sahara reveal the extent of the LTTE's vulnerability to military attack. Tamil Eelam was not regarded as a legitimate candidate for external self-determination. Nor were escalating tensions in Sri Lanka likely to precipitate major power intervention. As such, political contestation around government action was confined to the question of whether violence would secure Colombo's authority over the contested territory. There was less contestation around the question of whether the government was entitled to try a violent solution.

International law in an (un)contested state: *jus in bello*

Because fighting took place within Sri Lanka's borders and the conflict met the threshold and organization requirements of the Tadić criteria, it was regulated by the Laws of Non-International Armed Conflict (NIAC). NIAC is less restrictive than the Laws of International Armed Conflict (IAC), partly because it dispenses with the concept of legal symmetry between combatants. While a captured LTTE combatant was theoretically protected under international human rights law, they could not claim the protections of prisoner of war status. Meanwhile, government officials could not be prosecuted for 'grave breaches' of the Geneva Conventions. If 'grave breaches' were applicable, we could plausibly view the government IDP (internally displaced persons) camps as examples of 'unlawful confinement of civilians' as well as 'torture' (Mettraux 2005: 44–46). Such offences had led to convictions in the Celebici case during the International Criminal Tribunal for the former Yugoslavia (ICTY 1998). Other cases of contested statehood also implicate more restrictive legal paradigms. When the ICC prosecutor applied for arrest warrants in connection to the current Israeli assault on Gaza, he cited the existence of war crimes in an *international* armed conflict between Israel and Palestine (Khan 2024). Similarly, in Western Sahara, the 1974 ICJ ruling suggests that Moroccan and Polisaro armed clashes should fall under Additional Protocol I – wars of decolonization and, by extension, the laws of IAC. For a government fighting separatist groups, political contests over the status of a particular territory have significant flow on effects for the question of how those conflicts can be waged.

Killing en masse: disengagement from, and reengagement with, the law

In Sri Lanka's justifications for its onslaught during the final months of the war, the law of armed conflict was put to use for the purposes of rationalizing the enormous death toll. This strategic invocation of law did not occur straight away. Initially, the Sri Lankan government sought to disengage the law by narrating its military action so as to render the principles of distinction and proportionality irrelevant. In the face of robust contestation, this initial strategy gave way to a form of legal re-engagement whereby the government sought to present its actions as proportionate. Efforts at establishing accountability have been frustrated by the Rajapaksas' post-war stranglehold on Sri Lankan politics. In the event that the issue finds its way to some kind of tribunal, the Sri Lankan government's efforts to engage the law may very well enable them to avoid taking responsibility for a significant proportion of the 40,000 or so civilian casualties.

In its initial strategy of legal disengagement, the Sri Lankan government practised what Ian Clark and his colleagues call a denialist approach to the laws of war. In denialist strategies, actors supply their own version of events to curtail the reach of a given law or legal principle (Clark et al 2018: 319–343). For instance, states often seek to bolster their armed capabilities by backing non-state rebel groups. This strategy entails a measure of risk because, under the laws of armed conflict, where it is accepted that governments 'control' a group, they can be held responsible for its crimes. When faced with such accusations, a common response is to contest the existence of ties or of ties amounting to control. In other instances, denialism takes an even more radical form. States simply contest the very existence of events. In the case of recent massacres in Bucha, Ukraine, Russian officials claimed that Western countries had 'staged' the event to make Russia look bad (Reuters 2022). In this example, Russia depicted the key events so that the relevant legal principles could not be made to assess its actions.

The Sri Lankan government deployed its own strategy of denialism during the final months of the conflict when it sought to narrate the events of Mullaitivu. According to government accounts, Sri Lanka aimed to 'rescue' the trapped civilians with 'zero civilian casualties'. As Rajapaksa informed journalists: 'On my instructions, due to the priority given to the policy of zero civilian casualties the security forces are limiting themselves to rescue operations of the entrapped civilians held hostage as a human shield by the LTTE' (Rajapaksa 2009a). By the terms of this account, Sri Lanka was going above and beyond the requirements of proportionality. Indeed, Sri Lankan officials categorically denied using heavy weaponry (Samarasinghe 2009). If civilians were endangered, Sri Lankan officials insisted it was because the LTTE had used civilians as 'human shields', and shot them if they attempted to flee. The government buttressed this narrative by vigorously contesting figures like the civilian casualty rate and the number of trapped civilians. The 2012 UN internal review report notes that '[t]he Government's harsh reaction to even the suggestion that there were civilian casualties led the United Nations in Colombo to limit the sharing of information on the casualties' (Petrie 2012: 65). Similarly, in early May 2009, the government claimed there were only 10,000 trapped civilians. UN estimates at that time put the figure at over 100,000 though even this UN figure fell far short of the tally. At the conclusion of fighting, over 295,000 civilians emerged from the battle zone (Petrie 2012: 35). In the government's denialist narrative, its action could not be assessed according to the criteria of distinction or proportionality because the LTTE had killed the civilians.

A range of actors contested Sri Lanka's denialist strategy (Human Rights Watch 2009; International Crisis Group 2010; Channel 4 2011; Weiss 2012). In 2010, the UN Secretary General commissioned the Panel of Experts to compile a report into the events of the final months of the conflict. Published the following year, the UN Panel of Experts Report determined there were credible allegations against the LTTE for six potentially serious violations: '[U]sing civilians as a human buffer; (ii) killing civilians attempting to flee LTTE control; (iii) using military equipment in the proximity of civilians; (iv) forced recruitment of children; (v) forced labour; and (vi) killing of civilians through suicide attacks' (UN POE 2011: iiv–iv). However, and against the notion of a 'zero civilian casualty' approach, the report found that throughout the hostilities of 2009, Sri Lankan armed forces used heavy weaponry including in the so-called no fire zones (UN POE 2011: ii). The report acknowledged there were difficulties in estimating the civilian casualty rate. Limited surveys conducted after the conflict indicated that a high percentage of people had reported their relatives were among the dead. These surveys informed the report's assertion that 40,000 was a credible estimate (UN POE 2011: 40). The Panel of Experts also alleged that government shelling had caused the *majority* of these civilian casualties (UN POE 2011: 49). Against the 'hostage rescue' narrative, the authors pointed out that many of the civilians feared the government (UN POE 2011: 19). Finally, against the narrative of 'liberation', they pointed out that the 295,000 surviving civilians were detained en masse in closed IDP sites that became rife with abuses such as forced disappearances (UN POE 2011: 44). In other words, the report seemed to reject every premise of Sri Lanka's denialist claim.

The Panel of Experts report placed the spotlight back on the Sri Lankan government. In response, the government established its own Presidential Commission of Inquiry, which enlisted the help of a distinguished cast of international legal experts.[2] David Crane and Sir Desmond de Silva were among these lawyers. Crane was the former chief prosecutor of the Special Court for Sierra Leone, while de Silva was the former UN chief war crimes prosecutor. They submitted a joint opinion that exonerated the

---

[2] Neve Gordon and Nicola Perugini (2020) also provide an account of this phase of Sri Lanka's justificatory strategy in their book on the history of human shields.

Sri Lankan government. In contrast to the denialist narrative, Crane and de Silva re-engaged IHL by arguing that the government's military action was proportionate: 'If there were as many as 40,000 killed ... this would be a loss of approximately 12% of that population. Whatever the figure in terms of a hostage rescue operation where some 295,000 were saved – it is a successful operation' (Crane and de Silva 2015). In the denialist strategy, the government had not killed any civilians. In Crane and De Silva's opinion, it might have killed as many as 40,000 civilians but, in that event, those casualties were proportionate to the 295,000 it 'saved'.

As part of their argument about proportionality, Crane and de Silva drew on legal debates around human shielding. Referring to credible evidence that the LTTE had prevented civilians from leaving, they argued that the Sri Lankan government was entitled to adjust the proportionality calculation and, in effect, kill more people. In cases where the civilians were not coerced, Crane and de Silva suggested that many were liable to be killed because they stayed with the LTTE 'voluntarily':

> As a matter of logic, there is a powerful case for saying that it is extremely unlikely that some 20,000 cadres of LTTE, at that stage, could have taken up to 330,000 hostages against their will. The probability is that a large section of the civilians went voluntarily with the LTTE in order to play a part, albeit passive, in the LTTE war effort. (Crane and de Silva 2015)

This explanation positioned the civilians as 'voluntary shields'. Crane and de Silva went on to argue that, in cases of voluntary shielding, the government was not responsible for the civilian deaths because those civilians could conceivably be understood as legitimate targets. In other words, Crane and de Silva's legal reasoning relaxed the criteria of proportionality *and* converted a significant portion of the civilians from immune to liable.

Crane and de Silva had glossed over much. In their account, the government could take credit for saving hundreds of thousands of civilians. Yet it is worth pointing out that those same 'saved' civilians found themselves in the equivalent of a prison. Moreover, the government's methods of 'saving' them displayed manifold contempt for their welfare. For instance, the UN Panel of Experts allege the government deliberately underestimated the number of trapped civilians in order to reduce the flow of humanitarian aid (UN POE 2011: 39). As Gordon and Perugini point out, to accept Crane and de Silva's argument about the significance of the military objective, one has to assume that 300,000 or so civilians would have perished if the government had not shelled them (Gordon and Perugini 2020: 19). In relation to the question of voluntary shielding, escaping civilians often needed to move in the direction of oncoming fire

(UN POE 2011: 19). In any case, if the civilians volunteered to act as shields, then they arguably did not require 'rescuing'. Crane and de Silva had paradoxically characterized a significant portion of civilians as hostages *and* willing participants.

For all its wrongheadedness, unlike Sri Lanka's earlier strategy of legal disengagement, Crane and de Silva's opinion bore a slightly less surreal relationship to events. They did not contest allegations the government killed most of the 40,000 civilian casualties. Instead, their strategy of legal re-engagement rested on the assertion that the government was not legally responsible for those deaths. Significantly, *the law provides for this kind of argument*. Indeed, it is possible that Crane and de Silva were comfortable working for the Sri Lankan government because exonerating them did not require a wholly flagrant transgression of the legal terrain. On a basic level, the Additional Protocols to the Geneva Conventions enshrine the principle of 'double effect' (Kaempf 2009: 668). As such, the government never needed to invoke the phrase 'zero civilian casualties'. On the issue of human shields, Crane and de Silva's strategy of legal engagement played on an ambiguity in the law. Additional Protocol I to the Geneva Conventions prohibits the use of human shields (Additional Protocols 1977). Yet there are no treaty norms that specifically stipulate the attacker's obligations when its adversary employs the tactic (Schmitt 2009: 292). A widely held view is that the presence of involuntary human shields does not alter the attacker's legal obligations (Haque 2015: 394; Cohen and Zlotogorski 2021: 332).[3] Yet some legal scholars have contested this view, arguing that, if armed groups compel civilians to act as human shields, the attacking group should be permitted to relax assessments of proportionality (Dinstein 2004: 131; Rubinstein and Roznai 2011: 112). This latter view can be found in the UK's 2004 *Joint Service Manual of the Law of Armed Conflict* (Joint Doctrine and Concepts Centre 2015) and in the updated version of the 2015 US Department of Defense *Law of War Manual* (Office of General Council 2015). Such accounts can be read to support the basic premise of Crane and de Silva's argument – that the Sri Lankan government could be held to a different standard of proportionality if the LTTE coerced a portion of the civilians into serving as shields.

The question of 'passive voluntary shielding' also engages ongoing debates among legal scholars. The ICRC Interpretive Guidance on Direct Participation in Hostilities states that voluntary human shields can become

---

[3] The Additional Protocols (1977) appear to support this view: 'Any violation of these prohibitions shall not release the Parties to the conflict from their legal obligations with respect to the civilian population and civilians, including the obligation to take the precautionary measures provided for in Article'.

legitimate targets but only in circumstances where they create a physical barrier to an enemy attack (for example, physically blocking the path of advancing ground forces). If the civilian presence only affects the attacker's capacity to adhere to the principle of distinction, then they retain their protected status. These circumstances typically arise when the advancing forces employ heavy artillery as human beings cannot physically impede such fire power (Melzer 2009: 56–58). Crane and de Silva appeared to acknowledge that the civilians in the Sri Lankan case were at best a legal rather than physical barrier. Yet they pointed out that some scholars have contested the ICRC guidance. Emphasizing the importance of deterring human shielding, one such group argues that civilians should be understood as direct participants (Dinstein 2004: 130; Schmitt 2009: 326).[4] These arguments have significant implications for the Sri Lankan case. In the event the government successfully characterizes a portion of the civilians as 'voluntary shields' then, on their logic, those civilians would be responsible for their *own* deaths.

There is an ongoing contest to characterize the legitimacy of Sri Lanka's actions. The Sri Lankan government did face some condemnation over its final shelling campaign in the Wanni. After an uncritical initial reaction, in 2015, the UN Human Rights Council adopted a resolution supporting the establishment of a hybrid tribunal (UN Human Rights Council 2009; 2015). The UN Panel of Experts Report also prompted a period of reflection among UN agencies over their reticence to criticize the Sri Lankan government during the crisis (Petrie 2012). Proposals for a hybrid tribunal have been stymied principally because the Rajapaksa family has controlled the Sri Lankan government for much of the post-war era. Yet the issue of accountability has not disappeared. In 2019, Gotobaya Rajapaksa was served with papers for a US civil law suit related to accusations of torture and murder (Ives and Bastians 2019). In 2021, the UN Human Rights Council voted to provide funding for a team of investigators to collect and preserve evidence connected to the civil war (Cummings-Bruce 2021). In January 2023, the Canadian government imposed targeted sanctions against two Rajapaksa brothers and senior military officers while the United States imposed targeted sanctions against Lieutenant General Savendra Silva in 2020 (Gunasekara and Mashal 2023). The quest for legal accountability remains alive.

---

[4] Another group of scholars regards voluntary shields as a potential cause for adjusting the proportionality criteria. Cohen and Zlotogorski (2021: 153) propose a sliding scale of proportionality based on the degree of voluntariness. Haque (2015: 397–398) suggests that harming voluntary shields is more permissible than harming ordinary citizens but stresses that voluntary shields do not forfeit the right to immunity from attack.

In any future contestation over the legitimacy of Sri Lanka's shelling campaign, existing ambiguities and debates on human shielding offer officials a potential avenue to minimize their culpability. At the very least, doubt could work in their favour. Crane and de Silva were alert to the enabling effects of legal ambiguity when they ventured that 'uncertainties in international law could not have made it easy for Sri Lankan field commanders' (Crane and de Silva 2015). If anything, doubt has given way to an increasingly permissive attitude towards civilian casualties in circumstances of alleged human shielding. Saudi Arabia, Syria, Israel, and Russia have all justified civilian casualties by lamenting the difficulties created by human shields. Importantly, even when these military operations are condemned, the legal substance of the human shielding claim is less robustly challenged (Gordon and Perugini 2022). Tellingly, prior to the 2015 *Law of War Manual* (Office of General Council 2015), no US military manual outlined the attacker's obligations in circumstances of human shielding. In other words, the US position has shifted from one of ambiguity to an explicitly stated permissiveness (Gordon and Perugini 2020: 131). If they are aiming to avoid taking responsibility for civilian casualties, then these developments bode well for Sri Lankan officials. The strategy of legal engagement certainly has a better chance of reducing their culpability than prior attempts at legal disengagement.

'But it worked': constituting a notion of efficacy

Though the Sri Lankan government attempted to characterize its conduct as lawful, key officials triumphantly asserted that their action should be judged primarily on the basis of whether it 'worked' (DeVotta 2010: 342; Tikku 2016: 259). For instance, during his interview with *Time* magazine reporter Jyoti Thottam, the president gave this response when asked if he was worried about a diplomatic fallout with Western states: 'They're the people who encouraged us to defeat terrorism. We followed what [George W.] Bush said. We accomplished what he wanted: eliminate terrorism. They must give credit to us. We fought their war. We showed that you can defeat terrorism' (Rajapaksa 2009b). For Rajapaksa, a military victory in the war on terror was surely to be admired. These kinds of statements went hand in hand with instructions not to dwell on the events of the conflict: 'Then you will have the north and the south fighting each other again; you can't have that again. I don't want to dig into the past and open up this wound' (Rajapaksa 2009b). The conflict was a temporary state of suffering that Sri Lanka could move beyond if it focused on the future. The combined effect of this emphasis on victory and looking forward was to say, 'we might have acted illegally, but it is over, and it was worth it'.

There was an international audience for this emphasis on results. For instance, in May 2009, the government shared messages of congratulations from Vietnam, Iran, and Pakistan (Ministry of Defence 2009; Ministry of Foreign Affairs 2009a; 2009b). Meanwhile, *The Washington Post* published an op ed calling on the US president to 'learn some significant lessons from Sri Lanka's victory' (Leitner 2009). Writing in 2016, former Australian Prime Minister Tony Abbott described Sri Lanka's onslaught as a series of 'tough but probably unavoidable actions taken to end one of the world's most vicious civil wars' (Abbott 2016). The Sri Lankan government asked the world to focus on the fact that it achieved a military victory, and that message did resonate with some.

We might make sense of the emphasis on victory by viewing it as an attempt to render the law of armed conflict irrelevant. Yet international law nonetheless helped make this triumphalism conceivable. Notions of efficacy or 'what works' are not divorced from social dynamics. In order to agree that a measure has 'worked' we need to agree on the aim. As Finnemore puts it, '[e]ffectiveness always must have a referent' (Finnemore 2005: 200). International law helped constitute this shared understanding. At this point, we come full circle to themes from the chapter's section on the Sri Lankan government's *jus ad bellum* claims. The LTTE were an extreme case of *vulnerability by law*. They were regarded as a non-state 'terrorist' group fighting to carve out territory which no international actor recognized. It is not that international law directly licensed Sri Lanka's shelling campaign. Rather, in attaching meaning to the central actors and constituting their authority, it provided the raw materials for a narrative that would rationalize enormous bloodshed.

Conclusion

International law is often seen as a project to civilize international affairs and bring a modicum of decency to warfare. This notion of 'law as a project' leads to a couple of conclusions about its influence. For IR realists, international law is relatively ineffectual compared to domestic law because there is no one to enforce agreements. For rationalists, law constrains actors in circumstances where they see instrumental value in the legal institution. In occasionally intersecting inquiries, constructivist IR theorists and critical legal theorists have uncovered law's constitutive effects. This has led to a focus on how the law might be implicated in enabling violence.

The Sri Lankan government sought to militarily crush the LTTE. In so far as there are dominant interpretations of international law, those interpretations largely suited the government. Of the territories covered in this edited volume, Tamil Eelam was the *least* recognized. They garnered no great power support (for example, Taiwan), and possessed no favourable ICJ ruling (for example, Western Sahara). Further, the LTTE were an international pariah. This position of non-recognition made the LTTE more vulnerable to open military attack than secessionists in other cases. Outside states could stress the importance of finding a political solution but they could not effectively contest the proposition that Sri Lanka was legally entitled to fight the LTTE. Finally, the LTTE's position of *vulnerability by law* lent some legitimacy to the government's 'any means necessary' approach to eliminating them.

Because the medium of international law has the capacity to bestow action with legitimacy, its meaning is often hotly contested. In the realm of *jus in bello*, there has been a long-running political battle to hold the Sri Lankan government to account for its abuses. In this context, it is easy to forget that, in its strategy of legal re-engagement, the government also wielded the discourse of law. It treated the law as a means of jettisoning what was arguably a compelling obligation to exercise more care. The concerning thing is that this strategy might gain some traction. We can find permissive attitudes to civilian casualties in cases of human shielding in UK and US military manuals. If international law is a moving feast then, since the violence of the 2009 civil war, it has potentially rendered Sri Lanka's actions more and not less explicable.

References

Abbott, T. (2016). Abbott: I Was Right on National Security. *Quadrant*, 26 March, https://quadrant.org.au/opinion/qed/2016/03/abbott-right-national-security/.

Additional Protocols (1977). Article 51 – Protection of the Civilian Population, https://ihl-databases.icrc.org/en/ihl-treaties/api-1977/article-51#:~:text=7.,favour%20or%20impede%20military%20operations.

Bogollagama, R. (2007). Sri Lanka Looking Beyond Terrorism: A Road Map to Peace, https://slembassyusa.org/new/media-center/news/221-27sri-lanka-looking-beyond-terrorism-a-road-map-to-peace.html.

Bukovansky, M. (2002). *Legitimacy and Power Politics: The American and French Revolutions in International Political Culture*. Princeton: Princeton University Press.

Byers, M. (2005). Not Yet Havoc: Geopolitical Change and the International Rules on Military Force. *Review of International Studies*, 31, 51–70.

Channel 4 (2011). Sri Lanka's Killing Fields. *Channel 4*, www.channel4.com/programmes/sri-lankas-killing-fields.

Clark, I., Kaempf, S., Reus-Smit, C. and Tannock, E. (2018). Crisis in the Laws of War? Beyond Compliance and Effectiveness. *European Journal of International Relations*, 24 (2), 319–343, https://doi.org/10.1177/1354066117714528

Cohen, A. and Zlotogorski, D. (2021). Human Shields and Proportionality. In: A. Cohen and D. Zlotogorski (eds), *Proportionality in International Humanitarian Law*. Oxford: Oxford University Press, 145–154. https://doi.org/10.1093/oso/9780197556726.003.0009.

Committee on Foreign Relations (2009). *Sri Lanka: Recharting US Strategy After the War*, www.govinfo.gov/app/details/CPRT-111SPRT53866/CPRT-111SPRT53866.

Crane, D.M. and de Silva, D. (2015). Opinion to the Commission from Professor DM Crane and Sir Desmond de Silva, QC re. *Lankaweb*, www.lankaweb.com/news/items/2015/03/20/what-the-international-experts-say-3-war-crimes-in-sri-lanka/.

Cummings-Bruce, N. (2021). U.N. to Gather Evidence of Atrocities in Sri Lanka Civil War. *The New York Times*, 23 March, www.nytimes.com/2021/03/23/world/asia/sri-lanka-civil-war-un-investigation.html?searchResultPosition=17.

DeVotta, N. (2010). From Civil War to Soft Authoritarianism: Sri Lanka in Comparative Perspective. *Global Change, Peace & Security*, 22 (3), 331–343, https://doi.org/10.1080/14781158.2010.510268.

Dinstein, Y. (2004). *The Conduct of Hostilities under the Law of International Armed Conflict*. Cambridge: Cambridge University Press.

Feigenbaum, E. (2008). Evan Feigenbaum, Deputy Assistant Secretary for South and Central Asian Affairs Interview with Shakuntala Perera, The Daily Mirror Colombo, Sri Lanka, 3 July, https://2001-2009.state.gov/p/sca/rls/2008/106943.htm.

Finnemore, M. (2005). Fights About Rules: The Role of Efficacy and Power in Changing Multilateralism. In: D. Armstrong, T. Farrell, and B. Maiguashca (eds), *Force and Legitimacy in World Politics*. Cambridge: Cambridge University Press, 187–206.

Glazier, P.D.W. (2010). *Military Commissions Under the Obama Administration*. Legal Studies Paper No. 2010–32. Loyola Law School, Los Angeles.

Gordon, N. and Perugini, N. (2020). *Human Shields: A History of People in the Line of Fire*. Oakland: University of California Press.

Gordon, N. and Perugini, N. (2022). Why We Need to Challenge Russia's Human Shields Narrative. *Al Jazeera*, 3 April, www.aljazeera.com/opinions/2022/4/3/why-we-need-to-challenge-russias-human-shields-narrative.

Gunasekara, S. and Mashal, M. (2023). Sri Lanka's Former President Ordered to Pay Victims of 2019 Bombings. *The New York Times*, 1 December, www.nytimes.com/2023/01/12/world/asia/sri-lanka-former-president-compensation-bombings-2019.html?searchResultPosition=3.

Haque, A.A. (2015). Human Shields. In: S. Lazar and H. Frowe (eds), *The Oxford Handbook of Ethics of War*. Oxford: Oxford University Press, 383–400.

Human Rights Watch (2009). *War on the Displaced: Sri Lankan Army and LTTE Abuses against Civilians in the Vanni*, www.hrw.org/sites/default/files/reports/srilanka0209web_0.pdf.

Hurd, I. (2018). The Empire of International Legalism. *Ethics & International Affairs*, 32 (3), 265–278.

Hurd, I. (2020). *How to Do Things with International Law*. Princeton: Princeton University Press.

ICTY (1998). Celebici Case: The Judgement of the Trial Chamber. United Nations: International Criminal Tribunal for the former Yugoslavia, www.icty.org/en/press/celebici-case-judgement-trial-chamber-zejnil-delalic-acquitted-zdravko-mucic-sentenced-7-years.

International Crisis Group (2010). *War Crimes in Sri Lanka*, www.crisisgroup.org/asia/south-asia/sri-lanka/war-crimes-sri-lanka.

Ives, M. and Bastians, D. (2019). Sri Lankans Accuse Him of Wartime Atrocities. California May Decide. *New York Times*, 19 April, www.nytimes.com/2019/04/19/world/asia/sri-lanka-war-crimes-lawsuit.html.

Joint Doctrine and Concepts Centre (2015). *The Joint Service Manual of the Law of Armed Conflict*, https://assets.publishing.service.gov.uk/media/5a7952bfe5274a2acd18bda5/JSP3832004Edition.pdf.

Kaempf, S. (2009). Double Standards in US Warfare: Exploring the Historical Legacy of Civilian Protection and the Complex Nature of the Moral–Legal Nexus. *Review of International Studies*, 35 (3), 651–674, https://doi.org/10.1017/S0260210509008699.

Keethaponcalan, S. (2011). The Indian Factor in the Peace Process and Conflict Resolution in Sri Lanka. In: J. Goodhand, J. Spencer, and B. Korf (eds), *Conflict and Peacebuilding in Sri Lanka: Caught in the Peace Trap?* Routledge: London, 39–53.

Kennedy, D. (2009). *Of War and Law*. Princeton: Princeton University Press.

Khan, A. (2024). *Statement of ICC Prosecutor Karim A.A. Khan KC: Applications for arrest warrants in the situation in the State of Palestine*. International Criminal Court, www.icc-cpi.int/news/statement-icc-prosecutor-karim-aa-khan-kc-applications-arrest-warrants-situation-state.

Koskenniemi, M. (2011). The Politics of International Law. In: *The Politics of International Law*. Oxford: Oxford University Press, 33–61.

Leitner, P. (2009). Lessons from Sri Lanka. *The Washington Post*, 22 June, www.washingtontimes.com/news/2009/jun/22/lessons-from-sri-lanka/?

Lunstead, J. (2011). Superpowers and Small Conflicts: the United States and Sri Lanka'. In: J. Goodhand, J. Spencer, and B. Korf (eds), *Conflict and Peacebuilding in Sri Lanka: Caught in the Peace Trap?* Routledge: London, 54–73.

McMahan, J. (2009). *Killing in War*. Oxford and New York: Clarendon Press.

Meisels, T. (2014). Fighting for Independence: What Can Just War Theory Learn from Civil Conflict?. *Social Theory and Practice*, 40 (2), 304–326, https://doi.org/10.5840/soctheorpract201440218.

Melzer, N. (2009). *Interpretive Guidance on the Notion of Direct Participation in Hostilities under International Humanitarian Law*. Geneva: International Committee of the Red Cross.

Mettraux, G. (2005). *International Crimes and Ad Hoc Tribunals*. Oxford: Oxford University Press.

Ministry of Defence (2009). Vietnam Welcomes the Victory of the Government and People of Sri Lanka, https://web.archive.org/web/20110511194957/http:/defence.lk/new.asp?fname=20090526_04.

Ministry of Foreign Affairs (2009a). Iran Congratulates Sri Lanka on Defeating Terrorism, https://web.archive.org/web/20090523161801/http:/www.defence.lk/new.asp?fname=20090519_11.

Ministry of Foreign Affairs (2009b). Pakistan Felicitates Sri Lanka on Great Victory Over Terrorism, www.lankaweb.com/news/items/2009/05/22/pakistan-felicitates-sri-lanka-on-great-victory-over-terrorism/.

Office of General Counsel (2015). *Department of Defense Law of War Manual (Updated December 2016)*, https://dod.defense.gov/Portals/1/Documents/pubs/DoD%20Law%20of%20War%20Manual%20-%20June%202015%20Updated%20Dec%202016.pdf.

Petrie, C. (2012). *Report of the Secretary-General's Internal Review Panel on United Nations Action in Sri Lanka*. https://digitallibrary.un.org/record/737299?ln=en.

Price, M. (2022). *International Legitimacy and the Domestic Use of Force*. Milton: Taylor and Francis, https://doi.org/10.4324/9781003167228.

Rajapaksa, M. (2008). Address by His Excellency Mahinda Rajapaksa, President of the Democratic Socialist Republic of Sri Lanka at the Sixty-Third Session of the United Nations General Assembly, www.un.org/en/ga/63/generaldebate/pdf/srilanka_en.pdf.

Rajapaksa, M. (2009a). Address by H.E. President Mahinda Rajapaksa to the Diplomatic Community in Colombo on Current Developments in Sri Lanka, www.srilankaembassy.be/old/HomePagePhoto/May2009/07-05-2009/07-05-2009-01.pdf.

Rajapaksa, M. (2009b). Q&A: The Man Who Tamed the Tamil Tigers. *Time*, https://content.time.com/time/world/article/0,8599,1910095,00.html.

Ratner, S.R. (2012). Accountability and the Sri Lankan Civil War. *American Journal of International Law*, 106 (4), 795–808, https://doi.org/10.5305/amerjintelaw.106.4.0795.

Reus-Smit, C. (2014). International Law and the Mediation of Culture. *Ethics & International Affairs*, 28 (1), 65–82, https://doi.org/10.1017/S0892679414000069.

Reuters (2022). Russia Denies Killing Civilians in Ukraine's Bucha. *Reuters*, 3 April, www.reuters.com/world/europe/russia-denies-killing-civilians-ukraines-bucha-2022-04-03/.

Rubinstein, A. and Roznai, Y. (2011). Human Shields in Modern Armed Conflicts: The Need for a Proportionate Proportionality. *Policy Review*, 22 (1), 93–128.

Samarasinghe, M. (2009). Mahinda Samarasinghe, HARDtalk Interview, http://news.bbc.co.uk/1/hi/programmes/hardtalk/7921185.stm.

Samaraweera, M. (2006). Terrorism, Peacemaking and Democracy – Remarks by Minister of Foreign Affairs, Hon. Mangala Samaraweera at the Japan Institute of International Affairs (JIIA) on 18 May 2006'.

Schmitt, M.N. (2009). Human Shields in International Humanitarian Law. *Columbia Journal of Transnational Law*, 47 (2), 293–338.

Scott, S.V. (1994). International Law as Ideology: Theorizing the Relationship between International Law and International Politics. *European Journal of International Law*, 5 (3), 313–325, https://doi.org/10.1093/oxfordjourn als.ejil.a035873.

Sørbø, G. et al (2011). *Pawns of Peace: Evaluation of Norwegian peace efforts in Sri Lanka, 1997–2009*. Commissioned by Norad Evaluation Department.

Tikku, M.K. (2016). *After the Fall: Sri Lanka in Victory and War*. Oxford: Oxford University Press, https://doi.org/10.1093/acprof:oso/ 9780199463503.001.0001.

UN Human Rights Council (2009). 11th Special Session of the Human Rights Council: 'The Human Rights Situation in Sri Lanka', www.ohchr. org/en/hr-bodies/hrc/special-sessions/session11/th-special-session.

UN Human Rights Council (2015). Resolution A/HRC/30/L.29 Promoting Reconciliation, Accountability and Human Rights in Sri Lanka, https://ap.ohchr.org/documents/dpage_e.aspx?si=A/HRC/30/L.29.

UN POE (2011). *Report of the Secretary-General's Panel of Experts on Accountability in Sri Lanka*, www.securitycouncilreport.org/atf/cf/%7B6 5BFCF9B-6D27-4E9C-8CD3-CF6E4FF96FF9%7D/POC%20Rep%20 on%20Account%20in%20Sri%20Lanka.pdf.

Walzer, M. (2006). *Just and Unjust Wars: A Moral Argument with Historical Illustrations*. 4th edn. New York: Basic Books.

Weiss, G. (2012). *The Cage the Fight for Sri Lanka and the Last Days of the Tamil Tigers*. 1st edn. New York: Bellevue Literary Press.

4

Russia-Manufactured 'Secessions' in Ukraine: The Attempted Ambiguity of Status, Kosovo, and International Law

Júlia Miklasová

Introduction

In his speech following the annexation of Crimea on 18 March 2014, the president of the Russian Federation, Vladimir Putin, underlined:

> [T]he Crimean authorities referred to the well-known Kosovo precedent – a precedent our western colleagues created with their own hands in a very similar situation, when they agreed that the unilateral separation of Kosovo from Serbia, exactly what Crimea is doing now, was legitimate and did not require any permission from the country's central authorities. (Putin 2014a)

Kosovo's declaration of independence on 17 February 2008 (Kosovo Declaration of Independence 2008), and the 2010 advisory opinion of the International Court of Justice (ICJ) assessing the accordance of this declaration with international law (Accordance with International Law of the Unilateral Declaration of Independence in Respect of Kosovo 2010), have loomed large in international relations. This is particularly true for the developments in Ukraine, which has witnessed a world record of purported unilateral declarations of independence. Since 2014, the so-called Republic of Crimea, Donetsk People's Republic (DPR), Luhansk People's Republic (LPR), and the Zaporizhzhia and Kherson Regions have all purportedly declared independence as sovereign states.[1] Russia's recognition and the admission of these so-called 'independent' states to the Russian Federation followed. While the overwhelming majority of the international community sees these developments as illegal annexations of Ukrainian territory by Russia, separatists and Russia claim that these acts are perfectly in line with international law.

Importantly, at a closer look, Russia did not simply annex the five Ukrainian regions straightaway but, together with its local allies, engaged in a (convoluted) three-step scheme, ultimately resulting in an unlawful annexation of these territories: (1) holding a unilateral referendum presented as resulting in the overwhelming success of the vote in favour of independence and joining of the Russian Federation; (2) issuing a declaration of independence by the respective territories and populations and recognition of new 'states' by the Russian Federation; (3) concluding and ratifying the purported international treaties between these new 'states' and the Russian Federation and adopting the Russian law admitting new subjects to the Russian Federation (Pursiainen and Forsberg 2019: 223; Miklasová 2022b; Miklasová 2023: 119).

This scheme is highly formalized, legalistic, and mechanical. Ostensibly, it puts the tools and language of international law of statehood to the forefront but crucially omits the consequences of Russia's use of force or its own support and control of the purportedly secessionist actions. Notably, as the above quote highlights, the Kosovo case has featured highly in this rhetoric. This element underscores the dimension of *agency* at play, specifically that of governmental legal experts,[2] who present international law to justify actions concerning statehood on the international stage.

This chapter, therefore, zooms in on and analyzes the role played by the Kosovo case and the *Kosovo* advisory opinion in formulating the arguments and the policy of the Russian Federation regarding the purported 'secessions' in Ukraine. Given the specific character of international law as a primarily horizontal and decentralized legal order, the chapter focuses on how the states have used the arguments based on international law in the outlined cases, assesses their normative impact, and asks what broader implications on the rules governing secession can be drawn from them.

The chapter proceeds as follows. It first gives an overview of the background to the Kosovo case and outlines the implications of various positions advanced by the states vis-à-vis its independence and the *Kosovo* advisory opinion. Second, it traces the evolution of Russia's legal narratives

---

[1] The chapter uses these denominations without the adjective 'so-called' to facilitate reading the text.
[2] See the Introduction to this volume.

on secession and the specific references to the Kosovo case or the advisory opinion to justify the purported secessions of the Ukrainian territories. It then assesses this Russian rhetoric against the backdrop of the arguments presented in the context of the Kosovo case. Third, it evaluates the legal status of the separatist territories in Ukraine and distinguishes these cases from Kosovo. Lastly, it offers some conclusions.

Kosovo's declaration of independence and Advisory Opinion

The following section provides a brief overview of the events leading up to and surrounding Kosovo's declaration of independence in 2008. It then centres on the legal arguments presented to justify Kosovo's recognition, those advanced during the *Kosovo* advisory proceedings and the advisory opinion itself. The advisory opinions are rendered by the ICJ – the principal judicial organ of the United Nations. Unlike the judgments issued in contentious proceedings between states, advisory opinions can be requested only by the UN Security Council or the UN General Assembly (UNGA) on 'any legal question' or by other UN bodies or specialized agencies 'on legal questions arising within the scope of their activities' (UN Charter 1945, Art. 96). As their designation suggests, the opinions are advisory and thus non-binding. However, they carry significant legal weight as they clarify the relevant aspects of international law. The section situates the legal positions and the finding of the ICJ in a wider normative context of the international legal rules governing secession.

Background to the Kosovo case

It is beyond this contribution's scope to detail a complicated history leading up to Kosovo's declaration of independence in February 2008 (Vidmar 2022: 168–169). However, the revocation of Kosovo's autonomy within the Socialist Federal Republic of Yugoslavia (SFRY) in the late 1980s, the unilateral declaration of Kosovo in 1991 (recognized only by Albania), the Serbian discrimination of the Kosovo Albanians in the province, the armed operations of the Kosovo Liberation Army (KLA), and escalation in Serbia's violent response ultimately led to a humanitarian catastrophe (Weller 2009: 53, 60–64, 67–68, 77–78; Ker-Lindsay 2013: 843–844; Vidmar 2022). The worsening of the situation provoked the displacement of the Kosovo Albanian population; there were reports of ethnic cleansing (Weller 2009; Hughes 2013: 1001). Against this backdrop and after the Former Republic of Yugoslavia (FRY) refused to sign the attempt at political settlement proposed in the Rambouillet Accords (which, among others, stressed the FRY's territorial integrity), the North Atlantic Treaty Organization

(NATO) started its bombing campaign against Serbia in March 1999 (Ker-Lindsay 2013: 844; Vidmar 2022: 169–170). Despite the invocation of the humanitarian intervention, NATO's air war was not based on any lawful exceptions to the prohibition of the use of force; it is generally viewed as illegal under international law (Vidmar 2022: 170).

On 10 June 1999, following the cessation of hostilities, acting under chapter VII of the UN Charter, the UN Security Council (UNSC) adopted Resolution 1244 (still in force today) (ibid; UNSC 1999). This resolution placed Kosovo under the regime of international territorial administration (Vidmar 2022: 170). According to Professor Falk, '[a]ll in all, it is hard to negative the conclusion that in Resolution 1244 the United Nations confirmed Serbia's claim to sovereignty over Kosovo' (Falk 2011: 51 fn 4; see UNSC Resolution 1244: preambular paras 2, 4, 10, operative paras 4 and 10; Kohen and Del Mar 2011: 123–124). Vidmar points out that the resolution 'nevertheless created an effective situation in which the FRY *exercised* no sovereign powers in Kosovo' (Vidmar 2022: 171, emphasis added). The resolution foresaw 'a political process designed to determine Kosovo's future status, taking into account the Rambouillet accords' (UNSC Resolution 1244: para. 11(e)).

Ker-Lindsay argues that at the time, 'the international community appeared to have little appetite for an independent Kosovo state' (Ker-Lindsay 2013: 844). While acknowledging certain pro-independence elements in the US administration, Ker-Lindsay claims that the change in a mainstream Western position in favour of independence came about in response to the massive outbreak of violence in the province in 2004, exposing the limits of the international administration (Ker-Lindsay 2009: 150–153). In his view, the states supporting humanitarian intervention in 1999, now supported the independence 'to extricate themselves from the situation before they too became seen as some form of neo-colonial occupier' (Ker-Lindsay 2009: 155; Oeter 2015: 72).[3]

In 2005, the UN secretary-general appointed its Special Envoy for the future status process for Kosovo, Martti Ahtisaari (UNSC 2005; Ker-Lindsay 2009: 845–846). In March 2007, the special envoy presented his report, which determined that 'the negotiations' potential to produce any mutually agreeable outcome on Kosovo's status is exhausted' and that 'the only viable option for Kosovo is independence, to be supervised for an initial period by

---

[3] However, according to Falk, 'the states favoring humanitarian intervention expected and wished that Kosovo would be severed from Serbia in the future' (Falk 2011: 57). In 2000, the Independent International Commission on Kosovo, established in the aftermath of the NATO bombing campaign by the government of Sweden and composed of several experts (including Professor Falk), recommended 'conditional independence as the future status of Kosovo' (Independent International Commission on Kosovo 2000).

the international community' (Report of the Special Envoy of the Secretary-General on Kosovo's Future Status 2007: paras 3 and 5). On 17 February 2008, Kosovo declared independence (Kosovo Declaration of Independence 2008; Fabry 2012: 666). The Serbian authorities invalidated this act (Vidmar 2022: 175 fn 77). Subsequently, they initiated the diplomatic campaign at the UNGA to refer the question concerning the Kosovo declaration of independence to the ICJ for an advisory opinion. Among other things, Serbia viewed this step as a way to stall the pace of recognitions of Kosovo in the wake of its declaration of independence (Ker-Lindsay 2015: 12). A direct legal challenge against Kosovo at the ICJ was not possible, given Serbia's position on Kosovo's lack of statehood (Ker-Lindsay 2015: 13) and because Kosovo was not a member of the United Nations and the party to the Statute of the ICJ. Other options, such as contentious proceedings against recognizing states, were discarded as politically risky (Ker-Lindsay 2015: 13–14). In many instances, this path would also face the problem regarding the ICJ jurisdiction, which rests on the parties' consent. Following fervent Serbian diplomatic activity, the UNGA, on 8 October 2008, ultimately adopted the resolution referring the question 'Is the unilateral declaration of independence by the Provisional Institutions of Self-Government of Kosovo in accordance with international law?' to the ICJ (UNGA Resolution 63/3). Significantly, Serbia itself preferred this more equivocal question, assuming that it would mitigate the possibility of an opinion clearly unfavourable to it (Ker-Lindsay 2015: 16). In 2010, the ICJ issued its advisory opinion on the matter (Accordance with International Law of the Unilateral Declaration of Independence in Respect of Kosovo 2010). Up to today, 113 states have recognized Kosovo as a state.[4]

Several factors determined that Kosovo has become an emblematic point of friction between the West and the Russian Federation in the post-Cold War era. Since the 1990s, the Russian position favouring Serbia's territorial integrity was in line with the secessionist challenges inside Russia, especially in Chechnya (Hughes 2013: 998). The journalist Masha Gessen argues that Russia 'did not have a direct stake in Kosovo, aside from a vague, sentimental idea of affinity with the Serbs because they are, like Russians, Eastern Orthodox' (Gessen 2022). 'In Russian memory, however, the NATO [1999] war was an attack on Russia – because it showed that Russia no longer mattered' (Gessen 2022; see further Roy 2013: 44 et seq.) Mälksoo argues:

> The Russian government has construed the NATO military intervention in Kosovo in 1999 as the 'original sin' of post-Cold War

---

[4] A total number of recognizing states has, however, decreased, given that at least ten states have withdrawn their recognition (Vidmar 2022: 167).

international law ... To use military force against a sovereign nation without UN SC authorization and essentially notwithstanding the veto power meant rendering Russia's privileges and status in the post-1945 international community without substance. (Mälksoo 2015: 173 and 174)[5]

Implications of legal arguments, and the Kosovo Advisory Opinion

Several political and legal arguments were advanced through the years to justify Kosovo's independence. Precisely to limit the precedent-creating factor of Kosovo's recognition vis-à-vis other similar scenarios, its (Western) proponents claimed that Kosovo was a unique (*sui generis*) case (Peters 2015: 300–304; Hughes 2023: 6; Report of the Special Envoy of the Secretary-General on Kosovo's Future Status 2007: para. 21; Ker-Lindsay 2013: 845–851). Kosovo's supposed uniqueness essentially revolved around the following factors: (1) the context of Yugoslavia's breakup; (2) massive human rights violations in Kosovo (echoing the right of remedial secession (Vidmar 2009: 817–818; Vidmar 2010: 47–50; Ker-Lindsay 2013: 848–849); (3) the internationalization of the situation through UNSC Resolution 1244 (Fabry 2012: 666–667; Ker-Lindsay 2013: 847; Peters 2015: 301–304; Ingimundarson 2022).

Many scholars have criticized the legal quality and relevance of the elements of the *sui generis* argumentation extensively (Ker-Lindsay 2013: 854; Peters 2015: 304). Moreover, given the timing of the Kosovo declaration of independence in 2008, Ker-Lindsay underscored that:

> In this sense, the decision to support statehood was not about recognizing the unique case created by the break up of Yugoslavia or the fighting of 1998–99, as was later claimed. Had that been the case, the best option would have been to pursue independence in 1995, at the time of Dayton, or in 1999, as has been widely suggested. At that time, when Milošević was still in power, the political costs would have been lower, and the justification greater. (Ker-Lindsay 2009: 155, fnn omitted)[6]

---

[5] In this context, in 2000, President Yeltsin is quoted as saying that 'all the rules that had been established by the UN during the long post-war decades collapsed' (Yeltsin quoted in Hughes 2013: 1003).

[6] Oeter highlights that at the relevant time in 2008, due to the loss of emergency, the remedial secession argument to justify secession seems difficult to sustain (Oeter 2015: 62–67).

On the other hand, 'Russia was the most vociferous international critic not only of Kosovo's recognition without Serbia's consent, but also of the territory's purported exceptionality' (Fabry 2012: 667; Ker-Lindsay 2013: 853–854). After the declaration of independence, the Russian representative in the UNSC claimed: 'The 17 February declaration by the local assembly of the Serbian province of Kosovo is a blatant breach of the norms and principles of international law – above all of the Charter of the United Nations – which undermines the foundations of the system of international relations' (UNSC 2008; see Peters 2015: 304).

Just one month before the Georgia–Russia war in August 2008, then President Dmitry Medvedev stated, '[w]e consider the Kosovo precedent as extremely dangerous and unsuccessful. We don't consider the decision made on this issue as a *causus sui generis*, but as an absolute precedent' (Tanjug 2008; see further Lundstedt 2019: 209, especially fn 80).

Notably, concerning the advisory proceedings before the ICJ, Milanovic notes that, while the supporters of Kosovo independence raised the 'unpalatable' *sui generis* argument, their primary claim was 'the absence of prohibition directly addressed to non-state actors' (Milanovic 2015: 35). Similarly, the supporters of Kosovo's statehood invoked the right of peoples to self-determination or remedial secession *only* in the second place (if at all) Milanovic 2015: 44). Ultimately, on the issue of the right to remedial secession, out of a total number of 43 states participating in three rounds before the court, 14 held that the right existed, 14 opposed its existence and 25 remained neutral (ibid: 43). Thus, this question has remained 'inconclusive' (ibid: 43; see Accordance with International Law of the Unilateral Declaration of Independence in Respect of Kosovo 2010: para. 82). However, in a total break with its previous legal position – heralded already in its 2008 recognition of Abkhazia and South Ossetia, discussed later in the chapter – Russia claimed that a limited right of remedial secession existed, but it was subject to strict conditions (Written Statement of the Russian Federation 2009: para. 88). It argued, nevertheless, that in February 2008, these conditions were not fulfilled in the case of Kosovo (ibid: para. 101).[7]

Ultimately, the ICJ, in its Kosovo advisory opinion, held that 'general international law contains no applicable prohibition of declarations of independence' (Accordance with International Law of the Unilateral Declaration of Independence in Respect of Kosovo 2010: para. 81). The court found that the prohibition of the declaration of independence cannot

---

[7] 'There are no reasonable grounds whatsoever to consider that in 2008, or currently, a threat of extreme – and of any – oppression by Serbia against Kosovo Albanians existed or exists' (Written Statement of the Russian Federation 2009: para. 101).

be inferred from and, thus, it did not violate the *lex specialis* of the UNSC Resolution 1244 or the Constitutional Framework established by the UN Interim Administration Mission in Kosovo (UNMIK) (ibid: paras 118–119 and 120–121). However, the court famously 'determined that the question of whether the independence declaration was 'in accordance with' international law only required an examination of whether the declaration was 'in violation of' international law (Wilde 2011: para. 6; Accordance with International Law of the Unilateral Declaration of Independence in Respect of Kosovo 2010, para. 56). This contested and criticized reasoning allowed the court to focus only on a narrow issue (i.e. the declaration's 'compliance with any negative obligations') and not on the questions such as whether there was any positive entitlement to create a new state, especially under the right of peoples to self-determination, 'or whether other norms at an intermediate position between prohibition and entitlement were in operation' (Wilde 2011: para. 14; see also Kohen and Del Mar 2011).

As argued by Peters, it is exactly this substantive sparseness of the opinion (in other words, an unwillingness to draw 'a line between inadmissible and admissible secessions') that 'has the unfortunate effect … of not preventing subsequent (erroneous) reliance on its narrow findings' (Peters 2015: 293 and 299).[8] According to Ker-Lindsay, 'it was hardly surprising that the opinion was quickly endorsed by a number of other secessionist, or potentially secessionist territories' (Ker-Lindsay 2013: 852 and 839–842).[9]

More broadly, the acceptance of unilateral secession of Kosovo by a significant number of states signified a serious shift in what had been a constant practice. Until then, states refused to recognize entities that emerged from unilateral non-colonial secession (Ker-Lindsay 2013: 854; Oeter 2015: 69).[10] Therefore, even though the individual and divisive case of Kosovo did not arguably affect the rules governing secession (Peters 2015: 308; see below), it has had destabilizing reverberations on the law of statehood more generally. Especially, the *sui generis* arguments justifying Kosovo's declaration of independence have had such an eroding effect. Peters and Coppieters stress how these claims undermined the idea of generality and

---

[8] Another point raised by Milanovic and Wood is that 'the minimalist Court was perhaps not minimalist enough' (Milanovic and Wood 2015: 6).

[9] Falk raised the point as to why should the political secessionist actors 'bother' to differentiate between the finding that the Kosovo declaration of independence as not prohibited under international law and it being 'in accordance with international law' (Falk 2011: 52; and see 58).

[10] 'Since 1945 no State which has been created by unilateral secession has been admitted to the United Nations against the declared wishes of the government of the predecessor State' (Crawford 2006: 390). See on the case of Bangladesh, which could be seen as an aberration from this paradigm, Vidmar (2010: 42–43) and Miklasová (2024a: 208).

universality of law as such (Coppieters 2006; Peters 2015: 310). On another level, the unique case argument also brings the risk of double standards to the fore: 'the core element of the rule of law, namely the principle that like cases must be treated alike, is at stake' (Peters 2015: 311). Indeed, Mälksoo concludes that '[t]he West did indeed have certain double standards when the cases of Kosovo and Chechnya are compared' (Mälksoo 2015: 176).

Echoes of Kosovo in Russia's recognition practice

The chapter now turns to Russia's policy and positions concerning secession. It first highlights the change in its *legal* stance in the wake of Kosovo's declaration of independence while underscoring the continuity in its *actual policy* of supporting secessionists across the post-Soviet space. The chapter then details the arguments referring to Kosovo presented by Russian officials to justify Russia's recognition of the Ukrainian territories. Lastly, it assesses Russian rhetoric against the backdrop of the implications of the Kosovo case.

Change of the Russian legal position in the post-2008 period

Before August 2008, Russia had 'consistently advocated against the right to unilateral secession' and refused to recognize the post-Soviet separatist territories – Transnistria, Abkhazia, and South Ossetia (Lundstedt 2019: 205–208; Poghosyan 2021: 188; Ingimundarson 2022: 6; Miklasová 2024b). In fact, in the wake of the dissolution of the Soviet Union, Russia undertook in bilateral and multilateral treaties to respect the territorial integrity of the newly emerged successor states (former federal republics) in their former federal borders (Miklasová 2023: 116–118). The underlying principle was *uti possidetis juris* according to which the 'former federal borders determined the borders of newly independent states' (the 1991 *uti possidetis* border *status quo*) (Mälksoo 2015: 173; Miklasová 2023: 105 et seq.).

However, despite this clear *legal* position, in practice, Russia had *covertly* contributed to creating the separatist entities in the post-Soviet space through military interventions and helped them survive through its political, economic and other support (Mälksoo 2015: 173 and 179; Miklasová 2024a: 407–569). Several judgments of the European Court of Human Rights (ECtHR) found Russia exercising 'effective control' over these entities even before 2008, triggering the applicability of the European Convention of Human Rights (ECHR) for Russia in these areas beyond its sovereign borders (*Ilaşcu and Others v Moldova and Russia* 2004: para. 392; *Mamasakhlisi and Others v Georgia and Russia 2023*: para. 339). Thus, Russia had violated the territorial integrity of the ex-Union republics already before 2008 and cannot be seen as a *law-abiding* state (Miklasová 2023: 122–123). Nevertheless, despite these covert violations, Russia maintained its unequivocal legal stance.

As will be shown below, the same pattern continued even after 2008 – Russia supported and controlled the purported Ukrainian separatist territories even after their recognition as independent states (see below).

Following the Kosovo declaration of independence, however, Russia changed its *legal* narrative and overall strategy. Admittedly, this change must be seen in a larger context of Russia's aims to keep ex-Union republics – Georgia and Ukraine – in its sphere of influence, including by obstructing their NATO membership (Ingimundarson 2022: 6). For example, while politically the decision of the Bucharest April 2008 NATO summit – agreeing that Georgia and Ukraine will become NATO members without setting a specific pathway to it – was undeniably a relevant factor (Lundstedt 2019: 210; Ingimundarson 2022: 10), the Kosovo case played a primordial (but not exclusive) role for construction of a new *legal* narrative.

In fact, after Kosovo's declaration of independence, Russia made a legal u-turn 'from a strict anti-secessionist attitude towards a selective recognition of post-Soviet separatist entities' (Mälksoo 2015: 182; Miklasová 2023: 118; Miklasová 2024b). Immediately after the declaration of independence of Kosovo, it formally lifted its participation in a longstanding sanction regime of the Commonwealth of Independent States (CIS) vis-à-vis Abkhazia and after the August 2008 Georgia–Russia war, it recognized Abkhazia and South Ossetia as independent states relying on the arguments echoing the Western arguments on Kosovo (Frear 2014: 6).[11] In fact, 'South Ossetia and Abkhazia were Russia's response to Kosovo' (Mälksoo 2015: 180). The hallmark of this transformation was Russia's position presented during the Kosovo advisory proceedings in 2009 mentioned earlier when it claimed that the right of remedial secession exists, but 'should be limited to truly extreme circumstances, such an outright armed attack by the parent state, threatening the very existence of the people in question' (Written Statement of the Russian Federation 2009: para. 88). Thus, the legal argumentation, which would be fully employed later in Ukraine, was first conceptualized shortly after the Kosovo declaration of independence.

Kosovo in Russian rhetoric on 'secessions' in Ukraine

The Kosovo case is reflected in the Russian justifications concerning the recognition of the purported separatist territories of Ukraine since 2014 in

---

[11] The then Russian President Medvedev claimed, among others, that 'Saakashvili opted for genocide to accomplish his political objectives' and that the objective of Georgia's actions in the 2008 war was 'annexing South Ossetia through the annihilation of a whole people' (Medvedev 2008).

two ways (Ingimundarson 2022: 5).[12] First, there is a repeated reference to an apparent 'genocide' allegedly perpetrated by Ukraine's central government to justify the recognition of purported new states (echoing the Western arguments on the right of remedial secession of Kosovo and Russia's arguments already used to justify recognition of South Ossetia). Second, there is an *explicit* reference to the Kosovo advisory opinion and Kosovo precedent – either to highlight the supposed double standards of the West or to simply incorrectly take the advisory opinion as the relevant point of reference to justify its actions.

The Kosovo 'precedent' and the ICJ's advisory opinion were explicitly mentioned in the declaration of independence of the purported 'Republic of Crimea' (Declaration of Independence of the Autonomous Republic of Crimea and City of Sevastopol 2014). President Putin extensively relied on them in his speech on 18 March 2014:

> [T]he Crimean authorities referred to the well-known Kosovo precedent – a precedent our western colleagues created with their own hands in a very similar situation, when they agreed that the unilateral separation of Kosovo from Serbia, exactly what Crimea is doing now, was legitimate and did not require any permission from the country's central authorities. Pursuant to Article 2, Chapter 1 of the United Nations Charter, the UN International Court agreed with this approach and made the following comment in its ruling of July 22, 2010, and I quote: 'No general prohibition may be inferred from the practice of the Security Council with regard to declarations of independence,' and 'General international law contains no prohibition on declarations of independence.' Crystal clear, as they say. (Putin 2014a)

President Putin also explicitly quoted from the US written statements before the ICJ, according to which the declarations of independence did not violate international law and added, '[t]he actions of Crimean people completely fit in with these instructions, as it were. For some reason, things that Kosovo Albanians (and we have full respect for them) were permitted to do, Russians, Ukrainians and Crimean Tatars in Crimea are not allowed. Again, one wonders why' (ibid). Putin also disputed the special case argument based on the high number of victims, saying, '[a]ccording to this logic, we have to make sure every conflict leads to human losses' (ibid). In a later interview, Putin also claimed that, in comparison with Kosovo, Crimea's

---

[12] Bieber considers it a 'central' argument of Russia 'to justify recognizing secessionist territories since 2008' (Bieber 2022: 182). Russia, relied on other justifications under international law, for example the role of referenda.

secession was even more in line with international law given that it was supported by a 'stunning' majority expressed in referendum, which did not take place in Kosovo (Putin 2014c; for the same reasoning Putin 2014b). In September 2014, Russian Foreign Minister Lavrov – apparently echoing the *sui generis* arguments regarding Kosovo – said that 'Crimea is a special unique case from all points of view. Historically, geopolitically, patriotically, if you like' (ITAR-TASS 2014). Later on, to justify the recognition of the DPR and LPR on 21 February 2022 – preceding the Russian aggression against Ukraine – President Putin made claims regarding 'genocide, which almost 4 million people are facing' (Putin 2022a; see also Miklasová 2022a). Referring to the right of remedial secession, Putin added that '[t]o put an end to this genocide, Russia recognized the people's republics of Donbass and signed treaties of friendship and mutual aid with them' (Putin 2022b; see also Ingimundarson 2022: 11–12). In this context, Russia also invoked the supposed impossibility of finding a solution to the conflict through the Minsk II ceasefire agreement, which may relate to the last resort requirement of the remedial secession as well as to the Kosovo case (Miklasová 2022a). During the meeting with UN Secretary-General Antonio Guterres, President Putin said, '[i]f this [Kosovo] precedent was set, the republics of Donbass could do the same' (TASS 2022).

Mirroring and inconsistencies in Russia's rhetoric on Kosovo

Against this backdrop, several scholars have linked Russia's pseudo-legal arguments justifying the purported secession of Crimea and other Ukrainian territories (even though they ultimately do not hold up legal scrutiny) to the previous practice of Western states (Marxen 2014: 389; Oeter 2015: 73). According to Milanovic and Wood, '[a]t a normative or even purely rhetorical level, the secession of Crimea was at least partly facilitated by the Kosovo "precedent"' (Milanovic and Wood 2015: 4). According to Fabry, '[t]here can be no question that Kosovo encouraged the aspirations of various secessionist entities and that it created a permissive environment for Russia to recognize two of them, South Ossetia and Abkhazia' (Fabry 2012: 671).

Russia's arguments have not been accidental; they show a strategy, among others, of exploiting the arguments opened by the Kosovo case and, more generally, a perceived weakening of the international law of statehood. Indeed, many commentators highlight Russia's mirroring of the claims raised in the context of Kosovo (Bieber 2022: 183): 'Moscow first of all responded to Western claims and arguments in international law, in other words symmetry with the West became part of its ideology of international law' (Mälksoo 2015: 180 and 185). Moreover, Borgen argues that this mirroring was aimed at making it more difficult for the United States to criticize Russia's actions, 'understanding that the legal fine points of distinguishing the cases of Kosovo and Crimea would be lost in the rough sport of political argument' (Borgen 2015: 235). '[I]t was simply too easy for other powers, most notably Russia, to present the unique case argument as an example of Western hypocrisy' (Ker-Lindsay 2013: 854). Similarly, Russia has explicitly invoked the Kosovo opinion on several occasions to justify its recognition policy while omitting to mention its narrow focus and nuances. Given Russia's institutional apparatus in foreign affairs and legal counselling, such a misconstruction of the opinion could not have been unintentional.

Regardless of how unsubstantiated Russia's 'argument' based on international law governing secession was, it has served several functions. First, it allowed Russia to project an air of lawfulness (rather than lawfulness) or at least ambiguity. This has been an important element for domestic and international audiences and the legitimation strategy.[13] If these regions truly became new sovereign states (which they did not, as demonstrated below), their sovereign prerogative would include the decision to merge with another state (Miklasová 2024b). Their incorporation by Russia would thus not violate international law. Without the interpolation of the secessionist arguments, the acts in question by Russia amount to illegal annexation (as they do, as detailed below) (Miklasová 2024b). Second, Russian domestic legislation *only* allows for the admission to the Russian Federation of a foreign state or its part upon mutual consent pursuant to an international treaty concluded between this *state* and the Russian Federation (Law No. 6-FKZ, as amended, Art. 4(2)). The existence of a *state* willing to give such consent and conclude such an international treaty is thus a necessary formal precondition for triggering this constitutional procedure.[14] Third, arguably, the reliance on the law of secession allows Russia claiming that it did not undermine the overall 1991 *uti possidetis* border *status quo* in the post-Soviet space mentioned earlier; instead, the scheme targets the borders of the specific states, especially Ukraine (Miklasová 2023). Arguably, this sketchy and instrumental argument resulting in speeches and press releases was 'good enough for Putin to save his face while acting as a regional hegemonial power', at least until the annexation of Crimea (Marxsen 2014: 389).

---

[13] 'Legitimation is the process by which actors come to believe in the normative legitimacy of an object. Legitimation may occur as the result of a conscious effort to influence beliefs about what is normatively justified' (Thomas 2023: 16).

[14] The amendment to this law was proposed in the Russian Duma in the spring 2014 according to which, in case of 'the absence of efficient sovereign state government in the foreign state' the admission of a part of a foreign state can be based on the referendum conducted in the relevant part of the foreign state or on the basis of local authorities' request, but the amendment was withdrawn on 20 March 2014 (Venice Commission 2014: para 9). This amendment would be in a clear violation of international law (Bílková 2016: 196–197).

Moreover, notwithstanding the unlawfulness of its actions and the irrelevance of its arguments, the Russian legal rhetoric is internally incoherent. Poghosyan argues that 'after having opposed recognition of Kosovo's independence and having blamed the Western states for opening a Pandora's box of secessionist movements, Russia employed the same argument to justify annexation of Crimea, in a way contradicting its previous words and actions' (Poghosyan 2021: 191). Thus, while Russia keeps reiterating 'its opposition to Kosovo's independence, it relies on the case of Kosovo to justify its own military interventions and territorial revisions in post-Soviet states' (Ingimundarson 2022: 6). Furthermore, Russia's claims are not only inconsistent with its pre-2008 legal positions but are also not applied consistently in the post-2008 period (Mälksoo 2015: 179–180 and 182; Lundstedt 2019: 214–215; Miklasová 2024b).

Status of the Ukrainian territories is not ambiguous

Against this backdrop, it must be reiterated that Russia's arguments to justify its recognitions of the Ukrainian territories do not hold up to legal scrutiny for several reasons and on multiple levels.[15] First, the arguments echoing the right to remedial secession have never been factually substantiated, as no evidence supports the claims of genocide in these regions before Russia's recognitions (Miklasová 2022a; Miklasová 2022b: 8–9 and 13). Second, it is doubtful that Russia can even rely on this right. As highlighted in the volume's introduction regarding the *ambiguity* dimension regarding the contested states in war and law, the doctrine of remedial secession is extremely contested in international law – a single and rather controversial Kosovo case arguably could not have affected the rules on secession (Peters 2015: 308, see later).

Moreover, an additional crucial difference exists between the purported secessions of the Ukrainian territories and Kosovo (Peters 2015: 308). Unlike in Kosovo, Russia's illegal force was used to facilitate the referenda and the purported separatist movements in the Ukrainian territories. It is generally accepted that the 1999 NATO illegal bombing of Yugoslavia 'did not lead directly to the independence of Kosovo, neither was it aimed at ensuring it' (D'Aspremont 2007: 663). Rather, it paved the way for establishing its international administration (D'Aspremont 2007). Vidmar argues that Resolution 1244, which placed Kosovo under the regime of international territorial administration, likely disrupted the connection between the unlawful use of force and secession (Vidmar 2022: 178). This is also implicitly

---

[15] This author has extensively argued this point elsewhere. See in detail Miklasová (2024a: 407–478).

confirmed by the *Kosovo* advisory opinion (Accordance with International Law of the Unilateral Declaration of Independence in Respect of Kosovo 2010: para. 81; Vidmar 2022: 178).

On the other hand, Russia's illegal use of force was instrumental to the separation and ongoing survival of these purported separatist territories (Miklasová 2024a: 407–569; UNGA 2014, Resolution 68/262; UNGA 2022a, Resolution ES-11/1; UNGA 2022b, Resolution ES-11/4).[16] Under the principle of *ex injuria jus non oritur*, the effective entities created in violation of a *jus cogens* prohibition of the use of force are precluded from becoming States (Crawford 2006: 97–173). The five territories remain the *de jure* part of the Ukrainian territory (Miklasová 2022b: 11 and 14). Their status is not ambiguous. Russia's actions are undeniably illegal. Thus, despite its attempt at camouflaging its forcible annexations of five Ukrainian territories by the law of statehood, Russia's actions cannot be defined otherwise than serious violations of the peremptory norm of international law.

In addition, (even if accepted as valid) the claims of double standards do not justify further illegal conduct. 'Two wrongs do not make a right' (Christakis 2015: 78). From a legal perspective, only a formal change in the relevant rules matters. This has not occurred for several reasons. First, as mentioned earlier, one single and highly divisive case of Kosovo could not bring about any change in customary law governing secession (Peters 2015: 308). Second, while Russia has extensively relied on the rules governing secession and Kosovo to justify its recognitions, as shown, from a legal perspective, two cases are not identical. Moreover, the normative impact of Russia's claims has been nullified as the overwhelming majority of the international community rejected them and exposed the reality of Russia's blatant ambitions for territorial conquest of the Ukrainian territory (Miklasová 2024b).

However, as mentioned earlier, even without any formal change in customary law and the principles governing secession, some broader eroding effects cannot be denied. The Kosovo case marked the departure from the previous constant practice and *opinio juris* in the post-1945 era. The legal regime in this area, at minimum, appeared to be destabilized.[17] This

---

[16] While the ECtHR does not have a competence regarding the legality of the use of force, its factual findings concerning the unilateral use of force by Russia (direct or indirect) in support of the post-Soviet secessionist entities are relevant to the issue of status of these Ukrainian territories (*Ilaşcu and Others v Moldova and Russia* 2004: paras 380–382; *Mamasakhlisi and Others v Georgia and Russia* 2023: paras 323–324; *Georgia v Russia* (II) 2021: paras 166–174; *Ukraine v Russia (Re Crimea)* 2020: paras 317–335; *Ukraine and the Netherlands v Russia* 2023: paras 579–662).

[17] 'A legal argument is by definition inter-subjective – an appeal to standards that, at least in principle, apply to all who are similarly situated ... to express one's claims in legal terms means to signal which norms one considers relevant and to indicate which procedures one

implication could not have been contained by the unpersuasive *sui generis* arguments. Russia (already a *mala fide* actor due to its covert support of separatists) then used the arguments referring to the law regulating secessions to go as far as to disguise its own violations of *jus cogens* rules and attempts at territorial conquest. Moreover, this all has happened in the context of the escalating reciprocal charges of hypocrisy (Knox 2022: 28).[18] As highlighted by Knox, even though the accusations of hypocrisy are generally considered to operate on a political level, they also have several juridical implications (Knox 2022: 29). Given the essential distinction between international law and politics, invoking hypocrisy 'threatens this division by drawing attention to the "non-legal" reasons that underlie legal arguments' (Knox 2022:). Hughes demonstrates how such accusations undermine the function of international law when seen through the attributes of legitimacy, trust, communication, and effectiveness (Hughes 2023: 18–26). It is hard to deny that – while the formal normative impact was limited (Miklasová 2024b; see for contemporary regulation of secession Miklasová 2024a) – these wider undermining effects have been pertinent as far as the developments concerning the law governing secession are concerned.

Conclusion

There are no contested States in Ukraine. There is no *ambiguity* regarding their legal status, in other words they are the Ukrainian territories illegally annexed by the Russian Federation. Apart from other reasons, Russia's illegal use of force to facilitate these manufactured secessions in Ukraine distinguishes these cases from Kosovo.

However, the abundance of the instances in which Kosovo has been mentioned and relied upon by Russia to justify the purported secessions of the Ukrainian territories highlight the Kosovo precedent's central, albeit not exclusive, role in Russia's (legal) strategy. While Russia had already been violating the principles governing the law of secession ever since the Soviet Union break up (and thus acted as a *mala fide* actor), the chapter claims that it has deliberately profited from and abused the law of statehood outside decolonization (Miklasová 2024b) – previously weakened in the context of a supposed *sui generis* case of Kosovo. This reliance on Kosovo has benefited Russia in several ways.

---

intends to follow and would like others to follow' (Johnstone 2011: 23). The expectations of reciprocity are at the core of the emergence or change of customary international law. See Simma (2008: 3).

[18] Russia, however, never admitted the key underlying differences between these situations.

Specifically, mirroring the Western claims on Kosovo allowed Russia to expose alleged double standards. At the same time, Russia's positions echoing arguments in support of Kosovo – even when, in reality, they do not hold up under any legal scrutiny – have allowed it to project the air of lawfulness or at least ambiguity of its acts vis-à-vis the relevant international or domestic audiences. The form prevails over the substance in Russia's recognition policy.

More broadly, the chapter highlights how the destabilization of international law by dubious legal claims has led to its further subversion, thereby contributing to this legal order's vulnerability – another dimension explored throughout this volume (see also Oeter 2015: 74). Russia responded to the perceived double standards by removing any standards at all while still relying on the language of standards. A high quantity of references to international law did not trigger the change in the law governing secession. One single and highly divisive case of Kosovo did not lead to such a transformation (Peters 2015: 308). Moreover, the states have resolutely unmasked Russia's attempts at camouflaging its ambitions for territorial conquest of Ukraine through the unjustified and *mala fide* law of statehood justifications (Miklasová 2024b). However, even without a formal change in law, broader eroding effects on the law of statehood cannot be denied.

References

Accordance with International Law of the Unilateral Declaration of Independence in Respect of Kosovo (2010). *ICJ Rep* 403, www.icj-cij.org/sites/default/files/case-related/141/141-20100722-ADV-01-00-EN.pdf (accessed 10 July 2024).

Bieber, F. (2022). The Long Shadow of the 1999 Kosovo War. *Comparative Southeast European Studies*, 70 (2), 181–188.

Bílková, V. (2016). Territorial (Se)Cession in Light of Recent Events in Crimea. In: M. Nicolini, F. Palermo, and E. Milano (eds), *Law, Territory and Conflict Resolution*. Leiden: Brill, 194–218.

Borgen, C.J. (2015). Law, Rhetoric, Strategy: Russia and Self-Determination Before and After Crimea. *International Law Studies*, 91, 216–280.

Christakis, T. (2015). Self-Determination, Territorial Integrity and Fait Accompli in the Case of Crimea. *ZaöRV*, 75, 75–100.

Coppieters, B. (2006). The Kosovo Model. Four Lessons for the Caucasus. Committee of Foreign Affairs of the European Parliament, Brussels, 22 February, www.europarl.europa.eu/meetdocs/2004_2009/documents/dv/afet_220206_coppieters_present_r/afet_220206_coppieters_present_rev.pdf (accessed 26 April 2023).

Crawford, J. (2006). *The Creation of States in International Law*. Oxford: Clarendon Press.

D'Aspremont, J. (2007). Regulating Statehood: The Kosovo Status Settlement. *Leiden Journal of International Law*, 20, 649–668.

Declaration of Independence of the Autonomous Republic of Crimea and City of Sevastopol (2014). Adopted on 11 March 2014, www.rada.crimea.ua/news/11_03_2014_1 (accessed 7 February 2014).

Fabry, M. (2012). The Contemporary Practice of State Recognition: Kosovo, South Ossetia, Abkhazia and Their Aftermath. *Nationalities Papers*, 40 (5), 661–676.

Falk, R. (2011). The Kosovo Advisory Opinion: Conflict Resolution and Precedent. *American Journal of International Law*, 105 (1), 50–60.

Frear, T. (2014). The Foreign Policy Options of a Small Unrecognised State: The Case of Abkhazia. *Caucasus Survey*, 1 (2), 1–26.

Georgia v Russia (II) (2021). ECtHR, App no 38263/08, https://hudoc.echr.coe.int/fre#{%22itemid%22:[%22001-207757%22]} (accessed 10 July 2024).

Gessen, M. (2022). How the Kosovo Air War Foreshadowed the Crisis in Ukraine, *The New Yorker*, 15 February, www.newyorker.com/news/our-columnists/how-the-kosovo-air-war-foreshadowed-the-crisis-in-ukraine (accessed 11 May 2023).

Hughes, D. (2023). Does International Law Need a Theory of Hypocrisy? (manuscript on the file with the author).

Hughes, J. (2013). Russia and the Secession of Kosovo: Power, Norms and the Failure of Multilateralism. *Europe-Asia Studies*, 65 (5), 992–1016.

Ilaşcu and Others v Moldova and Russia (2004). ECHR 2004-VII, https://hudoc.echr.coe.int/fre#{%22itemid%22:[%22001-61886%22]} (accessed 10 July 2024).

Ingimundarson, V. (2022). The 'Kosovo Precedent': Russia's Justification of Military Interventions and Territorial Revisions in Georgia and Ukraine. *LSE Ideas Strategic Update*, www.lse.ac.uk/ideas/publications/updates/kosovo (accessed 11 May 2023).

Independent International Commission on Kosovo (2000). *The Kosovo Report: Conflict, International Response, Lessons Learned*. Oxford: Oxford University Press.

ITAR-TASS (2014). Russian Foreign Minister: Russia Prevented the Repetition of Maidan in Crimea, *Tass*, 10 September, https://tass.ru/politika/1433246 (accessed 13 May 2023).

Johnstone, I. (2011). *The Power of Deliberation: International Law, Politics and Organizations*. Oxford: Oxford University Press.

Ker-Lindsay, J. (2009). From Autonomy to Independence: The Evolution of International Thinking on Kosovo, 1998–2005. *Journal of Balkan and Near Eastern Studies*, 11 (2), 141–156.

Ker-Lindsay, J. (2013). Preventing the Emergence of Self-Determination as a Norm of Secession: An Assessment of the Kosovo 'Unique Case' Argument. *Europe-Asia Studies*, 65 (5), 837–856.

Ker-Lindsay, J. (2015). Explaining Serbia's Decision to Go to the ICJ. In: M. Milanovic and M. Wood (eds), *The Law and Politics of the Kosovo Advisory Opinion*. Oxford: Oxford University Press, 9–20.

Knox, R. (2022). Imperialism, Hypocrisy and the Politics of International Law. *TWAIL Review*, 3, 25–67.

Kohen, M.G. and Del Mar, K. (2011). The Kosovo Advisory Opinion and UNSCR 1244 (1999): A Declaration of 'Independence from International Law'?. *Leiden Journal of International Law*, 24 (1), 109–126.

Kosovo Declaration of Independence (2008). Adopted on 17 February 2008, www.refworld.org/docid/47d685632.html (accessed 11 May 2023).

Law No 6-FKZ on the Procedure of Admission to the Russian Federation and Creation of a New Subject within the Russian Federation (2010). Adopted on 17 December.

Lundstedt, T. (2019). The Changing Nature of the Contemporary Russian Interpretation of the Right to Self-Determination under International Law. In: P.S. Morris (ed.), *Russian Discourses on International Law: Sociological and Philosophical Phenomenon.* New York: Routledge, 197–219.

Mälksoo, L. (2015). *Russian Approaches to International Law*. Oxford: Oxford University Press.

Mamasakhlisi and Others v Georgia and Russia (2023). ECtHR, App Nos 29999/04 and 41424/04, https://hudoc.echr.coe.int/#{%22itemid%22:[%22001-223361%22]} (accessed 10 July 2024).

Marxen, C. (2014). The Crimea Crisis: An International Law Perspective. *ZaöRV*, 74, 367–391.

Medvedev, D. (2008). Statement by President of Russia Dmitry Medvedev. 26 August, http://en.kremlin.ru/events/president/transcripts/1222 (accessed 13 May 2023).

Milanovic, M. (2015). Arguing the Kosovo Case. In: M. Milanovic and M. Wood (eds), *The Law and Politics of the Kosovo Advisory Opinion*. Oxford: Oxford University Press, 21–59.

Milanovic, M. and Wood, M. (2015). Introduction. In: M. Milanovic and M. Wood (eds), *The Law and Politics of the Kosovo Advisory Opinion*. Oxford: Oxford University Press, 1–6.

Miklasová, J. (2022a). Russia's Recognition of the DPR and LPR as Illegal Acts under International Law. *Völkerrechtsblog*, 24 February, https://voelkerrechtsblog.org/russias-recognition-of-the-dpr-and-lpr-as-illegal-acts-under-international-law/ (accessed 26 April 2023).

Miklasová, J. (2022b). Post-Soviet Secession: Crimea and Eastern Ukraine Under International Law. In: K.W. Gray (ed.), *Global Encyclopedia of Territorial Rights*. Cham: Springer, 1–17.

Miklasová, J. (2023). Dissolution of the Soviet Union Thirty Years On: Re-Appraisal of the Relevance of the Principle of *Uti Possidetis Iuris*. In: J.E. Viñuales, A. Clapham, L. Boisson de Chazournes, and M. Hébié (eds), *The International Legal Order in the XXIst Century / L'ordre juridique international au XXIeme siècle / El órden jurídico internacional en el siglo XXI: Essays in Honour of Professor Marcelo Gustavo Kohen / Ecrits en l'honneur du Professeur Marcelo Gustavo Kohen / Estudios en honor del Profesor Marcelo Gustavo Kohen*. Leiden: Brill, 105–124.

Miklasová, J. (2024a). *Secession in International Law with a Special Reference to the Post-Soviet Space*. Leiden: Brill.

Miklasová, J. (2024b). Russian Approaches to Post-Soviet Secessions: Bad Faith Argumentation and Its Limits. *Baltic Yearbook of International Law*, 22 (1), 64–87, https://doi.org/10.1163/22115897_02201_005.

Oeter, S. (2015). The Kosovo Case – An Unfortunate Precedent. *ZaoeRV*, (75), 51–74.

Peters, A. (2015). Has the Advisory Opinion's Finding that Kosovo's Declaration of Independence was not Contrary to International Law Set an Unfortunate Precedent?. In: M. Milanovic and M. Wood (eds), *The Law and Politics of the Kosovo Advisory Opinion*. Oxford: Oxford University Press, 291–314.

Pursiainen, C. and Forsberg, T. (2019). The Principle of Territorial Integrity in Russian International Law Doctrine. In: P.S. Morris (ed.), *Russian Discourses on International Law: Sociological and Philosophical Phenomenon*. New York: Routledge, 220–242.

Poghosyan, S. (2021). Russian Approaches to the Right to Peoples to Self-Determination: From the 1966 United Nations Covenants to Crimea. *Juridica International*, 30, 183–193.

Putin, V. (2014a). Address by President of the Russian Federation, Moscow, 18 March, http://en.kremlin.ru/events/president/news/20603 (accessed 18 July 2021).

Putin, V. (2014b). Meeting of the Valdai International Discussion Club, 24 October, http://en.kremlin.ru/events/president/news/46860 (accessed 13 May 2023).

Putin, V. (2014c). Interview to German TV Channel ARD, 17 November, www.en.kremlin.ru/events/president/transcripts/interviews/47029 (accessed 13 May 2023).

Putin, V. (2022a). Address by President of the Russian Federation, 21 February. http://en.kremlin.ru/events/president/news/67828 (accessed 23 February 2022).

Putin, V. (2022b). Meeting on Socioeconomic Support for Regions, 16 March, http://en.kremlin.ru/events/president/news/67996 (accessed 6 March 2023).

Report of the Special Envoy of the Secretary-General on Kosovo's Future Status (2007). Adopted on 26 March 2007.

Roy, A. (2013). *Russia, the West and Military Intervention*. Oxford: Oxford University Press.

Simma, B. (2008). Reciprocity. In: R. Wolfrum (ed.), *Max Planck Encyclopedia of Public International Law*. Oxford: Oxford University Press.

Tanjug (2008). Medvedev: Kosovo Precedent Dangerous, 3 July, www.b92.net/eng/news/politics.php?yyyy=2008&mm=07&dd=03&nav_id=51597 (accessed 13 May).

TASS (2022). Putin Cites Precedent of Kosovo in Explaining Recognition of DPR, LPR. *Tass*, 26 April, https://tass.com/politics/1443661 (accessed 11 May 2023).

Thomas, C.A. (2023). The Concept of Legitimacy and International Law. LSE Legal Studies Working Papers No 12/2023.

United Nations General Assembly (2008). Resolution 63/3, adopted on 8 October 2008.

UNGA (2014). Resolution 68/262, adopted on 27 March 2014.

UNGA (2022a). Resolution ES-11/1, adopted on 2 March 2022.

UNGA (2022b). Resolution ES-11/4, adopted on 12 October 2022.

UN Charter (1945), adopted in San Francisco on 26 June 1945, entry into force: 24 October 1945.

UN Security Council (1999). Resolution 1244, adopted on 10 June 1999.

UN Security Council (2005). Presidential Statement 51, adopted on 24 October 2005.

UN Security Council (2008). Verbatim Record, 18 February 2008.

Venice Commission (2014). Opinion on 'Whether Draft Federal Constitutional Law No. 462741–6 On Amending the Federal Constitutional Law of the Russian Federation on the Procedure of Admission to the Russian Federation and Creation of a New Subject Within the Russian Federation Is Compatible with International Law', adopted on 21 March.

Ukraine and the Netherlands v Russia (2022). ECtHR, App nos 8019/16, 43800/14 and 28525/20, https://hudoc.echr.coe.int/eng#{%22appno%22:[%228019/16%22],%22itemid%22:[%22001-222889%22]} (accessed 10 July 2024).

Ukraine v Russia (Re Crimea) (2020). ECtHR, App nos 20958/14 and 38334/18, https://hudoc.echr.coe.int/eng#{%22appno%22:[%2220958/14%22],%22itemid%22:[%22001-207622%22]} (accessed 10 July 2024).

Vidmar, J. (2009). International Legal Responses to Kosovo's Declaration of Independence. *Vanderbilt Journal of Transnational Law*, 42, 779–851.

Vidmar, J. (2010). Remedial Secession in International Law: Theory and (Lack of) Practice. *St Anthony's International Review*, 6 (1), 37–56.

Vidmar, J. (2022). Secession of Kosovo. In: J. Vidmar, S. McGibbon, and L. Raible (eds), *Research Handbook on Secession*. Cheltenham: Edward Elgar, 167–183.

Weller, M. (2009). *Contested Statehood: Kosovo's Struggle for Independence*. Oxford: Oxford University Press.

Wilde, R. (2011). Kosovo (Advisory Opinion). In: R. Wolfrum (ed.), *Max Planck Encyclopedia of Public International Law*. Oxford: Oxford University Press.

Written Statement of the Russian Federation (2009). www.icj-cij.org/sites/default/files/case-related/141/15628.pdf (accessed 10 July 2024).

5

Legitimization of Violence and State Dissolution in Nagorno-Karabakh: A Critical Legal Analysis

Sheila Paylan

Introduction

As the disputed region of Nagorno-Karabakh is said to exist no more, the echoes of a protracted conflict resonate with a grim finality. The start of the year 2024 marked the closure to an entity that, while subjected to resumed hostilities since 2020, suddenly vanished in a manner that caught many observers off guard.

This chapter[1] seeks to unpack the layers of this complex dissolution of a region that many believed would endure despite the odds. It provides a critical legal analysis of the Nagorno-Karabakh conflict, emphasizing how international legal interpretations and their applications have facilitated acts of violence and led to the dissolution of this contested state. It explores the paradoxical role of international law in simultaneously restricting and enabling violence, often justified under the pretexts of sovereignty and territorial integrity. This analysis critiques the mainstream acceptance of such actions, which obscures the often-neglected interplay between human rights and territorial integrity, and highlights how these frameworks sometimes fail to address complex human dimensions.

---

[1] Research for this chapter was supported by a grant from the Armenian General Benevolent Union (AGBU). I would also like to express my gratitude to Mischa Gureghian-Hall for his invaluable assistance on specific aspects of this chapter. Any errors are mine alone.

Moreover, this chapter discusses the dynamics surrounding the recognition of contested states and the application of international humanitarian law in such conflict zones. It critiques the oversights in addressing human rights violations and war crimes, arguing that these omissions contribute to a selective historical narrative that legitimizes the suppression of the Nagorno-Karabakh entity. This effectively buries the true story of Nagorno-Karabakh, omitting significant human and cultural losses from global consciousness.

Furthermore, this chapter examines the delicate balance between self-determination and the sovereignty of states, alongside the legal underpinnings of self-defence in international conflicts. It also scrutinizes the interesting paradox whereby Azerbaijan, long arguing that the Nagorno-Karabakh Republic was non-existent, forced it to dissolve. Drawing on critical legal studies, this analysis challenges the conventional understanding that frames these actions within acceptable legal norms, revealing a darker, often overlooked side of international law that impacts real lives and geopolitical stability.

Background

The Nagorno-Karabakh conflict centres on a disputed region in the South Caucasus, to the east of Armenia, enclaved within the internationally recognized borders of Azerbaijan. This complex and protracted conflict has left deep scars in the region and remains a significant challenge for peace and stability in the South Caucasus. During the Soviet era, the Nagorno-Karabakh Autonomous Oblast (NKAO) was established and designated to the Azerbaijani Soviet Socialist Republic (SSR) in 1923, despite the region having a significant ethnic Armenian majority. This decision was part of the broader Soviet policy of nationalities under Joseph Stalin. This arrangement planted the seeds for future conflict, as the ethnic Armenians in the region feared marginalization.

As the Soviet Union neared its collapse in the late 1980s, the ethnic Armenians of Nagorno-Karabakh pursued independence, declaring themselves a separate entity to either unite with the Armenian SSR or achieve full sovereignty. This move led to heightened tensions and was met with opposition from the Azerbaijani SSR, marking the beginnings of what would become a civil war (Human Rights Watch 1991: 5). The Nagorno-Karabakh conflict thus initially involved mainly local ethnic Armenian forces and Azerbaijani forces. With the dissolution of the Soviet Union and the emergence of Armenia and Azerbaijan as independent states in 1991, the Nagorno-Karabakh conflict evolved into full-scale warfare as Armenia entered the theatre of war, supporting the Nagorno-Karabakh Armenians. This move was partly a response to the strategic and humanitarian needs of the ethnic Armenians in Nagorno-Karabakh, amid ongoing hostilities.

In 1994, local Armenian forces from Nagorno-Karabakh secured control over the region, as well as surrounding Azerbaijani territories, creating a buffer zone around the enclave. This action was primarily conducted by the Nagorno-Karabakh Defence Army, comprised of ethnic Armenians from the region itself, although supported by volunteers and resources from Armenia. The conflict was characterized by fierce combat, significant casualties, and substantial displacement on both sides, with hundreds of thousands of people – approximately 600,000 Azerbaijanis (International Crisis Group 2012) and 300,000–350,000 Armenians (Human Rights Watch 1994) – forced to leave their homes due to the fighting.

A ceasefire on 12 May 1994, brokered by Russia (Bishkek Protocol 1994), left Nagorno-Karabakh *de facto* independent and in control of seven surrounding territories (OSCE 2011). This *status quo* was maintained through a fragile peace, with the OSCE Minsk Group (co-chaired by the United States, Russia, and France) attempting to mediate a long-term resolution. However, peace efforts were repeatedly undermined by outbreaks of violence, mutual distrust, and a lack of compromise, leading to sporadic escalations throughout the years.

On 27 September 2020, the conflict reignited when Azerbaijan, backed by Turkey, launched a large-scale military offensive to reclaim territories lost in the early 1990s. After six weeks of heavy fighting, a Russia-brokered ceasefire was signed and came into effect on 10 November 2020 (President of the Republic of Azerbaijan et al 2020), which resulted in concessions of Armenian-controlled territory as well parts of Nagorno-Karabakh itself. The agreement also stipulated the deployment of Russian peacekeepers, further complicating the regional power dynamics.

On 19 September 2023, Azerbaijan launched its final military assault, quickly seizing full control of the rest of Nagorno-Karabakh. Over 100,000 ethnic Armenians (UNHCR 2023) were then forced to flee (Klonowiecka-Milart and Paylan 2023) Nagorno-Karabakh to Armenia, following a nearly ten-month blockade by Azerbaijan that led to a dire humanitarian crisis (OHCHR 2023) and widespread starvation which some experts deemed as amounting to genocide (for example, Moreno Ocampo 2023). The United Nations estimates as few as 50 Armenians remain in the region (UN 2023). The Nagorno-Karabakh conflict is now said to have ended on 1 January 2024, with the *de facto* Nagorno-Karabakh Republic considered to have ceased to exist (Uvarchev 2023).

The four UN Security Council resolutions

The UN Security Council (UNSC) passed four resolutions regarding the Nagorno-Karabakh conflict in 1993, during the most intense period of hostilities. Resolution 822 was adopted on 30 April 1993, after 'local Armenian forces' captured the town of Kelbajar, which lies outside the NKAO's borders but within Azerbaijan, creating a corridor linking Armenia to Nagorno-Karabakh, and leading to a significant displacement of civilians (UNSC 1993a, Res. 822). Resolution 853 was adopted on 29 July 1993, following the capture of Agdam, another territory outside of NKAO borders (UNSC 1993b, Res. 853). Resolution 874 was adopted on 14 October 1993, in response to continuing hostilities and efforts to mediate a peaceful resolution to the conflict (UNSC 1993c, Res. 874). Resolution 884 was passed on 12 November 1993, after the capture of Zangelan and Horadiz in Azerbaijan, leading to further displacement of civilians (UNSC 1993d, Res. 884).

The Armenian and Azerbaijani interpretations of these resolutions have differed significantly, reflecting their respective national narratives. Perhaps the most important significant difference in interpretation is the Azerbaijani stance that the resolutions establish Armenia as an aggressor and occupier, alleging that the conflict began with Armenia invading and then occupying Azerbaijani territory. However, this simplifies the complex dynamics of the conflict where local ethnic Armenian forces sought independence or unification with Armenia due to longstanding ethnic and territorial issues.

The resolutions do call for the withdrawal of 'occupying forces' and often express concern about the occupation of territories (UNSC 1993a, Res. 822, para. 1; UNSC 1993b, Res. 853, para. 1; UNSC 1993d, Res. 884, paras. 1, 4; see also UNSC 1993c, Res. 874, para. 5). They do not, however, explicitly state that the Republic of Armenia is the occupying force. Rather, the resolutions refer to 'local Armenian forces' as a distinct group within Azerbaijan (UNSC 1993b, Res. 853, preamble), and call on 'the Government of the Republic of Armenia to continue to exert its influence to achieve compliance by the Armenians of the Nagorny-Karabakh region of the Azerbaijani Republic with its resolution[s]' (UNSC 1993b, Res. 853, para. 9; see also UNSC 1993d, Res. 884, para. 2). This phrasing implies that the belligerent and occupying forces referred to therein are from Nagorno-Karabakh, not from the Republic of Armenia. By framing Armenia as the direct aggressor, Azerbaijan thus supports its narrative of territorial integrity and sovereignty being violated by another state, rather than addressing the internal separatist dynamics driven by the local Armenian population of Nagorno-Karabakh, ignoring the fact that the 12 May 1994 ceasefire agreement was signed by representatives of Armenia, Azerbaijan, *and* Nagorno-Karabakh (Bishkek Protocol 1994).

Azerbaijan's misinterpretations further stem from focusing on selective wording that supports the immediate withdrawal of 'occupying forces', while downplaying or ignoring parts that call for a negotiated peace, which considers the rights and security of the ethnic Armenian population in Nagorno-Karabakh. Such interpretations emphasize territorial integrity without equal consideration of self-determination and human rights stipulated in broader international law discussions, which the resolutions do not dismiss. The resolutions aim to address the conflict without overtly taking a side by naming a specific aggressor, focusing instead on the actions taken by local forces in the region. Azerbaijani officials have nonetheless often cited these resolutions to argue almost exclusively that the international community does not recognize Nagorno-Karabakh as separate from Azerbaijan and that *any* Armenian presence on these lands is considered an occupation.

The Azerbaijani government has also viewed these resolutions as supporting its right to reclaim control over these areas, including through military means. However, they repeatedly call for settlement through OSCE Minsk Group's mediation and emphasize the importance of achieving a peaceful resolution. This insistence on a diplomatic approach highlights a fundamental aspect of the resolutions: that they aim to set a framework for peace and negotiation, not endorse military action as a means of conflict resolution.

The (mis)interpretation of international judgments

Effective control at the European Court of Human Rights

In a similar fashion to the four UNSC resolutions, Azerbaijan advocates erroneous interpretations of other legal instruments in support of the purported partial occupation of its territory by Armenia. Chief amongst these is the 2015 judgment of the European Court of Human Rights (ECtHR) in *Chiragov and Others v Armenia*, in which the Grand Chamber determined that 'Armenia … exercises effective control over Nagorno-Karabakh and the surrounding territories' and, accordingly, that 'the matters complained of … come within the jurisdiction of Armenia for the purposes of Article 1 of the Convention' (para. 186). This judgment is often cited as purportedly establishing that Armenia occupied Nagorno-Karabakh.

However, the Grand Chamber took insufficient care to distinguish between the 'effective control' standard of the ECtHR to assess the extent of a state's extraterritorial jurisdiction under Article 1 of the European Convention on Human Rights (ECHR) (1950), on the one hand, and of international humanitarian law to determine situations of occupation, on the other. In particular, the 'effective control' test employed by the ECtHR is markedly less demanding.[2] By contrast, the 'effective control' test employed to attribute

---

[2] In *Catan and Others v Moldova and Russia* (ECHR 2012), the ECtHR Grand Chamber observed that 'the test for establishing the existence of "jurisdiction" under Article 1 of the Convention has never been equated with the test for establishing a State's responsibility for an internationally wrongful act under international law' (para. 115). Similarly, in *Georgia v Russia (II)* (ECtHR 2021), the Grand Chamber confirmed that 'the term "effective control" [within the meaning of Article 1 ECHR] is broader and covers situations that do not necessarily amount to a situation of "occupation" for the purposes of international

state responsibility under international humanitarian law is considered the appropriate standard for the determination of whether a state is occupying the territory of another (see, for example, ICJ 2024, *Palestine* Advisory Opinion, para. 90; ICJ 2004, *Wall* Advisory Opinion, para. 78; ICJ 2005, *Armed Activities*, paras 173–176; ICJ 1986, para. 115; ICJ 2007, *Bosnian Genocide*, paras 399–406). The ECtHR did not (nor did it need to) determine whether Armenia was, at the time relevant to the alleged violations of the ECHR, *occupying* Nagorno-Karabakh as defined under international humanitarian law.[3] Rather, the application of the far less demanding 'effective control' test was all that was necessary in order to establish extraterritorial Article 1 jurisdiction in *Chiragov*. Azerbaijan seizes upon this regrettable ambiguity, drawing a false equivalency between these standards.

Unblocking the Lachin corridor at the International Court of Justice

Another example of Azerbaijan's erroneous interpretations of international legal instruments involves the indication of provisional measures by the International Court of Justice (ICJ), especially concerning the blockade of the Lachin corridor. In 2023, the ICJ ordered Azerbaijan to ensure unimpeded movement along the corridor, a lifeline for the ethnic Armenian population in Nagorno-Karabakh (ICJ 2023, *Armenia v Azerbaijan*, para. 62). Despite this clear directive, Azerbaijani officials, including the agent of Azerbaijan before the ICJ and the Azerbaijani minister of foreign affairs, inaccurately claimed the ICJ's decision aligned with their stance on managing the protests blocking the Lachin corridor and continued to assert that no restrictions were placed there, contradicting the ICJ's findings of significant disruptions (Paylan 2023).

Azerbaijan's public statements and subsequent inaction evince a deliberate misreading and non-compliance with the ICJ's orders. By maintaining the blockade and blatantly misinterpreting a clear instruction, Azerbaijan deepened the crisis, compelling the Armenians of Nagorno-Karabakh to flee their homes under eventual bombardment and severe duress.

---

humanitarian law' (para. 196). Most recently, in *Ukraine v Russia (re Crimea)* (ECtHR 2024), the Grand Chamber found that even once 'effective control', within the meaning of Art. 1 is established, further factual evidence of control is required in order to establish a situation of belligerent occupation (par. 918). The ECtHR applied these principles to Nagorno-Karabakh explicitly in *Christian Religious Organization of Jehovah's Witnesses in the NKR v Armenia* (ECtHR 2022, para. 48).

[3] A '[t]erritory is considered occupied when it is actually placed under the authority of the hostile army' (Hague Regulations 1907, Art. 42). While the ECtHR did briefly recall potentially applicable norms of international humanitarian law (*Chiragov*, 2015, paras 96–97), it did not apply these rules in assessing the alleged human rights violations under the ECHR.

This scenario unfolded with little effective intervention from the international community. Notably, the UNSC, tasked with maintaining international peace and security, failed to enforce the ICJ's order. This allowed the situation to further deteriorate, which signals a troubling disregard for international judicial mechanisms, emboldening unilateral actions that contribute to ethnic displacements.

The (mis)application of international law

The principle of sovereignty, central to the understanding of international relations and law, has been the most contentious in the context of Nagorno-Karabakh. The dissolution of the Soviet Union activated a strong push for sovereignty and self-determination by the majority Armenian population in Nagorno-Karabakh, leading to a declaration of independence and secession that was not recognized by Azerbaijan or the broader international community. The principle of sovereignty and territorial integrity, by contrast, has been the cornerstone of Azerbaijan's legal and diplomatic, and ultimately military, efforts to reclaim control over Nagorno-Karabakh. Internationally, this principle is intended to prevent states from infringing on the territorial sovereignty of other states. However, in the case of internal conflict, such as that in Nagorno-Karabakh, territorial integrity is often cited to delegitimize secessionist movements.

The international community's adherence to a conservative interpretation of sovereignty that prioritizes state territorial integrity over the rights or aspirations of internal groups resulted in not a single UN member state (not even Armenia) ever recognizing Nagorno-Karabakh as an independent entity. In his 1994 analysis on the tension between a state-centric reading of self-determination and a revisionist reading thereof focused on peoples not yet endowed with statehood, Martti Koskenniemi noted that limiting the right to self-determination to contexts of decolonization has always seemed somehow arbitrary (Koskenniemi 1994: 242).[4] His analysis thus supports the position that self-determination must factor into any discussion of the Nagorno-Karabakh conflict, especially given that, having ignited in 1988, the conflict predates the independence of both Azerbaijan and Armenia, and

---

[4] The International Court of Justice has appeared sympathetic to this interpretation, framing self-determination as having 'developed in such a way as to create a right to independence for the peoples of non-self-governing territories and *peoples subject to alien subjugation, domination and exploitation*' (ICJ 2010, Kosovo Advisory Opinion, para. 79). Moreover, in its *Chagos* Advisory Opinion (ICJ 2019), the ICJ noted that, while the question before it was confined to self-determination in the decolonial context, 'the right to self-determination, as a fundamental human right, has a broad scope of application' beyond this specific area (para. 144).

the strong federal structure of the former Soviet Union does not necessarily lead to the assumption that it had to naturally dissolve into its SSRs. In this respect, Koskenniemi more specifically noted:

> The application of the *uti possidetis* principle in the determination of post-colonial boundaries lived always somewhat uneasily with the official ideology of decolonization as a restoration of authentic communities destroyed by alien rule. Can international lawyers now do better? How should we deal with the Armenian enclave in mountainous Karabagh in Azebeidzhan [*sic*]? (Koskenniemi 1994: 243)

Ultimately, the international community's choice to deal with Nagorno-Karabakh by adopting the conservative approach leading to non-recognition left Nagorno-Karabakh in a very vulnerable position. Moreover, the failure to adopt a human rights-based approach in addressing the Nagorno-Karabakh conflict has arguably contributed significantly to its perpetuation and the tragic ethnic cleansing witnessed in 2023. The longstanding consideration of sovereignty and territorial integrity as sacrosanct principles of international law and relations has overshadowed or sidelined crucial human rights considerations that are equally enshrined in the UN Charter. In the case of Nagorno-Karabakh, this has meant that the rights and securities of the ethnic Armenians have typically been acknowledged only as an afterthought in international discussions and resolutions. For instance, statements by major global actors regarding the behaviour of Azerbaijan post-2020 consistently emphasized the importance of respecting sovereignty and territorial integrity first, before finally addressing human rights abuses (for example, Council of the European Union 2023). This approach can be seen as contributing to an environment where aggressive actions are tolerated if they do not overtly transgress these 'higher' state-centric norms.

This skewed prioritization fails to address the root causes of such conflicts. By demoting the importance of human rights and self-determination, the international community left the Armenians of Nagorno-Karabakh with little recourse to peaceful advocacy for their rights and conditions that respect their identity and history. Moreover, the typical international response, which rigidly adheres to the principles of non-interference and State sovereignty, risks enabling States to manipulate these principles to justify or obscure their aggressive policies. This has been particularly evident in Azerbaijan's utilization of force under the pretext of reclaiming its territories, a justification seemingly endorsed by international inertia towards a rights-based resolution framework.

This skewed prioritization also fails to consider the tenets of the Declaration on Principles of International Law concerning Friendly Relations and Cooperation among States (UNGA 1970, Res. 2625 [XXV]). The seventh paragraph of the Declaration under the heading 'The principle of equal rights and self-determination of peoples' (the so-called 'safeguard clause'), provides that:

> Nothing in the foregoing paragraphs shall be construed as authorizing or encouraging any action which would dismember or impair, totally or in part, the territorial integrity or political unity of sovereign and independent States conducting themselves in compliance with the principle of equal rights and self-determination of peoples as described above and thus possessed of a government representing the whole people belonging to the territory without distinction as to race, creed, or colour.

The ICJ has repeatedly held the declaration is reflective of customary international law (for example, ICJ 1986, *Military and Paramilitary Activities*, para. 191; ICJ 2005, *Armed Activities*, para. 162; ICJ 2010, *Kosovo* Advisory Opinion, para. 80), and also of 'normative character under customary international law' with respect to the law of self-determination (ICJ 2019, *Chagos* Advisory Opinion 2019, para. 155; see also *Western Sahara* 1975, para. 58; ICJ *Wall* Advisory Opinion, para. 88; ICJ 2010, *Kosovo* Advisory Opinion, para. 80; Kohen 2020: 133). Significantly, the declaration goes further than the UN Charter 'in that it makes self-determination not only a foundational component but also a sufficiently concrete principle from which rights and obligations can be directly derived' (Abi-Saab 2020: 19). Accordingly, the safeguard clause effectively conditions a state's enjoyment of territorial integrity as a legal right on its compliance with the principle of equal rights and self-determination of peoples.

The application and misapplication of these principles in the context of Nagorno-Karabakh raise significant questions about the efficacy and fairness of international law. It may be argued that a rigid application of territorial integrity overlooks the nuances of self-determination and the historical contexts of disputed regions. This can lead to a perpetuation of conflict, as the underlying grievances and aspirations of the relevant populations are not adequately addressed. Azerbaijan has thus consistently portrayed its conflict with Nagorno-Karabakh's Armenian population as part of a broader irredentist conflict with Armenia. According to this view, there is no genuine independence movement in Nagorno-Karabakh; it is merely the result of external meddling. From the Azerbaijani perspective, the Nagorno-Karabakh Republic is merely a puppet state, comparable to the 'people's republics' in eastern Ukraine established by Russia, serving as a tool for annexation.[5]

---

[5] Discussed further in Miklasová, Chapter 4 of this volume.

As a result, the Nagorno-Karabakh conflict is further complicated by the potential for confusion or conflation with other regional conflicts involving Russian interference. In Ukraine, Russia has claimed to be supporting the self-determination of ethnic Russians and other minorities, but many international observers view these actions as pretexts for expanding Russian influence and control, thereby undermining the genuine application of self-determination in international law.

The case of Nagorno-Karabakh, by contrast, represents a genuine struggle for self-determination by the ethnic Armenian population, who have long expressed a clear and consistent will to determine their own political status and have sought to achieve this through established democratic processes, such as referendums. This movement arose from historical grievances and a deep-seated desire for autonomy, distinct from any aggressive foreign policy aims by an external state. The confusion or conflation of Russia's actions with those in Nagorno-Karabakh has misinterpreted the latter's aspirations as similar acts of aggression. This misunderstanding has diluted the unique aspects of the Nagorno-Karabakh situation, which in turn has led to international responses and policies that failed to recognize those unique aspects.

The (il)legality of the use of force by Azerbaijan

In the immediate aftermath of the 2020 Nagorno-Karabakh war, a spirited debate arose regarding the legitimacy of Azerbaijan's military actions starting on 27 September 2020, particularly its claim of self-defence (Permanent Representative of Azerbaijan to the UN 2020), to 'recover' Nagorno-Karabakh. Some experts assert that Azerbaijan's actions were justified, positing that an occupation resulting directly from an initial armed attack constitutes a 'continuing armed attack', thereby preserving the attacked state's enduring right to self-defence, regardless of the time elapsed (for example, Akande and Tzanakopoulos 2020; 2021). Conversely, other scholars argue that Azerbaijan's military engagement was not warranted, maintaining that the right to self-defence ceases to apply in situations where there is an established territorial *status quo*, marked by an extended period of non-combat and the peaceful governance of the disputed area (for example, Ruys and Rodríguez Silvestre 2020; 2021a; 2021b; Knoll-Tudor and Mueller 2020).

The debate over Azerbaijan's use of force in the 2020 Nagorno-Karabakh war revolved around the following legal question: Is it permissible under international law for a state to use armed force to reclaim territory that has been unlawfully occupied by another state, even if the latter has governed the territory peacefully for an extended period of time? This issue, not extensively explored in scholarly literature, accepts that, absent a UNSC authorization, the only lawful basis under the *jus ad bellum* (the law governing the use of force) for a state to recover occupied territory is the right of self-defence as articulated in Article 51 of the UN Charter (Ruys and Rodríguez Silvestre 2021a: 1288). It is also agreed that any exercise of this right must meet the criteria of immediacy, necessity, and proportionality (Kretzmer 2013: 242).

Illegal

Addressing this question, Ruys and Rodríguez Silvestre (2021a) argue against the legitimacy of invoking the right of self-defence to reclaim territory that has been occupied, irrespective of the circumstances of acquisition, where a territorial *status quo* has been established, marked by a long period without conflict and peaceful administration by the occupying state, as in the case of Nagorno-Karabakh (1287–1289, 1294). They assert that such a scenario fails to meet the immediacy requirement – often considered part of necessity – which mandates a close temporal connection between an armed attack and the defensive response (1288–1289). They also reference the principle prohibiting the use of force in territorial disputes, suggesting that it counters any entitlement to use force under self-defence in cases of longstanding, peacefully administered occupations (1292–1293). In their analysis, a state loses its right to self-defence if it does not act promptly after a new territorial *status quo* emerges, advocating that maintaining the *status quo* better serves the objective of prohibiting the use of force (1296–1297).

According to Knoll-Tudor and Mueller (2020), '[a]ny other result would challenge the overall architecture of peace preservation'. They argue:

> The massive use of force since 27 September [2020] could not be justified under a putative right to self-defence, as Azerbaijan claimed somewhat tongue-in-cheek, given problems in the areas of immediacy, necessity and proportionality. […] Likewise, Baku could not justify its 'war of liberation' with reference to the four Security Council resolutions of 1993. In these four resolutions […], the Council had urged those involved to cease the armed activities, to effectively enforce the cease-fire agreements, and to continue to seek a 'negotiated settlement of the conflict'. Of course, almost 30 years had lapsed without sensible progress having been made in terms of the settlement of the conflict, despite the work of the OSCE's Minsk Group. But this, in itself, should not – and could not – imply that Azerbaijan had a right to resort to self-help and impose its position by recourse to violence. A valid claim over the land does not justify the use of force.

These views are supported by earlier analyses that suggest once hostilities have ended and there has been a significant period without conflict, states are not permitted to restart hostilities – including in cases of unlawful occupation – unless a new legal justification emerges under the *jus ad bellum*, such as a UNSC authorization or a fresh armed attack (for example, Yiallourides et al 2018, paras 152, 157–158, 161, and references cited therein). Another scholar advocating for setting a time limit on the right to self-defence, even in scenarios involving occupation, has noted:

> In most cases, irredentist demands for lost territory or claims for restoration of the status quo ante are based on attacks that occurred many years, even decades, ago. To extend self-defence to such cases is to stretch the notion of defence far beyond its essential sense of a response to an attack or immediate threat of attack. (Schachter 1985: 292)

Legal

By contrast, Akande and Tzanakopoulos (2021) argue in favour of Azerbaijan's legitimacy of invoking the right of self-defence to reclaim Nagorno-Karabakh, contending that an occupation resulting directly from an unlawful armed attack constitutes a continuing armed attack, thus preserving the attacked state's right to self-defence indefinitely (1299–1307). They differentiate between territorial disputes and situations where occupation results from an armed attack (1301–1302), suggesting that, where years pass between the initial armed attack and the later use of force by the victim state to recover its unlawfully occupied territory, that may suggest that there is no other reasonable means of bringing the unlawful occupation to an end, rendering the use of force to recover the lost territory necessary (1305–1306). In their view, time disadvantages the aggressor rather than providing them with benefits (1299, 1306).

Although Akande and Tzanakopoulos do not stand alone in the constitutive elements of their position,[6] a review of the literature suggests that theirs forms the minority opinion. This is significant in determining who is, in fact, is the aggressor and thereby the wrongful party in this latest phase of the conflict. Questions of guilt, responsibility and reparations for loss of life and property all tie into who 'started it'.

---

[6] For instance, Dinstein (2005) posits that the suspension of hostilities, such as through a truce or ceasefire, should not be confused with their termination, and that a ceasefire violation is thus irrelevant to the determination of armed attack and self-defence (47–48, 54–55). Similarly, Longobardo (2018: 121) argues that unlawful occupation is not subject to the immediacy principle because it allegedly constitutes a continuing armed attack.

Consequences

Soon after the September 2023 final assault ended with the Armenians of Nagorno-Karabakh being forced to leave, Azerbaijani President Ilham Aliyev (2023b) stated: 'Many reiterated there is no military solution to this conflict. We have shown that there is. And we have shown it again recently. This topic is now closed! The subject of the Karabakh conflict is closed once and for all!' Aliyev now regularly boasts the use of military force to get what he wants (for example, Aliyev 2023c). As shown above, however, the international legal framework still unequivocally condemns the settlement of international disputes by force, a principle enshrined in the UN Charter.

As the Ethiopia–Eritrea Claims Commission (2009) found, 'the practice of States and the writings of eminent publicists show that self-defence cannot be invoked to settle territorial disputes' (para. 10). This precedent is directly applicable to the Nagorno-Karabakh situation given that Azerbaijan invoked the right of self-defence to restore its territorial integrity in launching the 2020 Nagorno-Karabakh War (see Permanent Representative of Azerbaijan to the UN 2020). The Commission further noted that 'border disputes between States are so frequent that any exception to the prohibition of the threat or use of force for territory that is *allegedly occupied unlawfully* would create a large and dangerous hole in a fundamental rule of international law' (Ethiopia–Eritrea Claims Commission 2009, para. 10, emphasis added).

Both sides of the debate start from the premise that Armenia was an occupying state. But the characterization of whether Armenia's involvement in the Nagorno-Karabakh conflict can be described not only as an 'occupation' but also an 'illegal' one is complex and depends on the perspective and legal criteria being applied. Armenia has historically emphasized the self-defence efforts of the Nagorno-Karabakh Armenians against Azerbaijani persecution, while Azerbaijan has accused Armenia of aggression and occupation from the early stages of the conflict. The position of Akande and Tzanakopoulos (2020; 2021) that 'occupation that is a direct consequence of an armed attack by another state is a "continuing armed attack"' in the context of the Nagorno-Karabakh conflict touts the Azerbaijani stance that the conflict started with Armenia attacking Azerbaijan first. However, the authors fail to provide any support or reference for such a factual premise.

The Nagorno-Karabakh conflict is widely recognized as having begun on 20 February 1988, when the NKAO independently proclaimed its intention to separate from the Azerbaijani SSR and join the Armenian SSR (for example, De Waal 2005: 14). The violence that ensued between Azerbaijani and local Armenian forces has been described by Human Rights Watch (1991: 5) as having escalated 'to a point approaching civil war'. It was not until 1991 that a newly independent Armenia entered the conflict, after extreme acts of persecutory violence had been committed against Armenians throughout the Azerbaijani SSR (Derrida et al 1990). The conflict then escalated significantly in 1992 when Armenia's support for Nagorno-Karabakh Armenians became more direct and substantial.

Armenia's involvement in the war thus evolved over time. That the conflict ceased in 1994 with Armenians in control of the former NKAO and several surrounding territories bordering Armenia for the next 26 years is not contestable. The conclusion that such control amounted to occupation, especially of the surrounding territories, is not unreasonable. But to claim that such control or occupation originated from an Armenian invasion to conquer Azerbaijani territory is not only baseless but also recklessly disregards the nuanced historical context and unfairly biases the narrative.

Akande and Tzanakopoulos (2021: 1306) also take issue with the passage of time, arguing that '[s]urely, when something lasts for a quarter of a century, then its "temporary" character can be called into question', in line with the Azerbaijani position that 26 years of peace negotiations was too long to wait thus justifying its resort to the use of force. Such an observation, again, ignores that a peaceful resolution of disputes will surely take more time than a militarily forced one. It took 27 years for Greece and (now North) Macedonia to resolve their dispute, and that was just over a name. If it were Armenia's intention to render the situation in and around Nagorno-Karabakh permanent, then it would have officially recognized Nagorno-Karabakh's independence. It did not. Instead, Armenia sought to reach an appropriate compromise short of Azerbaijan's maximalist demands that would provide a status for Nagorno-Karabakh's ethnic Armenian population to guarantee their rights and security. Akande and Tzanakopoulos' position appears to suggest that there is a time limit for that.

The results of supporting Azerbaijan's position and failing to hold it accountable for resorting to the use of force in 2020 are now clear. The international community was unable to prevent the ethnic cleansing of Nagorno-Karabakh, which Azerbaijan continued to justify in the name of sovereignty, territorial integrity, and acting in purported self-defence (for example, Suleymanov 2023), while holding no apparent regard for the lives or basic human rights of the Armenian population. Despite Azerbaijan's actions in 2023 having been met with worldwide condemnation, including by the European Parliament (2023) and members of the UNSC (2023), the lack of more robust consequences for Azerbaijan's breaches of international law, including the use of force to obliterate the dispute over the status of Nagorno-Karabakh, not only undermines the international legal order but also sets a dangerous precedent for repeat behaviour.

Indeed, Aliyev's success in using force to take Nagorno-Karabakh has emboldened him to now lay claim to Armenia proper, including Yerevan (for example, Aliyev 2024), as historic Azerbaijani land, dubbing it 'Western Azerbaijan' (Aliyev 2023a). Aliyev has been invading Armenia since May 2021 (see Macron 2021), with a major offensive in September 2022 having resulted in further war crimes (for example, Human Rights Watch 2022) and, according to the Armenian government, the occupation of over 200 square kilometres of Armenian sovereign territory (Armenpress 2023). Aliyev's actions in Nagorno-Karabakh having gone unpunished, there are now clear signs that Azerbaijan is gearing up for full-scale war and forcing Armenia to hand over more territory (Avetisyan 2024; Gavin 2024).

The forced dissolution of Nagorno-Karabakh as recognition thereof

On 1 January 2024, the Nagorno-Karabakh Republic is said to have officially ceased to exist (see Urvachev 2023). The final president of the self-proclaimed republic, Samvel Shahramanyan, ordered its dissolution through a decree dated 28 September 2023. This decree was a condition of the ceasefire agreement that concluded Azerbaijan's rapid military operation to subdue the Nagorno-Karabakh Republic, which occurred on 19–20 September 2023.

The forced dissolution of the Nagorno-Karabakh Republic presents a paradoxical yet pivotal moment in the history of the conflict, highlighting an inconsistency in Azerbaijan's longstanding policies and international legal positions. For years, Azerbaijan steadfastly denied the existence of Nagorno-Karabakh as a separate entity, dismissing its declarations of independence and self-governance as illegitimate. Yet, the circumstances surrounding the dissolution of Nagorno-Karabakh reveal a tacit acknowledgment of its entity status, fundamentally contradicting Azerbaijan's previous stance.

The final assault on Nagorno-Karabakh by Azerbaijani forces culminated not merely in a military victory but in a political act that inadvertently recognized the very existence of the Nagorno-Karabakh Republic. The coerced signing of the dissolution decree by the Nagorno-Karabakh authorities was procured under extreme duress and threats of further violence, challenging the legality of such actions under international law, specifically the Vienna Convention on the Law of Treaties (VCLT) (1969). According to Article 52 of the VCLT, any treaty that is procured by the threat or use of force is void. Since going into exile, President Shahramanyan has accordingly reneged on the validity of the decree ordering the dissolution of Nagorno-Karabakh, declaring it null and void (France 24 2023).

This introduces a legal anomaly where the act of dissolution itself, while intended to erase Nagorno-Karabakh from political maps, simultaneously legitimizes its existence as a contractual party capable of engaging in and being coerced into international agreements. Furthermore, this act of forced dissolution under duress raises significant concerns about the genuine acknowledgment of Nagorno-Karabakh's sovereign capabilities. By necessitating a formal agreement to dissolve, Azerbaijan may have unintentionally affirmed the government of Nagorno-Karabakh's authority to represent its people and to engage in treaty acts – a right typically reserved for recognized sovereign entities. This acknowledgment, whether intentional or not, pivots from Azerbaijan's longstanding narrative that Nagorno-Karabakh was merely a rebellious region within its territorial boundaries without any legitimate autonomous or governmental structure.

This development exposes the complex interplay between *de facto* state functions and international recognition. The international community, while largely supporting Azerbaijan's territorial claims, has not addressed the implications of such a dissolution under coercive conditions. This oversight may set a precarious precedent where the dissolution of an entity under duress is viewed as a legitimate means of conflict resolution, potentially encouraging similar strategies in other protracted conflicts worldwide.

The paradox of Nagorno-Karabakh's forced dissolution as a form of recognition by Azerbaijan offers a unique case study in the inconsistencies of international responses to self-determination, sovereignty, and state dissolution. It prompts a re-evaluation of how entities under duress are treated under international law and the moral and legal obligations of the international community to safeguard the rights and dignities of such entities and their populations.

The case of Nagorno-Karabakh and its ultimate demise thus challenges the global legal framework to better accommodate the realities of entities that exist at the margins of statehood and international law, ensuring that their rights and statuses are not overshadowed by the geopolitical agendas of more powerful states.

Conclusion

The case of Nagorno-Karabakh exemplifies the ways in which international law can be manipulated to serve national agendas, and sheds light on a critical paradox in the international legal framework, where the principles of sovereignty and self-determination are often in conflict. The scales, however, tend to tip towards the principles of sovereignty and territorial integrity, often at the detriment of the legitimate aspirations of distinct ethnic groups. This bias is evident in the selective engagement of international actors and in the rigid interpretations of international laws, which, in this case, facilitated the erosion of a community's hope for recognized autonomy and contributed to the demise of its *de facto* state entity.

The resolution of the Nagorno-Karabakh conflict, particularly through Azerbaijan's forceful reclamation of the territory and the subsequent coerced dissolution of the Nagorno-Karabakh Republic, illuminates a disconcerting readiness to accept a 'might is right' approach to the settlement of territorial disputes. Moreover, the handling of the Nagorno-Karabakh situation reveals a broader issue of international law potentially being manipulated to validate aggressive state actions under the guise of legal norms, thus sidelining the crucial aspects of human rights and ethnic identity.

Reflecting on these developments, the international legal framework requires substantial reform to better balance the principles of sovereignty, territorial integrity, and self-determination and to protect the rights and identities of peoples and minority populations against dominant geopolitical agendas. Moreover, the legal rationale used to justify such actions – namely the principle of territorial integrity – often overshadows crucial considerations of human rights and historical context, which should also hold significant weight in international discourse. The Nagorno-Karabakh conflict thus stands as a lesson on the often overlooked dark underbelly of current international legal norms, and showcases the urgent necessity for more nuanced and equitable approaches.

References

Abi-Saab, G. (2020). The System of the Friendly Relations Declaration. In: J.E. Viñuales (ed.), *The UN Friendly Relations Declaration at 50*. Cambridge: Cambridge University Press, 12–22.

Akande, D. and Tzanakopoulos, A. (2020). Use of Force in Self-Defence to Recover Occupied Territory: When Is It Permissible? *EJIL:Talk!*, 18 November, www.ejiltalk.org/use-of-force-in-self-defence-to-recover-occupied-territory-when-is-it-permissible/ (accessed 26 August 2024).

Akande, D. and Tzanakopoulos, A. (2021). Legal: Use of Force in Self-Defence to Recover Occupied Territory. *European Journal of International Law*, 32 (4), 1299–1307.

Aliyev, I. (2023a). *Speech by President of Azerbaijan Ilham Aliyev at the Extraordinary Summit of the Organization of Turkic States*. 16 March, Ankara, Turkey, https://president.az/en/articles/view/59186/print (accessed 26 August 2024).

Aliyev, I. (2023b). The subject of the Karabakh conflict is closed once and for all! *Twitter/X*, 17 October, https://x.com/presidentaz/status/1714323834134773774 (accessed 26 August 2024).

Aliyev, I. (2023c). We restored our territorial integrity and sovereignty by use of force and in line with international law and the UN Charter, and we feel proud of that. *Twitter/X*, 9 November, https://x.com/presidentaz/status/1722614957500694847 (accessed 26 August 2024).

Aliyev, I. (2024). In the 20th century the lands of Azerbaijan were given to Armenia in parts. *Twitter/X*, 13 January, https://x.com/presidentaz/status/1746075298863456373 (accessed 26 August 2024).

Armenpress (2023). Approximately 200 Square Kilometers of Armenian Territory is under Azeri Control – FM. *Armenpress*, 3 November, https://armenpress.am/en/article/1123429 (accessed 26 August 2024).

Avetisyan, A. (2024). Armenian PM Says Azerbaijan Gearing up for 'Full-Scale War'. *Eurasianet*, 16 February, https://eurasianet.org/armenian-pm-says-azerbaijan-gearing-up-for-full-scale-war (accessed 26 August 2024).

Bishkek Protocol (1994). 5 May, amended 8 May 1994, signed 9, 10 and 11 May 1994, https://www.peaceagreements.org/viewmasterdocument/990 (accessed 26 August 2024).

Council of the European Union (2023). *Press Remarks by President Charles Michel following Trilateral Meeting with President Aliyev of Azerbaijan and Prime Minister Pashinyan of Armenia.* 15 July, www.consilium.europa.eu/en/press/press-releases/2023/07/15/press-remarks-by-president-charles-michel-following-trilateral-meeting-with-president-aliyev-of-azerbaijan-and-prime-minister-pashinyan-of-armenia/ (accessed 26 August 2024).

De Waal, T. (2005). The Nagorny Karabakh Conflict: Origins, Dynamics and Misperceptions. In: L. Broers (ed.), *The Limits of Leadership: Elites and Societies in the Nagorny Karabakh Process.* London: Conciliation Resources: 12–17.

Derrida, J., Berlin, I., Finkielkraut, A., Gadamer, H.-G., Habermas, J., Wiesel E., et al (1990). An Open Letter on Anti-Armenian Pogroms in the Soviet Union. *New York Review of Books*, 37 (14), 27 September, www.nybooks.com/articles/1990/09/27/an-open-letter-on-anti-armenian-pogroms-in-the-sov/ (accessed 26 August 2024).

Dinstein, Y. (2005). *War, Aggression and Self-Defence.* 5th edn. Cambridge: Cambridge University Press.

Ethiopia–Eritrea Claims Commission (2009). *Partial Award: Jus ad Bellum – Ethiopia's Claims 1–8.* Award of 19 December 2009. *Reports of International Arbitral Awards*, 26, 457–469.

European Convention for the Protection of Human Rights and Fundamental Freedom (ECHR), adopted in Rome on 4 November (1950). Entered into force 3 September 1953.

ECHR (European Court of Human Rights) (2012). *Catan and Others v Moldova and Russia.* Application Nos 43370/04, 18454/06, and 8252/05. Grand Chamber Judgment of 19 October 2012.

ECtHR (2015). *Chiragov and Others v Armenia.* Application No. 13216/05. Grand Chamber Judgment of 16 June 2015.

ECtHR (2021). *Georgia v Russia (II).* Application No. 38263/08. Grand Chamber of 21 January of 2021.

ECtHR (2022). *Christian Religious Organization of Jehovah's Witnesses in the NKR v Armenia.* Application No. 41817/10. Judgment of 22 March 2022.

ECtHR (2024). *Ukraine v Russia (re Crimea).* Application Nos 20958/14 and 38334/18. Grand Chamber Judgment of 25 June 2024.

European Parliament (2023). Resolution on the Situation in Nagorno-Karabakh after Azerbaijan's Attack and the Continuing Threats Against Armenia (2023/2879[RSP]). *Official Journal of the European Union*, 2024, Series C, 1188–1194.

France 24 (2023). *Nagorno-Karabakh Dissolution Not Valid, Says Armenian Separatist Leader. France 24*, 22 December, www.france24.com/en/asia-pacific/20231222-nagorno-karabakh-dissolution-not-valid-says-armenian-separatist-leader (accessed 26 August 2024).

Gavin, G. (2024). Armenian PM: We'll Hand Azerbaijan Some Territory to Avoid a New War. *Politico*, 19 March, www.politico.eu/article/armenia-pm-nikol-pashinyan-hand-azerbaijan-some-territory-avoid-new-war/ (accessed 26 August 2024).

Hague Regulations (1907). Hague Convention (IV) Relative to the Laws and Customs of War on Land. Annex: Regulations Respecting the Laws and Customs of War on Land, adopted in The Hague on 18 October. Entered into force 26 January 1910. *Consolidated Treaty Series*, 205, 277 et seq.

Human Rights Watch (1991). *Conflict in the Soviet Union: Black January in Azerbaidzhan*. New York: Human Rights Watch, www.hrw.org/reports/pdfs/u/ussr/ussr915.pdf (accessed 26 August 2024).

Human Rights Watch (1994). *Azerbaijan: Seven Years of Conflict in Nagorno-Karabakh*. New York: Human Rights Watch, www.hrw.org/reports/AZER%20Conflict%20in%20N-K%20Dec94_0.pdf (accessed 26 August 2024).

Human Rights Watch (2022). *Video Shows Azerbaijan Forces Executing Armenian POWs*. 14 October, www.hrw.org/news/2022/10/14/video-shows-azerbaijan-forces-executing-armenian-pows (accessed 26 August 2024).

ICJ (1975). *Western Sahara*. Advisory Opinion of 16 October 1975. *ICJ Reports*, 12–82.

ICJ (1986). *Military and Paramilitary Activities in and against Nicaragua (Nicaragua v. United States of America)*. Merits, Judgment of 27 June 1986. *ICJ Reports*, 14–150.

ICJ (2004). *Legal Consequences of the Construction of a Wall in the Occupied Palestinian Territory*. Advisory Opinion of 9 July 2004. *ICJ Reports*, 136–203 (*Wall* Advisory Opinion).

ICJ (2005). *Armed Activities on the Territory of the Congo (Democratic Republic of the Congo v. Uganda)*. Merits, Judgment of 19 December 2005. *ICJ Reports*, 168–283.

ICJ (2007). *Application of the Convention on the Prevention and Punishment of the Crime of Genocide (Bosnia and Herzegovina v. Serbia and Montenegro)*. Merits, Judgment of 26 February 2007. *ICJ Reports*, 43–240 (*Bosnian Genocide*).

ICJ (2010). *Accordance with International Law of the Unilateral Declaration of Independence in Respect of Kosovo*. Advisory Opinion of 22 July 2010. *ICJ Reports*, 403–453 (*Kosovo* Advisory Opinion).

ICJ (2019). *Legal Consequences of the Separation of the Chagos Archipelago from Mauritius in 1965*. Advisory Opinion of 25 February 2019. *ICJ Reports*, 95–141 (*Chagos* Advisory Opinion).

ICJ (2023). *Application of the International Convention on the Elimination of All Forms of Racial Discrimination (Armenia v Azerbaijan)*. Provisional Measures, Order of 23 February 2023. *ICJ Reports*, 14–30.

ICJ (2024). *Legal Consequences arising from the Policies and Practices of Israel in the Occupied Palestinian Territory, including East Jerusalem*. Advisory Opinion of 19 July 2024 (*Palestine* Advisory Opinion).

International Crisis Group (2012). *Tackling Azerbaijan's IDP Burden*. Europe Briefing No. 67, 27 February, www.crisisgroup.org/europe-central-asia/caucasus/azerbaijan/tackling-azerbaijan-s-idp-burden (accessed 26 August 2024).

Klonowiecka-Milart, A. and Paylan, S. (2023). Forced Displacement of Armenians from Nagorno-Karabakh: A Response. *Opinio Juris*, 6 November, https://opiniojuris.org/2023/11/06/forced-displacement-of-armenians-from-nagorno-karabakh-a-response/ (accessed 26 August 2024).

Knoll-Tudor, B. and Mueller, D. (2020). At Daggers Drawn: International Legal Issues Surrounding the Conflict in and around Nagorno-Karabakh. *EJIL:Talk!*, 17 November, www.ejiltalk.org/at-daggers-drawn-international-legal-issues-surrounding-the-conflict-in-and-around-nagorno-karabakh/ (accessed 26 August 2024).

Kohen, M.G. (2020). Self-Determination. In: J.E. Viñuales (ed.), *The UN Friendly Relations Declaration at 50*. Cambridge: Cambridge University Press, 133–165.

Koskenniemi, M. (1994). National Self-Determination Today: Problems of Legal Theory and Practice. *The International and Comparative Law Quarterly*, 43 (2), 241–269.

Kretzmer, D. (2013). The Inherent Right to Self-Defence and Proportionality in *Jus Ad Bellum*. *European Journal of International Law*, 24 (1), 235–282.

Longobardo, M. (2018). *The Use of Armed Force in Occupied Territory*. Cambridge: Cambridge University Press.

Macron, E. (2021). Azerbaijani armed forces have crossed into Armenian territory. They must withdraw immediately. I say again to the Armenian people: France stands with you in solidarity and will continue to do so. *Twitter/X*, 14 May, https://x.com/EmmanuelMacron/status/1392965873187659778 (accessed 26 August 2024).

Moreno Ocampo, L. (2023). Starvation as a Means of Genocide: Azerbaijan's Blockade of the Lachin Corridor Between Armenia and Nagorno-Karabakh. *Just Security*, 11 August, www.justsecurity.org/87574/starvation-as-a-means-of-genocide-azerbaijans-blockade-of-the-lachin-corridor-between-armenia-and-nagorno-karabakh/ (accessed 26 August 2024).

OHCHR (2023). *UN Experts Urge Azerbaijan to Lift Lachin Corridor Blockade and End Humanitarian Crisis in Nagorno-Karabakh*. 7 August, www.ohchr.org/en/press-releases/2023/08/un-experts-urge-azerbaijan-lift-lachin-corridor-blockade-and-end (accessed 26 August 2024).

OSCE (2011). *Report of the OSCE Minsk Group Co-Chairs' Field Assessment Mission to the Occupied Territories of Azerbaijan Surrounding Nagorno-Karabakh*, https://www.osce.org/mg/76209 (accessed 26 August 2024).

Paylan, S. (2023). When Might Is Wrong: Addressing Azerbaijan's Refusal to Comply with the ICJ's Order to Unblock the Lachin Corridor. *Opinio Juris*, 16 March, http://opiniojuris.org/2023/03/16/when-might-is-wrong-addressing-azerbaijans-refusal-to-comply-with-the-icjs-order-to-unblock-the-lachin-corridor/ (accessed 26 August 2024).

Permanent Representative of Azerbaijan to the United Nations (2020). *Letter Addressed to the Secretary-General*, 27 September. UN Doc. A/75/357–S/2020/948, Annex.

President of the Republic of Azerbaijan, Prime Minister of the Republic of Armenia, and President of the Russian Federation (2020). *Statement by President of the Republic of Azerbaijan, Prime Minister of the Republic of Armenia, and President of the Russian Federation*. UN Doc. S/2020/1104, Annex, https://documents.un.org/doc/undoc/gen/n20/307/34/pdf/n2030734.pdf (accessed 26 August 2024).

Ruys, T. and Rodríguez Silvestre, F. (2020). The Nagorno-Karabakh Conflict and the Exercise of 'Self-Defense' to Recover Occupied Land. *Just Security*, 10 November, www.justsecurity.org/73310/the-nagorno-karabakh-conflict-and-the-exercise-of-self-defense-to-recover-occupied-land/ (accessed 26 August 2024).

Ruys, T. and Rodríguez Silvestre, F. (2021a) Illegal: The Recourse to Force to Recover Occupied Territory and the Second Nagorno-Karabakh War. *European Journal of International Law*, 32 (4), 1287–1297.

Ruys, T. and Rodriguez Silvestre, F. (2021b). Military Action to Recover Occupied Land: Lawful Self-defense or Prohibited Use of Force? The 2020 Nagorno-Karabakh Conflict Revisited. *International Law Studies*, 97, 665–738.

Schachter, O. (1985). The Lawful Resort to Unilateral Use of Force. *Yale Journal of International Law*, 10 (2), 291–294.

Suleymanov, E. (2023). Azerbaijan is Acting in Self-Defence. *The Guardian*, 10 November, www.theguardian.com/world/2023/nov/10/azerbaijan-is-acting-in-self-defence (accessed 26 August 2024).

UN (2023). UN Karabakh Mission Told 'Sudden' Exodus Means as Few as 50 Ethnic Armenians May Remain, 2 October, https://news.un.org/en/story/2023/10/1141782 (accessed 26 August 2024).

UNGA (1970). Resolution 2625 (XXV): Declaration on Principles of International Law concerning Friendly Relations and Co-operation among States. UN Doc. A/RES/2625(XXV), Annex. 24 October.

UNHCR (2023). *Refugees Find Safety in Armenia, but the Future Remains Uncertain*. 20 October, www.unhcr.org/news/stories/refugees-find-safety-armenia-future-remains-uncertain (accessed 26 August 2024).

UN Security Council (1993a). Resolution 822. UN Doc. S/RES/822, 30 April.

UN Security Council (1993b). Resolution 853. UN Doc. S/RES/853, 29 July.

UN Security Council (1993c). Resolution 874. UN Doc. S/RES/874, 14 October.

UN Security Council (1993d). Resolution 884. UN Doc. S/RES/884, 12 November.

UN Security Council (2023). *Latest Clash between Armenia, Azerbaijan Undermines Prospects of Peace, Speakers Warn Security Council, Calling for Genuine Dialogue to Settle Outstanding Issues.* Press Release SC/15418, 21 September, https://press.un.org/en/2023/sc15418.doc.htm (accessed 26 August 2024).

Uvarchev, L. (2023) The Head of Nagorno-Karabakh Signed a Decree on the Termination of the Existence of the Republic (translated from Russian). *Kommersant*, 28 September, www.kommersant.ru/doc/6239337 (accessed 26 August 2024).

Vienna Convention on the Law of Treaties (VCLT) (1969). Adopted in Vienna on 23 May 1969, entry into force 27 January 1980. *United Nations Treaty Series*, 1155, 331–353.

Yiallourides, C., Gehring, M., and Gauci, J-P. (2018). *The Use of Force in Relation to Sovereignty Disputes over Land Territory*. London: British Institute of International and Comparative Law.

PART II

Vulnerability and Agency on the Ground: People and Institutions Navigating War and Law

6

Contested Statehood, Ambiguities and Volatility: The Effects of Lawfare and Warfare in the Western Sahara Conflict

Irene Fernández-Molina

Introduction

The long-frozen conflict over Western Sahara has thawed and heated up since late 2020. Back then, it was stirred up by a spiral of destabilization on the ground, with the return of armed confrontation after three decades of ceasefire, and also on the regional and international scale, with the shock waves sent by US President Donald Trump's proclamation of recognition of Moroccan sovereignty over the territory. The berm dividing the western three-quarters of Western Sahara annexed by Morocco and the eastern strip controlled by the Polisario Front has thereafter been witnessing what the UN describes as 'low-intensity hostilities'.

This chapter examines the ambiguity and volatility associated to contested statehood by looking at the intersection between politics, law and violence in the case of Western Sahara. It will start by discussing the political, analytical, and legal grey areas that surround both Western Sahara as a territory and the Sahrawi Arab Democratic Republic (SADR) as a contested state. Such ambiguities include the SADR's outlier position as a non-secessionist contested state whose people enjoy a widely accepted right to self-determination. This is also an entity that operates as a hybrid between a state-in-exile and a *de facto* state, with the ensuing strengths and weaknesses of its statehood claim from constitutive and declaratory perspectives. A third duality concerns the relationship between the international legal regime applied by default to this territory and conflict, namely decolonization law based on the right to self-determination, and international humanitarian law including the law of occupation. The chapter will subsequently focus on the agency displayed in tandem by SADR and the Polisario Front – the national liberation movement internationally recognized as the representative of the Sahrawi people – in order to counter their own vulnerability, the asymmetry of the conflict, and international conflict management ambiguities in international conflict management that are detrimental to their interests. Such agency has materialized in new strategies of lawfare (legal activism) and warfare that the Polisario Front/SADR have pursued since the mid-2000s and 2020, respectively. The former has sought to hold the EU institutions accountable for the existing territorial undifferentiation practices in their economic relations with Morocco – the *de facto* inclusion of Western Sahara in all EU–Morocco bilateral cooperation agreements – while the latter has led to the return to armed struggle in the hope of drawing red lines, regaining international attention, and unblocking an ever-stalled conflict resolution process

Ambiguities

Both Western Sahara as a territory and the SADR proclaimed in 1976 by the Polisario Front display significant elements of ambiguity at the political, analytical and legal levels. To start with, as all the cases examined in this book, the dispute over the status of such piece of land appears as a conflict in the 'grey zone' of statehood (see the Introduction of this volume). From a political science and international relations (IR) perspective, the SADR fits comfortably in the broad and variegated category of 'contested states' given the 'internationally contested nature of [its] purported statehood' (Geldenhuys 2009: 3). It also shares a number of features with the narrower group of '*de facto* states', including the definitional conditions of having an organized political leadership that enjoys popular support, the capacity to provide governance to a certain population, the self-assigned capacity to enter into relations with other states, and the aim to achieve widespread international recognition of its sovereignty (Pegg 1998: 26). The same applies with some nuances to the usual conceptualizations of 'unrecognised states' (Caspersen and Stansfield 2011; Caspersen 2012) and 'quasi-states' (Kolstø 2006).

However, in a comparative light, the SADR is at most an outlier or a hybrid in relation to – if not outright excluded from – the last three overlapping categories. This is because of three fundamental reasons. First, the contestation of statehood here does not stem from secessionism but from foreign occupation by a legally separate neighbouring state in the context of a thwarted decolonization and self-determination process. Second, the SADR has not achieved *de facto* independence in as much as it does not exercise effective rule over the territory it claims (Kolstø 2006: 725–726; Caspersen 2012: 8). This is due to Morocco's *de facto* control over and formal annexation of three-quarters thereof upon its two-step takeover in 1975–1976 (following Spain's withdrawal) and 1979–1980 (following Mauritania's withdrawal from the southern part). As a result, the SADR operates on a primarily extraterritorial basis, as a state-in-exile (Wilson 2016: 10; see also McConnell 2016), from the Sahrawi refugee camps near Tindouf in south-western Algeria. Third, the SADR has not been overall 'unable to achieve any degree of substantive recognition' from the international society (Pegg 1998: 26). Since its foundation it has been recognized by 84–85 UN member states, and at present it maintains diplomatic relations with around 40 of them. This substantial, if partial, degree of international recognition reflects its sheltering by the principle of self-determination. Altogether, the combination of a widely accepted right to self-determination, foreign occupation, and extraterritoriality accentuates Western Sahara and SADR's position as a borderline case of contested statehood, showing some specific parallels solely with Palestine. Such conditions have mixed effects on the SADR's sovereignty and statehood claims referring to the constitutive and declaratory theories of state recognition in international law (Crawford 2006; Oeter 2015).

On one hand, SADR's hand is significantly stronger than that of than typical secessionist contested states from a constitutive perspective – i.e. based on external legitimacy and collective endorsement – due to its enjoyment of 'titular recognition', defined as the 'wide formal acceptance (at multilateral level) of an entity's *right* of or title to statehood' (Geldenhuys 2009: 25, emphasis in original). Here, such an entitlement relies on the principle of self-determination. Titular recognition stems from the UN's designation of colonial Spanish Sahara as a non-self-governing territory in 1963, which entailed an UN General Assembly demand for Spain, the administering power, to arrange 'a referendum under [UN] auspices with a view to enabling the indigenous population of the Territory to exercise freely its right to self-determination' (A/RES/2229(1966)). The fact that the Madrid regime delayed and eventually abandoned plans to hold such referendum – as Spain irregularly withdrew from the territory transferring its administration to Morocco and Mauritania in November 1975 – pushed the Polisario Front to proclaim the SADR's independence in February 1976, referring to UN General Assembly resolution 1514 (Polisario Front 1976). Due to this unique genealogy and firm grounding in decolonization law, while self-determination through a referendum was deferred and remains yet to be realized today, the SADR's declaration of independence was not generally regarded as challenging international legality or a majority of the international community. This is what sets this case of contested statehood apart from breakaway entities, and completely turn the tables regarding what Krasner (1999) calls 'international legal sovereignty'. Furthermore, in practice, the added layer of ambiguity posed by the apparent contradiction between the Western Sahara territory's non-self-governing status and the SADR's statehood claim has been more of an asset than a problem for the Polisario Front/SADR 'state-movement' duo (Wilson 2016), which have mobilized one or another depending on contexts, audiences, and their respective roles. While the Polisario Front has always enjoyed much wider international recognition as a national liberation movement, the proclamation of the SADR allowed most notably for its admission into the Organization of African Unity (OUA) as a full-blown member state in 1982.

On the other hand, going back to doctrinal legal approaches to statehood, the SADR's prevailing extraterritoriality, while not being absolute given its control over the so-called 'liberated zone' comprising the easternmost 25 per cent of Western Sahara, still substantially weakens its statehood according to the functional or effectiveness criteria prioritized by the declaratory theory. The SADR has an overall reduced ability to exercise actual 'domestic sovereignty' and 'Westphalian sovereignty' (Krasner 1999) in Western Sahara itself. Regardless, elements of declaratory statehood have been consciously cultivated and invoked by the SADR leadership. Making a virtue of necessity, their broad strategy regarding the state-in-exile vs *de facto* state and constitutive vs declaratory statehood ambiguities has been to try and have it both ways.

In the domain of international law, besides the implications of the SADR's political hybridity between a state-in-exile and a *de facto* state, there are also some further ambiguities as to the status of and the regime applicable to the territory this contested state claims, i.e. Western Sahara (Fernández-Molina and Ojeda García 2020: 86). The fundamental, unchanged international consensus and UN position since the 1960s is that the former Spanish colony constitutes a non-self-governing territory subject to decolonization law and pending the fulfilment of its people's right to self-determination. On this point, a noteworthy element of exceptionality and controversy is the lack of indication of who is Western Sahara's administering power on the UN list of non-self-governing territories, since Spain declared itself 'exempt from any responsibility of any international nature in connection with the administration of the Territory' in early 1976.[1] Yet, the Polisario Front/SADR, along with an important number of legal scholars and a 2014 decree from the Spanish National Court (Audiencia Nacional), maintain that, while not *de facto*, Spain continues to be the *de jure* administering power due to the legal nullity and no effect of the 1975 Madrid Accords (Kassoti

---

[1] See the UN official webpage on Non-Self-Governing Territories: www.un.org/dppa/decolonization/en/nsgt).

2017b: 33). The African Union and its special envoy for Western Sahara Joaquim Chissano have also advocated this position in the past decade. The opposing view contends that Morocco should be acknowledged as the *de facto* administrator of the territory (Torres-Spelliscy 2014: 236) – as done explicitly at times, most notably, by EU representatives (Fernández-Molina 2017: 221, 224; see below).

The second legal ambiguity concerns the international legal regime(s) applicable to the Western Sahara territory and the conflict over it. The prevailing consensus prioritizes their falling under the framework of decolonization law based on the right to self-determination (Articles 73–74 of the UN Charter on non-self-governing territories as well as the two UN human rights covenants of 1966). In addition, regarding the past and present hostilities, the self-determination element entitles Western Sahara to be treated as an international armed conflict (IAC) for the purposes of international humanitarian law – unlike most wars pitting (secessionist) *de facto*/contested states against their parent states, which are regarded as non-international armed conflicts (NIACs). This extends the rights and protections of *jus in bello* to Western Sahara's civilian population and those fighting on its behalf in the exercise of their right to self-determination, who are considered as lawful combatants and enjoy, among other things, the guarantees attached to the prisoner of war status (Introduction to this volume; see Additional Protocol I to the Geneva Conventions of 1977). This categorization and recognition from international humanitarian law reduces the legal vulnerability of the Polisario Front, and the so-called Sahrawi People's Liberation Army in particular. For this reason, in 2015 the Polisario Front made a unilateral declaration committing itself to apply to the Western Sahara conflict the four Geneva Conventions and Protocol I, as enabled by Article 96.3 of the latter (Swiss Federal Department of Foreign Affairs 2015).

However, in the policy practice, international humanitarian law has been invoked to a very limited extent in the most significant UN documents dealing with the Western Sahara conflict: resolutions from the Security Council and reports of the secretary-general. This seems a logical consequence of the scarce attention and number of documents devoted by the UN to this issue during the years of open warfare (1996–1991) and especially until 1983 – the year when Morocco consolidated its military control over the annexed territory and the intensity of armed combat substantially decreased to a below-war level of fatalities.[2] Instead, the OUA was the international organization that took the lead in peace-making efforts

---

[2] See Correlates of War (COW) War Data, 1816–2007 (v4.0) (https://correlatesofwar.org/data-sets/cow-war/).

during this first stage of the war. The UN only took over the process in the late 1980s (Zunes and Mundy 2022: 174–180). As a result, aside from three resolutions passed in October–November 1975, at the time of the Moroccan invasion of the territory (S/RES/377[1975]; S/RES/379[1975]; S/RES/380[1975]), the first UN Security Council intervention on this matter dates back to September 1988 (S/RES/621). The first UN secretary-general report is from June 1990 (S/21360[1990]).

Since that time, references to international humanitarian law in UN Security Council resolutions on Western Sahara have focused exclusively on the release of prisoners of war. Interestingly, this was one of the measures for the post-ceasefire 'transitional period' under the UN Settlement Plan accepted by Morocco and the Polisario Front in 1991, which became the primary framework of reference – rather than international humanitarian law – in the 1990s. For example, in its resolution from May 1996, the Council

> [called] upon the parties, as a demonstration of good will, to cooperate with the United Nations in the implementation of certain aspects of the Settlement Plan, such as the release of Saharan political prisoners and the exchange of prisoners of war on humanitarian grounds, as soon as possible, to accelerate implementation of the Settlement Plan in its entirety. (S/RES/1056[1996])

However, the Polisario Front delayed this step arguing that the United Nations was not implementing the other Settlement Plan measures for the 'transitional period' – a refusal that deepened in the early 2000s as preparations for the self-determination referendum were abandoned and the United Nations attempted to broker a 'political solution' through the Baker Plans I (2001) and II (2003) (Besenyő, Huddleston and Zoubir 2023: 28–29). It was as a result of this shift that, between 2002 and 2005, the UN Security Council calls for the Polisario Front to 'release without further delay all remaining prisoners of war' started to be justified 'in compliance with international humanitarian law' (S/RES/1429[2002]; S/RES/1495[2003]; S/RES/1598[2005]; S/RES/1634[2005]).

In the case of the reports of the UN secretary-general on the Western Sahara conflict, references to international humanitarian law have a similarly narrow focus on the issue of prisoners of war – with two strong appeals for the Polisario Front to release them 'in compliance with international humanitarian law' in January and April 2005 (S/2005/49; S/2005/254), the year when this issue was eventually settled – as well as on 'persons unaccounted for in the conflict'. All reports since 2014 have included, under the section covering humanitarian activities and human rights, a brief point highlighting the International Committee of the Red Cross' continuing work on 'cases of persons still unaccounted for in relation to the past hostilities'.

On the other hand, the specific – and politically most sensitive – branch of international humanitarian law that is hardly mentioned in the UN discourse on Western Sahara is occupation law, including instruments such as the Hague Regulations annexed to the 1907 Hague Convention respecting the Laws and Customs of War on Land, the 1949 IV Geneva Convention relative to the Protection of Civilian Persons in Time of War and Additional Protocol I to the latter (see Saul 2015). The UN General Assembly described the presence of Morocco in Western Sahara as 'occupation' in two successive resolutions following Mauritania's withdrawal from, and Morocco's takeover of, the southern half of the territory in 1979 and 1980. These resolutions referred, in particular, to 'the continued occupation of Western Sahara by Morocco and the extension of that occupation to the territory recently evacuated by Mauritania' (A/RES/34/37[1979]; A/RES/35/19[1980]). Yet, since then, there has been no consideration of Western Sahara as a matter of occupation and annexation at the UN level, including both the General Assembly – the only body that has kept passing resolutions annually on this question – and the Security Council (Smith 2020). This suggests a gradual international coming to terms with facts on the ground, or at least dwindling consensus and firmness on the unacceptability of Morocco's position since the consolidation of its military control in 1983. Even the influential legal opinion on Western Sahara delivered by UN Under-Secretary for Legal Affairs Hans Corell in 2002 (see below) failed to refer to occupation law.[3]

The extent to which the term 'occupation' has become pretty much a taboo for the United Nations was demonstrated by the unprecedented diplomatic crisis unleashed when, as an exception and maybe in a slip of the tongue, Secretary-General Ban Ki-moon used the word during a visit to the region in March 2016 (UN Secretary-General 2016a). Outraged, Morocco accused the United Nations of abandoning its 'neutrality, objectivity and impartiality'. The Rabat government stated it '[noted] with astonishment that the Secretary General used the term "occupation" to qualify Morocco's recovery of its territorial integrity, which deviates drastically from the terminology traditionally used by the UN' (MAP 2016), and expelled most of MINURSO (United Nations Mission for the Referendum in Western Sahara) civilian staff from Western Sahara in response (Fernández-Molina and Porges 2019: 384). In what seemed a rectification, the secretary-general then went back to the usual UN line stressing that 'the status of the Western Sahara territory remains to be decided, as it is a non-self-governing territory' (UN Secretary-General 2016b).

In fact, besides the broader question as to who determines whether there is a foreign occupation, the avoidance of occupation law in this case in not

---

[3] Similarly, the CJEU has not considered this branch of law in any of its judgments.

the result of any legal incompatibility or mutually exclusive relationship with decolonization law. Most international legal scholars agree that 'Western Sahara is also a non-self-governing territory, akin to colonies, but that does not change its status as occupied' (Wrange and Helaoui 2015: 40; see alsoSoroeta Liceras 2014; Kassoti 2017a: 352; 2017b: 29; Besenyő, Huddleston and Zoubir 2023: 87–89). Likewise, at the African Union level, a judgement of the African Court on Human and Peoples' Rights (2022) emphasized that 'both the UN and the AU recognize the situation of SADR as one of occupation and consider its territory as one of those territories whose decolonisation process is not yet fully complete'. In other words, the limited UN and Western treatment of Western Sahara as a case of occupation is first and foremost a consequence of the international politics and the deep asymmetry of the conflict. These international actors opt for the default, less controversial position prioritizing the decolonization legal framework in order to avoid alienating the stronger conflict party, Morocco. By contrast, the Polisario Front/SADR have consistently asserted that Western Sahara is a matter of both decolonization and occupation law, and that Spain remains the territory's *de jure* administering power. These are matters on which clarity plays in their favour.

Lawfare

One way in which the Polisario Front/SADR has strived to counter such asymmetry and dispel some of the legal ambiguities surrounding the conflict, since the turn of the millennium has been by resorting to a type of legal activism that may be viewed as lawfare. As the implementation of the UN Settlement Plan and the conflict resolution process stalled, two problematic side effects of Western Sahara's protracted occupation and annexation came to the fore: Morocco's human rights violations and economic exploitation of its natural resources (Fernández-Molina 2019a). There lay the basis for a new Sahrawi 'low politics' international strategy (Fernández-Molina 2017). Much of this has been pursued through parliamentary and judicial routes, by using legal instruments 'as a substitute for traditional military means' (Dunlap 2008: 146) to achieve political or operational goals in a conflict context, which fits into a descriptive and non-normative concept of lawfare. Introduced into the legal and IR scholarship in the early 2000s following a winding and contradictory conceptual journey,[4] in its value-neutral understanding – deprived of the connotations of illegitimacy prevalent in other contexts – lawfare is

---

[4] See Werner (2010) for a critical reconstruction of this evolution and discussion of the problematic aspects of normative and non-normative uses of the term.

simply defined as the 'use of law as a weapon of war' (Kittrie 2016: 1). That makes it particularly suitable to refer to legal activism in a context of armed conflict.

As an additional element relevant to the case here, US administrations in that decade started to increasingly regard, and decry, lawfare as a 'strategy of the weak' in the hands of victim groups, human rights advocates and government critics (Werner 2010: 68–69). Whatever its ends and targets, being less deadly, less costly, and yet sometimes more effective than conventional warfare, lawfare appears as a particularly attractive tool for disempowered conflict actors. According to Kittrie (2016: 41), if asymmetric warfare consists of 'attempts to circumvent or undermine an opponent's strengths while exploiting his vulnerabilities using methods that differ significantly from the opponent's usual mode of operations' – for example, guerrilla warfare, terrorism, and cyberwarfare – then lawfare may well be considered a 'subset' thereof. As such, the types of actors that typically wage instrumental lawfare include contested states, non-governmental organizations (NGOs), and advocacy networks, such as the Palestinian Authority and Palestinian and allied NGOs (Kittrie 2016: 11–12; see also Castan Pinos and Friis Hau 2023).[5]

In the case of Western Sahara, the main target of Sahrawi lawfare has been the European Union (EU), whose manifold bilateral economic and sectoral cooperation agreements with Morocco have for decades failed to make any differentiation between the internationally recognized territory of this country and that of Western Sahara – thus including the latter by default within their scope. The Polisario Front/SADR and NGOs such as Western Sahara Resource Watch (WSRW) started to challenge such territorial undifferentiation practices following in the steps of Palestinian strategies, and encouraged by the groundbreaking 2002 'Corell opinion' on contracts between Morocco and foreign companies to explore for mineral resources in the annexed territory. The most consequential points of this UN legal opinion were the conclusions that the people of Western Sahara legally retain 'permanent sovereignty over natural resources' and therefore, 'if further exploration and exploitation activities were to proceed in disregard of the interests and wishes of the people of Western Sahara, they would be in violation of the international law principles applicable to mineral resource activities in Non-Self-Governing Territories' (UN Security Council 2002; see Hagen 2015: 379).

---

[5] Attempts to draw a conceptual line between lawfare and 'legal mobilization' – where the former denotes illegitimate legal instrumentalism that 'sustains hegemonic power' whereas the latter refers to the 'legitimate use of the law by rights claimants to advance human rights and social justice' – have not gone uncontested (Matthews 2023: 27–28).

Upon this new normative basis, a novel lobbying campaign of the Polisario Front/SADR and WSRW with the European Parliament resulted in the latter's rejection, in December 2011, of the protocol of extension of the 2006 EU–Morocco fisheries agreement on the legal grounds, among other arguments, that it included Western Sahara's waters without its direct benefits for the local population having been sufficiently demonstrated (Fernández-Molina 2017; Bouris and Fernández-Molina 2018: 317). However, the limits of the parliamentary route became soon apparent, as in 2012 and 2013 the same European Parliament gave its consent to the 2010 EU–Morocco agricultural trade agreement (Council of the EU 2012b) and a revamped fisheries protocol (EU–Morocco 2013) despite the fact that both deals continued to automatically include Western Sahara's territory. EU normative change was aborted and ambiguity persisted at this point: 'There was no cascade of the budding territorial differentiation norm, and no change whatsoever in the domain of practices' (Bouris and Fernández-Molina 2024: 9). At the time, though, undifferentiation seemed more of a default set of practices – the result of intergovernmental influence, institutional path dependence and the inability to formulate a coherent joint position – than of a fully deliberate EU policy.

This pushed Sahrawi actors to focus their lawfare on the judicial route, initiating a number of legal actions at the Court of Justice of the EU (CJEU) from 2012 onwards. Such strategy, which was formally led by the Polisario Front because of the national liberation movement's recognition by the UN General Assembly as 'the representative of the people of Western Sahara' (A/RES/34/37(1979)), would prove to be highly fruitful. As a result, firstly, after admitting the Polisario Front's legal personality and capacity to bring proceedings before EU courts – in an example of the politics of international courts navigating and adjudicating tricky status questions – the CJEU annulled the EU–Morocco agricultural trade agreement in so far as it applied to Western Sahara due to the Council's failure to examine whether the exploitation of the territory's natural resources was 'likely to be to the detriment of its inhabitants and to infringe their fundamental rights' (Court of Justice of the EU 2015). Secondly, in the final ruling on the same case one year later, the CJEU modified its previous judgment to specify that, more fundamentally, Western Sahara has a 'separate and distinct status' and hence, in order for its inclusion in EU–Morocco agreements to be legal, 'the people of Western Sahara must be regarded as a "third party"' from which the implementation of the agreement 'must receive the consent' (Court of Justice of the EU 2016; see Ferrer Lloret 2017: 21; Flavier 2017: 4; Kassoti 2017a: 340; Kalimo and Nikoleishvili 2022: 378–384). Thirdly, in February and July 2018, two further CJEU rulings on two separate cases concluded, for the same reasons, that the EU–Morocco fisheries agreement is valid in itself but not applicable to the waters adjacent to the territory of Western

Sahara (Court of Justice of the EU 2018a; Court of Justice of the EU 2018b). Fourthly, in November of the same year, the CJEU likewise decided that the EU–Morocco Aviation Agreement should not cover Western Sahara either (Court of Justice of the EU 2018c).

In sum, from late 2015 we started to see a swift norm cascade that dispelled ambiguity and consolidated Morocco-Western Sahara territorial differentiation through accumulating case-law within the EU judiciary. The success of Sahrawi lawfare as a form of asymmetric struggle was demonstrated by its capacity to trigger an unheard-of three-year diplomatic crisis between Rabat and Brussels. In February 2016, Rabat announced the suspension of all contacts with the EU institutions in protest of the 'highly political nature' and the 'biased logic' of the first CJEU ruling on this matter (Royaume du Maroc 2016). On the other hand, the reach of the norm cascade was limited at the EU's inter-institutional level, given the European Commission and Council's reluctance to further alienate Morocco by putting territorial differentiation down on paper and into practice. During the new negotiations on the CJEU-required adaptations of the EU–Morocco agricultural trade and fisheries agreements' protocols in 2017 and 2018, the Commission and the European External Action Service (EEAS) conducted consultations with a range of stakeholders from Moroccan-annexed Western Sahara so as to claim they had secured the 'consent' of 'concerned populations' – though the Polisario Front and pro-independence Sahrawi civil society organizations declined to participate in what they saw as a prejudiced process against their interests (Court of Justice of the EU 2021). At this point it became evident that the EU executive institutions' continuing ambiguity on the status of Western Sahara had turned into a policy by design which put the stability of relations with Morocco first.

In formally acknowledging the CJEU rule, the most recent agricultural trade and fisheries deals – passed by the European Parliament in February and March 2019 respectively – significantly reduced the EU's ambiguity on the status of the territory of Western Sahara *on paper*. Both the EU and Morocco stated in accompanying exchanges of letters that these agreements had been concluded 'without prejudice to the respective positions' (EU–Morocco 2019a), including an EU reference to Western Sahara as a 'non-self-governing territory' with the 'right to self-determination' under international law (EU–Morocco 2019b). At the same time, *in practice*, the purpose remained that the existing territorial undifferentiation stay unchanged, for example that agricultural 'products originating in Western Sahara subject to controls by customs authorities of the Kingdom of Morocco […] benefit from the same trade preferences as those granted by the EU to products covered by the Association Agreement [with Morocco]' (EU–Morocco 2019a; see also Suárez-Collado and Contini 2022). In fact, the CJEU was to again annul the two agreements in September 2021, arguing that the EU consultations with 'concerned populations' did not amount to a legally valid expression of the 'consent' of the 'people' of Western Sahara based in these two terms' definitions in international law, and that the criterion of the benefits for the populations concerned could not replace such consent (Court of Justice of the EU 2021). Despite the clarity gradually achieved since 2015, legal uncertainty and lawfare over Western Sahara still had a long way to go ahead.

Volatility and warfare

In parallel to Sahrawi lawfare, in late 2020 escalating tensions on the ground, coupled with destabilization at the regional and international levels, resulted in a violent thawing of the long-frozen conflict of Western Sahara. Hostilities between the parties resumed after nothing less than 30 years of compliance with the 1991 ceasefire. This demonstrates the extent to which volatility is inherent to contested statehood. Contested states remain highly volatile and prone to quick escalation even after periods of calm and apparent compromise. In addition, from the perspective of the Polisario Front/SADR, the return to armed struggle has been largely a strategic choice seeking, like lawfare, to counter a perceived growing asymmetry, and ambiguities in the international engagement with this conflict that are detrimental to their position. The intersection between ambiguities, volatility, and warfare may be observed by reconstructing three major developments on the local, international, and regional levels: the crisis at the border crossing of Guerguerat in October–November 2020, the US proclamation of recognition of Moroccan sovereignty over the territory in December 2020 and the breakdown of diplomatic relations between Algeria and Morocco in August 2021.

The Guerguerat crisis started with a Sahrawi civilian protest that blocked a section of road crossing the UN-monitored demilitarized buffer strip between the far south of Moroccan-annexed Western Sahara and Mauritania. This was eventually suppressed through a Moroccan military operation beyond the dividing line – and thus in breach of the terms of the ceasefire – which in turn led the Polisario Front/SADR to declare the end of its commitment to such ceasefire (International Crisis Group 2021: 1–2). Three key decisions intervened in this escalatory process.

Firstly, the Polisario Front/SADR's call for a sustained protest that disrupted Moroccan–Mauritanian land traffic and transport may be understood as stemming from a combination of rational choice and a more desperate, existential struggle for international visibility in a context in which Morocco appeared to be winning on nearly all fronts. This also coincided with the years following a turnover in the Sahrawi national leadership, after the passing of the four-decade Polisario Front secretary-general and SADR president, Mohamed Abdelaziz, and his replacement by Brahim Ghali in July 2016.

The negative picture for Sahrawi nationalists at the time was to a large extent a product of the UN Security Council resolutions' creeping ambiguity as to the centrality of self-determination and a referendum for the resolution of the Western Sahara conflict, as well as about which were exactly 'the parties and neighbouring states' among the four participants in the Geneva process, that is, the UN-convened negotiations that took place in 2018–2019 between Morocco, the Polisario Front, Algeria, and Mauritania (S/RES/2548[2020]). By avoiding clarity about the status of Algeria and Mauritania in those roundtable talks, the latest UN Security Council resolutions were contributing to blurring the conflict's internationally recognized two-party structure and thereby played in the hands of Morocco, which views this as a primarily regional confrontation with rival Algeria. This muddling was coupled with the anomalously long vacancy of the post of personal envoy of the secretary-general for Western Sahara since Horst Köhler stepped down in May 2019 – a vacuum that the Polisario Front/SADR also perceived to be against its interests – and the end of the dynamism of the Geneva process following Trump's firing, in September 2019, of US National Security Advisor John Bolton – who had shown an extraordinary level of personal investment in this issue (Fernández-Molina 2019b; Besenyő, Huddleston and Zoubir 2023: 70–73). The Polisario Front/SADR's attention-seeking and threats of resuming armed struggle had intensified in the face of all these adverse developments.

Secondly, another crucial contributing factor to escalation in late 2020 was the Moroccan decision to clear the Sahrawi protest by military force and crossing the ceasefire line (i.e. violating military agreement No. 1 between MINURSO and each the two conflict parties).[6] This involved ruling out a more restrained approach such as the one followed in a previous border crisis in Guerguerat between August 2016 and February 2017, which ended with Morocco's unilateral withdrawal from the buffer strip at the UN secretary-general's request (S/2017/307: 1–3). Morocco's new brinkmanship was driven by an unprecedented self-perception of strength and foreign policy assertiveness. In addition to the UN-level developments described above, Rabat felt empowered by its success in securing membership of the African Union in January 2017 – putting an end to over three decades of absence from pan-African regionalism with the ultimate aim of neutralizing diplomatic support for the SADR in this organization, if not in getting the SADR expelled thereof – the weakening of Algeria's rival regional influence due to the negative impact of the large-scale domestic unrest caused by the Hirak protest movement, as well as Morocco's reconciliation with the EU, in its

---

[6] See the MINURSO page of ceasefire monitoring (https://minurso.unmissions.org/ceasefire-monitoring).

own terms, after the 2016–2019 bilateral crisis caused by Sahrawi lawfare. Last, but not least, the longstanding international consensus on avoiding any diplomatic presence in the annexed Western Sahara territory to signal the formal non-recognition of Morocco's sovereignty claims was shaken by a wave of openings of 16 African and two Arab consulates in the cities of Laayoune and Dakhla between December 2019 and December 2020 (International Crisis Group 2021: 6–7). In the wake of such accumulating diplomatic gains, Rabat's military operation in Guerguerat sought to establish new facts on the ground, including its full control over this strategic border crossing point and the development of new logistic infrastructure.

Thirdly, and finally, in response to the Moroccan violation of the ceasefire, on 14 November 2020, the Polisario Front/SADR issued a decree declaring the end of its commitment to such an agreement and the 'consequent resumption of armed struggle' (S/2021/843: 1–3). This decision had the strategic goal of raising the conflict's international profile by reverting to a state of 'war'. A good deal of rhetorical entrapment as well as domestic legitimacy and mobilization needs were also arguably involved. Indeed, since the Guerguerat crisis, the Polisario Front/SADR has maintained that the entire territory of Western Sahara has become a 'zone of open war'. This contrasts with denial declarations on the side of Rabat. The same strategic motivations that encourage Sahrawis to disseminate a 'state of war' narrative in front of international diplomats and media lead Morocco to pretend the 'total absence of any armed conflict' (S/2021/843: 3, 6). The latter calculated ambiguity seems to be actually in line with a broader pattern. As argued by Fazal (2018: 5–6), the development of international humanitarian law over the twentieth century has disincentivized recognized states from declaring war, which entails an expectation of compliance with rising legal standards, while belligerents such as secessionist rebel groups remain eager to abide by the laws of war as part of their search for international legitimacy and recognition of statehood. According to the United Nations, the reality of the past five years has been a situation of sustained 'low-intensity hostilities' and regular reports of 'shots fired across the berm' by both parties. The UN secretary-general's report on Western Sahara of October 2021 further specified that, 'according to MINURSO calculations based on reporting by the parties, the incidence of reported firing has decreased since January [2021] and has primarily been concentrated in the north of the Territory near Mahbas' (S/2021/843: 3). On the other hand, the October 2022 report mentioned a growing number of Moroccan drone strikes 'east of the berm' (18 reported over the previous year) (S/2022/733: 7), which hit Algerian civilian trucks in addition to Sahrawi targets.

An additional complicating factor at the international level, less than one month after the resumption of hostilities, was the US presidential proclamation recognizing 'Moroccan sovereignty over the entire Western

Sahara territory' (White House 2020). This came as part of a trilateral transactional deal brokered by the Trump administration whereby, in exchange for Washington's concession, Rabat committed itself to normalizing its bilateral relations with Israel[7] following in the steps of the Abraham Accords concluded by United Arab Emirates, Bahrain, and Sudan. The unilateral US recognition, which deviated from the international/UN consensus and legal parameters on this conflict, constituted a diplomatic victory without comparison or precedent for Morocco – the achievement of its longstanding top foreign policy priority – and created the expectation in Rabat that other Western countries would follow suit shortly. These maximalist hopes turned soon into frustration, resulting in severe destabilization of Morocco's bilateral relations with key European states such as Germany, Spain, and France, which were subject to unparalleled pressure to shift their position on Western Sahara. Rabat recalled its ambassadors to the first two countries in May 2021 (MAP 2021a; 2021b), and furthermore orchestrated a 'coercive engineered migration' crisis (Greenhill 2010) by allowing some 10,000 migrants to cross the border into the Spanish North African city/enclave of Ceuta later in the same month (Economist 2021).

Finally, the breakdown of relations between Algeria and Morocco in August 2021 was both a byproduct and an accelerator of mounting instability on the regional scale. It occurred in the context of Algiers' anxiety about both the US recognition of Western Sahara's Moroccanness and the Moroccan-Israeli rapprochement, the latter of which was depicted as a direct threat to Algerian national security. This state's decision to cut diplomatic ties itself was officially justified by a long list of grievances (APS 2021), chief among which was Morocco's abandonment of its 1988 commitment (stated in a joint communiqué with Algeria) to support 'a just and final settlement to the conflict over Western Sahara through a proper and free referendum on self-determination' (UN General Assembly 1988). On the other hand, its timing suggested a different, non-Western Sahara-related trigger, i.e. Rabat's perceived interference in Algerian domestic affairs and support for the self-determination of the Kabylie – or the Movement for the Self-determination of Kabylie (MAK) – which a Moroccan diplomat had indeed provocatively stated in a document distributed in a previous Non-Aligned Movement UN meeting. In any case, as put by the UN secretary-general's 2021 report: 'Neighbouring states have a vital role in the achievement of a solution to the question of Western Sahara. In this connection, the deterioration in relations between Morocco and Algeria is of concern' (S/2021/843: 14).

---

7   See Trump tweets on X (https://twitter.com/realDonaldTrump/status/1337067019385057290 and https://twitter.com/realDonaldTrump/status/1337067073051238400).

Going back to the ongoing hostilities between the Polisario Front/SADR and Morocco, it is worth considering their further implications for the ambiguities surrounding the conflict, especially in legal terms. This remains a grey-area situation in itself, in that only one of the parties acknowledges and strives to overstate the level of armed confrontation while the other one keeps it quiet. With the UN peacekeeping mission MINURSO's freedom of movement and ability to observe the situation in the territory increasingly curtailed by the two parties, independent monitoring has been very limited. In any case, there is sufficient evidence of two new developments in Rabat's operational strategy that may, in the long run, contribute to reshaping the conflict in both spatial/geopolitical and legal terms: the willingness to establish new facts on the ground including through territorial expansion since the Guerguerat crisis and the (unacknowledged) attacks against targets in the strip controlled by the Polisario Front/SADR. If prolonged, these trends suggest a Moroccan ambition to assert control over a larger part or the entirety of the territory of Western Sahara, including the so-called 'liberated zone' currently in Sahrawi hands – which would deprive the SADR of its limited *de facto*, declaratory statehood, turning it closer to a full-blown state-in-exile.

Regarding the duality between decolonization law and international humanitarian law, the secondary place that the latter has occupied in the UN approach to the Western Sahara conflict since the late 1980s could be questioned in the event of more widespread and systematic targeting of civilians or escalation to large-scale war. Such a scenario of intensified warfare would raise issues concerning the distinction between combatants and non-combatants, the prohibition of deliberately targeting the latter, the treatment of potential new prisoners of war, and the prohibition of certain types of weapons. Whether the application of international humanitarian law to Western Sahara would then remain limited to its impartial and status-neutral humanitarian aspects, or furthermore bring occupation law back to the forefront, is an open question.

Conclusion

This chapter has unpacked the manifold political and legal ambiguities that surround contested statehood and conflict in Western Sahara, expounding how these have generally acted as sources of vulnerability for the Polisario Front/SADR and the Sahrawi people, but also elicited strategic responses from these disadvantaged actors in the form of lawfare (legal activism) and warfare. In this sense, as argued by Kittrie (2016: 41), these two avenues of agency may be seen as 'mutually reinforcing' forms of asymmetric conflict. That being said, their effects may differ and even contradict each other depending on the level of analysis and the time frame considered.

The Sahrawi lawfare currently appears as more successful internationally yet also more of a long-term effort, while warfare may meet more immediate domestic needs for the Polisario Front/SADR leadership. Furthermore, consequences are certainly divergent in terms of the volatility engendered.

As a way of conclusion, it is worth recapping what this case of contested statehood tells us about the relationship between ambiguity, vulnerability, and agency. On one hand, there are a number of political ambiguities that the Polisario Front/SADR has strategically assumed, if not capitalized on, over the course of this conflict. Making a virtue of necessity, the SADR has tried to have the best of both worlds in playing at once the game of states-in-exile and *de facto* states, and in building its constitutive and declaratory credentials for statehood. Something similar applies to the logical tension between the non-self-governing status of Western Sahara's territory and the SADR's statehood claim, which in turn relates to the symbiosis between the two components of the 'state-movement' (Wilson 2016) and their respective roles, benefits, and forms of recognition in the international sphere. Wearing the two hats has substantially enhanced the international agency of Saharawi national actors as a whole.

On the other hand, there are other legal and political ambiguities that the Polisario Front/SADR have always seen as detrimental to their interests and have consistently sought to dispel. Firstly, these include controversies on the international legal regime(s) applicable to Western Sahara, in which they have maintained a clear stance and strategic emphasis on the compatibility and complementarity between decolonization/self-determination and international humanitarian law including the law of occupation, as well as on Spain's continuing responsibility as the *de jure* administering power. Secondly, an increasingly glaring source of vulnerability for Sahrawis lies in the EU's ambiguity on the non-self-governing status of Western Sahara's territory and the conditions for the latter's legal inclusion in economic cooperation agreements with Morocco, including questions such as where lies the distinction between Western Sahara's people and local population, who are the actors entitled to represent this (these) collective(s), and how their consent is meant to be exercised. The EU's longstanding territorial undifferentiation practices – originally by default, increasingly by design – have been successfully challenged by the Polisario Front's lawfare at the CJEU, producing accumulating, compelling case-law.

Finally, another perceived disadvantage for the Polisario Front/SADR concerns broader international community and UN ambiguities about the nature and status of the Western Sahara conflict as such. Here, the liminality inherent to its three-decade status as a frozen conflict (no war, no peace) has been coupled with the UN Security Council's increasingly unclear language regarding self-determination as its defining feature, the referendum as the specific method for the Sahrawi people to exercise such right and even the recognized parties to the conflict – as opposed to 'neighbouring states'. These are the insidious ambiguities that, to a great extent, motivated the Sahrawi return to warfare in late 2020. Paradoxically, though, the ongoing low-intensity hostilities still remain in between the 'state of war' declared by the Polisario Front/SADR and 'total absence of any armed conflict' stated by Morocco.

References

African Court on Human and Peoples' Rights (2022). Judgement on Application No. 028/2018, 22 September, www.african-court.org/cpmt/storage/app/uploads/public/632/e0f/3ad/632e0f3ad580e748464681.pdf.

APS (2021). Déclaration de Lamamra sur la rupture des relations diplomatiques avec le Maroc, 24 August, www.aps.dz/algerie/126530-declaration-de-lamamra-sur-la-rupture-des-relations-diplomatiques-avec-le-maroc.

Besenyő, J., Huddleston, R.J. and Zoubir, Y.H. (eds) (2023). *Conflict and Peace in Western Sahara: The Role of the UN's Peacekeeping Mission (MINURSO)*. Abingdon and New York: Routledge.

Bouris, D. and Fernández-Molina, I. (2018). Contested States, Hybrid Diplomatic Practices, and the Everyday Quest for Recognition. *International Political Sociology*, 12 (3), 306–324.

Bouris, D. and Fernández-Molina, I. (2024). The International Norm-Practice Relationship, Contested States and the EU's Territorial (Un)Differentiation towards Palestine and Western Sahara. *Global Studies Quarterly*, 4 (2), 1–12.

Caspersen, N. (2012). *Unrecognized States: The Struggle for Sovereignty in the Modern International System*. Cambridge: Cambridge University Press.

Caspersen, N. and Stansfield, G. (eds) (2011). *Unrecognized States in the International System*. Abingdon and New York: Routledge.

Castan Pinos, J. and Friis Hau, M. (2023). *Lawfare: New Trajectories in Law*. Abingdon and New York: Routledge.

Council of the EU (2012b). Council Decision of 2 December 2010 on the Signature of the Agreement in the Form of an Exchange of Letters between the European Union and the Kingdom of Morocco Concerning Reciprocal Liberalisation Measures on Agricultural Products, Processed Agricultural Products, Fish and Fishery Products. *Official Journal of the European Union*, 7 September, https://eur-lex.europa.eu/legal-content/EN/TXT/?uri=CELEX%3A32012D0496.

CJEU (2015). Judgement of the General Court (Eighth Chamber), Case T-512/12, 10 December, https://eur-lex.europa.eu/legal-content/EN/TXT/?uri=CELEX%3A62012TJ0512&qid=1678043196481.

CJEU (2016). Judgement of the Court (Grand Chamber), Case C-104/16 P, 21 December, https://eur-lex.europa.eu/legal-content/GA/TXT/?uri=CELEX:62016CJ0104.

CJEU (2018a). Judgment of the Court (Grand Chamber), Case C-266/16, 27 February, https://eur-lex.europa.eu/legal-content/EN/TXT/?uri=CELEX%3A62016CJ0266.

CJEU (2018b). Order of the General Court (Fifth Chamber, Extended Composition), Case T-180/14, 19 July, https://eur-lex.europa.eu/legal-content/EN/TXT/?uri=CELEX%3A62014TO0180%2802%29.

CJEU (2018c). Order of the General Court (Fifth Chamber), Case T-275/18, 30 November, https://eur-lex.europa.eu/legal-content/EN/TXT/?uri=CELEX:62018TO0275.

CJEU (2021). Judgement of the General Court (Ninth Chamber), 29 September, https://eur-lex.europa.eu/legal-content/en/TXT/?uri=CELEX:62019TJ0344.

Crawford, J.R. (2006). *The Creation of States in International Law*. 2nd edn. Oxford: Oxford University Press.

Dunlap, C.J. (2008). Lawfare Today: A Perspective. *Yale Journal of International Affairs*, 3 (1), 146–154.

Economist (2021). King Muhammad of Morocco Weaponises Migration. *Economist*, 22 May, www.economist.com/middle-east-and-africa/2021/05/22/king-muhammad-of-morocco-weaponises-migration.

EU–Morocco (2013). Protocol between the European Union and the Kingdom of Morocco Setting Out the Fishing Opportunities and Financial Contribution Provided for in the Fisheries Partnership Agreement. *Official Journal of the European Union*, 7 December, https://eur-lex.europa.eu/legal-content/EN/TXT/?uri=CELEX%3A22013A1207%2801%29.

EU–Morocco (2019a). Agreement in the Form of an Exchange of Letters between the European Union and the Kingdom of Morocco on the Amendment of Protocols 1 and 4 to the Euro-Mediterranean Agreement Establishing an Association between the European Communities and their Member States, of the One Part, and the Kingdom of Morocco, of the Other Part. *Official Journal of the European Union*, 6 February, https://eur-lex.europa.eu/legal-content/EN/TXT/?uri=uriserv:OJ.L_.2019.034.01.0004.01.ENG.

EU–Morocco (2019b). Sustainable Fisheries Partnership Agreement between the European Union and the Kingdom of Morocco. *Official Journal of the European Union*, 20 March, https://eur-lex.europa.eu/legal-content/EN/TXT/?uri=uriserv:OJ.L_.2019.077.01.0008.01.ENG.

Fazal, T.M. (2018). *Wars of Law: The Unintended Consequences in the Regulation of Armed Conflict*. Ithaca: Cornell University Press.

Fernández-Molina, I. (2017). The EU, the ENP and the Western Sahara Conflict: Executive Continuity and Parliamentary Detours. In D. Bouris and T. Schumacher (eds), *The Revised European Neighbourhood Policy: Continuity and Change in EU Foreign Policy*. New York: Palgrave Macmillan, 219–238.

Fernández-Molina, I. (2019a). Bottom-up Change in Frozen Conflicts: Transnational Struggles and Mechanisms of Recognition in Western Sahara. *Review of International Studies*, 45 (3), 407–430.

Fernández-Molina, I. (2019b). Momentum for Negotiations on Western Sahara Will Fade. *Oxford Analytica*, 8 November, https://dailybrief.oxan.com/Analysis/DB247626/Momentum-for-negotiations-on-Western-Sahara-will-fade.

Fernández-Molina, I. and Porges, M. (2019). Western Sahara. In G. Visoka, J. Doyle and E. Newman (eds), *Routledge Handbook of State Recognition*. Abingdon and New York: Routledge, 376–390.

Fernández-Molina, I. and Ojeda-García, R. (2020). Western Sahara as a Hybrid of a Parastate and a State-in-exile: (Extra)territoriality and the Small Print of Sovereignty in a Context of Frozen Conflict. *Nationalities Papers*, 48 (1), 83–99.

Ferrer Lloret, J. (2017). El conflicto del Sahara Occidental ante los tribunales de la Unión Europea. *Revista General de Derecho Europeo*, 42, 15–64.

Flavier, H. (2017). La Cour de justice, juge du droit international? Réflexions sur l'affaire Front Polisario. *Journal d'Actualité des Droits Européens*, 4, 1–15.

Geldenhuys, D. (2009). *Contested States in World Politics*. New York: Palgrave Macmillan.

Greenhill, K.M. (2010). *Weapons of Mass Migration: Forced Displacement, Coercion, and Foreign Policy*. Ithaca: Cornell University Press.Hagen, E. (2015). Saharawi Conflict Phosphates and the Australian Dinner Table. *Global Change, Peace & Security*, 27 (3), 377–393.

International Crisis Group (2021). *Time for International Re-engagement in Western Sahara*. Brussels: International Crisis Group.

Kalimo, H. and Nikoleishvili, S. (2022). Sovereignty in the Era of Fragmentation: EU Trade Agreements and the Notion of Statehood in International Law. *Duke Journal of Comparative & International Law*, 32 (2), 353–407.

Kassoti, E. (2017a). The Front Polisario v. Council Case: The General Court, Völkerrechtsfreundlichkeit and the External Aspect of European Integration (First Part). *European Papers*, 2 (1), 339–356.

Kassoti, E. (2017b). The Council v. Front Polisario Case: The Court of Justice's Selective Reliance on International Rules on Treaty Interpretation (Second Part). *European Papers*, 2 (1), 23–42.

Kittrie, O.F. (2016). *Lawfare: Law as a Weapon of War*. Oxford: Oxford University Press.

Kolstø, P. (2006). The Sustainability and Future of Unrecognized and Quasi-States. *Journal of Peace Research*, 43 (6), 723–740.

Krasner, St.D. (1999). *Sovereignty: Organized Hypocrisy*. Princeton: Princeton University Press.

MAP (2016). Le Gouvernement du Royaume du Maroc exprime les plus vives protestations contre les propos du SG de l'ONU sur la question du Sahara Marocain (communiqué), 8 March, www.mapexpress.ma/actualite/activite-gouvernementale/gouvernement-du-royaume-du-maroc-exprime-les-vives-protestations-contre-les-propos-du-sg-lonu-question-du-sahara-marocain-communique/.

MAP (2021a). Morocco Recalls HM the King's Ambassador in Berlin for Consultation. *MAP*, 6 May, www.mapnews.ma/en/actualites/politics/morocco-recalls-hm-kings-ambassador-berlin-consultation.

MAP (2021b). Moroccan Ambassador to Spain has been Recalled for Consultations in Connection with Crisis that Goes Back to mid-April: FM. *MAP*, 20 May, www.mapnews.ma/en/actualites/politics/moroccan-ambassador-spain-has-been-recalled-consultations-connection-crisis-goes.

Matthews, T. (2023). Interrogating the Debates Around Lawfare and Legal Mobilization: A Literature Review. *Journal of Human Rights Practice*, 15 (1), 24–45.

McConnell, F. (2016). *Rehearsing the State: The Political Practices of the Tibetan Government-in-Exile*. Chichester: Wiley-Blackwell.

Oeter, Stefan (2015). (Non-)Recognition Policies in Secession Conflicts and the Shadow of the Right of Self-Determination. In C. Daase, C. Fehl, A. Geis, and G. Kolliarakis (eds), *Recognition in International Relations: Rethinking a Political Concept in a Global Context*. Basingstoke: Palgrave Macmillan, 125–140.

Pegg, S. (1998). *International Society and the de Facto State*. Farnham: Ashgate.

Polisario Front (1976). Carta de Proclamación de la Independencia de la República Árabe Saharaui Democrática, 27 February, https://frentepolisario.es/carta-proclamacion-independencia-rasd/.

Royaume du Maroc (2016). Déclaration de M. le ministre de la Communication Porte-parole du Gouvernement au sujet de l'évolution des relations entre le Royaume du Maroc et l'Union européenne, 25 February, www.maroc.ma/fr/actualites/declaration-de-m-le-ministre-de-la-communication-au-sujet-de-levolution-des-relations.

Saul, B. (2015). The Status of Western Sahara as Occupied Territory under International Humanitarian Law and the Exploitation of Natural Resources. *Global Change, Peace & Security*, 27 (3), 301–322.

Smith, J.J. (2020). A Four-Fold Evil? The Crime of Aggression and the Case of Western Sahara. *International Criminal Law Review*, 20 (3), 492–550.

Soroeta Liceras, J. (2014). *International Law and the Western Sahara Conflict*. Oisterwijk: Wolf Legal Publishers.

Suárez-Collado, Á. and Contini, D. (2022). The European Court of Justice on the EU-Morocco Agricultural and Fisheries Agreements: An Analysis of the Legal Proceedings and Consequences for the Actors Involved. *The Journal of North African Studies*, 27 (6), 1160–1179.

Swiss Federal Department of Foreign Affairs (2015). Notification to the Governments of the States parties to the Geneva Conventions of 12 August 1949 for the Protection of War Victims, 26 June, www.eda.admin.ch/content/dam/eda/fr/documents/aussenpolitik/voelkerrecht/geneve/150626-GENEVE_en.pdf.

Torres-Spelliscy, G. (2014). The Use and Development of Natural Resources in Non-self-governing Territories. In A. Boukhars and J. Roussellier (eds), *Perspectives on Western Sahara: Myths, Nationalisms, and Geopolitics*. Lanham: Rowman and Littlefield, 235–260.

UNGA (1988). Letter dated 17 May 1988 from the Permanent Representatives of Algeria and Morocco to the United Nations addressed to the Secretary-General, 17 May, https://digitallibrary.un.org/record/38851.

UN Secretary-General (2016a). Secretary-General's Remarks to Press with Foreign Minister of Algeria, 6 March, www.un.org/sg/en/content/sg/press-encounter/2016-03-06/secretary-generals-remarks-press-foreign-minister-of-algeria-scroll-down-for-qa-english.

UN Secretary-General (2016b). Note to Correspondents in Response to Questions on Western Sahara, 9 March, www.un.org/sg/en/content/sg/note-correspondents/2016-03-09/note-correspondents-response-questions-western-sahara.

UN Security Council (2002). Letter Dated 29 January 2002 from the Under-Secretary-General for Legal Affairs, the Legal Counsel, addressed to the President of the Security Council, S/2002/161, 12 February, https://digitallibrary.un.org/record/458183?ln=en.

Werner, W.G. (2010). The Curious Career of Lawfare. *Case Western Reserve Journal of International Law*, 43 (1), 61–72.

White House (2020). Proclamation on Recognising the Sovereignty of the Kingdom of Morocco over the Western Sahara, 10 December, https://trumpwhitehouse.archives.gov/presidential-actions/proclamation-recognizing-sovereignty-kingdom-morocco-western-sahara/.

Wilson, A. (2016). *Sovereignty in Exile: A Saharan Liberation Movement Governs*. Philadelphia: University of Pennsylvania Press.

Wrange, P. and Helaoui, S. (2015). *Occupation/Annexation of a Territory: Respect for International Humanitarian Law and Human Rights and Consistent EU Policy*. Brussels: European Parliament.

Zunes, S. and Mundy, J. (2022). *Western Sahara: War, Nationalism and Conflict Irresolution*. 2nd edn. New York: Syracuse University Press.

7

Hardening Ceasefire Lines in Protracted Secessionist Conflicts: From the Negotiating Table and International Law to Realities on the Ground in the Case of the Abkhaz–Georgian War

Giulia Prelz Oltramonti and Gaëlle Le Pavic

Introduction

Ceasefire agreements (CfAs) represent formal commitments between conflicting parties to halt ongoing hostilities. While the primary aim of a CfA is to cease warfare temporarily, the specific contents of such agreements can vary widely, encompassing clauses related to guarantees, negotiating formats, institutional arrangements, monitoring frameworks, and more. The efficacy of these mechanisms in facilitating a transition towards a more enduring peace is debated (Fortna 2018), as is their interplay with wartime governance structures and state-building efforts (Sosnowski 2023). In the case of territorial disputes, including separatist conflicts, CfAs typically incorporate a territorial dimension. This dimension often reflects the respective territorial holdings of each side at a given moment or outlines specific arrangements – such as withdrawal from or demilitarization of particular areas – that have been mutually agreed upon.

While CfAs are typically perceived as temporary measures, their duration can vary significantly. Some CfAs are short-lived, broken by one or more

---

Both authors contributed equally to the chapter.

parties involved, but others evolve into enduring arrangements. For instance, the Korean CfA has endured since 1953, and similar agreements in conflicts involving contested territories and states have also persisted for considerable periods. For example, the UN Security Council Resolution 186 in 1964 led to the establishment of the United Nations Peacekeeping Force in Cyprus (UNFICYP) and intensive negotiations among warring parties in Cyprus, resulting in an arrangement that continues to this day, albeit with evolutions. Similarly, the Agreement on the Principles for a Peaceful Settlement of the Armed Conflict in the Dniester Region of the Republic of Moldova has endured since 1992.

When these agreements last in time, their territorial dimension transitions from temporary to increasingly permanent. Ceasefire lines (or security zones, among other appellations), initially serve to demarcate the geographical boundary of hostilities cessation. However, they gradually acquire additional functions, characteristics, and symbolic significance. This evolution is evident in the case of the ceasefire line (CfL) between Georgia and Abkhazia, which largely follows the Enguri/Ingur[1] River in its southmost segment.[2] The 1994 Agreement on a Cease-Fire and Separation of Forces between Georgia and Abkhazia centred on military positions and separation of (military) forces in a particular (security) zone and contained very few non-military provisions, vague at best.

This is where the consensus between parties ends as to the nature and the management of the divide. The protracted Abkhaz–Georgian conflict revolves around different interpretations of what this dividing line is. For Georgians, it represents a CfL along an internal administrative boundary established within Georgia in 1991 and it should be referred to as an administrative boundary line (ABL). This ABL splits the region of Samegrelo, which the central government controls, from the region of Abkhazia, which it does not control and, since 2008, considers occupied by Russia. In contrast, Abkhaz authorities view the divide as a CfL along the national border of the state that they claim to have established in 1994. Both sides have strived to shape the resulting security area and CfL in accordance with the significance that they give it. They have devised distinct legal frameworks and alternatively encouraged or repressed informal practices that influenced the hardening or softening of the boundary.

---

[1] Throughout the chapter, the names are marked inclusively to include the Georgian and Abkhaz denominations, respectively Enguri and Ingur. Gal/i and Sukhum/i reflect the distinction between the Abkhaz denominations: (Gal and Sukhum) and the Georgian ones (Gali and Sokhumi). However, we acknowledge the limits of this inclusive writing.

[2] Aside from the segment running along, or close to, the Enguri/Ingur River, the boundary between Abkhazia and Tbilisi-controlled Georgia runs into mountainous and largely impassable terrain.

This chapter examines the transformations and evolutions of this CfL through time. While the overarching international law framework remains relatively stable, the interpretations that various actors give it have evolved. International law has been used to justify the different understandings of what the CfL is and what it stands for, as well as the evolving provisions governing it and governing around it. As one would expect, this has had profound impacts on the populations of the borderlands, as well as on their strategies of interaction and navigation. The chapter explores both claims across three levels of analysis: the juridical dimension of borders and ceasefire lines; the legal frameworks and practices developed by Georgian, Abkhaz, and Russian authorities; and the inhabited dimension of the borderland (Wilson and Donnan 2005; Orsini et al 2019).

How borders and ceasefire lines (do not) come to be

In the case of the protracted Abkhaz–Georgian conflict, two distinct dimensions, related to boundaries, borders, and CfLs, are often conflated. The first concerns the rules governing border creation after the dissolution of the Soviet Union. This includes the acceptance of such rules, the related practices, and the evolution of both acceptance and practices since 1991. The second hinges on the content of the CfAs and the provisions governing CfLs, which are relevant for as long as the conflict continues. These two dimensions are unpacked in turns.

International law and post-Soviet borders creation

Recent scholarship on borders and boundaries reflects a noticeable shift away from solely examining the physical and territorial aspects of borders, toward exploring the diverse ways in which different actors influence them in more intangible ways. Scholars are increasingly investigating how states, communities, and individuals shape social dynamics in borderlands, as well as the strategies employed by various actors to respond to external bordering practices (Yuval-Davis et al 2019; Edenborg 2020; von Löwis et al 2023). Despite this interdisciplinary exploration, social sciences still fail to engage with the legal dimension of borders. Few studies delve into the reason why certain actors are recognized as legitimate bordering agents, while others are not, underscoring a broader lacuna in the literature where international law's conception of borders and its impact on people's lives remain largely unexplored (Kesby 2007: 102). Legal analyses often focus on how states exercise their right to establish border and unfolding bordering practices, manifested by their laws, policies, and practices such as control policies, migration regulations, and citizenship laws (Jones 2012; Bigo 2014). Some post-Westphalian scholars advocate for a rethinking of the nature and functions of borders in an evolving global context, yet these studies often overlook the legal frameworks underlying border establishment and the unfolding social consequences.

International law dictated the rules that governed the dissolution of the Soviet Union and the establishment of post-Soviet borders. It was also extensively used to justify various positions regarding state status and the delineation of borders (Lynch 2002; Levinsson 2006; Minakov 2019). Overall, two conflicting interpretations of international law have been advanced since the outbreak of the Abkhaz–Georgian War, reflecting the divergent positions of the two conflicting parties. According to mainstream interpretations of international law, which Georgia embraces, Abkhazia is part of Georgia, making the management of the boundary along the Enguri/Ingur River a matter of Georgian internal affairs (Shanahan Cutts 2007). Conversely, a dissenting (and largely outnumbered) interpretation, championed by Abkhazia, claims that, as new borders were established following the dissolution of the Soviet Union, the Enguri/Ingur River should serve as one such border (Chirikba 2009). Both positions are developed more thoroughly in this section, with the addition of Russia's evolving interpretation of international law in line with its shifting geopolitical interests in the region.

The first interpretation is championed by the Georgian authorities, which have presented various arguments asserting their territorial rights over Abkhazia, including claims of historical control (Wright et al 2003). The legal arguments advanced by Georgia since its independence in 1991 aligned with a prevailing interpretation of international law regarding border creation. Upon independence, the borders of Georgia were established based on several key principles enshrined in international law. Foremost among these is the *uti possidetis* principle, rooted in Roman law and holding significant weight as a customary principle in international law (Lalonde 2002). The *uti possidetis* principle emphasizes the stability and finality of boundary determination. Additionally, the principle of 'territorial integrity', as included in UN declarations concerning the self-determination of peoples (United Nations 1960; see General Assembly resolution 1514, point 6), further underscores Georgia's territorial rights. While these principles are well-established, it is important to note that they were codified in international law primarily during the decolonization process of mostly non-contiguous empires, following World War II. Many foundational texts, legal cases, and scholarly analyses surrounding these principles stem from this specific historical context. Nonetheless, these principles have continued to be reaffirmed in the adjudication of border disputes before the International Court of Justice (Ratner 1996; Lalonde 2002; Emeziem 2021), highlighting their enduring relevance in international law.

In the case of the Soviet Union's dissolution, the *uti possidetis* principle was interpreted to signify that the former boundaries between constituent units of federalism would serve as borders between newly sovereign states (Mirzayev 2014; Malksoo 2020; Miklasová 2023). In the early 1990s, amid the disintegration of the Soviet Union, a widely accepted understanding of international law held that the administrative boundaries within former federal states should be adopted as the borders for (re)emerging sovereign nations. This implied that the borders of an independent Georgia would correspond to the previous administrative boundaries of the federative Georgian Soviet Socialist Republic, which was formed in 1921.

However, this widely embraced interpretation of international law has been contested by Abkhazia and, since the late-2000s, by Russia. For Abkhazia, and Russia since its recognition of Abkhazia as a sovereign state in 2008, the demarcation with Georgia is an international, albeit contested, border. However, the rationales behind this claim differ between Abkhazia and Russia.

Just as Georgia has used historical arguments to support its claim for sovereignty and borders aligned with its Soviet administrative boundaries, Abkhazia has similarly drawn upon historical narratives (Ó Beacháin 2016). Specifically, Abkhazian authorities refer to the period between 1921 and 1931, when Abkhazia functioned as a Soviet Socialist Republic (SSR Abkhazia), albeit with an ambiguous status as a treaty republic associated with the Georgian Soviet Socialist Republic. Joseph Stalin, himself from Georgia, ended this status in 1931 (Ó Beacháin 2016). In addition to these historical arguments, Abkhazia asserts its right to legitimize its statehood, which it initially established through military means, on the grounds of a democratic process of state-building (Ó Beacháin 2012; Ó Beacháin et al 2016).

While Abkhazia's stance is primarily driven by its pursuit of separation from Georgia and recognition of independence, Russia's position is more complex. Russian authorities have not unequivocally accepted the *uti possidetis* principle (Malksoo 2020). They argue that international law is imbued with strong national and regional components, often overlooked in the prevailing Western-centric discourse on universal norms and rights (Malksoo 2020). Russia advocates for its regional conception of international law – framed as Eurasian international law – as opposed to Western universalism.[3]

---

[3] An extensive review of this literature is included in Malksoo 2020. It is important to note that the concept of Eurasia is multifaceted, serving various purposes, such as criticizing Eurocentric narratives of culture and economic modernity. Moreover, it can encompass the 15 republics succeeding the Soviet Union, or specifically designate Russia and the five Central Asian Republics (Bringa and Toje 2016: 6–7) as part of part of Eurasianism ideology (Tsygankov 2003). This ideology emphasizes a dissociation between Russia and Europe, rejecting the understanding of Russia as European and advocating for its distinct civilization, rooted in the union of Slavic and Turko-Mongol steppe peoples (Humphrey 2002: 263).

Russian literature has raised doubts regarding the universality of the *uti possidetis* principle as a fundamental tenet of international law (Malksoo 2020). While the Russian Federation has consistently adhered to the *uti possidetis* principle regarding its own territories, it rejects it as universally binding. Instead, it asserts its prerogative to make exceptions to this principle, even if those exceptions lack recognition from the majority of other states. This underscores the tension between the universalistic conception of international law, which promotes universal legal principles, and the exceptionalist approach taken by a former empire towards its former imperial territories. Madina Tlostanova has examined the Soviet Union, and Russia as the successor state, through the lens of a 'Janus-faced empire', a term denoting its dual orientation: one towards the perceived success and modernity of 'the west', to which Russia is a colony, and the other towards its own (former) colonies (Tlostanova 2008), including Georgia, and where the Abkhaz–Georgian CfL is situated. This analysis highlights Russia's contradictory position, oscillating between mimicking Western hegemony, albeit contesting it superficially, and rejecting what is framed as 'Western values' (Tlostanova 2017; Edenborg 2018).

The concept of dual colonialism, wherein Russia is viewed as both a subaltern and imperialist actor, provides insight into its rejection of the *uti possidetis* principle as a 'Western imperialist principle' while simultaneously reproducing imperialistic tendencies within its former empire, of which its war in Ukraine is one of the last tragic iterations. This framework is particularly relevant in the context of Russia's role in shaping the evolution of the Abkhaz–Georgian CfL, notably through its recognition of Abkhazia as an independent country in 2008. Paradoxically, this recognition was met with ambivalence in Abkhazia and marked the beginning of a heightened presence of Russia in Abkhazia. While use of the Russian rouble and the issuance of Russian passports to Abkhaz residents predates recognition, after 2008 Russia proceeded to deploy Russian Federal Security Service (FSB) agents in Abkhazia, including along the CfL. The practical consequences of this arrangement are explored in more detail in the following section, while the next sub-section focuses on ceasefire agreements and the practical aspects of ceasefire lines with the specific case of the Abkhazian–Georgian CfL.

The establishment of ceasefire lines in the Abkhazian–Georgian case: lines of separation and security zones

In addition to the divergent interpretations of international law principles governing the establishment and maintenance of international borders, the Abkhaz–Georgian case hinges on the arrangements that govern the Abkhaz–Georgian CfL. In 1994 and 2008, representatives from Georgia and Abkhazia signed two different CfAs with territorial dimensions, primarily focused on military dispositions and troop separation. While pivotal in halting high-intensity hostilities, these agreements, particularly the 2008 agreement, remain vague concerning the separation line.

The 1994 Agreement on a Ceasefire and Separation of Forces, mediated by the Russian Federation, was signed by Jaba Ioseliani, representing Georgian President Eduard Shevardnadze, and by Sokrat Jinjolia, representing Vladislav Ardzinba, the leader of the self-proclaimed Republic of Abkhazia. Signed in Moscow on 14 May 1994, this agreement established a 'security zone' between two lines, roughly equidistant to the Enguri/Ingur River, and stretching into Abkhazia on one side of the river and into Samegrelo on the other side. It delineated an area between lines B and D as the security zone.[4] This agreement aimed at creating a buffer between the conflicting sides, comprising a narrower security zone and a wider restricted weapons zone. A peacekeeping force of the Commonwealth of Independent States (CIS) was mandated to patrol the entire area to monitor compliance with the CfA. In turn, the UN Observer Mission in Georgia oversaw the implementation of the agreement and monitored the operation of the CIS forces.[5] While the Enguri/Ingur River was not intended as a dividing line, it served as the territorial central reference point of this conflict-management agreement.

In August 2008, high-intensity conflict resumed in the form of the Russo-Georgian War. This ended with the brokering of a CfA known as the Medvedev–Sarkozy six-point agreement, mediated and signed by the president of France, Nicolas Sarkozy, representing the European Union, the president of Russia, Dimitri Medvedev, and the president of Georgia, Mikheil Saakashvili. While the agreement does not explicitly mention the names of the Abkhaz and South Ossetian leaders, their signatures are present on the document. Notably, Sergei Bagapsh, who served as the *de facto* president of Abkhazia at the time, signed the six-point agreement on behalf of Abkhazia.[6]

---

[4] See the map on p. 5 of the Agreement on a Ceasefire and Separation of Forces, in its Russian original version: Соглашение о прекращении огня и разъединении сил: https://peacemaker.un.org/sites/peacemaker.un.org/files/GE_940514_Agreement CeasefireSeparationOfForces%28ru%29.pdf – this pictorial map is notably unclear and unprecise with regards to the delimitations of Georgian and Abkhaz territorial control and the force(s) exerting this control.

[5] Because of limited space, this chapter does not develop further how a range of additional international actors navigated and shaped the CfL, including the CIS peacekeeping force and the UN Observer Mission in Georgia until 2008 and the EU monitoring mission afterwards.

[6] Bagapsh's role as Abkhazia's *de facto* president is a position and term that is strongly contested by Georgia and many other actors; it is worth noting that the agreement does not specify this role, but reads instead that his signature stands 'for the Abkhazian side'.

Points 4 and 5 of the agreement verge, respectively, on Georgia's commitment to return its troops to their normal quarters and on Russia's commitment to return to its positions prior to the start of hostilities. They are glaringly ambiguous regarding the exact locations of Georgian forces' 'normal quarters' and Russian forces' 'positions prior to the start of the hostilities',[7] giving significant latitude to all parties involved, particularly Russia, whose forces were granted the authority to 'implement additional security measures'. However, this ambiguity facilitated a swift agreement and halted the progression of Russian troops towards the Georgian capital, Tbilisi.

Both CfAs fail to characterize the status of the Enguri/Ingur River, the demarcation between the involved parties, as well as the management of the area, in anything other than military matters, reflecting a dual challenge of concessions based on military positions while ensuring acceptability to all parties. Both agreements are based on a minimal, common denominator phrased in terms of 'lines', indicating a consensus on lines of division among the different warring sides. On paper, representatives agreed on where these lines, or areas between lines, should stand. However, the nature and functions of these lines beyond their military significance remain uncharacterized. This ambiguity enabled various interpretations and had implications for the enforcement of the agreements, particularly evident in the 2008 CfA, which lacks operationalization details and guarantees.

Moreover, limiting the understanding of the area concerned as only a zone of division among warring parties failed to account for the various functions of this area of contact and division, especially given their long-term existence. The CfL affected much more than military deployments. More than 200,000 people fled across this line in 1993. For Georgia, they are internally displaced persons (IDPs), having fled within Georgia; Abkhaz authorities consider them refugees, having crossed what they consider to be an international border. In the following years, some of them attempted to return to their homes or established coping strategies based on seasonal migration from one side to the other of the Enguri/Ingur River. The civil and property rights that they can count on depend on the interpretation by Georgian and Abkhaz authorities of what kind of boundary exists along the Enguri/Ingur River. The CfL affected and continues to affect people's mobility, as well as commercial ties between the two sides, economic activities, transport, communication, and many more areas of life. However, given that no provision regulating flows was included in the CfAs, the functions that the CfLs progressively acquired were independently developed by the

---

[7] See the original version of the CfA in its original languages (French and Russian): Peace Agreement, Database of the University of Edinburgh, Protocol on Agreement (The Medvedev–Sarkozy–Saakashvili plan), www.peaceagreements.org/view/724.

authorities in control of each side, in line with their own interpretations of the rules governing border creation after the dissolution of the Soviet Union.

Legal frameworks and official practices shaping the Abkhaz–Georgian CfL

The different interpretations of international law outlined above, and the varied understandings of CfAs among involved parties, significantly shape the content of national laws and the practices of respective authorities. Georgian authorities have grappled with managing the boundary along the old Soviet administrative line and with legislating on the basis of the principle that it remains an administrative boundary, albeit one that they control only on one side. Conversely, Abkhaz authorities have aimed to establish a national border along the Enguri/Ingur River, shaping their legislation and administrative practices accordingly. While Abkhaz authorities aimed to establish a border along the Enguri/Ingur River, Georgian authorities endeavoured to prevent such an outcome. However, neither of these two processes unfolded seamlessly or without contradictions, but two distinct periods can be observed: the boundary was rather permeable before 2008 and has hardened since the 2008 Russo-Georgian War.

A permeable boundary: pre-2008

The CIS imposed sanctions on Abkhazia in January 1996.[8] While the 'Decision by the Council of the CIS Heads of State on Measures to Settle the Conflict in Abkhazia' covered a range of topics, it focused on limitations on 'trade-economic, financial, transport or other operations with authorities of the Abkhaz side', as well as on military equipment. Initially, however, both Georgian and Russian authorities expanded the interpretation of the terms of the agreement to include an array of goods: chemicals used in agriculture, which could potentially be used by the military, as well as white goods and medicines.

These restrictions had significant repercussions on everyday life in Abkhazia, resulting in regular interruptions in electricity delivery, the closure of Sukhum/i airport, and disruptions in railroad operations (Hopf 2005; Kvarchelia 2008). Furthermore, in January 1996, Georgia adopted a

---

[8] The original text of the Decision of the Council of the Heads of States of CIS of 19 January 1996 ('РЕШЕНИЕ о мерах по урегулированию конфликта в Абхазии, Грузия') is published in the digital database of the CIS (https://cis.minsk.by/reestrv2/doc/541#text). Interestingly, it is not included in a parallel English-language database of CIS legislation (https://cis-legislation.com), but an unofficial translation is available here: https://civil.ge/archives/114457.

presidential decree stating that 'Sukhumi, seaport, port points, sea border and Georgian-Russian border in the territory of Abkhazia will be closed for any kind of international transport except the transportation of humanitarian cargoes carried out according to this decree' (Punsmann 2009). As a result, the port of Sukhum/i was shut down, halting maritime traffic, particularly with Turkey, with whom trade ties were bolstered by a substantial Abkhaz diaspora (Smolnik et al 2017).

The consequences of these sanctions were harsh on the population of Abkhazia, especially as they came amid the destruction caused by the war and the disruption brought about by the dissolution of the Soviet Union, as well as on the back of a series of unilateral measures implemented by Russia in the same period. In 1994, amid allegations of Chechen fighters being trained in Abkhazia, Russia closed its border to all men between the ages of 16 and 60 (Le Huérou et al 2014). In 1997, long-distance telephone lines, which linked Abkhazia to the rest of the world via Russia, were cut (Garb 1999). In addition, Soviet passports gradually expired, leaving the residents of Abkhazia with no documents to travel, as most of them did not apply for Georgian passports. The 1990s are widely seen in Abkhazia as the era of the 'Georgian embargo', irrespective of whether travel limitations on people and isolation were a consequence of CIS trade restrictions or imposed by Russia.

The embargo aimed to isolate and pressure the self-declared state of Abkhazia into accepting a resolution on Georgians' terms. However, it did not achieve its objective and was gradually eased, notably by Russia from the 2000s onwards, coinciding with Vladimir Putin's election as president of the Russian Federation. Nonetheless, some restrictions, such as the closure of Sukhum/i airport and maritime traffic, remain in place to date.[9] Abkhaz scholar Liana Kvarchelia argued that this approach has only increased Abkhazia's dependency on Russia, making it the 'only outside world' with which Abkhazia could communicate (Kvarchelia 2008, 72). Tellingly, Russia unilaterally withdrew from the framework in March 2008, five months before the start of the 2008 Russo-Georgian War.

The Georgian authorities refrained from imposing any restrictions on the movement of people across the Enguri/Ingur River, arguing that, since Abkhazia is an integral part of Georgia, circulating between Abkhazia and the Samegrelo region, and then further into Georgia, should be deemed an internal movement. While Abkhaz authorities consistently checked documents at the Enguri/Ingur bridge crossing point, Georgian authorities did so only sporadically, indicating their reluctance to recognize it as an

---

[9] Moscow and Sukhum/i have been discussing the possibility of reopening the Sukhum/i airport (Zavodskaya 2023), the exploitation of which, without the approval of Georgia, would be in breach of the Chicago Convention of 1944 that governs civil aviation.

official border of Georgia. During the 1990s and early 2000s, informal trade between Abkhazia and Georgia flourished across the CfL due to the limited capacity and, often, the unwillingness of both parties to exert control over the dividing line (Prelz Oltramonti 2017). While Georgian authorities neither passed legislation nor implemented any border management practices, Abkhaz authorities focused on the security function of what they considered the southern border of their newly independent state. Border guards symbolically enacted document verification at the Enguri/Ingur bridge, but this was not matched by the capacity effectively to manage the flow of goods and people elsewhere along the river. Until well into the early 2000s, they struggled to control the entire borderland region along the ceasefire line.

A hardened boundary: post-2008

The 2008 August War, which primarily centred on South Ossetia and which led to direct confrontation between Russian and Georgian armed forces, led to a decisive evolution in boundary management on both sides of the Enguri/Ingur River.[10] In this volume, Júlia Miklasová plunges earnestly into Russia's engagement with international law and how it has used it to justify the evolution of its practices on the ground. A review of Russia's arguments has also been carried out in the first part of this chapter. But outlining the kind of implications that the Russian volte-face brought about is still missing. Following the 2008 war and Russia's recognition of Abkhazia's independence, an agreement was reached between Moscow and Sukhum/i for what they regarded as the border management of the northern side of the CfL. During the 2008 war, Russian troops had pushed far into the Samegrelo region. When they retreated behind the Enguri/Ingur River, following the CfA brokered by the EU presidency, they consolidated their positions there. This new arrangement highlighted the fact that, according to Russia, the management of the border could now depend on bilateral agreements between Moscow and Sukhum/i. Russia, which had recognized Georgia's sovereignty over Abkhazia until 2008, claimed that Abkhaz border management was no longer a matter concerning Tbilisi.[11] While officially

---

[10] The war was preceded by a series of skirmishes, including at the Abkhazian–Georgian contested border. In the summer of 2006, Georgians launched a military campaign in the Kodor/i Gorge (Kvarchelia 2008; Garb 2012). In April and May 2008, Georgia claimed that Russian military planes shot down Georgian unmanned aerial vehicles over the Kodor/i Gorge (Garb 2012, 95).

[11] Pushing this logic further, in 2011 Russia also attempted to challenge a mountainous stretch of the old Georgian–Russian border, established during the Soviet Union, which would have led to the annexation of up to 160 square km in the vicinities of the Olympic venues at Krasnaya Poliana (Suleimanov 2011).

Russia's enhanced role in border management along the Enguri/Ingur River emanated from a bilateral agreement between Russia and Abkhazia, doubts linger over whether Abkhaz authorities could request the departure of Russian troops, raising questions about the degree of independence achieved through Russia's recognition.

The presence of the Russian troops along the CfL and the arrival of Russian FSB forces sealed the *de facto* border much more effectively than the Abkhaz *de facto* border guards were ever able to do before 2008. Trading across the river, outside the official checkpoint, became extremely difficult; the circulation of residents between Samegrelo and the Gal/i district, which previously took place with the assent of Abkhaz *de facto* border guards and was facilitated by the payment of small bribes, ended. This forced all those who wanted to cross from Abkhazia to Samegrelo, or vice versa, to take long detours to reach the bridge on the Enguri/Ingur River. Symbolically, maintaining control over the contested border was of paramount importance for the Abkhaz. This prompted the Abkhaz authorities and acting border guards to oversee the checkpoint on the bridge until October 2012. Subsequently, this responsibility was shared with Russian personnel, although the predominant influence of the latter became evident during crossings.

In the face of Russian continuous presence in Abkhazia, the parliament of Georgia (2008) adopted the Law on Occupied Territories, which denounced '[Russia's] illegal military occupation of the territory of a sovereign country', aimed at 'defin[ing] the status of territories that have been occupied as a result of military aggression by the Russian Federation, and establish a special legal regime for these territories' (Parliament of Georgia 2008, Art. 1), and unveiled a number of measures to contribute to the 'the process of de-occupation' (Parliament of Georgia 2008, Art. 11). The measures included in the law span a rather vast range of fields, impacting the legality of most economic and administrative activities in Abkhazia. In addition, and as a central element of the law, Georgia legislated that the only legal way in and out of Abkhazia is from Georgia. With this law, entering and exiting Abkhazia from Russia or the sea becomes a criminal offence, a provision that the government of Georgia struggles to enforce, lacking control over that part of its international border. Although the law never mentions the CfL, which in other instances the government of Georgia refers to as the administrative boundary line, it legislates against all mobility to and from Abkhazia, except for cross-CfL movement.

Because of its provisions on the illegality of economic and administrative activities in Abkhazia, the law deepens the divide between Abkhazia (and what it designates as the other occupied territory of South Ossetia) and the rest of Georgia. It implicitly recognizes a profound difference between one side and the other of the CfL and codifies provisions aimed at rendering everyday activities in Abkhazia illegal. The spirit of this law was to undermine

Abkhazia's viability but, because of the wider context, Abkhaz authorities consolidated their power within Abkhazia in the subsequent period, especially in the Gal/i region, abutting the CfL.

While the law contributed to a deepening of the cleavage between the two banks of the Enguri/Ingur River, by creating two distinct juridical spaces, the changes that it brought about were rather theoretical, because of scant enforcement. More impactfully, the Georgian authorities' practices of control along the CfL evolved and contributed to the hardening of the boundary between Abkhazia and Samegrelo. New border-like measures included increasingly systematic registrations and checks at the Enguri/Ingur main crossing point. From the 2010s onwards, controls have been carried out by both Georgian police and authorities. Nowadays, agents in Georgian police uniforms and plainclothes agents monitor the crossing (author's observations, 2022). While Georgian authorities justify these measures on security grounds, the extensive controls inadvertently make the divide more prominent and border-like, despite the official Georgian rhetoric framing Abkhazia as an 'autonomous region of Georgia'.

Interestingly, the presence and activities of the Georgian police at the Enguri/Ingur bridge crossing point contrast with the absence of any Georgian authorities at the only other open controlled crossing point at the time of writing, located between the villages of Pakhuliani on the Georgian-controlled side and Saberio on the Abkhaz one. When one of the authors questioned this discrepancy, she was told that the presence of Georgian police would imply the existence of a border, where there is none; and that controls were taking place at the main crossing only to accommodate the crossing of Russian citizens, who were barred from crossing at Pakhuliani (interview with Georgian official, 2022, Pakhuliani). Hence, the Georgian legal instruments and practices of control performed along the Enguri/Ingur River contribute to the evolution of the CfL as a hardened boundary divide, but this evolution is not uniformly happening along its whole length. Yet Georgian authorities keep denying that such a divide is a border as this would be in contradiction not only of international law but also with Georgian public opinion, for which Abkhazia remains a part of Georgia, albeit one occupied by Russia.

The inhabited dimension of the borderland

Against this backdrop of hardening of the CfL, the inhabited dimension of the CfL reflects the necessity, as well as the ability, of a range of actors to navigate the crossing, to maintain links and, sometimes, to exploit the divide. Cooperation between Abkhaz and Georgians exists in several areas, including more or less formal and/or official ones. One enduring example revolves around the Enguri/Ingur River hydroelectric power station.

Constructed in 1961, the dam is located in Georgia's Samegrelo region, while the power station is in Abkhazia's Gal/i district. It plays a critical role in supplying electricity to both the Georgian-controlled territory and Abkhazia but, for it to work, both sides must agree on financing, sharing the output, and personnel circulation across the CfL. Also, while some of these forms of cooperation entail navigating the CfL, others revolve around avoiding it, by establishing contacts and activities in third countries.[12]

Trade between Abkhazia and Georgia has been a feature of the CfL since the establishment of the first CfA. To survive, Abkhaz residents relied on 'petty cross-border trade' not only with Russia (Kvarchelia 2008), but also with Georgia (Prelz Oltramonti 2017). Many different types of local actors – including authorities, 'civil servants' (чиновники/chinovniki), violence entrepreneurs and traders – played a key role in this trade flow across the Abkhaz-Georgian contested border (Prelz Oltramonti 2020). Our previous research documented that activities such as small-scale cross-CfL trade or subsistence farming, with cash crops such as hazelnuts cultivated on the Abkhaz side and sold across the CfL, represented half of the income of the Gal/i residents throughout the 1990s and 2000s, at a time when formal employment remained low (Prelz Oltramonti 2015, 298). Nevertheless, trading was never straightforward: violence abounded, confidence between communities had been frayed by the war (Mirimanova 2006), and Abkhaz authorities repeatedly tried to clamp down on the traffic, including in 2007, by introducing an embargo on goods from Georgia in 2007 (JAMnews 2023).

The arrival of Russian forces along the CfL in 2008 reduced its permeability and made trading across the Enguri/Ingur River, outside the official checkpoints, challenging, and disrupting informal trading practices, including small (bribe) payments. The reduction of space for negotiation coupled with an increased physical materialization of the contested border on the Abkhaz side, marked by fences, ditches, barbed wire, and watchtowers, further impedes crossing despite enduring socio-economic ties on both sides. Consequently, individuals wishing to cross between Abkhazia and Georgia were compelled to take lengthy detours to reach the main bridge on the Enguri/Ingur River which made trade more costly. Many gradually gave up.

Aside from a Russian militarization of the boundary, Abkhaz authorities seek to develop standard features of borders along the Enguri/Ingur River. In 2021, Abkhaz *de facto* Prime Minister Alexander Ankvab permitted the company Apsny DewT to open a duty-free shop 'within the boundaries of the checkpoint "Ingur" in the village of Khitskha of the Gal district' (Zavodskaya 2022). The Abkhaz authorities intend 'to mark the entry into

---

[12] This is most notably the case of civil society organizations (Le Pavic et al 2024).

new territory for representatives of international organizations who all enter Abkhazia via the Ingur-controlled crossing point' (Zavodskaya 2022).

While some Abkhaz consider cross-CfL trade as 'trad[ing] with the enemy', others argue that illicit trade is happening anyway, feeding corruption, and that regularization would instead contribute to the Abkhaz budget (Gogoryan 2021). To circumvent sanctions imposed on Russia following its full-scale invasion of Ukraine, more goods entered Abkhazia through Georgia and were then moved onwards to Russia. On 31 March 2023, the *de facto* acting president of Abkhazia, Aslan Bzhaniya, approved a list of 14 items (such as agricultural machinery, cars spare parts, and motor oils) that could be imported across the CfL (JAMnews 2023). On the Georgian side, trade with Abkhazia contributes to economic dynamism, particularly in Samegrelo as well, where the bustling Zugdidi market attracts sellers and buyers from Abkhazia. Going shopping in Georgia is one of the motivations for Abkhaz to cross the CfL, although most of them keep a low profile about this practice to avoid social stigma within the Abkhaz society (Peinhopf 2022).

The concept of borderland is useful to better understand the social dynamics occurring along the Abkhaz–Georgian CfL. A borderland is where two (or more) socio-economically interconnected spaces are divided by a (contested) border, profoundly impacting everyday life through both symbolic and tangible bordering practices (Orsini et al 2019). The latter encompasses the 'everyday construction of borders through ideology, cultural mediation, discourses, political institutions, attitudes and everyday forms of transnationalism' (Yuval-Davis et al 2018: 2). The contested border significantly influences social dynamics in the Gal/i district of eastern Abkhazia and the Samegrelo region in western Georgia, where the divide cuts across two regions linked by strong ethnic bonds, being populated by Mingrelians, a sub-group of Georgians (Broers 2012) who maintain dense social ties (Kabachnik 2012). The borderland's influence extends beyond these regions, encompassing Abkhaz residing in the six other districts under Abkhaz control and Georgians spread throughout Georgia, and further abroad.

Some Georgians continue crossing the CfL, while others refuse, citing their reluctance to 'go to their occupied homeland' (Peinhopf 2021) or engage with Abkhaz authorities for documentation. An Abkhaz national (internal) passport printed since 2006, an Abkhaz resident permit, or an Abkhaz administrative document commonly called 'form number 9' are the documents enabling the crossing. Abkhaz passports written in Abkhaz and Russian stipulate the ethnicity of the holder, as Soviet passports did. While ethnic Georgians with Abkhaz passports find crossing easier, many IDPs from the Samegrelo region face challenges, ranging from not having the required documentation to denial of entry to the Abkhaz-controlled territory by the 'border guards' (pogranitchniki/**пограничники**).

The evolution of boundary regimes is recent enough that residents of the borderlands still recall a before and after:

> We used to go [to Gal/i] like partisans [как партизаны/kak partizani] crossing through woods and the river. [...] We visited our relatives like this for a while. We spent many summers there. It changed in 2008, after the war it became impossible to cross as we did before, Russian soldiers arrived and prevented us from crossing. (Interview conducted by one of the authors, Svaneti, 2022)

As Russia's full-scale invasion of Ukraine unfolds, the sentiment among interviewees, particularly among the IDPs, unable to cross into Abkhazia, reflects a lingering hope that 'the victory of Ukraine' will facilitate their return 'home'. The reference to 'their home in Abkhazia' remains prevalent among the interviewed IDPs, even though some were born in Georgia.

Conversely, from an Abkhaz perspective, crossing the CfL from Abkhazia to Samegrelo is rarely expressed openly, because Georgia is framed by some as an 'enemy' and a social stigma arises toward those going there (Peinhopf 2022: 2). While most Abkhaz exit Abkhazia by crossing the Psou River checkpoint with Russia, some go to Samegrelo or Tbilisi for various reasons, including trade or access to free healthcare programmes. Abkhaz crossing the CfL have mixed experiences: some express pride in presenting their passport at checkpoints, while others emphasize the stress of enduring multiple controls. In many instances Abkhaz individuals who cross the CfL into Georgia are interviewed by the Abkhaz State Security Service, a process described by one of our interviewees as 'humiliating'.

Conclusion

The uninitiated reader would have assumed that international law and CfAs provide straightforward and undisputable tools to manage war and the lines of division that are established when high-intensity fighting stops. This chapter has shown how, especially in the case of protracted secessionist conflicts, this assumption is far removed from the reality, for a number of reasons.

First, key principles of international law are interpreted differently by various parties. A universal consensus, around the very crucial element of what makes a state and who is entitled to claim and recognize statehood, is frayed, occasioning a deep ambiguity with regards to what the established dividing lines are, and which actors can manage them legitimately.

Second, CfAs are limited in scope and focus on a military dimension. Avoiding all references to the issue of statehood (or non-statehood) is what makes them acceptable to all parties; at the same time, such vagueness opens a wide door for different interpretations of the terms and of the beyond, in function of the interests of the signatories and third parties.

Third, the policies and practices that are developed around the management of the CfL are neither unequivocally in line with a mainstream interpretation of international law, nor with the interpretation of the various parties. States and contested states are constrained by their limited capacity to implement policies in line with their official position on statehood, or are spurred by practical considerations that transcend status.

This results in a wide misalignment between international law, the results of the negotiating table, and realities on the ground. This mismatch entails an augmented vulnerability for those who would have been protected by a unique and straightforward interpretation and implementation of the guiding principles of IL. This is true for (contested) states and residents of the borderland alike. As shown repeatedly in the chapter, authorities of all sides develop ad hoc policies and implementation strategies that are in contradiction with those of their adversaries, trying either to exploit the divergence or to limit their loss of authority over the dividing line. Residents do just the same: they navigate the CfL, looking for opportunities and weary of the vulnerability that the ambiguity around the dividing line engenders.

References

Bigo, D. (2014). The (in) Securitization Practices of the Three Universes of EU Border Control: Military/Navy–Border Guards/Police–Database Analysts. *Security Dialogue,* 45 (3), 209–225.

Bringa, T. and Toje, H. (2016). *Eurasian Borderlands: Spatializing Borders in the Aftermath of State Collapse.* New York: Springer.

Broers, L. (2012). Two Sons of One Mother: Nested Identities and Centre-Periphery Politics in Post-Soviet Georgia. In Andreas Schönle (ed.), *When the Elephant Broke Out of the Zoo: A Festschrift for Donald Rayfield.* Stanford: Stanford University Press, 234–267.

Chirikba, V. (2009). The International Legal Status of the Republic of Abkhazia in the Light of International Law. *Abkhaz World,* 2.

Edenborg, E. (2018). Homophobia as Geopolitics: 'Traditional Values' and the Negotiation of Russia's Place in the World. *Gendering Nationalism: Intersections of Nation, Gender and Sexuality,* 67–87.

Edenborg, E. (2020). Saving Women and Bordering Europe: Narratives of 'Migrants' Sexual Violence' and Geopolitical Imaginaries in Russia and Sweden. *Geopolitics,* 25 (3), 780–801.

Emeziem, C. (2021). Beyond Formalism and Uti Possidetis The International Court of Justice and Boundary Disputes in Africa. In M. Ndulo and C. Emeziem (eds), *The Routledge Handbook of African Law.* Abingdon: Routledge, 580–608.

Fortna, V.P. (2018). *Peace Time: Cease-Fire Agreements and the Durability of Peace*. Princeton: Princeton University Press.

Garb, P. (1999). The Inguri Power Complex. In *A Question of Sovereignty: The Georgia–Abkhazia Peace Process*. London: Conciliation Resources.

Garb, P. (2012). Civil Society and Conflict Transformation in the Georgian–Abkhaz Conflict: Accomplishments and Challenges. *European Security*, 21(1), 90–101.

Gogoryan, A. (2021). 'Все Равно Торгуют, Все Равно По Факту Это Происходит, Доходы Уходят в Тень» / [All the Same They Trade, All the Same in Fact It Happens, Incomes Go into the Shadow]. *Eko Kavkas*, 9 February, www.ekhokavkaza.com/a/31094441.html.

Hendl, T., Burlyuk, O., O'Sullivan, M., and Arystanbek, A. (2023). (En) Countering Epistemic Imperialism: A Critique of 'Westsplaining' and Coloniality in Dominant Debates on Russia's Invasion of Ukraine. *Contemporary Security Policy*, 1–39.

Hopf, T. (2005). Identity, Legitimacy, and the Use of Military Force: Russia's Great Power Identities and Military Intervention in Abkhazia. *Review of International Studies*, 31 (S1), 225–243.

Humphrey, C. (2002). 'Eurasia', Ideology and the Political Imagination in Provincial Russia In C.M. Hann (ed.) *Postsocialism: Ideals, Ideologies, and Practices in Eurasia*. London: Routledge.

JAMnews (2023). Due to Anti-Russian Sanctions, Abkhazia Partially Lifts Embargo on Goods from Georgia, 14 April, https://jam-news.net/embargo-on-goods-from-georgia/.

Jones, R. (2012). *Border Walls: Security and the War on Terror in the United States, India, and Israel*. London: Bloomsbury Publishing.

Kabachnik, P. (2012). Shaping Abkhazia: Cartographic Anxieties and the Making and Remaking of the Abkhazian Geobody. *Journal of Balkan and Near Eastern Studies*, 14 (4), 397–415.

Kesby, A. (2007). The Shifting and Multiple Border and International Law. *Oxford Journal of Legal Studies*, 27 (1), 101–119.

Kvarchelia, L. (2008). Sanctions and the Path Away from Peace. In A. Griffiths & C. Barnes (eds), *Powers of Persuasion: Incentives, Sanctions and Conditionality in Peacemaking*. London: Conciliation Resources, 66–68.

Lalonde, S.N. (2002). *Determining Boundaries in a Conflicted World: The Role of Uti Possidetis*. Montréal: McGill-Queen's Press-MQUP.

Le Huérou, A., Merlin, A., Regamey, A., and Sieca Kozlowski, E. (2014) *Chechnya at War and Beyond*. Abingdon-on-Thames: Routledge

Le Pavic, G., Orsini, G., Bossuyt, F., and Lietaert, I. (2024). Negotiating de Facto Borders: The Case of Social Services Provision in Abkhazia and Transnistria. *Eurasian Geography and Economics*.

Levinsson, C. (2006). The Long Shadow of History: Post-Soviet Border Disputes – The Case of Estonia, Latvia, and Russia. *Connections*, 5 (2), 98–110.

Löwis, S. von, Eschment, B., and Khutsishvili, K. (2023). Dynamics of Bordering in the Post-Soviet Space over the Last 30 Years. In S. von Löwis and B. Eschment (eds), *Post-Soviet Borders*. Abingdon: Taylor & Francis.

Lynch, D. (2002). Separatist States and Post-Soviet Conflicts. *International Affairs*, 78 (4), 831–848.

Malksoo, L (2020). Post-Soviet Eurasia, Uti Possidetis and the Clash between Universal and Russian-Led Regional Understandings of International Law. *New York University Journal of International Law and Politics*, 53, 787.

Miklasová, J. (2023). Dissolution of the Soviet Union Thirty Years On: Re-Appraisal of the Relevance of the Principle of Uti Possidetis Iuris. In J.E. Viñuales, A. Clapham, L. Boisson de Chazournes, and M. Hébié (eds), *The International Legal Order in the XXIst Century/L'ordre Juridique International Au XXIeme Siècle/El Órden Jurídico Internacional En El Siglo XXI*. Brill: Nijhoff, 105–124.

Minakov, M. (2019). On the Extreme Periphery. The Status of Post-Soviet Non-Recognised States in the World-System. *Ideology and Politics Journal*, 12 (1), 39–72.

Mirimanova, N. (2006). *Corruption and Conflict in the South Caucasus*. London: International Alert.

Mirzayev, F.S. (2014). *Uti Possidetis v Self-Determination: The Lessons of the Post-Soviet Practice*. Leicester: University of Leicester.

Ó Beacháin, D. (2012). The Dynamics of Electoral Politics in Abkhazia. *Communist and Post-Communist Studies*, 45 (1–2), 165–174.

Ó Beacháin, D. (2016). Elections and Nation-Building in Abkhazia. In R. Isaacs and A. Polese (eds), *Nation-Building and Identity in the Post-Soviet Space*. Abingdon: Routledge, 208–227.

Ó Beacháin, D., Comai, G., and Tsurtsumia-Zurabashvili, A. (2016). The Secret Lives of Unrecognised States: Internal Dynamics, External Relations, and Counter-Recognition Strategies. *Small Wars & Insurgencies*, 27 (3), 440–466.

Orsini, G., Canessa, A., Gonzaga Martínez del Campo, L., and Ballantine Pereira, J. (2019). Fixed Lines, Permanent Transitions. International Borders, Cross-Border Communities and the Transforming Experience of Otherness. *Journal of Borderlands Studies*, 34 (3), 361–376.

Parliament of Georgia (2008). Law on Occupied Territories. *LHG*, 28, 30 October, https://web.archive.org/web/20140624083638/http://www.smr.gov.ge/docs/doc216.pdf.

Peinhopf, A. (2021). The Curse of Displacement: Local Narratives of Forced Expulsion and the Appropriation of Abandoned Property in Abkhazia. *Nationalities Papers*, 49 (4), 710–727.

Peinhopf, A. (2022). Crossing the Conflict Divide: De Facto Borders, State Belonging, and the Changing Dynamics of Enemy Relations in Abkhazia. *Ethnopolitics*, 1–18.

Prelz Oltramonti, G. (2015). The Political Economy of a de Facto State: The Importance of Local Stakeholders in the Case of Abkhazia. *Caucasus Survey*, 3 (3), 291–308.

Prelz Oltramonti, G. (2017). Trajectories of Illegality and Informality in Conflict Protraction: The Abkhaz–Georgian Case. *Caucasus Survey*, 5 (1), 85–101.

Prelz Oltramonti, G. (2020). Viability as a Strategy of Secession: Enshrining De Facto Statehood in Abkhazia and Somaliland. In R.D. Griffiths and D. Muro (eds), *Strategies of Secession and Counter-Secession*. Old Heath: ECPR Press.

Punsmann, B.C. (2009). Questioning the Embargo in Abkhazia: Turkey's role in integrating into the Black Sea region. *Turkish Policy Quarterly*, 8(4), 77–88.

Ratner, S.R. (1996). Drawing a Better Line: Uti Possidetis and the Borders of New States. *American Journal of International Law*, 90 (4), 590–624.

Shanahan Cutts, N.M. (2007). Enemies through the Gates: Russian Violations of International Law in the Georgia/Abkhazia Conflict. *Case Western Reserve Journal of International Law*, 40, 281.

Smolnik, F., Weiss, A., and Zabanova, Y. (2017). Political Space and Borderland Practices in Abkhazia and Adjara: Exploring the Role of Ottoman Legacies and Contemporary Turkish Influences. *Eurasian Geography and Economics*, 58 (5), 557–581.

Sosnowski, M. (2023). *Redefining Ceasefires: Wartime Order and Statebuilding in Syria*. Cambridge: Cambridge University Press.

Souleimanov E. (2011). Russia and Abkhazia Dispute Border Delimitation. *CACI Analyst*, 11 May, www.cacianalyst.org/publications/analytical-artic les/item/12283-analytical-articles-caci-analyst-2011-5-11-art-12283.html (accessed 12 January 2015).

Tlostanova, M. (2008). The Janus-Faced Empire Distorting Orientalist Discourses: Gender, Race and Religion in the Russian/(Post) Soviet Constructions of the 'Orient.' *Worlds and Knowledges Otherwise*, 2 (2), 1–11.

Tlostanova, M. (2017). Postsocialist≠ Postcolonial? On Post-Soviet Imaginary and Global Coloniality. In D. Kołodziejczyk and C. Şandru (eds), *Postcolonial Perspectives on Postcommunism in Central and Eastern Europe*. Abingdon: Routledge, 28–40.

Tsygankov, A.P. (2003). Mastering Space in Eurasia: Russia's Geopolitical Thinking after the Soviet Break-Up. *Communist and Post-Communist Studies*, 36 (1), 101–127.

UN (1960). Declaration on the Granting of Independence to Colonial Countries and Peoples. General Assembly Resolution 1514 (XV), www. ohchr.org/en/instruments-mechanisms/instruments/declaration-grant ing-independence-colonial-countries-and-peoples.

Wilson, T.M. and Donnan, H. (2005). Territory, Identity and the Places in-between: Culture and Power in European Borderlands. In H. Donnan and T.M. Wilson (eds), *Culture and Power at the Edges of the State. National Support and Subversion in European Border Regions*. Munster: LIT Verlag and Transaction Publishers, 1–31.

Wright, J., Schofield, R., and Goldenberg, S. (2003). *Transcaucasian Boundaries*. Abingdon: Routledge.

Yuval-Davis, N., Wemyss, G., and Cassidy, K. (2018). Everyday Bordering, Belonging and the Reorientation of British Immigration Legislation. *Sociology*, 52 (2), 228–244.

Yuval- Davis, N., Wemyss, G., and Cassidy, K. (2019). *Bordering*. London: John Wiley & Sons.

Zavodskaya, E. (2022). **Беслан Цвинария: «Значит Ли Это, Что Будет Открыто Движение**? [Beslan Tsvinaria: 'Does This Mean That There Will Be an Open Movement?] *Ekho Kavkaza*, 16 June, www.ekhokavkaza.com/a/31900913.html.

Zavodskaya, E. (2023). **Сухумский аэропорт обретет российского инвестора**. *Ekho Kavkaza*, 26 July, www.ekhokavkaza.com/a/32521503.html?mc_cid=f3b390f4d1&mc_eid=d00e5cff3b.

8

Sovereign Experimentation by Separatist Insurgencies: A Performative Perspective

Bart Klem

Introduction

This chapter analyzes the Tamil nationalist militancy in Sri Lanka to illustrate how a performative perspective helps us grapple with some of the omissions, biases, and circular logics that afflict the existing scholarship on separatist movements and *de facto* states. Such political entities confront us with the tensions and contradictions inherent to the nature of sovereign states. As indicated in this book's first section, the ambiguous status of these entities spawns questions of veracity and authenticity – are the institutions and laws of incompletely recognized states like Abkhazia or Turkish Republic of Northern Cyprus real? Are they legitimate? Are they legal? Such an inquiry cannot remain restricted to questions about these supposed anomalies because it inevitably prompts questions about the benchmarks of normalcy. And this then directs us to interrogate the foundations of recognized sovereign states.

Sovereignty is ultimately a self-referential quality (Hansen and Stepputat 2005; Gilmartin et al 2020). The sovereign assertion on which national states are premised tends to be legitimated with reference to legal foundations, the political demarcation of a national community, and interrelationships with other sovereign states. But through these registers of legitimation, the referent of sovereignty is endlessly deferred, and the historical origins of such chains of deferral are typically clouded in violent impositions that thwarted alternative interpretations of sovereignty.

My vantage point in this chapter is that it is futile to try and resolve the arbitrariness of sovereign demarcation and that we should instead make the irresolvable nature of contentions around the correct or legitimate demarcation of sovereignty central to our analysis of *de facto* states. Moving beyond the dichotomy of declarative and constitutive convocations of sovereignty, this chapter explores the incremental nature of sovereign articulation. To grapple with the interpretative dilemmas of studying *de facto* states, I draw on anthropological scholarship that conceptualizes political and legal institutions as contingent performances for diverse audiences (Navaro-Yashin 2007; McConnell 2016; Wilson 2016; Bobick 2017; Klem and Maunaguru 2017; Bryant and Hatay 2020; Reeves & Bryant 2021; Rutherford 2012). Sovereignty does not instantaneously appear through military imposition, political declaration, or formal diplomatic recognition (Ker-Lindsay 2015; Kyris 2022). It matures through forms of encroachment, ambiguous overlaps, the stabilization of routines, tacit acknowledgment, and implied recognition – combined with the ability to project violent force.

This chapter examines the analytical merits of taking a performative perspective on the legal and political articulations of separatist insurgencies and *de facto* states. I argue that this sheds light on these contested political entities, because it debunks the purportedly fixed attributes of statehood – the law, a territory, a national people, the architecture of state entities – and conceptualizes these as claims that are enacted for a particular audience with a contingent degree of potency, credibility, and legitimacy. As such, this chapter speaks to all three dimensions of contested states – ambiguity, vulnerability, and constrained agency – discussed in this book's introduction (Grzybowski et al, this volume). I illustrate my argument by drawing on the Tamil nationalist movement in Sri Lanka, a sovereign experiment that failed to graduate into a consolidated *de facto* state (let alone a recognized *de jure* state). The Tamil separatist militancy was comprehensively defeated by the Sri Lankan military in May 2009 (see Price, this volume).

The two sections that comprise the first half of this chapter elaborate my conceptual point with reference to broader thematic scholarship. The second half offers an empirical illustration, presented across three sub-sections that seek to capture the *longue durée* of Tamil nationalism in Sri Lanka.

The conceptual problem

The conceptual problem at the heart this chapter is rooted in the ambiguous status of *de facto* states, elaborated in Part 1 of this book. Rather than focusing on strategic implications (Chu, this volume) and the legal-military affordances (Henderson, this volume; Miklasová, this volume; Price, this volume) of this ambiguity, I focus on more rudimentary analytical and descriptive aspects. Whether or not we consider a particular political entity to be a sovereign state or not has profound ramifications for the way we describe it. Sovereign states collect taxes, they write laws, they draft armed forces, and they maintain law and order. If other political entities try to do similar things, they extort money, they make up rules, they engage in forced abduction and armed intimidation. Which idiom we choose has major analytical and normative implications. To describe a *de facto* state, be it an incipient, a consolidated or a collapsing one, thus requires us to decide – right from the start – whether to depict it as what it purports to be (a state) or as an anomaly that lacks validity (an illegal political entity).

Most authors seek to circumnavigate this terminological dilemma with recourse to prefixes (*pseudo*-ministry, *quasi*-court) or scare quotes (the Tamil 'state', the North-Cypriote 'Prime Minister', Sahrawi 'law'). While these are useful qualifications, they side-step the interpretative issue. The political work that such prefixes and scare quotes do therefore merits more scrutiny. After all, they still imply that there is in the end a firm basis to distinguish between the validity of these states-in-the-making (as assertions that require scare quotes or qualifying prefixes) and that of established sovereign states (as real entities that require no typographical disclaimer). The analytical problem that I confront in this text stems from the realization that this basis is lacking. Each of the three main anchors for sovereign claim making – the legal foundation of the state, the political demarcations of people and territory, and recognition by other sovereign states – sets in motion an infinite regression where legitimacy is endlessly deferred. I will discuss these three dimensions in very broad strokes, but I hope the reader will tolerate this bold outset to make a preambular point: that the demarcation of sovereign states ultimately pivots on circular reasoning.

First, the sovereignty of states is codified in law. States derive their prerogatives from the laws they write, which are in turn validated by a constitutional settlement. Separatist contenders to such states typically break these state laws or are altogether criminalized and may thus be discredited as illegal groups that require a law-and-order solution. When such groups start governing people or territory, they may be described as *de facto* sovereign rather than de jure sovereign (Hansen and Stepputat 2005). However, the laws that validate the state are only legal because they derived from prior laws. And those prior laws would have had to derive from prior laws. This yields an infinite regression, where the origin of law could never itself have been legal. The law, to use Brilmayer's (1989) phrase, was 'bootstrapped' into a legal existence – and more often than not, this bootstrapping had colonial dimensions, at least somewhere down the line (Anghie 1999). If a separatist group with sovereign aspirations initiates its own laws and legal institutions, it engages in a similar kind of bootstrapping (Provost 2021, see also Fernández-Molina's discussion of the Sahrawi case in this volume). And arguably it is no longer merely *de facto* sovereign, but *de facto de jure* sovereign as well.

Second, sovereignty derives from the mandate of a national people, in whose name the state governs – the *demos*. Attempts by a minority community to secede are often invalidated as undemocratic. Separatist groups place themselves democratically out of bounds and are called on to rejoin the democratic stream to pursue their objectives. However, the demarcation of the *demos* is not itself a democratic outcome, as Whelan's (1983) seminal essay pointed out. Any attempt to democratically draft the boundaries of the *demos* – who is in and who is out? – would require a prior *demos* to mandate such a demarcation. Another infinite regression emerges. Contemporary authors (Bloemraad 2018; Ochoa Espejo 2020) have complicated and nuanced Whelan's democratic boundary problem (why for example can there not be different overlapping *demoi*?), but for political communities that aspire to an independent state, the rules of the democratic order rarely offer a viable trajectory. If we take their secessionist demarcation of the *demos* as a vantage point, the democratic legitimation of sovereignty is turned on its head.

Third, sovereignty is consolidated through external recognition. Being treated as an equal of sorts within the international community of states is a hallmark of sovereignty, and it is indispensable to fulfil essential state roles (Caspersen 2012). Even a state that struggles to maintain basic governance and enforce rules, such as Somalia, retains a semblance of *de jure* sovereignty, because other states recognize it as such. Political entities that lack recognition from key states (or from any state) may thus be depicted as non-sovereign or not fully sovereign, even if other states engage with them in ways that imply some form of endorsement (Ker-Lindsay 2015; Kyris 2022). However, a state's potency to impart sovereign status on another entity through formal recognition derives from that state being sovereign itself. And that sovereign status is derived from the recognition of another sovereign state, which ... *ad infinitum*. This referential pyramid scheme of sovereign recognition is similarly entangled with the history of colonialism (Anghie 1999; Hansen 2021). Many *de facto* states fulminate against a sovereign arrangement that emerged from this imperial history. Rejecting their validity based on the lack of acceptance from the cartel of established states would be ironic: the same constellation of power that stands at the root of separatist grievances is used to disqualify them.

Summing up, neither the foundation of law, nor the bounds of democracy, nor the mutuality of international recognition offer us a firm analytical basis to assess the validity and legitimacy of sovereign aspirants, because each of these pathways to sovereign legitimation is ultimately based on a circular logic. Recourse to the self-referential schemata that distinguish recognized sovereign states from unrecognized non-sovereign states has problematic effects. It tends to treat sovereign aspirants as anomalies and ascribe legitimacy and normalcy to recognized states, even in cases where this is dubious. Moreover, such schemata are poorly equipped to describe what *de facto* states look like in practice, what they mean to the people concerned, and how they undergo a trajectory of incremental advancements, ruptures and consolidation or demise.

A performative perspective

The analytical problem, which I have admittedly sketched in truncated and perhaps overly stark terms, may be confronted in various ways. I will advance the claim that the literature on performative politics offers us a helpful vantage point to do so. Evidently, this does *not* imply that such an approach is the only solution or that it resolves all the issues at hand, but I will argue that it offers us a heuristic idiom that helps us grapple with the blurry boundaries and referential loops around the conduct of *de facto* states. The literature on performative politics is inspired by Goffman's dramaturgical approach (1959), which pertained to individual human interaction and the way we enact ourselves, depending on the circumstances, in everyday life. Subsequent work in political anthropology has applied this perspective to the conduct of states, political leaders, and authority figures (Spencer 2007; Rutherford 2012). The work that concerns us here has expanded this approach to institutional politics in contested states, including breakaway *de facto* states.

The central conceptual move that this scholarship makes is that we must resist the inclination to understand the meaning, role and significance of an institution in terms of its official mandate, in other words, as what it is supposed to be in legal terms. After all, as citizens across the globe well know, it is quite possible for an officially credited institution to be rendered impotent, while agencies with weak, disputable, or non-existent mandates can grow into potent bodies. Governments invent new authorities to render existing departments irrelevant (Spencer 2007; Piliavski 2014). Presidents start acting like kings, and people help them keep up such appearances by engaging in 'as-if politics' (Wedeen 1999). Leaders feel compelled to perform a particular repertoire because of the gaze of their subject audience (Rutherford 2012) or – vice versa – face humiliation when they become the subject of humour and satire (Bhungalia 2020). Supposedly extra-political repertoires of violent spectacle, religious conduct, public protest and martyrdom yield powerful political capital (Degregori 2012; Dimova and Cojocaru 2013; Michelutti et al 2018).

Instead of looking at formal mandates, a performative perspective invites us to consider institutions in dramaturgical terms: as what they are *enacted* to be and how this enactment is *experienced*. Political leaders and government bodies often behave according to a particular script, they stage their work in a more or less deliberate manner, and they do so for different kinds of audiences. That script may be perfectly in line with their legal mandate, somewhat detached, or at odds with it. Such performance may assume symbolic or ritualistic qualities, and there are often differences between what happens front stage and backstage. In many contexts, elections herald a period of excitement and upheaval: the heightened state of agitation on the streets, the stage-fight dynamic during rallies, the spatial politics of campaigning, the dressing up to vote, and the rituals around victory and defeat (Bertrand et al 2007; Spencer 2007; Banerjee 2014; Klem 2015). It makes little sense to describe this political carnival from the vantage point that elections merely comprise the exercise of franchise to establish the composition of the legislative or executive. A lot more is going on.

Many separatist groups face the predicament of having to engage in politics within the democratic system that they fundamentally oppose and, as such, they face the risk of legitimizing the institutions that they want abolished by participating in them. As a result, their political endeavour assumes a schizophrenic character, where they operate through the trappings of the state that they are simultaneously fighting against. This schizophrenic plight also opens up new political space. Winning a seat in parliament affords opportunities for radical opposition: to voice principled dissent, to demonstratively vacate it, or to refuse occupying it at all. Elections can be used to stage a principled boycott or an informal plebiscite, and political offices can be governed in a way that demonstrates the deficiency of the system (Paley 2008; Byrne 2021; Klem 2024).

When such movements evolve into *de facto* states with a consolidated degree of control over people and territory, a new set of institutional performances ensues. Rather than first establishing a legal foundation to then mount state institutions, militants start acting like states with an incremental institutional landscape in order to gain implied recognition and then grow legal roots to consolidate these institutions. They experiment with new offices, they establish provisional legal and diplomatic structures, they start issuing probationary legal identity documents (Bobick 2017; Prelz Oltramonti 2017; Sosnowski and Klem 2023) and, as such, they perform a 'dress rehearsal' (McConnell 2016, in relation to the Tibetan government-in-exile) and engage in 'make-believe' politics (Navaro-Yashin 2007, in relation to Northern Cyprus). This acting like a state is a form of citational practice (Weber 1995) or mimicry (Bhabha 1994). After all, for the institutions of a militancy to be recognizable as state-like, they must resemble what their audience (its subjects or external actors) knows states to look like. Importantly, such imitation is never quite the same as its model. Mimicry, Bhabha holds, yields a duplicate *but not quite*, and this 'not quite' opens up space for governing institutions to mutate or transform through subtle re-enactment. Invariably, this process involves not only the creation of new entities, but also a large measure of tactical restraint, tacit overlap, encroachment, and incrementalism vis-à-vis the state that an insurgency seeks to supplant. State departments may become co-opted or reoriented in pursuit of separatist ambitions, thus undermining the state that they are ostensibly part of.

Before I proceed, an important qualification with regard to reality and fiction is in order. First, a performative perspective could be taken to imply that we take any projection of sovereignty at face value. In other words, if an insurgent movement or *de facto* state presents a rule to be a law or an institution to be a court, then we should interpret it as such. Such an approach would embrace the self-representation of aspiring sovereigns a little too readily. Second, a performative perspective could be taken to imply a purely metaphorical interpretation. This risks reducing our analysis to a set of theatrical metaphors, which inadvertently reinscribe the dichotomy between the fictional (the performance) and the real (the actors, the audience and the reality that is enacted) that I seek to address.

The merit of a performative perspective lies precisely in the fact that it does not require us to pass *a priori* judgements of veracity but rather treat that question as a matter that is subjective and contingent. The perspective that I advocate hence *departs* from the idea that political performance takes place on a neatly delineated stage that separates fiction from reality: in other words, fictional is what happens on the stage during the performance (a pre-defined script enacted by characters with a *mise en scene*, a backdrop and props), and real is what happens around, before and after it (the screenwriter, the true stories on which the script may be based, the actors, the audience). Rather, the point is that such delineations are unsettled and never final. Performers can redirect the plot and a performance can assume new meaning when the backdrop or audience change. Fictional scripts can become real and real scripts can become fictional. Subtle changes can transform validating ceremonial conduct into a mockery or a farce, and farcical situations can spur people to assert themselves in an authoritative manner.

Bryant and Hatay (2020) use the term 'aporetic state' to grapple with the probationary character of the state in the Turkish Republic of Northern Cyprus. The assertion of an institutional architecture in pursuit of sovereign aspirations pivots on an inherent paradox: it establishes these institutions as fact, while it simultaneously calls them into question. The governing apparatus is presented as self-evident, but they derive significance and instil a sense of awe and amazement because it is *not* self-evident. The institutional structures of *de facto* states are inherently probationary and, because of this work-in-progress character, they exhibit their own incompletion and ambivalence. They must be provisional to be credible. A degree of ambiguity and inconsistency is needed to preserve the focus on unresolved grievances and unfulfilled aspirations. This realization, a recent collection edited by Reeves and Bryant (2021) posits, directs our attention from definitional status questions (What is sovereignty? Are these entities sovereign?) to a broader concern with what people expect from sovereignty and what they desire when they declare sovereign aspirations.

After all, many aspirations and assertions of sovereignty do not merely challenge the delineation of the sovereign state that they contest; they mobilize a political community that more fundamentally defies the trappings of modern statehood. Native American communities that straddle national jurisdictions (Simpson 2014; Lightfoot 2021) and aboriginal mobilization against the Australian state (Little 2020) project a set of claims in the name of a public. Neither these claims nor these publics fit the neat boxes of national government or constitutional law, but both are presented and experienced as sovereign. Democratic politics can be shaped to fundamentally redefine the state while steering clear of overt separatism, as the experiment with 'stateless democracy' in the Kurdish-controlled autonomous administration of Northeast Syria shows (Jongerden and Akkaya 2013). And even when a political movement does fit the contours of demanding independence in the form of a modern sovereign state – such as the Catalan movement or Tamil separatism in Sri Lanka – the affective political energy that radiates from these sovereign pursuits is not constrained to the legal or political accordance that they receive. It was through the staging of the Catalan nation as a discrete people in the political stand-offs around the 2017 referendum on independence that people perceived sovereign potency – regardless of the fact that the referendum was declared illegal (and thus never 'was') and the result was not implemented (Achniotis 2021; Byrne 2021). And it was through the ability of Tamil militants to create a Tamil space beyond the grasp of the Sri Lankan military that people first experienced a Tamil kind of sovereignty (Klem and Maunaguru 2017: 626). Sovereign experiences emanate from the struggle, even when the sovereign status that this struggle pursues remains firmly out of reach.

Performing sovereign aspirations before the war

In the second half of this chapter, I will illustrate the merits of a performative perspective with a discussion of the Tamil nationalist movement in Sri Lanka. While the set-up of this chapter leaves no space for a detailed description of empirical material, this analysis builds on my fieldwork experience over the last 20 or so years, especially in north and east Sri Lanka. As such, this section builds on my recent book (Klem 2024) and earlier work (Klem 2012; Klem and Maunaguru 2017). The first empirical section will consider the manoeuvring of Tamil nationalist parties in the 1970s (in other words, before the escalation into a full-blown civil war). For these earlier phases of the conflict, which predate my fieldwork, I have drawn on retrospective interviews, written sources, and the formidable existing academic scholarship. The next section will then discuss attempts by the Liberation Tigers of

Tamil Eelam (LTTE), which became the dominant armed group, to adopt a state-like posture during the war. The final section will then look attempt at continued (but heavily constrained) staging of Tamil aspirations after the 2009 defeat of the LTTE.

The Tamil nationalist movement may be depicted as an ethno-national struggle for self-determination within a majoritarian democratic post-colonial state. With a three-quarter Sinhalese majority, newly independent Ceylon was drawn into the orbit of ethno-nationalist politics, where efforts to rectify colonial injustices against the Sinhalese resulted in the discrimination of ethnic and religious minorities. A gradual erosion of the checks and balances in the constitutional settlement, an electoral dynamic of 'ethnic outbidding', and a sequence of scuttled power-sharing agreements yielded increasingly hard-nosed contentions. When Srimavo Bandaranaike became prime minister in 1970, she used her landslide parliamentary majority to mandate the drafting of a new constitution. As a capstone to the decolonization process, the 1972 constitution turned the commonwealth Dominion Ceylon into the Republic Sri Lanka. Most pertinent to this chapter, it also dismantled the remaining minority safeguards and, as such, it marked a turning point in the strategy of the Tamil parliamentarian leadership.

The Tamil political leadership comprises an anglicized polity from firmly high-class and high-caste backgrounds, marked out by an upper-class British accent and an Oxford law degree or equivalent. When Tamil concerns fell on deaf ears, Tamil leader S.J.V. Chelvanayakam stepped out of the constitutional drafting committee. His party publicly voiced its objections and reiterated that a constitution that lacked the consent of the Tamil nation would lack legitimacy and would therefore not apply to Tamils. When the new constitution precipitated the rebirth of parliament (the House of Representatives became the National State Assembly), Chelvanayakam demonstratively walked out. His vacant seat prompted a by-election in his constituency, which was held after much delay. Chelvanayakam ran for this election but on the explicit premise that these polls comprised a public plebiscite on the validity of the new constitution (Wilson 1994: 123–125; Edrisinha et al 2008: 232–247).

Soon after, all Tamil parties joined hands to formally declare their commitment to separatism (the so-called Vaddukoddai resolution of 1976). The government responded with more repression and criminalized the dissemination of this resolution or the ideas advanced in it. This then resulted in the arrest of the main Tamil leader, Appapillai Amirthalingam (who had replaced the aging Chelvanayakam). He was tried for advocating separatism in a special tribunal, created under the emergency provisions of the new constitution. Amirthalingam's oversized legal team (which comprised most of his fellow Tamil nationalist leaders) then used this tribunal as an elevated stage to discredit the new constitution, castigate its emergency provisions and reject the legality of the tribunal itself. Ironically, the court case became itself a privileged platform to advance the very thing that the defendant was on trial for: advocating separatism (Edrisinha et al 2008: 260–272). The court proceedings fizzled out when the government realized it had shot itself in the foot and withdrew the case. When new parliamentary elections followed in 1977, the Tamil nationalist party participated by informing its voters that the vote should be considered an opportunity for the popular endorsement of the Vaddukoddai resolution. In other words, their performative practice turned the elections into a referendum on a separate state. Tamils voted overwhelmingly in support of the nationalists, but the same election yielded a vast majority to the right-leaning Sinhala party, which pushed through its own presidential constitution, followed by a rapid a violent escalation and the 1983 anti-Tamil pogroms, which brought Sri Lanka to the precipice of civil war.

When we considered the dynamics of the 1970s from a formal institutional perspective, Sri Lanka experienced a sequence of elections and constitutional reforms. The Tamil parties voiced their concern, withdrew from parliament, broke the law by advocating separatism but were not convicted, and then got re-elected to parliament with a campaign centred on Tamil nationalist rhetoric. No big deal. Happens all the time. However, given the heated political dynamics and public sentiments and the resulting escalation into civil war, such a formal interpretation clearly misses the point. A performative perspective helps us see that a demonstrative walk-out from parliament is no withdrawal from politics but an escalation thereof. And while neither Chelvanayakam's by-election nor the 1977 general election were a referendum (respectively rejecting the 1972 constitution and endorsing a separatist course), the positioning of the Tamil nationalist party turned these elections into a political moment that resembled such a plebiscite, thus adding a gloss of democratic legitimacy to the party's demand for an independent Tamil state. Similarly, the court case against Amirthalingam became a performative stage to advance a meticulous legal-political case for Tamil self-determination. It became an arena where advocates of Tamil nationalism could dress up and perform like statesmen to articulate their aspirations in an uninterrupted manner in the national and international spotlights.

Performing the sovereign experiment of a nascent state

With the 1980s escalation of the war, armed Tamil youth militias wrested the political baton from Tamil parliamentarians. As that happened, the strategy of enacting transgressive politics from within Sri Lanka's institutional landscape mutated into a strategy of creating a different institutional landscape altogether. The sovereign experiment of gradually establishing Tamil Eelam – an independent homeland – began.

The LTTE became the dominant protagonist of Tamil nationalism in the mid-1980s. In that period, the Indian federal government attempted (unsuccessfully) to coerce the Sri Lankan government and the Tamil militants into a power-sharing arrangement using both military and diplomatic means. As part of that strategy, it tried to control the welter of Tamil militant groups with Machiavellian tactics. To avoid being outmanoeuvred, the LTTE violently crushed rival militant groups and subdued Tamil political parties. When the Indian army was forced to retreat in 1990, the LTTE gradually expanded its institutional experiment of governing the parts of Sri Lanka's north-east that it controlled. This nucleus of a state-to-come comprised a suite of bodies, departments, and legal institutions, as has been described by scholars of rebel governance in geography (Stokke 2006), political science (Mampilly 2011), and law (Provost 2021). Each of these studies offers a valuable and rich description by meticulously detailing the procedures and mandates of LTTE bodies with neat overviews, timelines, and organograms. This is very much in line with the image that the LTTE sought to project. But what such renditions fail to capture is the central dynamic of awe, amazement, and apprehension that surrounded the LTTE's sovereign experiment. For all the acting normal that the LTTE engaged in, the whole reason this experiment captured the imagination of so many was that it was not in fact normal at all. Tamil subjects were amazed, proud, angry, or scared (or all of these at the same time) because of the movement's ability to pull off what had seemed unthinkable. Just a few years earlier, this had been a group of boys on bicycles staging hit-and-run attacks; now they were running an incipient Tamil state with offices, uniforms, and national ceremonies in a territory sheltered from the Sri Lankan state.

The LTTE's state-building performance climaxed with the Norwegian-facilitated ceasefire and peace talks in the early 2000s. Norway's peace effort was highly internationalized due to the involvement of a Nordic monitoring mission, international 'co-chairs' to the peace process, and a welter of development donors. This offered the LTTE a conducive environment to continue its sovereign performance in the international arena. The ceasefire offered tacit acknowledgement of the LTTE and the territories it controlled. The movement consolidated its rule with official customs checkpoints at the border, and a rapid expansion of offices lining the main road in Kilinochchi, its provisional capital. LTTE delegations were flown around the world to consult with international actors. They presented themselves like diplomats and they sat on stage on par with the Sri Lankan government. The movement held international press conferences and fielded media teams to report on all the official visits and handshaking. A caravan of international convoys and foreign VIPs flurried into the Vanni (the northern region where the

LTTE's *de facto* state experiment was concentrated). This corroborated the movement's attempt at incremental normalization, and it was clear from the buzz in Colombo's expat circles that there was a high degree of fascination and amazement for the LTTE experiment. They were the talk of town. Among Tamils, the sense of pride and consternation took to a new level: 'the boys' (as they used to be known) were now flying round acting like suit-clad diplomats, shaking hands with dignitaries – without getting found out.

The target audiences of the LTTE, both locally and internationally, knew that the movement engaged a form of improvised theatre, but large constituents of their audience acted the part in this performative experiment (with the major exception of the Indian and US governments, which continued to proscribe the movement). Delegations came and went. Photo opportunities abounded. And in their interactions with LTTE representatives, visiting aid workers, journalists, diplomats, and academics engaged in 'as-if' politics (Wedeen 1999): treating the LTTE for what it enacted itself to be, a state-in-the-making. This form of participatory theatre was captivating, because a lot was at stake, and it was radically unclear how the plot would end. To stick with the theatrical idiom, the curtains could fall unexpectedly, and it was uncertain who would still be standing when they did – or indeed who would survive the next act. The LTTE dazzled some international observers with its sovereign performance, but it alarmed others. The implied legitimacy emanating from the LTTE's performance in international echelons with Norwegian support raised concern in New Delhi (which had definitively broken with the LTTE after the humiliating failure of India's peace efforts in the 1980s and the subsequent assassination of former Indian prime minister Rajiv Gandhi). When the peace process started to derail (in the period 2003 to 2006), a growing number of countries blacklisted the LTTE as a terrorist group.

As a consequence, the movement's international performance faced a rapidly changing audience. Its presentation as a legitimate state-like player was increasingly out of jar with international perceptions. When military violence escalated in 2006, the Sri Lankan government made steady territorial advances. The LTTE had shown little interest to expand its performative political overtures to the sphere of international law (unlike the Palestinian Authority, for example) and, in the absence of a strong regional human rights framework, the Tamil community living under LTTE rule was very vulnerable. Eleventh-hour protests aimed at the UNHRC proved ineffectual, and both the federal Indian government and Tamil Nadu rebuffed any pressure to step in. The LTTE was comprehensively defeated (see Price, this volume). Pictures of its slain *talaivar* (leader) Prabhakaran were put on display in the media. After the vanquishment of the LTTE, the government set out to inscribe its victory in the land in the former territories of Eelam with a triumphant Sinhala symbology of victory monuments, army camps, refashioned archaeological sites, and peasant colonization schemes.

One can dissect the institutional landscape established by the LTTE in the 1990s and 2000s from the perspective of rational governance. This yields an overview that matches the neat line-up of offices along the Kilinochchi main road, the hub of LTTE governance during the climax of its sovereign experiment in the early 2000s ceasefire period (Stokke 2006; Mampilly 2011). Similarly, one can seek to decipher the legal foundations of these institutions. These are clearly lacking in Sri Lankan domestic law, but one can resort to the norms and principles of international law to carve out some juridical space to countenance the LTTE's penal code, its courts, its law school, and its police (Provost 2021). Both perspectives have merit, but bereft of a performative interpretation, neither perspective accounts for the immense political energy around the LTTE's state-building effort. While it went to great lengths to normalize its governing efforts, its sovereign experiment derived potency from the fact that it was *extra*ordinary: a bold transgression of the legal and political strictures of the Sri Lankan state. It had a captivating and disciplining impact because it was capricious (Klem and Maunaguru 2017). LTTE institutions projected a form of power that could not be fully fathomed. There were rules, but they could change. Rule-breakers were subjected to the law, but outright traitors or enemies were not merely disciplined, they were obliterated. The bureaucratic trappings of the LTTE state-in-the-making were shrouded in a martial cult of violent force and sacrifice. And its defeat in 2009 was not simply followed by the resumption of normal governance. Rather, the Sri Lankan government staged the humiliating nemesis of Tamil sovereignty and reinscribed its power in the land.

Performing to international audiences after the 2009 Tamil defeat

The victory/defeat of 2009 comprises a monumental historical watershed for Sri Lanka, arguably even surpassing independence. The Sinhala-nationalist government of Mahinda Rajapaksa thrived on a discourse of crushing terrorism and kindling the flames of Sinhala-nationalist triumphalism. The remnants of the Tamil nationalist movement (the old guard of Tamil politicians) lacked the leverage that armed militancy had provided them, now that the LTTE was exterminated and its leader dead. They jostled to credibly present themselves as heirs of the struggle, but these were big shoes to fill. From the late 1990s onwards, Tamil parliamentarians had positioned themselves as extensions of the LTTE's sovereign experiment, as placeholders of the state-to-come. After the war, they could no longer draw on the LTTE's projection of power. How to pursue Tamil aspirations in a democratic landscape that allowed no space for it, without recourse to the LTTE? As a result of these constraints, the centre of gravity within Tamil nationalist politics shifted, as I will illustrate in this final section. The script shifted from projecting Tamil aspirations and prowess to the display of Tamil victimhood, expressed in the idiom of human rights. The performative cast shifted when diaspora actors came forward as primary protagonists. And as a result, the stage and the audience shifted to the international arena.

In terms of domestic political repertoires, this was a return to the 1970s: staging political aspirations and dissent through the fringes and affordance of Sri Lankan state institutions. This time, however, expectations were higher and political space was even more constrained. There were opportunity spaces that had not existed in the 1970s, though. One of these, if a highly ambivalent one, was the provincial council system. These councils were created through the Indian peace intervention of the 1980s. As a watered-down compromise of regional autonomy, Tamil nationalists despised the provincial council system as sabotage to the cause, and it never functioned as envisaged in the north and east. But after the war this system was arguably the only thing left, and if Tamil nationalists continued to boycott the provincial councils (as they had initially done), another faction would govern the northern and eastern provinces in their place, and they would risk rendering themselves irrelevant. As I argue elsewhere (Klem 2024: 127–155), the Tamil nationalists thus reluctantly participated in provincial elections and provincial governance, but they did so with a repertoire of anti-politics: a combination of oath-of-allegiance politics (rituals and ceremonial practices), politics of abstinence (electoral boycotts), and the performance of deficiency (governing the provincial councils to show their dysfunctionality).

This performance of deficiency was centrally oriented at an international audience: to show that everything had been tried but nothing had worked, and that it was thus warranted for international actors to step in and force the Sri Lankan government into a more reasonable compromise. Tamil diaspora groups were instrumental in delivering that message. The Sri Lankan Tamil diaspora is large and well-networked. During the war, the LTTE successfully percolated these dispersed communities to disseminate propaganda and extract financial resources. After the 2009 LTTE defeat, the diaspora community experienced fragmentation, disorientation, and internal competition (Thiranagama 2014), but the dominant groups managed to close the ranks on major issues. Within months after the LTTE defeat, diaspora groups initiated a (self-declared) procedure to establish a Transnational Constituent Assembly of Tamil Eelam (thus replicating the 1970s Sri Lankan government's skullduggery of unilateral constitution-making). Alongside this effort, these groups organized a global referendum in December 2009, by holding polls in countries with a large Sri Lankan Tamil community

(Canada, Australia, and several European countries). Over 99 per cent of the voters endorsed the statement:

> I aspire for the formation of the independent and sovereign state of Tamil Eelam in the north and east territory of the island of Sri Lanka on the basis that the Tamils in the island of Sri Lanka make a distinct nation, have a traditional homeland and have the right to self-determination.[1]

As with the above-mentioned 'referendums in the form of elections' of the 1970s, this plebiscite had no formal status. There was no voter list, so there was no way of calculating the turnout, and the polls excluded those who had the biggest stake, namely the Tamils living in Sri Lanka. Moreover, the poll comprised a statement that read like an oath of allegiance, an article of faith. Following the referendum, in May 2010, elections were held to populate the Transnational Constituent Assembly, which then yielded the declaration of a transnational government of Tamil Eelam.

From a formal institutional perspective, this was a non-entity, and the so-called referendum was a moot statement that made little sense because it lacked legal or political anchorage. But if we adopt such a vantage point and treat the poll as a non-event, how do we account for the significant amount of political excitement, spectacle, consternation, and dismay? The diaspora referendum powerfully staged the large transnational support base of Sri Lankan Tamil nationalism. It demonstrated that there was life for the Tamil struggle after the death of Velupillai Prabhakaran (the LTTE leader). It provided a channel to voice aspirations that the Sri Lankan democratic system had silenced. And it jumped scale from the national level, where space for Tamil aspirations had closed, to the international arena, where global legal and political norms could be leveraged to support the Tamil cause.

In synch with these efforts, the human rights community in Geneva emerged as the primary arena for Tamil nationalist politics. As a result of the immense human massacres in the final stages of the war (see Price, this volume), Sri Lanka attracted the attention of the UNHRC. During the final military campaign, the Sri Lankan government managed to counterpoise pressure from (mainly) European states, with an appeal to anti-terrorism and anti-colonial antipathy to Western norm-imposition on the Global South. The fact that Tamil activists continued to visibly align themselves with the LTTE, by then a proscribed terrorist organization in most Western countries, made it easy for Sri Lankan diplomats to discredit Tamil pleas. However,

---

[1] This text is widely available on the internet. See, for example, the Canadian Broadcasting Cooperation, www.cbc.ca/news/canada/toronto/tamil-canadians-vote-for-independent-state-in-sri-lanka-1.810846. The referendum was held in December 2009.

the legal-discursive battle over investigating war crimes by the Sri Lankan military continued in the years to follow. Every time the UNHRC turned its spotlight on Sri Lanka, this provided civil society organizations with an occasion to lambast the government, and it allowed Tamil diaspora groups to rearticulate the discursive frame. They argued that the violence at the end of the war in fact amounted to genocide, and they succeeded in latching on a much broader range of concerns than the forensic scrutiny of military conduct in 2008 and 2009.

In the immediate post-war years, the UNHRC debates thus emerged as a primary political stage. They were covered in detail by Sri Lankan media and there was a great deal of social media activism around it. This brought Tamil diaspora groups further to the forefront, thus weakening the positioning of Tamil politicians as the primary bulwark against the Sri Lankan state. One Swiss-based Tamil diaspora group claimed to have established a 'permanent representation for Tamil Eelam' in Geneva, and it successfully claimed consultative status with the UN Economic and Social Council (Thurairajah 2022: 35). Shifting Tamil nationalist politics to the UNHRC arena required adjustments. The narrative of Tamil separatist aspirations – with its routine references to the historical canon of the 'liberation struggle', to the heroism of the LTTE and to the right of self-determination – was inapt for the legal idiom that prevails in the UNHRC's periodic reviews. This narrative was therefore translated into the language of individual victimhood and human rights (Thurairajah 2022), which comprised different terminology, different symbols, and different evidence. Victim reports by selected individuals who had suffered the government's final military campaign became a vital discursive currency, while adulated leaders and martyrs seeped out of the plot. The new narrative required a severance from the LTTE. The movement's atrocious human rights record obstructed the rehinging of Tamil aspirations in human rights terms.

From an orthodox vantage point of international law, UNHRC debates occur within the firm clasp of the human rights framework. It designates space for civil society actors to hold states accountable to the treaties and covenants that they have ratified. Post-war Tamil activism shows that such an arena of international law also affords a stage for highly political performative interventions, where the language and protocols of human rights law are co-opted into an ethno-nationalist script aimed at advancing aspirations of self-determination and separatism.

Conclusions and implications

The examples from Sri Lanka's long history of conflict that I have discussed in this chapter can all be discussed from a formal institutional perspective. General elections serve to mandate the composition of parliament; a tribunal seeks to adjudicate unlawful propagation of separatism; the self-declared departments of the LTTE have no legal authority; their courts lack validity; a self-invented global diaspora referendum is an oxymoron; and attempts to abuse UNHRC debates for nationalist politics are a breach of human rights principles. However, in each of these cases, such a formalistic reading misses the point in terms of understanding what belligerents seek to accomplish, how they present their claims, how their acts are understood, and what political implications they have. A performative perspective helps us see that elections can embody the political energy of a referendum. A tribunal against separatism can be turned into a stage to advance it. Domestic and international audiences adopt an understanding of LTTE departments and courts as tentacles of a state-in-the-making. These institutions may lack an accepted legal basis, but they gain implied forms of recognition and, as such, they project an anticipation of graduating into a legally valid and politically recognized entity in the future. The post-war referendum among Tamil diaspora had no status, but it powerfully exhibited transnational support for Tamil aspirations. And the staging of Tamil victimhood in the UNHRC arena converted legal deliberations into political pressure.

These observations matter beyond the idiosyncrasies of the Sri Lankan case. My central claim – that the sovereign experimentation of Tamil nationalists must be understood as a radical form of sovereign mimicry, where a probationary institutional architecture is developed first and legal roots may then be grown later – resonates with scholarship in other parts of the world. The contradictions around LTTE institutions match Bryant and Hatay's (2020) analysis of the Turkish Republic of Northern Cyprus as a state enactment that simultaneously positions itself as fact and struggles against its own denial. Tamil nationalist attempts to gain implied recognition through these probationary tactics converge with the provisional stabilization of republican structures in Abkhazia (Prelz-Oltramonti 2017), north-east Syria (Jongerden and Akkaya 2013) and Transnistria (Bobick 2017).

Rather than attempting to settle the legal and political status of these aspirant sovereign states, the central analytical vantage point is that one can never quite be sure. Given the murky self-referential schemes of legitimation that underpin state sovereignty, we lack credible yardsticks to adjudicate assertions of sovereign statehood. What we observe are probationary experiments with institutional mimicry that encroach on established states. Whether or not these efforts will in hindsight prove to have been part of a legitimate state-building trajectory culminating in a legal and recognized state remains to be seen. The ambiguous non-yet-known validity of an entity like Taiwan or South Ossetia today, or Tamil Eelam during the war years, is no sign of our analytical deficiency; it is the point. It is because of this contingency that we see the dynamics that we see: institutional improvisation, struggles over implied recognition, awe and apprehension over self-declared authorities, and a continuous preoccupation with what might happen next. This of course leaves both the political entity and the people governed by it in a highly vulnerable position, because their plight depends in large measure on the degree to which international audiences buy their performative claims.

The implications of that contingency stand out in stark relief in the Sri Lankan case. As a defeated experiment in separatism, the plight of the Tamil nationalist movement resonates with the current dynamic in the recaptured territory of Nagorno Karabakh. And it highlights what is at stake for other states-in-the-making and, as such, it accounts for the anxiety around state conduct in Northern Cyprus, north-eastern Syria, and other politically unsettled territories. Everything that happened in the name of LTTE law, with the figure of Prabhakaran as its ultimate referent, retrospectively became null and void. During the tragic massacres in the final months of the war, Tamil nationalist claims to sovereignty offered neither political nor legal recourse, and the vulnerable nature of the LTTE's *de facto* state became exposed: the LTTE was obliterated, and the Tamil community suffered the biggest breach of human rights in modern Sri Lankan history. The violence deployed to crush the LTTE retrospectively became law-making violence that was foundational to the reasserted constitutional democratic order of the Sri Lankan state. Yet, as I have shown, the performative repertoires of sovereign aspiration do not simply end when an emerging *de facto* state is erased. They yield new forms of mimicry and citational practice, which may travel to new political arenas, with a not-yet-known outcome.

Acknowledgements

The author gratefully acknowledges the support from the many Sri Lankans who enabled this inquiry and the constructive feedback from the editors and fellow chapter authors of this book. This chapter is in part based on research conducted with funding from the Australian Research Council (grant number DE180101161). The conceptual reflections, participation in author workshops and writing were enabled by a grant from the Swedish Science Council (grant number 2020-03318_3).

References

Achniotis, P. (2021). Sovereign Days: Imagining and Making the Catalan Republic from Below. In M. Reeves and R. Bryant (eds), *The Everyday Lives of Sovereignty: Political Imagination beyond the State*. Ithaca: Cornell University Press, 175–196.

Anghie, A. (1999). Finding the Peripheries: Sovereignty and Colonialism in Nineteenth Century International Law. *Harvard International Law Journal*, 40 (1), 3–71.

Banerjee, M. (2014). *Why India Votes?* London: Routledge.

Bertrand, R., Briquet, J.-L. and Pels, P. (eds) (2007). *Cultures of Voting: The Hidden History of the Secret Ballot.* London: Hurst.

Bhabha, H. (1994). *The Location of Culture.* London: Routledge.

Bhungalia, L. (2020). Laughing at Power: Humor, Transgression, and the Politics of Refusal in Palestine. *Environment and Planning C: Politics and Space*, 38, 387–404.

Bloemraad, I. (2018). Theorising the Power of Citizenship as Claims-Making. *Journal of Ethnic and Migration Studies*, 44 (1), 4–26.

Bobick, M. (2017). Sovereignty and the Vicissitudes of Recognition: Peoplehood and Performance in De facto State. *PoLAR: The Political and Legal Anthropology Review*, 40 (1), 158–170.

Brilmayer, L. (1989). Consent, Contract, and Territory. *Minnesota Law Review*, 1795, 1–35.

Bryant, R. and Hatay, M. (2020). *Sovereignty Suspended: Building the So-Called State.* Philadelphia: University of Pennsylvania Press.

Byrne, S. (ed.) (2021). *Identity and Nation in 21st Century Catalonia: El Procés.* Cambridge: Cambridge Scholars Publishing.

Caspersen, N. (2012). *Unrecognized States: The Struggle for Sovereignty in the Modern International System.* Cambridge: Polity Press.

Degregori, C. (2012). *How Difficult It Is to Be God: Shining Path's Politics of War in Peru, 1980–1999.* Madison: University of Wisconsin Press.

Dimova, R. and Cojocaru, L. (2013). Contested Nation-Building within the International 'Order of Things': Performance, Festivals and Legitimization in South-Eastern Europe. *History and Anthropology*, 24 (1), 1–12.

Edrisinha, R., Mario Gomez, V.T. Thamilmaran and Welikala, A. (2008). *Power-Sharing in Sri Lanka: Constitutional and Political Documents 1926–2008.* Colombo and Berlin: Centre for Policy Alternatives and Berghof Foundation for Peace Support.

Gilmartin, D., Price, P. and Ruud, A.E. (eds) (2020). *South Asian Sovereignty: The Conundrum of Worldly Power.* London: Routledge.

Goffman, E. (1959). *The Presentation of Self in Everyday Life.* New York: Doubleday Anchor.

Hansen, T.B. (2021). Sovereignty in a Minor Key. *Public Culture*, 33 (1), 41–61.

Hansen, T.B. and Stepputat, F. (2005). *Sovereign Bodies: Citizens, Migrants, and States in the Postcolonial World.* Princeton: Princeton University Press.

Jongerden, J. and Hamdi Akkaya, A. (2013). Democratic Confederalism as a Kurdish Spring: The PKK and the Quest for Radical Democracy. In M. Ahmed and M. Gunter (eds), *The Kurdish Spring: Geopolitical Changes and the Kurds.* Costa Mesa: Mazda Publishers, 163–185.

Ker-Lindsay, J. (2015). Engagement without Recognition: The Limits of Diplomatic Interaction with Contested States. *International Affairs*, 91 (2), 267–285.

Klem, B. (2012). In the Eye of the Storm: Sri Lanka's Front-Line Civil Servants in Transition. *Development and Change*, 43 (3), 695–717.

Klem, B. (2015). Showing One's Colours: The Political Work of Elections in Post-War Sri Lanka. *Modern Asian Studies*, 49 (4), 1091–1121.

Klem, B. (2024). *Performing Sovereign Aspirations: Tamil Insurgency and Postwar Transition in Sri Lanka*. Cambridge: Cambridge University Press.

Klem, B. and S. Maunaguru (2017). Insurgent Rule as Sovereign Mimicry and Mutation: Governance, Kingship and Violence in Civil Wars. *Comparative Studies in Society and History*, 59 (3), 629–656.

Kyris, G. (2022). State Recognition and Dynamic Sovereignty. *European Journal of International Relations*, 28 (2), 287–311.

Lightfoot, S. (2021). Decolonizing Self-Determination: Haudenosaunee Passports and Negotiated Sovereignty. *European Journal of International Relations*, 27 (4), 971–994.

Little, A. (2020). The Politics of Makarrata: Understanding Indigenous–Settler Relations in Australia. *Political Theory*, 48 (1), 30–56.

Mampilly, Z. (2011). *Rebel Rulers: Insurgent Governance and Civilian Life during War*. Ithaca: Cornell University Press.

McConnell, F. (2016). *Rehearsing the State: The Political Practices of the Tibetan Government-in-Exile*. Chichester: Wiley Blackwell.

Michelutti, L., Hoque, A., Martin, N., Picherit, D., Rollier, P., Ruud, A.E., and Still, C. (2018). *Mafia Raj: The Rule of Bosses in South Asia*. Stanford: Stanford University Press.

Navaro-Yashin, Y. (2007). Make-Believe Papers, Legal Forms and the Counterfeit: Affective Interactions between Documents and People in Britain and Cyprus. *Anthropological Theory*, 7 (1), 79–98.

Ochoa Espejo, P. (2020). *On Borders: Territories, Legitimacy, and the Rights of Place*. Oxford: Oxford University Press.

Paley, J. (ed.) (2008). *Democracy: Anthropological Approaches*. Santa Fe: School of Advanced Research Press.

Piliavsky, A. (ed.) (2014). *Patronage as Politics in South Asia*. Cambridge: Cambridge University Press.

Prelz Oltramonti, G. (2017). Trajectories of Illegality and Informality in Conflict Protraction. *Caucasus Survey*, 4 (3), 85–101.

Provost, R. (2021). *Rebel Courts: The Administration of Justice by Armed Insurgents*. Oxford: Oxford University Press.

Reeves, M. and Bryant, R. (eds) (2021). *The Everyday Lives of Sovereignty: Political Imagination beyond the State*. Ithaca: Cornell University Press.

Rutherford, D. (2012). *Laughing at Leviathan: Sovereignty and Audience in West Papua*. Chicago: Chicago University Press.

Simpson, A. (2014). *Mohawk Interruptus: Political Life across the Borders of Settler States*. Durham: Duke University Press.

Sosnowksi, M. and Klem, B. (2023). Legal Identity in a Looking-Glass World: Documenting Citizens of Aspirant States. *Citizenship Studies*, 27 (7), 761–778.

Stokke, K. (2006). Building the Tamil Eelam State: Emerging State Institutions and Forms of Governance in LTTE-Controlled Areas in Sri Lanka. *Third World Quarterly*, 27 (6), 1021–1040.

Spencer, J. (2007). *Anthropology, Politics, and the State: Democracy and Violence in South Asia*. Cambridge: Cambridge University Press.

Thiranagama, S. (2014). Making Tigers from Tamils: Long-Distance Nationalism and Sri Lankan Tamils in Toronto. *American Anthropologist*, 116 (2), 265–278.

Thurairajah, T. (2022). Performing Nationalism: The United Nations Human Rights Council (UNHRC). and Sri Lankan Tamil Diasporic Politics in Switzerland. *The Geographical Journal*, 188, 28–41.

Weber, C. (1995). *Simulating Sovereignty: Intervention, the State and Symbolic Exchange*. Cambridge: Cambridge University Press.

Wedeen, L. (1999). *Ambiguities of Domination: Politics, Rhetoric, and Symbols in Contemporary Syria*. Chicago: Chicago University Press.

Whelan, F. (1983). Prologue: Democratic Theory and the Boundary Problem. *Nomos*, 25, 13–47.

Wilson, A. (2016). *Sovereignty in Exile: A Saharan Liberation Movement Governs*. Philadelphia: University of Pennsylvania Press.

Wilson, A.J. (1994). *S.J.V. Chelvanayakam and the Crisis of Sri Lankan Tamil Nationalism, 1947–1977: A Political Biography*. London: Hurst.

PART III

Contesting and Constructing States at International Courts

9

Contested States Framed by the European Court of Human Rights

Anne Lagerwall

Introduction

Life in contested states undoubtedly exerts a form of fascination. This curiosity goes beyond the academic community of political scientists and international lawyers to which the authors in this book largely belong. Among others, photographers have documented and questioned what life can look like in a state that exists in reality, if not formally.

For his project *De Facto Transnistria* shown in 2015, Belgian photographer Thomas van den Driessche visited the self-proclaimed Republic of Pridnestrovia during the celebration of the 25th anniversary of its independence. One can read on the website of the artist that 'this small territory located mostly between the Dniester River and the Ukrainian west border (half million inhabitants), has acquired all the attributes of a state (money, passport, parliament, government, hymn, etc) but without obtaining any international recognition' (van den Driessche 2015). Spanish photographer Alvaro Deprit had visited Nagorno-Karabakh a few years before for a similar project entitled *Black Garden* (Deprit 2010). Commenting on his photographs, Dana Stolzgen explains in *Burn Magazine* that:

> Inside the narrow valleys of the Caucasus Mountains there is a country not appearing in the maps: Nagorno-Karabakh, which name – a mixed of Russian, Turkish and Persian languages – means Mountainous Black Garden. This self-proclaimed republic is the result of a cruel conflict – 20 to 30 thousand victims – that started in 1988, when its majority Armenian population started demanding the independence from the Soviet Republic of Azerbaijan. People in Karabakh try to survive

as they can. The recognition of Kosovo's independence by Western powers as the recognition by Russia of South Ossetia and Abkhazia – two secessionist regions of Georgia – are the facts that made the Karabakhians think they could become a real country. (Stolzgen 2010)

Norwegian photographer Jonas Bendiksen had also developed a project in 2005 on yet another experience. His work entitled *Abkhazia: A Vacation in a Non-Existent Country* was notably prompted by the fact that '[he] was drawn to the ambiguity of life in a place not marked on a map' as he explains for his agency Magnum Photos. He pursued his research in Transnistria as well as Nagorno-Karabakh, and a series of photographs shot during seven years was published in a book entitled *Satellites* (Bendiksen 2006), which was depicted on the editor website as 'un voyage photographique dans des pays qui n'existent pas officiellement'. In 2019, Estonian photographer Silvia Pärmann finalized a project entitled *The Countries That Do Not Exist* (Pärmann 2020), introduced by the Juhan Kuus Documentary Photo Centre on its website as a project that

> follows everyday life in the countries and regions that have all the trappings of a real country – they have governments and an independent spirit, quite often their own currency and military, and sometimes they even issue visas and stamp passports on the border – but they don't officially exist. For various reasons, they are not allowed representatives in the United Nations and are ignored by most governments.

All these projects vary in style and content, a variation that might be understood in relation to the photographers' respective aesthetics and personal interests to the situations depicted but also to the characteristics of the situations themselves. Despite these differences, the projects share the intention to reveal what life may look like for the inhabitants of these contested states. By showing that life goes on in these places with its daily struggles and its joyful moments, the photographs somehow counter the sense of crisis or exceptionality which might accompany our understanding of such situations.

In *De Facto – Transnistria,* Thomas van den Driessche reveals a luminous reality, devoid of violence and brutality (van den Driessche 2015). The difficulties experienced by the inhabitants are not concealed, but there is calm, if not hope, emerging from his images. The aesthetics of Alvaro Deprit (2010) in *Black Garden* is very different – dark and disquieting. The pictures are shadowy, deserted, and convey a sense of despair, as if the photographer wanted to underline the uncertainties linked to the fate of Nagorno-Karabakh. You can nonetheless also distinguish roads and windows, signalling openings that might lead the inhabitants to better lives.

Alvaro Deprit (2010) wishes that one day they could have a 'real country'. Jonas Bendiksen (2015), as his editor puts it, adopts 'a look that is sometimes caustic, sometimes serious, always poetic at this troubled heritage'. His photographs translate the harsh conditions of existence, but also portray life with beauty and humour in what looks like stolen moments of laughter and joy. Silvia Pärmann seeks to unravel the interactions between people and offers a glance at how they relate to their environment. Looking at all these photographs, one might easily come to the conclusion that the people portrayed should enjoy the stability necessary to their well-being, a stability that could eventually be brought about by a universally recognized state. To that extent, the photographers take part in a conversation reminiscent of that entertained by international lawyers as well as international courts and tribunals as to the status of these contested states (Czaplinski and Kleczkowska 2019).

In her essays collected in a book relating to the images of wars, Judith Butler highlights the necessity of paying attention to the ways in which such images are framing our understanding of violence and its victims, by identifying what and who is pictured and what and who is left out of the images (Butler 2010). The photographs collected in the various projects mentioned above were made *in situ* and consequently depict the people living in these places today. People coerced to flee these territories during past or more contemporary conflictual episodes are thus absent. And so is, to a large extent, the violence that helped empowering decades ago the *de facto* authorities presently in control of the concerned territories, including the political and military violence used by third states. Could Judith Butler's invitation to reflect on frames of war be extended to decisions adopted by courts and tribunals in relation to events occurring on territories that once were – and sometimes still are – war-torn zones?

Since the 1990s, human rights violations committed on territories claimed or effectively controlled by contested states have been brought to the attention of the European Court of Human Rights (ECtHR). The ECtHR has been asked to rule on alleged violations committed in the 'Turkish Republic of Northern Cyprus', the 'Moldovan Republic of Transnistria', the 'Republic of Nagorno-Karabakh', the 'Republics of Abkhazia and South Ossetia', as well as the 'Peoples' Republics of Donetsk and Lugansk' in eastern Ukraine. How does the ECtHR frame these contested states? Are they understood as *de facto* authorities resulting from military operations pursued in violation to the UN Charter that should be, for that reason, denied any form of recognition? Are they shown as effective entities whose legislative, executive, and judicial organs should be viewed as functioning organs capable of guaranteeing or violating human rights of the concerned populations?

Through an analysis of its case-law, the contribution seeks to reveal how the ECtHR frames these contested states. It tends to show that, formally, the ECtHR does not recognize them as states, and sometimes explicitly denies the validity of their constitutional order (1). But the ECtHR nevertheless accepts to take into consideration their legislative, executive, or judiciary powers in certain circumstances, following lines of reasoning whose evolution or circumvolution might illustrate the uneasy position of a court called upon to study entities that exist in reality, but not formally (2). To that extent, their portrayal by the ECtHR may be perceived as legitimizing their existence. But the ECtHR has also denied recognition to the legal order of *de facto* entities because it was not deemed compatible with the tradition of human rights embodied in the European Convention of Human Rights. To decide that the juridical order of contested states might be considered as compatible with the European Convention tradition could, in principle, lead the ECtHR to monitor their conduct according to the same standards that the court uses in relation to states enjoying a perfectly valid title of sovereignty on their territory, as if the unlawful character of *de facto* authorities supported by a third state in violation of the UN Charter was irrelevant. Such a framing of contested states prompts troubling questions as to the role played by human rights in consolidating the *fait accompli* of military interventions and occupations, which certainly deserve attention.

Formally framing contested states as entities that should be denied recognition

The authority of contested states brought to the attention of the ECtHR has been established and maintained through military interventions by third states launched and pursued in violation of the principle prohibiting states to use force (Corten 2021, Corten and Ruys with Hofer 2017). This explains why the ECtHR has refused to endorse their independence and has generally recalled the identity of the legitimate government of the concerned territories. Without being too explicit on the unlawful character of *de facto* authorities, the ECtHR has revealed the extent to which they have always been, and still are, dependent on third states. In that, the ECtHR adopts a position that can be viewed in light of a duty firmly established in customary international law, a duty 'not to recognize as lawful any situation created by a serious breach' of fundamental principles of international law such as the prohibition to use force in international relations (International Law Commission 2001; Christakis 2006). But this position can also be understood in relation to the limits of the ECtHR's jurisdiction. The ECtHR can only determine whether states parties to the European Convention on Human Rights are responsible for human rights violations and may hold a state responsible for what occurs in these places, only if it can be proven that the state enjoyed an effective control over the territory or the victims of the said violations.

Framing the 'Turkish Republic of Northern Cyprus' as totally dependent on Turkey

The first prominent case in which the ECtHR was confronted with a *de facto* authority was the application brought by Titina Loizidou in the 1990s in relation to events occurring in the 'Turkish Republic of Northern Cyprus' (TRNC). Loizidou had been prevented from accessing her properties in Kyrenia by the Turkish forces stationed in the northern part of Cyprus since 1974 as a reaction to the *coup* ordered by the military junta in Greece. She argued that, as long as she could not enjoy her possessions peacefully and build her family house on the land she owned, her right to property as well as her right to private and family life was breached by Turkey. Turkey was claiming to have no responsibility whatsoever in the events taking place in the TRNC, a perfectly sovereign state. For Ankara, the TRNC had a constitution whose Article 159 provided that all property found 'abandoned' in the north was the property of the state. For that reason, there could not have been any violation of Loizidou's right to property or private and family life.

The ECtHR thus had to determine if the TRNC constitution could have validly given it a title of property on Loizidou's land. In its decision, the ECtHR took note of the UN Security Council resolutions considering the declaration to create the TRNC invalid and calling upon states not to recognize any Cypriot state other that the Republic of Cyprus (UN Doc. S/RES/541 1983, UN Doc. A/RES/550 1984). The ECtHR underlined that the Committee of Ministers of the Council of Europe had condemned the proclamation of independence and called upon states to deny any recognition to the TRNC, further joined by the European Community and the Commonwealth Heads of Government. In the light of these statements, the ECtHR considered that the TRNC could not be recognized as a state under international law and that its constitution was invalid:

> [I]t is evident from international practice and the various, strongly worded resolutions referred to above [...] that the international community does not regard the TRNC as a State under international law and that the Republic of Cyprus has remained the sole legitimate Government of Cyprus – itself, bound to respect international standards in the field of the protection of human and minority rights. Against this background the Court cannot attribute legal validity for purposes of the Convention to such provisions as Article 159 of the fundamental law on which the Turkish Government rely. (*Loizidou v Turkey* 1996 § 44)

This framing of the TRNC was reaffirmed by the ECtHR in every case that was brought to its attention since, systematically recalling that the government of Cyprus remains the sole legitimate government of the island (*Cyprus v Turkey* 2001 § 61, *Foka* 2008 § 84, *Demopoulos* 2010 § 96).

In the *Loizidou* case, and later in other cases, the ECtHR also described the extent to which the creation of the TRNC was subsequent to the invasion of the island by the Turkish troops in 1974. The ECtHR stated that Turkish armed forces of more than 30,000 personnel were stationed throughout Northern Cyprus and controlled the entire territory. This enabled the ECtHR to hold Turkey responsible for many of the alleged violations of the European Convention on Human Rights occurring in the TRNC.

Framing the 'Moldovan Republic of Transnistria' as totally dependent on Russia

The ECtHR was also invited to determine whether violations of human rights had occurred in the 'Moldovan Republic of Transnistria' (MRT), a *de facto* entity established in eastern Moldova since 1991 with the military assistance of Russia. Four Moldovan nationals, Mr Ilascu, Mr Lesco, Mr Ivantoc, and Mr Petrov-Popa, had been arrested, sentenced, imprisoned, and ill-treated in Tiraspol for political activities that were condemned as terrorism by a Transnistrian court following a procedure that was, according to the four applicants, contrary to their right to security and to a fair trial guaranteed by Articles 5 and 6 of the European Convention on Human Rights. They argued that both Moldova and Russia were responsible for what they endured, the former for not taking the necessary measures to secure their release promptly, the latter for being accountable of any decision taken by the MRT given the political, economic, and military support it provided to the MRT, including the assistance of the 14th Army of the military district of Odessa. Several thousand Russian soldiers, infantry units, and artillery were deployed in eastern Moldova in order to secure the MRT independence proclaimed by the Supreme Council in August 1991. Around 2,000 soldiers remained in the region after the conflict, positioned between Moldovan security forces and Transnistrian separatists during the 1991–1992 clashes, as part of a plan aimed at easing particularly tense hostilities. This explains why it was soldiers of the 14th Army who arrested and transferred Ilascu and his comrades to the Transnistrian authorities in June 1992. Before the ECtHR, Russia merely observed that the only legitimate government was the Moldovan government and that only Moldova could be held responsible for what had happened in Transdniestria as it was an integral part of its territory. Russia also argued that it did not enjoy any control over the region and that its troops remained stationed there with the consent of Moldova. Moldova affirmed, on the contrary, that it could not be held responsible for the fate of the applicants as its authorities were unable to exert any form of control over the events taking place or the people present in the region, which was *de facto* administered by the MRT regime backed by Russia.

In its decision, the ECtHR pictured the MRT as 'a region of Moldova which proclaimed its independence in 1991 but is not recognized by the international community' (*Ilascu and others v Moldova and Russia* 2004 §§ 2 and 30). The ECtHR underlined that 'the Moldovan Government, the only legitimate government of the Republic of Moldova under international law, does not exercise authority over part of its territory, namely that part which is under the effective control of the MRT', an assessment shared by all parties (*Ilascu* § 330). The ECtHR concluded:

> [T]he 'MRT', set up in 1991–92 with the support of the Russian Federation, vested with organs of power and its own administration, remains under the effective authority, or at the very least under the decisive influence, of the Russian Federation, and in any event it survives by virtue of the military, economic, financial and political support given to it by the Russian Federation. (*Ilascu* § 392)

This framing of the MRT as an entity entirely dependent on the Federation of Russia was consistently sustained by the ECtHR in all subsequent cases brought in relation to alleged violations of human rights committed in this region (*Ivantoc* 2011 §§ 116–120; *Catan* 2012 §§ 119–121; *Mozer* 2016 § 110; *Lypovchenko and Halabudenco* 2024 §§ 85–87). This enabled the ECtHR to hold Russia responsible for many of the alleged violations before 2022, since Russia then ceased to be a member of the Council of Europe and a state party to the European Convention on Human Rights (Council of Europe 2022; Leach 2022).

Framing the 'Republic of Nagorno-Karabakh' as totally dependent on Armenia

As for the 'Nagorno-Karabakh Republic' (NKR), the ECtHR has been seized of several applications relating to acts occurring on the territory of the self-proclaimed entity. It remains unclear whether the ECtHR will receive more applications relating to this *de facto* state, as its last leader adopted in 2023 a decree abolishing all government institutions and declaring that the NKR would cease to exist on 1 January 2024. It was argued that this was necessary to halt the 2023 military operations launched by Azerbaijan to recover its sovereignty over the region, forcing nearly all ethnic Armenians to flee the region. The leader has since appeared to annul the decree, leaving the current status of the NKR uncertain.

In particular, the ECtHR was seized in 2005 by six Azerbaijani nationals: Mr Elkhan, Mr Chiragov, Mr Gebrayilov, Mr Hasanof, Mr

Pashayev, and Mr Gabrayilov. They alleged that they had been prevented from returning to the district of Lachin and enjoying their properties as well as their homes because Armenia was occupying this Azerbaijani district, thus violating their right to private and family life recognized in Article 8 of the European Convention on Human Rights as well as their right to private property codified in Article 1 of Protocol 1 to the Convention. The ECtHR recalled that Nagorno-Karabakh was a former oblast of the Azerbaijan Soviet Socialist Republic. After demands for the incorporation of Nagorno-Karabakh into Armenia were rejected by the Azerbaijan Socialist Soviet Republic and the Soviet Union, the NKR was established in 1991 and declared its independence from Azerbaijan. Before the ECtHR, Armenia denied exerting any control over the territories or the persons in question as they were under the administration of the NKR.

The ECtHR noted that 'the self-proclaimed independence of the "NKR" has not been recognized by any State or international organisation' (*Chiragov and others v Armenia* 2015 § 28). The ECtHR recalled that the UN Security Council had adopted several resolutions by which the Council requested the immediate withdrawal of all occupying forces from the occupied areas of Azerbaijan (UN Doc. S/RES/822 1993; UN Doc. S/RES/853 1993; UN Doc. S/RES/874 1993; UN Doc. S/RES/884 1993) and that the General Assembly had, a few years later, asked for 'the immediate, complete and unconditional withdrawal of all Armenian forces from all occupied territories of the Republic of Azerbaijan' (UN Doc. A/RES/62/243 2008). On the basis of reports and documents submitted during the proceedings, the ECtHR stated that Armenia, through its military presence and the provision of military equipment and expertise, had been deeply involved in the Nagorno-Karabakh conflict. In its decision, the ECtHR affirmed:

> Armenia, from the early days of the Nagorno-Karabakh conflict, has had a significant and decisive influence over the 'NKR', that the two entities are highly integrated in virtually all important matters and that this situation persists to this day. In other words, the 'NKR' and its administration survive by virtue of the military, political, financial and other support given to it by Armenia which, consequently, exercises effective control over Nagorno-Karabakh and the surrounding territories, including the district of Lachin. (*Chiragov* 2015 § 186)

This stance was later confirmed by the ECtHR in several cases relating to acts occurring in the NKR (*Zalyan* 2016 § 214; *Muradyan* 2016 § 126; *Mirzoyan* 2019 § 54; *Avanesyan* 2021 §§ 36–37; *Nana Muradyan* 2022 § 91–92; *Hovhannisyan and Karapetyan* 2023 §§ 59–62; *Dimaksyan* 2023 §§ 42–44; *Hamzayan* 2024 §§ 24–28; *Varyan* 2024 §§ 67–70). This enabled the ECtHR to hold Armenia responsible for alleged human rights violations occurring in Nagorno-Karabakh, some of which concerned Armenian servicemen deployed in the NKR. Several cases are still pending before the ECtHR, including two interstate applications relating to human rights violations occurring during the resurgence of the conflict in the 2020s.

Framing the 'Peoples' Republic of Donetsk and Luhansk' as totally dependent on Russia

More recently, the ECtHR was invited to look into alleged human rights violations taking place on the territories of the 'People's Republics of Donetsk' (DPR) and the 'People's Republics of Lugansk' (LPR) since the declaration of their independence from Ukraine in 2014. Ukraine lodged nearly a dozen applications against Russia, one concerning possible abductions by armed separatists of groups of children and their transfer to Russia, and another concerning the downing in 2014 of Malaysia Airlines Flight 17, causing the deaths of almost 300 people on board. Ukraine argued that Russia exerted effective control over the region at the time of the events, both directly and through subordinate local forces. This understanding was shared by the Netherlands, which had lodged an application together with Ukraine for the downing of the flight, as most of the victims were Dutch nationals. Russia denied having any control over the Donbas Republics, which were functioning as independent states, an independence later recognized by Russia days before the launch of the so-called special military operation in February 2022 (Putin 2022).

In presenting the circumstances in which the DPR and the LPR came to existence, the ECtHR recalled the condemnation of their creation subsequent to the so-called 'independence referendums' in 2014 (*Ukraine and the Netherlands v Russia* 2022 § 190). The ECtHR did not make an assessment of the unlawfulness of the situation, but set out the position of the Netherlands:

> On 11 May 2014, among widespread international condemnation, an 'independence referendum' was held in the separatist-controlled parts of Donetsk province. Ukraine's acting President called the result of the referendum a 'farce' and stated that the referendum 'will have no legal consequences except the criminal responsibility for its organisers'. The spokesperson of the United States' Department of State declared that the referendum was 'illegal under Ukrainian law … and an attempt to create further division and disorder'. The President of France stated that the referendum 'had no legitimacy and no legality' and that it was 'null and void'. The United Kingdom's Foreign Secretary stated that the referendum was 'illegal by anybody's standards'. The EU declared

the referendum illegal and refused to recognise the outcome. (*Ukraine and the Netherlands v Russia* 2022 § 298)

The ECtHR then focused on the relationship between the republics and Russia. After studying a vast amount of documents and material, the ECtHR asserted that Russian soldiers were present in the Donbass from 2014 and that Russia had a significant influence on the military strategy of the separatists, supplied weapons and other military material to them on a significant scale, engaged in cross-border artillery attacks at their requests, and provided political support as well as economic assistance. In the end, the ECtHR considered:

> The vast body of evidence above demonstrates beyond reasonable doubt that, as a result of Russia's military presence in eastern Ukraine and the decisive degree of influence and control it enjoyed over the areas under separatist control in eastern Ukraine as a result of its military, political and economic support to the separatist entities, these areas were, from 11 May 2014 and subsequently, under the effective control of the Russian Federation. (*Ukraine and the Netherlands v Russia* 2022 § 695)

This allowed the ECtHR to hold Russia responsible for the violations of several human rights taking place in the Donbass and to declare several grounds of the application admissible.

In sum, by refusing to recognize formally *de facto* entities and by underlining their dependence on third states, the ECtHR rather frames these entities as puppet states enjoying very little autonomy, if any, on the international scene on which the court deploys its jurisdiction. This, however, does not preclude the court from granting some validity to the acts adopted by their legislative, executive or judicial organs, thus fuelling to a certain extent their legitimacy, as we shall now see.

Framing the contested states as actors able to ensure the respect of human rights if their practice reflects the tradition of the Convention

The ECtHR may participate in strengthening the legitimacy of contested states when coming to the conclusion that their organs can be considered as actors able to ensure the respect of human rights as long as their practice reflects a tradition compatible with the Convention, as the ECtHR did in relation to the TRNC. The ECtHR did not reach the same conclusion with regard to the MRT, without excluding the possibility of that being the case one day, thus adopting a framework that does not come to definitive conclusion on *de facto* authorities given the unlawfulness of their creation.

Accepting acts adopted within a legal order which reflects the tradition of the Convention: the 'Turkish Republic of Northern Cyprus'

The TRNC was never recognized by the ECtHR, nor was its constitution considered as validly conferring rights. The ECtHR did not want, however, to draw from this assessment a general conclusion as to the invalidity of all acts adopted by its organs. In its judgment relating to Loizidou, the ECtHR rather recalled the limited scope of a rule invalidating acts adopted by an unlawful authority. Quoting the International Court of Justice, which had decided that acts adopted by South Africa in relation to Namibia – a territory that South Africa did not have any right to administer after its mandate came to an end in 1970 – the ECtHR recalled:

> The Court [...] does not consider it desirable, let alone necessary, in the present context to elaborate a general theory concerning the lawfulness of legislative and administrative acts of the 'TRNC'. It notes, however, that international law recognises the legitimacy of certain legal arrangements and transactions in such a situation, for instance as regards the registration of births, deaths and marriages, 'the effects of which can be ignored only to the detriment of the inhabitants of the territory'. (*Loizidou* 1996 § 45)

This enabled the ECtHR to consider that the courts set up in TRNC could be recognized as 'domestic remedies' within the meaning of the European Convention on Human Rights (*Cyprus v Turkey* 2001 §§ 86 and 90–98; *Djavit An v Turkey* 2003 §§ 30–37; Report of the European Commission on Human Rights 1999 §§ 124–125). The rationale grounding this position was expressed in the following terms:

> [T]he obligation to disregard acts of *de facto* entities is far from absolute. Life goes on in the territory concerned for its inhabitants. That life must be made tolerable and be protected by the *de facto* authorities, including their courts; and, in the very interest of the inhabitants, the acts of these authorities related thereto cannot be simply ignored by third States or by international institutions, especially courts, including this one. To hold otherwise would amount to stripping the inhabitants of the territory of all their rights whenever they are discussed in an international context, which would amount to depriving them even of the minimum standard of rights to which they are entitled. (*Cyprus v Turkey* 2001 § 96)

The ECtHR thus accepted the validity of acts adopted by the TRNC authorities even though the laws grounding the powers of such authorities were based on a constitution that the ECtHR had initially stressed had no legal validity, adopting a rather paradoxical approach that was underlined by dissenting judges in the following terms:

> In the first place, any consideration of remedies gives rise to the obvious difficulty that the entire court system in the 'TRNC' derives its legal authority from constitutional provisions whose validity the Court cannot recognise – for the same reasons that it could not recognise Article 159 in the *Loizidou* case – without conferring a degree of legitimacy on an entity from which the international community has withheld recognition. An international court should not consider itself free to disregard either the consistent practice of States in this respect or the repeated calls of the international community not to facilitate the entity's assertion of statehood. Secondly, the Court cannot examine the remedies of the 'TRNC' in a vacuum, as if it were a normal Contracting Party, where it can be assumed that courts are 'established by law' or that judges are independent and impartial (absent evidence to the contrary). To attribute legal validity to court remedies necessarily involves the Court in taking stand on whether the courts are 'established by law' – something the Court should avoid doing if it is to respect the illegal status of the 'TRNC' regime and the declared stance of the international community. It is true that the concept of 'established by law' is an autonomous one. However, the Court should avoid putting itself in a position where, for supposedly laudable reasons, it is tempted to fashion a semblance of legality out of a clearly illegal situation. (Partly dissenting opinion of Judge Palm joined by Judges Jungwiert, Levits, Pantiru, Kovler, and Marcus-Helmons, *Cyprus v Turkey* 2001)

The ECtHR maintained its position in the following cases. In *Xenides-Arestis*, the ECtHR endorsed a compensation mechanism available in the TRNC to persons who had lost their property even if one could say, as Mrs Xenides-Arestis did, that the law establishing this mechanism could not be taken into consideration since its authority derived from the 'invalid' constitution (*Xenides-Arestis* 2006 § 19). The ECtHR also decided that arrests, pre-detentions, and detentions carried out by the police of the TRNC could be considered as 'lawful' within the meaning of Article 5 of the European Convention on human rights. In *Foka v Turkey*, Mrs Foka alleged that, as the TRNC was not a state under international law, no deprivation of liberty carried out by its agents might be regarded as 'lawful'. But the ECtHR held that 'when as in the instant case an act of the "TRNC" authorities is in compliance with laws in force within the territory of northern Cyprus, those acts should in principle be regarded as having a legal basis in domestic law for the purposes of the Convention' (*Foka* 2008 § 84). This was confirmed in other cases (*Protopapa* 2009; *Asproftas* 2010 §§ 70–78; *Petrakidou* 2010 §§ 69–77).

By accepting acts of the TRNC as 'lawful' or 'established by law', the ECtHR participates in legitimizing its *de facto* authorities and it comes as no surprise that the TRNC itself invokes this case-law to that effect (Immovable Property Commission, https://tamk.gov.ct.tr/en-us/). Such reasoning does not entail, however, that any law, administrative act, or judicial decision adopted in an unlawfully established entity may be considered as 'lawful', as we shall now illustrate.

Refusing acts adopted within a legal order which does not reflect the tradition of the Convention: the 'Moldovan Republic of Transnistria'

In the *Ilascu* case, the ECtHR was invited to decide whether the conviction of Ilascu and his comrades by the Supreme Court of the MRT was in conformity with the Convention. Romania, as third-party intervener, stressed that 'the applicants' detention had no legal basis, since they had been sentenced by an unlawfully constituted court' (*Ilascu v Moldova and Russia* 2004 § 458). Addressing the question, the ECtHR considered:

> In certain circumstances, a court belonging to the judicial system of an entity not recognised under international law may be regarded as a tribunal 'established by law' provided that it forms part of a judicial system operating on a 'constitutional and legal basis' reflecting a judicial tradition compatible with the Convention, in order to enable individuals to enjoy the Convention guarantees. (*Ilascu* 2004 § 460)

To the ECtHR, such conditions were not fulfilled before the MRT's 'Supreme Court'. The only persons authorized to enter the courtroom were Moldovan nationals residing in Transnistria. Police officers and soldiers were present on the stage where the judges sat, and Ilascu together with his comrades were not allowed to speak to their lawyers unless police officers were present. The ECtHR highlighted that one could find on the bench of the MRT's Supreme Court a 28-years old lawyer appointed after only one year at the Moldovan Procurator General's Office. In these circumstances, the ECtHR found that none of the applicants could be said to have been convicted by a 'court', and that a sentence of imprisonment passed by such a judicial body could not be regarded as a 'lawful detention' ordered 'in accordance with a procedure prescribed by law' (*Ilascu* 2004 § 462). More generally, the ECtHR found:

The 'Supreme Court of the MRT' which passed sentence on Mr Ilascu was set up by an entity, which is illegal under international law and has not been recognised by the international community. That 'court' belongs to a system which can hardly be said to function on a constitutional and legal basis reflecting a judicial tradition compatible with the Convention. That is evidenced by the patently arbitrary nature of the circumstances in which the applicants were tried and convicted, as they described them in an account which has not been disputed by the other parties [...], and as described and analysed by the institutions of the OSCE. (*Ilascu* 2004 § 436)

The ECtHR thus draws from the unlawful character of the MRT under international law and its non-recognition by the international community conclusions that can be directly related to the ability of its organs to guarantee the respect for human rights. But it does not constitute either the only or the dominant factor in such determination, nor has it been identified by the ECtHR as a factor that should systematically be taken into consideration. In *Mozer*, which related to the detention and conviction of a person by MRT authorities, the ECtHR relativized the importance to be given to the unlawful character of the entity under international law and held:

[I]t cannot automatically regard as unlawful, for the limited purposes of the Convention, the decisions taken by the courts of an unrecognised entity purely because of the latter's unlawful nature and the fact that it is not internationally recognised [...]. It is insufficient to declare that the Convention rights are protected on a certain territory – the Court must be satisfied that such protection is also effective. A primary role in ensuring that such rights are observed is assigned to the domestic courts, which must offer guarantees of independence and impartiality and fairness of proceedings. Consequently, when assessing whether the courts of an unrecognised entity satisfy the test established in its *Ilascu and others* judgement, namely whether they 'form part of a judicial system operating on a 'constitutional and legal basis' [...] compatible with the Convention', the Court will attach weight to the question whether they can be regarded as independent and impartial and are operating on the basis of the rule of law. (*Mozer v Moldova and Russia* 2016 §§ 142 and 144)

These cases illustrate that the ECtHR may also participate in delegitimizing an entity when coming to the conclusion that its organs do not reflect a tradition compatible with the Convention. But the ECtHR does not consider it to be the case only because of the unlawfulness of the authority exerted by *de facto* states in the light of international law. The ECtHR rather builds a framework of its own to make this assessment by studying the effective capacity of the concerned organs to work in conformity with human rights standards.

Conclusion

If the logic behind the ECtHR's acceptance of the legal order grounding unlawfully created entities is understandable, one might still feel uneasy towards the form of validation offered by the ECtHR to a legal system that might be compatible with the Convention, but that was nonetheless put in place following a war waged in violation of international law. This uneasiness is further reinforced by the idea that such a reasoning leads the ECtHR to judge the conduct of a state unlawfully supporting a secessionist entity abroad in terms that are similar to those used in relation to a sovereign state acting within its own territory.

Interestingly, the ECtHR recently adopted a slightly different approach in the case between Ukraine and Russia concerning alleged human rights violations in Crimea, which has been annexed by Russia since 2014 (Czapliński 2014; Milano 2014). To the ECtHR, the Russian laws in force in Crimea could only be considered as 'lawful' in relation to Crimea if they were adopted in conformity with international humanitarian law and, more precisely, with the rules framing the rights and duties of an occupying power. That framework had not been respected:

> [W]hen the respondent State extended the application of its law to Crimea, it did so in contravention of the Convention, as interpreted in the light of international humanitarian law. Accordingly, Russian law cannot be regarded as 'law' within the meaning of the Convention and any administrative practice based on that law cannot be regarded as 'lawful' or 'in accordance with the law'. (*Ukraine v Russia re-Crimea* 2024 § 946)

The reliance by the ECtHR on international humanitarian law might provide a firmer criteria to help determine which laws, administrative acts, or judicial decisions the ECtHR could consider as 'lawful' in such situations of territorial occupations, a criteria that might prove easier to handle than that of a legal order 'reflecting the tradition of the Convention'. It does, however, still prompt the question of the desirability of developing a case-law legitimizing occupations created or maintained through unlawful uses of force, as long as the occupied territories remain effectively governed in conformity with international humanitarian law. What is left of the principle *ex injuria jus non oritur* under which the right cannot arise from a wrong? (Lagerwall 2016b)

References

Bendiksen, J. (2006). *Satellites*. Paris: Textuel.
Butler, J. (2010). *Frames of War: When Is Life Grievable?*. London: Verso.
Czapliński, W. (2014). The Crimean Crisis and the Polish Practice on Non-Recognition. *Questions of International Law-Zoom-out*, 73–84.
Czapliński, W. and Kleczkowska, A. (2019). *Unrecognized Subjects in International Law*. Warsaw: Scholar Publishing House Ltd.
Christakis, T. (2006). L'obligation de non-reconnaissance des situations créées par le recours illicite à la force ou d'autres actes enfreignant des règles fondamentales. In C. Tomuschat and J.-M. Thouvenin (eds), *The Fundamental Rules of the International Legal Order: Jus Cogens and Obligations Erga Omnes*. Leiden and Boston: Martinus Nijhoff Publishers.
Corten, O. and Ruys, T., with Hofer, A. (2017). *The Use of Force in International Law – a Case-Based Approach*. Oxford: Oxford University Press.
Corten, O. (2021). *The Law against War*. 2nd edn. Oxford: Hart Publishing.
Council of Europe (2022). Resolution CM/Res(2022)2 on the cessation of the membership of the Russian Federation to the Council of Europe, 16 March, https://rm.coe.int/0900001680a5da51.
Deprit, A. (2010). Black Garden. https://www.alvarodeprit.com/blackgarden.
ECtHR (1996). *Loizidou v Turkey*, 18 December.
ECtHR (2001). *Cyprus v Turkey*, 10 May.
ECtHR (2003). *Djavit An v Turkey*, 20 February.
ECtHR (2004). *Ilascu and others v Moldova and Russia*, 8 July.
ECtHR (2006). *Xenides-Arestis v Turkey*, 7 December.
ECtHR (2008). *Foka v Turkey*, 24 June.
ECtHR (2009). *Protopapa v Turkey*, 24 February.
ECHR (2010). *Demopoulos and others v Turkey*, 1 March.
ECtHR (2010). *Asproftas v Turkey*, 27 May.
ECtHR (2010). *Petrakidou v Turkey*, 27 May.
ECtHR (2011). *Ivantoc and others v Moldova and Russia*, 15 November.
ECtHR (2012). *Catan and others v Moldova and Russia*, 19 October.
ECtHR (2015). *Chiragov and others v Armenia*, 16 June.
ECtHR (2016). *Mozer v Moldova and Russia*, 23 February.
ECtHR (2016). *Zalyan and others v Armenia*, 17 March.
ECtHR (2016). *Muradyan v Armenia*, 24 November.
ECtHR (2019). *Mirzoyan v Armenia*, 23 May.
ECtHR (2021). *Receipt of applications in two inter-State cases related to the conflict in Nagorno-Karabakh*, Press Release, ECHR 046, 4 February.
ECtHR (2021). *Avanesyan v Armenia*, 20 July.
ECtHR (2022). *Nana Muradyan v Armenia*, 5 April.
ECtHR (2022). *Ukraine and the Netherlands v Russia*, 30 November.
ECtHR (2023). *Dimaksyan v Armenia*, 17 October.

ECtHR (2023). *Hovhannisyan and Karapetyan v Armenia*, 17 October.
ECtHR (2024). *Hamzayan v Armenia*, 6 February.
ECtHR (2024). *Lypovchenko and Halabudenco v. Moldova and Russia*, 20 February.
ECtHR (2024). *Varyan v Armenia*, 4 June.
ECtHR (2024). *Ukraine v Russia (re-Crimea)*, 24 June.
Lagerwall, A. (2016a). *Le principe ex injuria jus non oritur en droit international contemporain*. Bruxelles: Bruylant.
Lagerwall, A. (2016b). Les républiques auto-proclamées non reconnues, saisies par la photographie comme par le droit?, https://cdi.ulb.ac.be/defacto-blackgarden-droit-lagerwall/.
Leach, P. (2023). A Time of Reckoning? Russia and the Council of Europe, *Strasbourg Observers*, 17 March, https://strasbourgobservers.com/2022/03/17/a-time-of-reckoning-russia-and-the-council-of-europe/.
Milano, E. (2014). The Non-Recognition of Russia's Annexation of Crimea: Three Different Legal Approaches and One Unanswered Question. *Questions of International Law-Zoom-out*, 35–55.
Pärmann, S. (2020). The Countries that Do Not Exist, https://dokfoto.ee/en/uritused/silvia-parmann-riigid-mida-pole-olemas/.
Putin, V. (2022). President Putin discourse on the decision to recognize the Donetsk and Lugansk People's Republics. 21 February, http://en.kremlin.ru/events/president/news/67828.
Stolzgen, D. (2010) Black Garden. *Burn Magazine*, www.burnmagazine.org/essays/2012/02/alvaro-deprit-black-garden/.
UN Doc. S/RES/541 (1983).
UN Doc. A/RES/550 (1984).
UN Doc. S/RES/822 (1993).
UN Doc. S/RES/853 (1993).
UN Doc. S/RES/874 (1993).
UN Doc. S/RES/884 (1993).
UN Doc. A/RES/62/243 (2008).
Van den Driessche, T. (2015). De Facto Transnistria, http://thestoryinstitute.com/de-facto/.

10

Hide and Seek: Bracketing and Projecting the States of Kosovo and Palestine at International Courts

Janis Grzybowski

Introduction

'A State is not a fact in the sense that a chair is a fact', as James Crawford once put it (2006: 5). It is 'a legal status attaching to a certain state of affairs by virtue of certain rules or practices' (2006: 5). From a realist perspective in international relations, this insistence on status might appear to miss a reality of "power" beyond the legal and social construction of statehood (Krasner 1999).[1] Yet the attribution of legal status – or lack thereof – is not socially detached from political reality. It has in fact important consequences for the constitution and survival of states. As established in the chapters of this volume, this is why disagreements over contested states entail particular vulnerabilities (Grzybowski et al, Introduction to this volume). Parent states dismiss contested states as rebels or even terrorists (Chapters 1, 3 and 5, this volume); some third states instead prop them up against the parent state's formal sovereignty (Chapters 4 and 5, this volume); and representatives of contested states themselves try to persuade local and international audiences that they are states, declared or otherwise (Chapters 2, 6 and 8, this volume). Taiwan, Western Sahara, Nagorno-Karabakh, the Tamil Tigers, and pro-Russian separatists in Crimea and the Donbass have straddled, in different

---

[1] For a 'classical realist' approach to '*de facto* states', see Knotter 2023. On the *entanglement* of law and power in the social construction of statehood, see Koskenniemi 1994; Biersteker and Weber 1996; Weber 1998; Aalberts 2012; Grzybowski and Koskenniemi 2015; dos Reis and Grzybowski 2021.

ways and to different degrees, the line between state and non-state. But they *also* illustrate the consequences of international responses by third states and others that imply, grant, or deny them state status. Ultimately, to say that an entity is a state or not is intertwined with making it so. And these evaluations are often justified in the idiom of international law.

Yet by speaking this idiom to make sense of their positions, the speakers also invoke a particular professional field (Bourdieu 1986), and 'culture of formalism' (Koskenniemi 2001: 494) that come with their own – socially constructed and evolving – rules, authorities, and 'bounds of (non)sense' (Kratochwil 2014: 261). Not every argument is equally valid or, at least, not equally persuasive at every moment. Moreover, interpretations can also be subjected to *interpretations of interpretations*, notably by international courts.[2] To be sure, this does not relieve the courts themselves from making legal arguments that are liable to charges of politics, nor does it necessarily mark the end of a dispute or contestation. Yet the turn to courts yields authority in interpretation to the judges, and their opinions or decisions can in turn affect the political and everyday dimensions of the conflict, including in situations involving contested states. It is to these court rulings and opinions that I turn in this chapter to explore how claims, attributions, and assumptions of statehood are considered or, more often, bracketed in ways that still pick up, disseminate, and entangle them within and beyond the law. That is, I am interested in how courts become – often reluctant, limited, and indirect – co-producers of statehood claims.

This is perhaps not straightforward. By touching on fundamental questions of general international law, conflicts over sovereignty, state creation, self-determination, and territorial integrity escape the direct purview of most international courts. An obvious exception is the International Court of Justice (ICJ), 'established by the Charter of the United Nations as the principal judicial organ of the United Nations' (UN Charter, Statute of the International Court of Justice, Art. 1), which has a preeminent role in these matters and which, upon request by the United Nations General Assembly (UNGA), provided notable advisory opinions on questions of self-determination and independence regarding Namibia (ICJ 1971), Western Sahara (ICJ 1975), Kosovo (ICJ 2010), and the Chagos Archipelago (ICJ 2019). Even the ICJ often does not approach statehood questions head-on, however, but indirectly, as in the case of Kosovo (ICJ 2010) and in the advisory opinions on Palestine (ICJ 2004; 2024). Other courts with more specialized and limited mandates also have come to grapple with contested statehood in specific areas of international law, but arguably even more

---

[2] This is arguably the core 'function of international law' (Lauterpacht 2011) in international relations.

indirectly so. For instance, the European Court of Human Rights (ECtHR) has done so when considering in its human rights jurisprudence the legal obligations of *de facto* authorities in Northern Cyprus, Crimea, Transnistria, and elsewhere (see Lagerwall, Chapter 9 in this volume). Similarly, the International Criminal Court (ICC) has been confronted with questions about its own jurisdiction in 'the territory of Palestine' following the admission of Palestine to the court and the request to open investigations into alleged international crimes. Given the foundational role of statehood in international law and the general taken-for-granted assumption that we know exactly *which* entities are states (see Grzybowski 2017), practical legal questions in international criminal or human rights law can indirectly raise questions, or imply limited attributions, of statehood. Courts tend to be conservative in this regard but, as I discuss below, even big brackets and small concessions allude to something lurking behind, and it is not certain that it can be concealed and contained.

The challenges arising from these issues are usually approached either in a general manner, insisting on the importance of determining statehood under general international law, or in a functional and pragmatic manner, suggesting a restricted attribution of statehood for particular legal regimes and purposes while remaining seemingly agnostic about the state's – general – existence. Capitalizing on the tension between the two approaches, I suggest that a third perspective allows for exploring how the assuming, hinting at, and bracketing of state status ties in with wider legal and political chains of signification that imply and project the existence of these states, if often in rather ghostly shape. That is, while courts that reflect on situations involving contested states seem to stand above the politics of status controversies, they also intervene in them, and thereby in the performative enactment of states.

To make my case, I focus on the illustrative controversies about the status of Kosovo and Palestine, both of which show how technical legal analyses by international courts – notably the ICJ and the ICC – can be read as indirect interventions in ongoing political debates that also involve the conflict dynamics on the ground, international organizations, and third states. For all their important differences, the ICJ in Kosovo and the ICC in Palestine have struggled with a similar problem, namely that, for various reasons, they could not affirm the existence of contested states but at the same time had to assume them indirectly. By doing so, they avoided drawing the opposite conclusion, namely that the territories of Kosovo and Palestine are under the sovereignty of other states, that is, Serbia and Israel, respectively. In different ways, the two cases therefore also showcase the possible implications of status questions for the legality of violence. Projecting and contesting states affect where and by whom what use of violence is legally authorized.

State status – contestable, functional, performative

Modern international law presupposes states as both its main authors and subjects. Yet it also aims to regulate the creation of new states and their endowment with formal status and legal personality. States make international law and international law makes states, at least in the legal imagination.[3] If the traditional tension between declarative and constitutive approaches to state recognition is haunted by politics – the politics of supposed facts and discrete decisions, respectively – then post-Kelsen and post-Lauterpacht international law has aimed to control politics for good by insisting on the *legal* character of statehood.[4] As Crawford's (2006: 5) aforementioned quote explains, the apparent facticity of statehood is not reducible to any obvious physical markers but describes 'a legal status attaching to a certain state of affairs by virtue of certain rules and practices'. At the same time, the application of these rules and practices cannot depend on the interpretation of existing states alone and, in the case of state creation, on their recognition. Therefore, Crawford adds, 'the status of an entity as a State is, in principle, independent of recognition' (2006: 28).

This suggests that there is a genuinely legal way to determine statehood beyond recourse to recognition by other states and facts on the ground alone – weighing instead the right to self-determination, territorial integrity, and the prohibition of the use of force, among other rules and rights under international law (Crawford 2006), as also epitomized by the increasing role of international courts in developing and applying the law of statehood (Besson 2019). However, legal considerations of state creation have remained haunted by the intrusion of supposed facts and decisions, as well as the politics of legal interpretation (Koskenniemi 2005: 272–282; d'Aspremont 2013; Grzybowski 2017). As revisited in the introduction to the edited volume (Grzybowski et al, Introduction in this volume), questions about who has a right to external self-determination and whether the use of force is deemed illegal can be legally contested in concrete instances, whether successfully or not. Since 'there is *no centralized law of persons* in the international legal system' (Portmann 2010: 9), perceptions about which entities constitute states can therefore also fundamentally differ. 'Contested states' illustrate as much, especially when the claims and counterclaims over state status are articulated in the idiom of international law (d'Aspremont 2013;

---

[3] It thus mirrors the bellicose dictum of Charles Tilly (1985) that 'war made states and states made war'.

[4] See, for instance, Kelsen 1941; Lauterpacht 1947; Crawford 2006; dos Reis and Grzybowski 2021.

Grzybowski and Koskenniemi 2015; Grzybowski 2017; 2019; Besson 2019; Vidmar 2021; Panepinto 2021).

Moreover, questions of contested status are not restricted to the immediate concern with state creation and recognition. Given the central role that states play in general international law and across specific domains and regimes, the attribution of rights, obligations, and jurisdiction in any of these areas often works through the assumption of the legal personality of individual states. It is, therefore, sometimes difficult to ignore open status questions even when considering other legal areas, from human rights law (Lagerwall, Chapter 9 in this volume; Müller 2021) to investment treaties (Happ and Wuschka 2016) to international criminal law (Panepinto 2021). From these perspectives, the determination of states is not the primary goal but an intermediate step to respond to a more specific legal question.

Yet a tension remains. Either statehood is established for specific purposes, contexts, and legal regimes without any implications for the entity's status elsewhere, or such a pragmatic reduction to functions of state status is rejected in favour of returning to the determination of state status under general international law. A functional notion suggests that there is no actual person behind the 'mask' of the 'persona', but just 'a bundle of rights, obligations, and competences' (Klabbers 2011: 15) directly derived from the law. It is the law that makes the legal person, not the other way around. If so, 'one can have personality in various gradations' (Klabbers 2011: 15), depending on the legal function in any particular context and perspective to avoid gaps in attribution and liability that emerge when non-state actors are only arbitrarily accounted for (Worster 2020; Vidmar 2021). In this vein, the ICJ can be credited with 'demonstrating a high degree of pragmatism within the parameters of its mandate to ensure the widest possible reach of international law' (Panepinto 2021: 137).

At least when it comes to statehood and sovereignty, however, this functional argument raises thorny questions about the coherence of international law, and the limits of its functional differentiation into distinct regimes.[5] After all, the status question is often only posed because the rights, obligations, and competences of any entity depend on their identification as legal persons in the first place. Indeed, it is usually not concluded that an entity is a state because it enjoys a right to territorial integrity and self-defence, but rather that it enjoys those rights because it is considered a state. Azerbaijan could claim to act in self-defence when militarily seizing control over Nagorno-Karabakh *because* it is widely recognized as a state whose sovereignty extends to this territory, while Nagorno-Karabakh was exposed to the use of force

---

[5] On the 'fragmentation' of international law, see the International Law Commission (UNGA 2006).

because it was not regarded as a state and other considerations, such as of human rights, were dismissed as secondary (see Payan, Chapter 5 in this volume). Taiwan's potential right to self-defence is equally tied up with the status attributed to it (Henderson, Chapter 1 in this volume), as is the widespread rejection of any claims to self-defence by the pro-Russian 'People's Republics' in Ukraine (Miklasová, Chapter 4 in this volume). Since states are construed as exclusively sovereign over their territories, overlapping claims to statehood and degrees of effective control raise questions about general state status beyond functional attributions. Of course, in the case of contested states, this determination of states was the problem to begin with. This leaves a tension between functional attributions of legal personality and general status. To say that 'whether […] [the functional attribution of limited statehood] suggests that all states are necessarily relative is an argument for another day' (Worster 2020: 98) is to shirk back from pushing a functionalist notion of statehood to its logical conclusion.

Apart from seeking to solve the question legally, however, we can also look at it from a more sociological, critical, or constructivist lens (Weber 1998; Biersteker and Weber 1996; Koskenniemi 2005; Aalberts 2012; Grzybowski and Koskenniemi 2015), asking how statehood is performatively enacted when attributed functionally and with professed 'agnosticism' (Panepinto 2021: 135) about its general status. What implications do functional attributions of statehood have and how do even limited attributions of statehood circulate within and beyond the law? Do functions beget functions, do limited attributions spill over? Indeed, rather than reduce state status either to a general affirmation or to mere functional premises in circumscribed contexts, its assumption might spread across different legal domains and regimes. If so, then the supposed agnosticism of functional attributions is productive beyond explicitly circumscribed contexts and restricted legal functions, by entangling presumptions of statehood *across* contexts, legally and politically. The following sections on Kosovo and Palestine at international courts illustrate different aspects of these intra- and extra-legal entanglements articulated through limited attributions of state status.

The state in the shadows: the ICJ Advisory Opinion on Kosovo

One of the most notorious cases of legally contested statehood is the longstanding conflict over the status of Kosovo. Once an autonomous province within Serbia with a limited status on the federal Yugoslav level, Kosovo's autonomy was dismantled by the Serbian government under Slobodan Milošević in the late 1980s and Kosovo was instead put under direct Serbian authority. Following the peaceful grassroots organization of a 'parallel state' in the early 1990s and armed rebellion by the Kosovo Liberation Army

(KLA) in the late 1990s, tensions with the Serbian authorities escalated into a civil war that was ultimately halted by the intervention of NATO forces in 1999, to the detriment of Serbia whose control over the territory was – if only temporarily – suspended by Security Council resolution 1244 (1999). A UN interim administration was put into place and, in 2005, status talks between Serbia and Kosovo were organized under auspices of the UN secretary-general, only to eventually end in deadlock. Frustrated by the seemingly inconclusive process, Kosovar members of the Kosovo Assembly – itself part of the Provisional Institutions of Self-Government (PISG) set up under S/RES/1244 (1999) by the UN interim administration – unilaterally declared Kosovo independent in 2008, a decision supported and recognized by Kosovo's Western backers, including the United States, but rejected by Serbia and others, including Russia and China. Against the background of a split international community, Serbia was supported by a majority of 77 member states in the UN General Assembly to submit to the ICJ the following question to be assessed in an advisory opinion: 'Is the unilateral declaration of independence by the Provisional Institutions of Self-Government of Kosovo in accordance with international law?' (ICJ 2010). In this pivotal moment of the longstanding conflict over Kosovo, with many states claiming that it had legally become a state and many others rejecting this position, all eyes turned toward the ICJ. Various written statements with the views of states were submitted to the court.

Yet if the question appears to straightforwardly ask the court to consider the claimed state status of Kosovo based on the legality of its unilateral declaration of independence, the court disagreed and infamously found a way around the state status question. Maintaining that 'the question is narrow and specific' and that it 'asks for the Court's opinion on whether or not the declaration of independence is in accordance with international law', it notably 'does not ask whether or not Kosovo has achieved statehood', 'nor does it ask about the validity or legal effects of the recognition of Kosovo by those States which have recognized it' (ICJ 2010: para. 51). According to the court, it does not ask about any 'legal consequences' (ICJ 2010: para. 51) of the unilateral declaration of independence (UDI) at all and there is also no direct connection between a declaration of independence and state creation. In fact, the court stated, '[s]ometimes a declaration resulted in the creation of a new State, at others it did not.' (ICJ 2010: para. 79) In other words, the court first stripped the UDI of legal significance to then argue that a simple declaration as such was not prohibited under international law (ICJ 2010: para. 84), period. By upholding this narrow focus, the court concluded that 'the adoption of that declaration did not violate any applicable rule of international law' (ICJ 2010: para. 122).

If the ICJ thus seemed to argue that as mere 'ink on paper' the UDI was not as such of any legal consequence, it also added a series of considerations that suggest that *if the UDI had the effect of creating a new state* or assisting in its creation, it would not have been illegal. To begin with, the notion that the UDI did not violate international law can also be read as a version of the *Lotus* principle, in that 'restrictions upon the independence of states cannot [...] be presumed' (PCIJ 1927, series A, no. 10) and, thus, what is not prohibited under international law is permissible (see Falk 2011). The *Lotus* principle applied to states, however, and whether or not Kosovo was a state was precisely the question.[6] Moreover, it is debated whether territorial integrity does not weigh against unilateral secession (Vidmar 2011), or at least against recognition of a new state before it is established beyond any doubt.[7] Nevertheless, secession as such has long been held to be in principle neither endorsed nor prohibited by international law, but a matter of fact (Cassese 2001: 12; see also Crawford 2006). At least the court leaves open the conclusion that if the UDI did lead to effective state creation, then this result was not necessarily a breach of international law. The state as potential fact outside the law is the first version in which the ICJ invoked the shadow of a Kosovar state.

Yet even if this permissive reading of state creation was accepted in general, Kosovo was under the regime mandated by S/RES/1244 (1999), which foresaw a temporary suspension of Serbian sovereignty over Kosovo, an interim administration under UN auspices, and final status talks between the two parties. Against this background, Serbia and others argued that a unilateral declaration of independence to settle the status question unilaterally was illegal. Neither were the Provisional Institutions of Self-Government (PISG) authorized to take such a step outside the provisions of S/RES/1244 (1999) under which they were created and to which they were bound, nor had status talks led to any agreement. The court, however, did not accept either obstacle to – potential – state creation. As for the status talks, they had in fact taken place, and that they had remained inconclusive did not mean that independence was precluded. Serbia had no veto right (ICJ 2010: para. 118). Indeed, the interim regime established by S/RES/1244 (1999) was not meant to last indeterminately, and it did not suspend the application of general international law. In this sense, it mattered that the 'authors of the declaration did not act, or intend to act, in the capacity of an institution created by and empowered to act within that legal order' (ICJ 2010: para. 105) of the regime and thus as *provisional* institutions of self-government or PISG. The 'Special Representative of the Secretary-General continues to exercise his functions in Kosovo' (ICJ 2010: para. 92), but it had not reacted

---

[6] On the argument that the ICJ did in fact *not* apply the *Lotus* principle, see also Christakis 2011.
[7] For this argument, see Lauterpacht 1947.

to the declaration of independence, which it could have vetoed had it been issued by the PISG (ICJ 2010: para. 108). Whether a state had been created by the UDI or not, it did not violate the framework of interim administration established under S/RES/1244 (1999).

If the court had thereby sought to argumentatively remove *obstacles* to a legal creation of statehood, it also hinted at the substantive subject plausibly creating such a state under modern international law, in other words, 'the people'. It notably did not take the controversial path of declaring a right to external self-determination on the basis of 'remedial secession'. In fact, it explicitly excluded any consideration of 'the extent of the right of self-determination and the existence of any right of "remedial secession"' because they touched upon 'the right to separate from a State', which was 'beyond the scope of the question posed by the General Assembly.' (ICJ 2010: para. 83) However, the court then reintroduced the question of the people by the backdoor, arguing that the UDI had not been issued by the PISG but by 'representatives of the people of Kosovo' (ICJ 2010: para. 109). There was thus, so the court implied, a 'people of Kosovo' distinct from that of Serbia. Whether it had a right to external self-determination or not was carefully left aside. But, since any legal obstacles to the UDI and state creation had been removed, one can conclude that the court both opened the gates of lawful state creation and envisioned the state-like subject walking through them, in however shadowy shape.

Apart from discussing some technical aspects of the legal constraints imposed by S/RES/1244 (1999) and a few other related questions, the advisory opinion largely develops a permissive argument under general international law that does not establish a right to state creation but focuses on its principal legality. It has stirred controversy for its lack of direct engagement with crucial questions of state creation, for its argument of permissibility, and for the implications for other cases, all talk about its 'sui generis' character notwithstanding (Christakis 2011; Falk 2011; Hannum 2011; Ker-Lindsay 2011; Milanović and Wood 2015). Russia, for instance, has – controversially – interpreted the advisory opinion as permission to recognize Abkhazia and South Ossetia as independent states, not to mention its intervention on behalf of pro-Russian 'Peoples' Republics' of the territory of Ukraine, which Russia has equally justified by an expansive view of self-determination and the use of force (see Miklasová, Chapter 4 in this volume). Yet the ICJ's advisory opinion had eschewed general questions of state creation, and instead removed legal obstacles while invoking a Kosovar 'people' ready to declare and establish a state. The Kosovar state was thereby assumed into possible existence, with plausible deniability.

This position of hinting at a new but somewhat concealed state rather than openly declaring or validating its existence was eagerly picked up by Kosovo's supporters as vindication of its statehood bid and their recognition of Kosovo as a state. It also increased the cascade of incoming recognition statements by other third states. At the same time, it could not overcome the resistance by Serbia, Russia, China, and many others who were arguably wary of the implications for the legality and potential recognition of secessionists elsewhere, including their own territories. As such, it also failed to lead to universal recognition or full UN membership; Kosovo remains a contested state. Nevertheless, in the ceaseless efforts of Kosovar politicians and diplomats to 'entangle' Kosovo in international relations (Visoka 2018), the court opinion picked up, tied in with, and further disseminated the assumption that Kosovo was a state, if one always in the shadows and internationally 'negotiated' at a 'cost' (Kursani 2024).

The state in brackets: Palestine between the UNGA, ICJ, and ICC

It is a tragic irony that, while Palestinian statehood further fades on the ground as a result of the war in Gaza since 2023, the international persona of the 'State of Palestine' continues to take hold in international fora. It has come a long way from the recognition of the Palestinian right to self-determination and of the Palestinian Liberation Organization (PLO) as its sole representative in 1974 (UNGA resolution 3236 [1974]) to the 1988 declaration of the State of Palestine to the 2012 admission as non-member observer state in the UNGA. Its future is uncertain amid war, continued occupation, and expanding settlement. Yet once again the Palestinian Authority (PA) is turning to international fora, including international courts and the UNGA. In fact, as a notorious case of denied self-determination and occupation, the situation of Palestine has been discussed in international law for long, in terms of state creation, recognition, and self-determination as well as international humanitarian, human rights, and criminal law. Moreover, it has been through international courts, alongside the United Nations, that the PA has put Palestinian statehood – and its denial – time and again on the agenda.

An important step was the 2004 ICJ Advisory Opinion on Israel's construction of a wall that partly runs through occupied Palestinian territory (ICJ 2004). Israel had justified the building of this wall as a security measure meant to curb infiltration by attackers during the second intifada. In response, the General Assembly asked the court to clarify the 'legal consequences arising from the construction of the wall being built by Israel […] considering the rules and principles of international law, including the Fourth Geneva Convention of 1949, and relevant Security Council and General Assembly resolutions' (ICJ 2004). Although these consequences were expressed mainly in terms of violations of international humanitarian and human rights law, the key to these considerations was the affirmation of Palestine's right to self-determination. Not only was the construction of the wall through

Palestinian territory in the borders of 1967 directly contrary to the right to self-determination and amounted, by its enclosure of Israeli settlements, to illegal annexation (ICJ 2004).[8] The application of important parts of international humanitarian and human rights law was in turn dependent on the status of the territories as occupied territories of a state – or people with a right to self-determination. The court rejected Israel's argument that the Fourth Geneva Convention was not applicable to the Palestinian territories because of the 'lack of recognition of the territory as sovereign prior to its annexation by Jordan and Egypt' and inferring that it is 'not a territory of a High Contracting Party as required by the Convention' (ICJ 2004: para. 90). As the court noted, 'the existence of a 'Palestinian people' is no longer in issue' (ICJ 2004: para. 118) and Israel must therefore be regarded as the occupying power, with all implications for the applicability of international humanitarian and human rights law, as well as the obligation to respect the right to self-determination itself. The 2004 advisory opinion had not considered the question of whether or not Palestine was – already – a state, but the affirmation of the status of Palestinians as a people and of their right to self-determination implied at least a 'quasi-state identity as a self-determination unit' (Burgis-Kasthala 2014: 680). The attribution of this identity was the basis for considering other legal regimes or particular provisions of them applicable to the case.

In the case of the ICC, the question of state status itself appeared at stake for the establishment of the ICC's jurisdiction in the case (see Grzybowski and dos Reis 2024). Although the 'State of Palestine' had already in 2009 lodged a declaration under Article 12(3) of the Rome Statute that retrospectively granted the ICC jurisdiction over international crimes committed in Palestine, ICC Prosecutor Luis Moreno Ocampo declined considering the situation of Palestine in April 2012 on the ground that Palestine was not considered a state (ICC OTP 2012). More specifically, the Office of the Prosecutor (OTP) argued that 'The Rome Statute provides no authority for the Office of the Prosecutor to adopt a method to define the term "State"' and – a hint, perhaps – it was 'for the relevant bodies at the United Nations or the Assembly of States Parties to make the legal determination whether Palestine qualifies as a State for the purpose of acceding to the Rome Statute' (ICC OTP 2012: 2). In November 2012, the PA achieved a diplomatic victory by seeing the 'State of Palestine' admitted to the UN General Assembly as a 'non-member observer state' (UNGA resolution 67/19,

---

[8] As the court notes, in UNSC 446 (1979) of 22 March 1979 the Security Council considered that those settlements had 'no legal validity', which was reaffirmed in resolutions UNSC 452 (1979) of 20 July 1979 and UNSC 465 (1980) of 1 March 1980. See also UNSC/RES/681 (1990), UNSC/RES/799 (1992), and UNSC/RES/904 (1994).

4 December 2012). This admission has not widely been credited with *creating* statehood (Vidmar 2013). Yet in January 2015 the State of Palestine again asked the ICC to open investigations as well as formally accept it as a state party, the latter of which was granted by the Assembly of State Parties to the Rome Statute (ICC 2015). Implying statehood rhetorically, if not legally (Vidmar 2013), the UNGA had turned the tide for Palestine at the ICC, which in turn would help to – self-referentially – imply it again in the ICC proceedings themselves and elsewhere.

ICC Prosecutor Fatou Bensouda preliminarily examined the situation in Palestine and confirmed in December 2019 that the criteria for opening a formal investigation were met. However, due to the contested status question, and open Israeli rejection of both Palestinian statehood and the ICC's jurisdiction, the prosecutor requested the court to assess whether and in what territory of Palestine the ICC had jurisdiction. Pre-Trial Chamber I of the court delivered its assessment on 3 March 2021 (ICC 2021a). It affirmed with a 2–1 vote that, first, the court had jurisdiction in this case and, second, that the territory of Palestine was defined by the borders of 1967, thus comprising the West Bank, the Gaza Strip, and East Jerusalem (ICC 2021a: para. 87). The chamber explicitly excluded the 'political' question of state creation to focus on the 'legal' question of the court's 'territorial jurisdiction in Palestine' (paras 53–58). That is, it sought to bracket and functionally restrict the question of statehood for the purpose of establishing and circumscribing the ICC's jurisdiction. Likewise, the chamber maintained that 'any territorial determination by the Chamber for the purpose of defining its territorial jurisdiction for criminal purposes has no bearing on the scope of Palestine's territory' (ICC 2021a: para. 62).[9] Yet as the dissenting opinion by Judge Kovács (ICC 2021b) and wider controversy show, this functional restriction of state status and territory was not merely technical, but arguably invoked a Palestinian state in ways that point beyond the specific purposes of international criminal law.

The two questions addressed by the court merit separate consideration. First, the majority decision maintained that since the 'State of Palestine' was a 'State Party' to the Rome Statute and had acceded to the Statute according to its proper procedures, it should be treated like any other state party. Therefore, establishing Palestine's status under the Rome Statute 'does not [...] require a determination as to whether that entity fulfils the prerequisites of statehood under general international law' (ICC 2021a: para.

---

[9] The reasoning has been expressed in another decision of the pre-trial chamber (ICC 2018) and cites further in support the decision of the Permanent Court of International Justice in the *Lotus* case (PCIJ 1927). But see Ambos 2021 for a critique of the chamber's reference to the *Lotus* principle.

93).¹⁰ However, via a detour through the Vienna Convention on the Law of Treaties (1969), the UN secretary-general as depository of treaties, and the role of the UN General Assembly in determining whether an entity constitutes a state and could accede to treaties (ICC 2021a: paras 94–98), the chamber regarded General Assembly Resolution 67/19 (4 December 2012) as a sufficient basis for treating Palestine as having legally acceded to the Rome Statute as a state party. Moreover, it explicitly rejected going back beyond the accession of Palestine to consider its statehood under general international law and instead read the notion of ' "[t]he State on the territory of which the conduct in question occurred" in article 12(2)(a) of the Statute' as referring to 'the territory of a State Party for the purpose of establishing individual criminal responsibility for the crimes within the jurisdiction of the Court' (ICC 2021a: para. 103).

Yet according to Judge Kovács' dissenting opinion, the legal authority of the UN General Assembly to determine states under general international law was contestable (ICJ 2021b: para. 219) and the notion that Palestine was a state because it was a 'state party' to the Rome Statute was circular (ICJ 2021b: para. 17). It did not establish that Palestine was, generally, a state. For Kovács, whether Palestine truly was a state could not be bracketed; it was the 'real question' (ICJ 2021b: para. 26). The majority, however, had effectively circumvented the general status question.

Regarding the territorial scope of the ICC's jurisdiction, statehood raised important questions that the chamber could only superficially shirk by insisting on its functional approach. It is an international court whose jurisdiction depends on the jurisdiction of the states by whom and in whose *territory* international crimes are investigated, subject to qualifications of complementarity and other relevant principles. That is, state territory is crucial for delineating the ICC's jurisdiction. Hence the OTP's request for clarification. Drawing again on UNGA resolution 67/19, which affirmed 'the right of the Palestinian people to self-determination and to independence in their State of Palestine on the Palestinian territory occupied since 1967' (ICC 2021a: paras 116–117), as well as other UNGA resolutions emphasizing 'that the Palestinian people have the right to [...] sovereignty over their territory' (cit. in ICC-PTC I 2021, para. 117; see also Heinsch and Pinzauti 2020; Pertile 2020), the majority of the chamber concluded that 'the Court's territorial jurisdiction in the Situation in Palestine extends

---

¹⁰ In fact, the chamber cites ICJ advisory opinions discussed above to foster its functional interpretation of statehood, arguing that 'in its advisory opinions on the *Kosovo Declaration of Independence* and the *Wall*, the International Court of Justice refrained from determining whether Kosovo or Palestine were "States" under public international law' (ICC 2021a: 40 fn 266).

to the territories occupied by Israel since 1967, namely Gaza and the West Bank, including East Jerusalem' (ICC 2021a: para. 118). The state in brackets has a territory too.

By contrast, for Judge Kovács, Palestine is only a 'state *in statu nascendi*' (ICC 2021b: para. 267), and the right to self-determination determined neither state status nor the scope of its territory and jurisdiction. Specifically, any jurisdiction it could have delegated to the ICC would have been restricted to the designated areas for which the PA had explicitly obtained jurisdiction in the Interim Agreement of the Oslo Accords (ICC 2021b: para. 282 ff.). Palestine could therefore not delegate criminal jurisdiction in areas for which Israel had explicitly retained it in the Oslo Accords. Yet this argument overlooked that, as Panepinto (2021: 154) points out, Palestine had only 'agreed to a temporary arrangement with an expiry date which Israel has not respected' (see also Ronen 2014: 23; Al-Khudayri 2020). More generally, while belligerent occupation interferes with the effectiveness of statehood (Ronen 2020), this does not mean that it precludes it as such (Heinsch and Pinzauti 2020). As an institution of the laws of war, the occupation of a state's territory by another state does not amount to annexation but is subject to rules specified under international humanitarian law. The ICJ advisory opinion on the *Wall* (2004) reiterates this in the case of Palestine, and the pre-trial chamber could cite this opinion in turn (ICC 2021a: para. 121).

Palestine's functionally assumed status proliferates further. For instance, the 2014 accession of the 'State of Palestine' to international human rights treaty bodies entangled and projected state status through yet another legal regime (Haddad and Jasper 2025). A contentious case at the ICJ against the United States for moving its embassy in Israel to Jerusalem is still pending and raises the stakes further because only 'states' can be parties in such cases before the ICJ (Panepinto 2021: 142). In the meantime, on 10 May 2024 the UNGA adopted a resolution (UNGA/R/ES-10/23) that '*[d]etermines* that the State of Palestine is qualified for membership in the United Nations in accordance with Article 4 of the Charter of the United Nations and should therefore be admitted to membership in the United Nations', although the Security Council did not confirm Palestinian membership. Individual states, however, including Norway, Spain, and Ireland, moved to recognize Palestine as a state, bringing recognitions up to 145. On 19 July 2024, the ICJ (2024) further determined in its advisory opinion on the *Legal Consequences arising from the Policies and Practices of Israel in the Occupied Palestinian Territory, including East Jerusalem* that Israel had 'annexed' and 'asserted permanent control over the Occupied Palestinian Territory', as well as denied 'the right of the Palestinian people to self-determination', thereby violating 'fundamental principles of international law' and rendering 'Israel's presence in the Occupied Palestinian Territory unlawful' (ICJ 2024: para. 261). While indicating the ongoing momentum of the State of Palestine's diplomatic and legal campaign, the

2024 UNGA and ICJ decisions, as well as new state recognitions, also reaffirm longstanding condemnations of Israel's illegal annexation, pointing to what remains materially denied on the ground. The pending contentious case between the State of Palestine and the United States at the ICJ as well as ongoing criminal investigations of the ICC prosecutor will show how and to which degree the state status of Palestine proliferates further, or not, and with what consequences.

Functional attributions of statehood have travelled from site to site. Clearly, however, these chains of signification are embedded in a wider social and political environment in which claims and contestations of statehood are maintained by other means than legal attributions alone. International recognition despite the occupation has also curtailed the local legitimacy of the PA and led to its increasing fragmentation (Olsson 2025, forthcoming). Contradictions thus persist (see also Kursani 2024; Lefteratos 2025).

Conclusion

The rigid designation of states under general international law poses legal and political problems in cases of contested states. At the same time, the determination of states cannot be easily brushed aside by functional attributions that are independently derived for particular contexts and legal regimes. It is true that, in the case of Palestine, the ICC and the ICJ 'have shown pragmatism in fulfilling their mandates within the letter and spirit of their respective constitutive documents' (Panepinto 2021: 158), indicating that they both 'have ample scope to exercise their jurisdiction in relation to Palestine *regardless* of its formal status as a state' (Panepinto 2021: 159). The same can be said about the ICJ advisory opinion in the case of Kosovo. Yet this agnosticism does not actually operate without any attributions or assumptions of statehood. It casts shadows of the state, and leaves brackets to trap them. They seep and slip through, however. The Kosovo opinion drew on and confirmed notions of a Kosovar people, a stalemate over status, and missing restraints on secession. In the case of Palestine, 'Over the past 10 years a number of symbolic events have indicated an acceleration of the process' of crediting Palestine with statehood, 'despite the continuing doctrinal (and political) debates' (Panepinto 2021: 159). Indeed. International courts play a part in disseminating – not merely functional – attributions of statehood, from self-determination to international criminal jurisdiction. As such, professed agnosticism for limited legal purposes can at the same time be part of performative enactment in the wider social and political context.

To be sure, any such enactment through status attributions by international courts is always only part of state creation. In particular, it obviously matters what status is accepted by the governments of parent states, occupying powers, third states, and international organizations. Limited international recognition has at the same time 'tamed' (Kursani 2024) the Palestinian Authority, and undermined its domestic legitimacy (Olsson 2025, forthcoming), just as it enticed Kosovo to concede a 'negotiated' (Kursani 2024) form of statehood. Moreover, hostile governments use their diplomatic clout or military wherewithal to craft international alliances against contested states, hold their territory occupied, or engage in campaigns of annexation and displacement. Still, even powerful states wishing to crush their sovereignty-aspiring opponents struggle with the stubborn performances of a statehood that is projected and entangled locally and internationally, including in the sphere of international law and courts, where it can be both hidden and sought out.

References

Aalberts, T. (2012). *Constructing Sovereignty between Politics and Law.* London: Routledge.

Al-Khudayri, Y. (2020). Procedural Haze: The ICC's Jurisdiction over the Situation in Palestine. *The Palestine Yearbook of International Law Online*, 20 (1), 117–147.

Ambos, K. (2021). Solid Jurisdictional Basis'? The ICC's Fragile Jurisdiction for Crimes Allegedly Committed in Palestine, *EJIL Talk!*, 2 March 2021, www.ejiltalk.org/solid-jurisdictional-basis-the-iccs-fragile-jurisdiction-for-crimes-allegedly-committed-in-palestine/.

Besson, S. (2019). International Courts and the Jurisprudence of Statehood. *Transnational Legal Theory*, 10 (1), 30–64.

Biersteker, T.J. and Weber, C. (eds) (1996). *State Sovereignty as Social Construct.* Cambridge: Cambridge University Press.

Bourdieu, P. (1986). The Force of Law: Toward a Sociology of the Juridical Field. *Hastings Law Journal*, 38, 805.

Burgis-Kasthala, M.L. (2014). Over-stating Palestine's UN Membership Bid? An Ethnographic Study on the Narratives of Statehood. *European Journal of International Law*, 25 (3), 677–701.

Cassese, A. (2001). *International Law.* Oxford: Oxford University Press.

Christakis, T. (2011). The ICJ Advisory Opinion on Kosovo: Has International Law Something to Say about Secession? *Leiden Journal of International Law*, 24 (1), 73–86.

Crawford, J. (2006). *State Creation in International Law.* 2nd edn. Cambridge: Cambridge University Press.

d'Aspremont, J. (2013). The International Law of Statehood: Craftsmanship for the Elucidation and Regulation of Births and Deaths in the International Society. *Connecticut Journal of International Law*, 29, 201–224.

dos Reis, F. and Grzybowski, J. (2021). The Matrix Reloaded: Reconstructing the Boundaries between (International) Law and Politics. *Leiden Journal of International Law*, 34 (3), 547–570.

Falk, R. (2011). The Kosovo Advisory Opinion: Conflict Resolution and Precedent. *American Journal of International Law*, 105(1), 50–60.

Grzybowski, J. (2017). To Be or Not to Be: The Ontological Predicament of State Creation in International Law. *European Journal of International Law*, 28(2), 409–432.

Grzybowski, J. (2019). The Paradox of State Identification: De Facto States, Recognition, and the (Re-)production of the International. *International Theory*, 11(3), 241–263.

Grzybowski, J. and dos Reis, F. (2024). After States, before Humanity? The Meta-politics of Legality and the International Criminal Court in Iraq, Afghanistan, and Palestine. *Review of International Studies*, 50 (2), 354–372.

Grzybowski, J. and Koskenniemi, M. (2015). International Law and Statehood: A Performative View. In: R. Schuett and P.M.R. Stirk (eds), *The Concept of the State in International Relations: Philosophy, Sovereignty and Cosmopolitanism*. Edinburgh: Edinburgh University Press, 23–47.

Haddad, M. and Jasper, A. (2025). In Pursuit of Statehood: Palestinian Performativity in Human Rights Treaty Bodies. *Law & Social Inquiry*, 1-30.

Hannum, H. (2011). The Advisory Opinion on Kosovo: An Opportunity Lost, or a Poisoned Chalice Refused? *Leiden Journal of International Law*, 24 (1), 155–161.

Happ, R. and Wuschka, S. (2016). Horror Vaccui: or Why Investment Treaties Should Apply to Illegally Annexed Territories. *Journal of International Arbitration*, 33 (3), 245–268.

Heinsch, R. and Pinzauti, G. (2020). To Be (a State) or Not to Be? The Relevance of the Law of Belligerent Occupation with Regard to Palestine's Statehood before the ICC. *Journal of International Criminal Justice*, 18 (4), 927–945.

ICC (2015). Assembly of States Parties to the Rome Statute of the International Criminal Court, resumed Thirteenth Session, The Hague, 24–25 June, Official Records, https://asp.icc-cpi.int/sites/asp/files/asp_docs/ASP13/OR/ICC-ASP-13-20-Add1-ENG.pdf.

ICC (2021a). *Pre-Trial Chamber I. 2021. Situation in the State of Palestine*. ICC-01/18.

ICC (2021b). *Pre-Trial Chamber I, Partly Dissenting Opinion Judge Kovaćs. 2021. Judge Péter Kovaćs' Partly Dissenting Opinion*. ICC-01/18 Annex.

ICC OTP (2012). *Situation in Palestine*, www.icc-cpi.int/sites/default/files/NR/rdonlyres/C6162BBF-FEB9-4FAF-AFA9-836106D2694A/284387/SituationinPalestine030412ENG.pdf.

ICJ (1971). *Legal Consequences for States of the Continued Presence of South Africa in Namibia (South West Africa) notwithstanding Security Council Resolution 276 (1970)*. Advisory Opinion – ICJ 1971 21 June No. 352.

ICJ (1975). *Western Sahara*. Advisory Opinion – ICJ 1975 16 October No. 414.

ICJ (2004). *Legal Consequences of the Construction of a Wall in the Occupied Palestinian Territory.* Advisory Opinion – ICJ 2004 9 July No. 883.

ICJ (2010). *Accordance with international law of the unilateral declaration of independence in respect of Kosovo.* Advisory Opinion – ICJ 2010 22 July No. 997.

ICJ (2018). *Relocation of the United States Embassy to Jerusalem (Palestine v. United States of America).* Order – ICJ 2018 15 November No. 1154.

ICJ (2019). *Legal Consequences of the Separation of the Chagos Archipelago from Mauritius in 1965.* Advisory Opinion – ICJ 1970 25 February No. 1164.

ICJ (2024). *Legal Consequences arising from the Policies and Practices of Israel in the Occupied Palestinian Territory, including East Jerusalem.* Advisory Opinion – ICJ 2024 19 July General List No. 186.

Kelsen, H. (1941). Recognition in International Law. *American Journal of International Law*, 35 (4), 605–617.

Ker-Lindsay, J. (2011). Not Such a 'Sui Generis' Case After All: Assessing the ICJ Opinion on Kosovo. *Nationalities Papers*, 39 (1), 1–11.

Klabbers, J. (2011). The Concept of Legal Personality. In: F. Johns (ed.), *International Legal Personality*. London: Routledge.

Knotter, L. (2023). *A Theory of De Facto States: Classical Realism and Exceptional Polities.* London: Routledge.

Koskenniemi, M. (1994). The Wonderful Artificiality of States. *Proceedings of the Annual Meeting (American Society of International Law)*, 88, 22–29.

Koskenniemi, M. (2001). *The Gentle Civilizer of Nations: The Rise and Fall of International Law: 1870–1960.* Cambridge: Cambridge University Press.

Koskenniemi, M. (2005). *From Apology to Utopia: The Structure of International Legal Argument, 2nd edition.* Cambridge: Cambridge University Press.

Krasner, S. (1999). *Sovereignty: Organized Hypocrisy.* Princeton: Princeton University Press.

Kratochwil, F. (2014). *The Status of Law in World Society: Meditations on the Role and Rule of Law.* Cambridge: Cambridge University Press.

Kursani, S. (2024). Costs of International Recognition: Palestine's and Kosovo's Struggle with Negotiated Statehood. *Geopolitics*, 29 (1), 174–202.

Lauterpacht, H. (1947). *Recognition in International Law.* Cambridge: Cambridge University Press.

Lauterpacht, H. (2011). *The Function of Law in the International Community.* Oxford: Oxford University Press.

Lefteratos, A. (2025). Palestine's Post-2012 External Statehood Performativity: Diplomatic Agency and International Discourse. *Geopolitics*, 1–30.

Milanovic, M. and Wood, M. (eds) (2015). *The Law and Politics of the Kosovo Advisory Opinion.* Oxford. Oxford University Press.

Müller, A. (2021). De Facto Independent Regimes and Overarching Human Rights Duties. *Hague Yearbook of International Law/Annuaire de La Haye de Droit International*, 32, 31–68.

Olsson, C. (2025, forthcoming). Between the 'Dome of the Rock' and a Hard Place: Fatah and the Trade-Off between Armed Struggle and International Legitimacy. In: K. Schlichte and S. Hensell (eds), *Armed Non-State Actors and the Politics of Recognition*. Oxford: Oxford University Press.

Panepinto, A. (2021). International Courts and Contested Statehood: The ICJ and ICC in Palestine. *Hague Yearbook of International Law/Annuaire de La Haye de Droit International*, 32, 135–174.

PCIJ (1927). *The Case of the SS 'Lotus' (France v Turkey)*, Judgment, 7 September, PCIJ Series A. No. 10.

Pertile, M. (2020). The Borders of the Occupied Palestinian Territory Are Determined by Customary Law: A Comment on the Prosecutor's Position on the Territorial Jurisdiction of the ICC in the Situation Concerning Palestine *Journal of International Criminal Justice*, 18(4), 967–983.

Portmann, R. (2010). *Legal Personality in International Law*. Cambridge: Cambridge University Press.

Ronen, Y. (2020). Palestine in the ICC: Statehood and the Right to Self-Determination in the Absence of Effective Control. *Journal of International Criminal Justice*, 18(4), 947–966.

Ronen, Y. (2014). Israel, Palestine and the ICC – Territory Uncharted but Not Unknown. *Journal of International Criminal Justice*, 12(1), 7–25.

Tilly, C. (1985). War Making and State Making as Organized Crime. In: D. Rueschemeyer, T. Skocpol, and P.B. Evans (eds), *Bringing the State Back In*. Cambridge: Cambridge University Press, 169–191.

UNGA (2006). *Report of the Study Group of the International Law Commission on Fragmentation of International Law: Difficulties Arising from the Diversification and Expansion of International Law* (13 April) UN Doc. A/CN.4/L.682.

UNGA/R/ES-10/23 (2024), 10 May 2024.

UNSC/RES/446 (1979), 22 March.

UNSC/RES/465 (1980). 1 March 1980.

UNSC/RES/681 (1990). 20 December.

UNSC/RES/799 (1992). 18 December.

UNSC/RES/904 (1994). 18 March.

UNSC/RES/1244 (1999). 10 June.

UNGA/RES/3236 (1974). 22 November.

UNGA/RES/67/19 (2012). 4 December.

Vidmar, J. (2011). The Kosovo Advisory Opinion Scrutinized. *Leiden Journal of International Law*, 24 (2), 355–383.

Vidmar, J. (2013). Palestine and the Conceptual Problem of Implicit Statehood. *Chinese Journal of International Law*, 12 (1), 19–41.

Vidmar, J. (2021). The Structural Crack of the International Legal System: What Happens with Unattributed Conduct? *Hague Yearbook of International Law/Annuaire de La Haye de Droit International*, 32, 1–29.

Vienna Convention on the Law of Treaties (1969). Done at Vienna on 23 May 1969. Entered into force on 27 January 1980. United Nations, Treaty Series, vol. 1155, 331.

Visoka, G. (2018). *Acting Like a State: Kosovo and the Everyday Making of Statehood*. London: Routledge.

Weber, C. (1998). Performative States. *Millennium*, 27 (1), 77–95.

Worster, W.T. (2020). Functional Statehood in Contemporary International Law. *Brooklyn Journal of International Law*, 46, 39.

PART IV
Conclusions

11

Four Normative Positions on the Contestation of Statehood in War and Law

Bruno Coppieters

Introduction

The term 'contested state' points to a wide variety of disputes, whose subjects range from the appropriateness of applying the traditional legal criteria for statehood to a self-proclaimed independent entity, to the questions of whether, when, and how such an entity may legitimately be subdued by the central government, or even annihilated, through the use of force. The present chapter categorizes some of the main arguments regarding such disputes that are addressed in this volume.[1] Contested states claim to possess all the rights and duties that go together with statehood, while this is categorically denied by the states they have broken away from. A distinction is drawn between the continuity, remedial, choice, and effectivist positions on the contestation of statehood. The four-way typology of normative positions presented in this concluding chapter covers the main principles active in such disputes.

The typology applied to the contributions in this volume draws on the literature on international law and the ethics of secession. Each of these disciplines has its own way of classifying justifications of claims to statehood. In determining the extent to which the principle of territorial integrity limits the application of the principle of national self-determination,

---

[1] The four positions have been applied in a previous publication of the author's on Soviet and post-Soviet discussions on secession, which includes a moral assessment of these positions: Coppieters (2018).

international lawyers establish a basic distinction between a colonial and a non-colonial context. In a colonial context, the principle of territorial integrity does not cancel out the right of national liberation movements to create an independent state, but for movements striving for secession in a non-colonial context, the principle of territorial integrity rules out any recognition of independent statehood that is not agreed to by the parent state. This approach accounts for the first type of justification of claims to statehood in international law. The second type is the remedial approach to secession. It allows for an exception to the rule that, outside the colonial context, the recognition of a new state by the parent state is generally required, stating instead that claims to statehood may be justified by the experience of severe forms of injustice. This entitlement is disputed, but it nonetheless receives substantial support from international lawyers. Their support is, however, marginal when it comes to the plebiscitary or choice theory. A unilateral declaration of independence (UDI) based on a majority decision by the population of a territory is not considered to be in conflict with international law with regard to its unilateral character (Vidmar 2013), but nor does it create the legal rights or duties associated with statehood.

The literature on the ethics of secession classifies arguments relating to non-consensual ways of creating independent statehood according to their moral justification. For the construction of the typology presented below, this discipline is no less important than international law. Its literature offers a differentiated range of views, which leaves room for approaches generally regarded as marginal in international law. This is the case, for instance, with the choice theory. Christopher Heath Wellman distinguishes a 'choice' position on the right to secession, which he prefers to a 'statist' or a 'nationalist' position (Wellman 2010) – a classification useful for identifying the author's personal stance more precisely. One must bear in mind, however, that a particular term used in a classification based on international law – such as a 'remedial' right to secession – will be given a different meaning in a classification based on the ethics of secession. In presenting a particular categorization, individual authors in each discipline will, moreover, highlight the characteristics they consider important.

Both legal and moral arguments are central to the four positions described here. In contrast to the juxtapositions of various types to be found in the literature on international law and the ethics of secession, however, this chapter does not aim to explore the extent to which their defence corresponds to international law, or to demonstrate the moral superiority of one argument over the others. Rather, it aims at a descriptive analysis of the presence of the four positions in the disputes on statehood dealt with in this volume.

Four positions

The continuity, remedial, choice, and effectivist positions diverge in defining the nature of a conflict and the principles that would give a breakaway entity the right to sovereign statehood. Accordingly, these positions differ on the conditions under which a claim to sovereign and independent statehood may be considered legitimate and when a breakaway state is entitled to it.

The continuity position is relevant in a situation where a state, a colonial regime, or a federation enters a crisis so severe that it is unable to halt the withdrawal of a territory or territories that it previously held under its control. This position defends the need to create or recognize a new independent state, or new independent states, when the revolutionary overthrow of a state, the dissolution of a colonial empire or the dismembering of a federation/confederation are considered necessary and/or inevitable, but it also aims at the preservation of continuity with the previous situation. This is the case for instance in a decolonization process where the principle of national self-determination is applied to the population of a colony without, however, challenging its boundaries. National liberation from the yoke of colonialism must then take place within the existing division of territories, in line with the *uti possidetis* principle. The continuity position is primarily concerned with the preservation of international stability, rather than the correction of all previous or present injustices, such as the division of ethnic groups resulting from colonial policies. There is, however, deep concern about the injustices that may result from destabilization.

Striving at continuity is also a major issue when it comes to the dissolution of a federation, which ends its legal personality (Chan 2009: 478). The federation's constitution will no longer be in force, but it will still be taken as a guideline by third parties developing their recognition and non-recognition policies: in making their choice, they will look at how the constitution addressed the question of sovereignty. This approach preserves a certain degree of continuity, and thus stability, but it has also preserved the legacy of, for instance, the Soviet and Yugoslav constitutions with respect to the hierarchy between the various levels of their federations – constitutions that were the product of subjugation rather than of freely accepted compromises.

The correction of past and present injustices is prominent in the remedial position. This holds that a nation is entitled to independent statehood if it has been, or still is, a victim of severe injustice at the hands of the authorities of the state from which it wants to separate. Colonization, illegal occupation, massive human rights violations, genocide, ethnic cleansing, violations of international humanitarian law, or the forcible suppression of legitimate claims to national self-determination are mentioned in this context. Independent statehood offers a certain amount of protection in the event of aggression, so this position takes into account the need to prevent a resurgence of injustice.

The choice position is not primarily concerned with the question of international stability (in contrast to the continuity position) or the restoration of justice (in contrast to the remedial position). It holds that the population of any given territory is entitled to organize a referendum on sovereign statehood and, where this option is backed by a majority vote, to secede unilaterally. The freedom of collective choice is at the heart of the interpretation of the principle of national self-determination upheld by the choice position.

Finally, the effectivist position grounds policies of recognition and non-recognition on pragmatic considerations and practical results, rather than on firm principles (Coppieters 2018). It looks at the threat that unresolved conflicts over sovereignty represent for third states and the international order generally. Counter-secession policies are considered ineffective, and even harmful to the international order, if they are unlikely to achieve reunification in the foreseeable future through negotiations or the use of military force. The effectivist position further assumes that any member of the international community is entitled to recognize a contested state as sovereign if a number of criteria are met, such as domestic legitimacy and effective control over a territory, and if non-recognition policies are unable to bring about the reintegration of the breakaway entity. A policy of recognition must prevent the conflict from spilling over into the international order. Here, too, the risk of destabilization lies at the heart of the argumentation – not the correction of previous or present injustices.

The application of each of the four positions may, in addition, take the prudential principles of last resort, likelihood of success, and proportionality into account. Each of these positions will then give a different meaning to these three principles.

Each of the four positions is a particular product of the interaction between law, ethics, and politics. This exchange takes place in what the editors of this volume describe in their introduction as 'spaces for agency', which can engender 'creative strategies' for the conflicting parties to 'help them cope with, challenge, or exploit the blurring of conventional distinctions and legal regimes'. Each of these four positions may be combined imaginatively with others in policies of recognition or non-recognition aimed at persuading and mobilizing. Arguments and principles highlighted in one position reinforce arguments and principles that are central to another position. With the help of the material presented in this volume, this chapter enquires how positions are mingled in particular cases. Each of the disputes investigated here presents such creative mixtures. A similar lack of systematization is characteristic of governments' policies on the (non-)recognition of statehood, which are not based on coherent doctrines but vary considerably from case to case, leaving room for the best defence of state interests and for diplomatic negotiations. Policies of recognition and non-recognition are, moreover, not an exclusive concern of governments, but involve public arguments in a broader societal context. The scholarly arguments reflected upon in this volume, and those defended by its authors, diverge widely in combining normative positions, even when, in a particular case, they are defending a common cause either for or against recognition.

Taiwan

Christian Henderson (Chapter 1) and Ming-Chin Monique Chu (Chapter 2) explore the applicability of international law to the use of force against Taiwan. According to Henderson, with respect to the application of rights and obligations, the status of the contested state of Taiwan is uncertain. There is no agreement between legal scholars on this issue. Regarding the constraints on Taiwan's agency, and its vulnerability, some scholars assume a customary form of the right to self-defence, but they do not say on which legal grounds such a right would apply to contested states. Henderson moreover sees hesitancy among lawyers regarding the right of third states to act in collective self-defence of Taiwan.

Henderson's analysis of the various legal opinions and rules that either support or deny the applicability of the *jus ad bellum* rights and obligations closely examines the One-China policies of the United States and other governments. These policies recognize only the government in Beijing as representing China. But the United States, in its policy, also states that Taiwan has the right to defend itself against any attempt by Beijing to bring about reunification with the island by force, and Washington supports Taiwan with vast programmes of military aid for that purpose. In Henderson's view, this entails a certain contradiction with the One-China policy, as it makes support for Taiwan's right to self-defence through the 'supply of arms potentially a violation of the principle of non-intervention and the prohibition of the use of force'.

In terms of the four-way typology presented above, it could be said that China and the United States defend the continuity position on the non-recognition of Taiwan as a sovereign and independent state, but that their interpretations of it diverge widely. The continuity position – with different interpretations – is also clearly dominant in the China policies of the international community. Even the recognition policies of the governments that have established diplomatic relations with the authorities in Taipei do not necessarily conflict with the continuity position: they may be seen as a particular interpretation of it. According to Henderson, it is indeed not clear whether the governments currently conducting diplomatic relations with Taiwan deal with it 'in its capacity as an independent state or as [if it is] hosting the legitimate government of China'.

Henderson does not reflect on arguments that represent the choice position – which is quite prominent in the discourses of the Taiwanese Democratic Progressive Party (DPP), with its claim that the people of Taiwan have a democratic right to determine the future of the island, but is marginal in international law debates on the use of force. The author is, however, attentive to arguments in line with the remedial position. He writes that 'all states are under an obligation not to suppress or support the suppression of the right of self-determination through forcible means'. Such a statement is not unequivocal, however, when applied to Cross-Strait relations, considering that this right applies to a 'people' – the meaning of which is disputed in the context of Taiwan. The remedial position is also present in Henderson's analysis of the potential outcome of the use of force by China against Taiwan. If such an attack were to happen, the United States would be confronted with the question of whether it could act in collective self-defence of Taiwan. Henderson then sees the possibility of a military escalation in which – and here he is quoting from a book by Olivier Corten – 'Taiwan would either be characterised as a State or at least assimilated to a State' by the United States (Corten 2021: 164). In such a hypothetical case, the option of direct US involvement in collective self-defence of Taiwan would be based on the remedial position, and in opposition to the continuity position, which entails the non-recognition of Taiwan.

Chu, in her chapter, examining the potential use of force against Taiwan, looks at arguments and policies in line with the continuity position. She quotes a senior European diplomat who said that 'everybody here functions within the context of the one-China policy'. She also refers to the argument – often heard in Taiwan – that the People's Republic of China never exercised jurisdiction over Taiwanese territory. This allows for an interpretation of the One-China policy that differs from Beijing's understanding of it.

Chu writes that Taiwan's status remains ambiguous and vulnerable in terms of international law, but she also supports the view that Taiwan is a rights holder in terms of the use of force. First, in her opinion the Taiwanese population qualifies in international law as a people possessing the right to self-determination. Second, Taiwan is a stable *de facto* regime that cannot be changed by force. Third, Chinese military intervention would disrupt international peace and security. The first argument is in accord with the choice position, the two others with the remedial position. But Chu does not address the issue of Taiwan's vulnerability solely from an international law perspective: according to her reading of international relations literature, the military capacity of the United States to intervene in an armed conflict across the Taiwan Strait is decreasing. It could be added to her analysis that this trend requires all actors involved in this dispute to pay additional attention to the prudential principles of last resort, likelihood of success, and proportionality, irrespective of the normative positions on which their policies are based.

Nagorno-Karabakh

Nagorno-Karabakh was described in the Soviet constitution as a region (*oblast*) that was part of Azerbaijan. This subordinated status made the contested state of Nagorno-Karabakh, as it emerged from the 1994 ceasefire, deeply vulnerable in terms of international law. It was destroyed in 2023 in a military assault by Azerbaijan. Sheila Paylan, in her contribution to this volume (Chapter 5), states that here the international community favoured a conservative interpretation of international law that defends the principles of state sovereignty and territorial integrity to the detriment of human rights, historic grievances, and the principle of national self-determination, neglecting the numerous arguments advanced by Nagorno-Karabakh in favour of independence – or, at least, of what she calls 'recognized autonomy'. According to the typology introduced in the present chapter, the (non-)recognition policies that Paylan criticizes are firmly linked to the continuity position. This position focuses on stability but was, in the case of Nagorno-Karabakh, ultimately unsuccessful in achieving a peaceful resolution of the conflict. It also failed to bring about a firm international condemnation of the use of force by Azerbaijan, of the destruction of this contested state or of the displacement of its entire population. Policies in line with the continuity position were supportive of what Paylan describes as 'the paradoxical role of international law in simultaneously restricting and enabling violence'.

Paylan also engages critically with legal arguments advanced by Azerbaijan against the occupation of a large part of its territory. Here Azerbaijan is supporting a 'narrative of territorial integrity and sovereignty being violated by another state'. In her view, these arguments wrongly endorse a recourse to violence as a means of conflict resolution. Such arguments are in line with the remedial position: Azerbaijan is thus combining the continuity with the remedial positions to strengthen its justification of the use of force.

Abkhazia

The Georgian–Abkhaz ceasefire line along the Ingur/Enguri River, whose management and political significance are the theme of the contribution to this volume from Giulia Prelz Oltramonti and Gaëlle Le Pavic (Chapter 7), demarcates a territory that is controlled by Abkhazia and whose status is disputed between the two sides from a territory that is undisputedly part of the Georgian state. The ceasefire line between these two territories was agreed between the two sides in 1994. The authors describe how what was intended to be a temporary separation of military forces turned into a permanent one, and how this transformation increased the vulnerability of the local population on both sides of the line, despite all the creative strategies they deployed in their daily lives to survive economically. In contrast to Paylan's analysis of the failure to resolve the Nagorno-Karabakh conflict peacefully, Prelz Oltramonti and Le Pavic do not regard the (non-)recognition policies of the international community on the basis of the continuity position as questionable. On the contrary, they see Russia's recognition of Abkhazia, going against the continuity position, as a decisive factor in the hardening of the border and the negative transformation of the ceasefire line.

As we are reminded by these two authors, the Georgian authorities consider the border with Abkhazia to be purely administrative and domestic, referring to it as an 'administrative boundary line'. This fits in with the continuity position of Georgia, which views Abkhazia as having always belonged to its territory, and of the international community, which regards Abkhazia as subordinated to Georgia in the Soviet constitution. It could be added to their analysis of the Georgian view that Tbilisi also refers to the border in remedial terms as an 'occupation line', given the current Russian military presence in Abkhazia. The Abkhaz, by contrast, refer to it as a 'state border'. This tallies with a historical narrative in line with the remedial position which asserts that Abkhazia's integration into Soviet Georgia was unjustly imposed. Such contradictory interpretations confirm Prelz Oltramonti and Le Pavic's thesis of 'a deep ambiguity with regards to what the established dividing lines' are.

Tamil Eelam

Since their foundation in 1976, the Liberation Tigers of Tamil Eelam (LTTE) have claimed that the Tamils are the legitimate rulers of a 'traditional homeland' in north-eastern Sri Lanka. This view of the Tamils as a distinct nation, separate from the Sinhalese, with their own ancestral territory, emerged shortly after independence (Samarasinghe 1990: 3; Silva 1990: 35–36). According to this application of the remedial position, a Sinhalese policy of colonization and repression marginalized the Tamils in their own homeland. The destruction of the contested state known as Tamil Eelam (the final battles took place in 2009) extinguished all practical prospects of the restoration of this homeland.

Megan Price examines how international law was invoked to legitimize the use of force by Sri Lanka and its destruction of the contested state of Tamil Eelam in the period 2006–2009 (Chapter 3). Internationally, Tamil Eelam was, as she explains, generally not considered 'a legitimate candidate for external self-determination'. The war against it was seen as being governed by the laws of non-international armed conflict, which are less restrictive than those of international armed conflict. Moreover, the government of Sri Lanka weakened the constraining effect of international law on military policies by situating its counter-secession policies within the global war on terror. Price explains that the United States was unwilling to counter this discourse, especially at a time when it was itself involved in foreign wars in the name of that same war against terror. All these factors made the LTTE even 'more vulnerable to open military attack than secessionists in other cases'. Price also examines how the government of Sri Lanka used legal arguments to defend the 'any means necessary' approach in military operations, and denied responsibility for the harm these operations caused to the civilian population. In her view, the existing *in bello* constraints on war are too indeterminate to prevent misinterpretation, for example through a denialist strategy of contesting the existence of key events. Law was 'implicated in enabling violence'. This demonstrates that the legal vulnerability of the population of a contested state not only stems from the ambiguity inherent in the contested nature of statehood, as is demonstrated in other disputes analyzed in this volume, but can also be brought about by the interpretation of law itself. Price writes that 'the LTTE were an extreme case of vulnerability by law'.

Bart Klem's contribution (Chapter 8) proposes a performative perspective on what he describes as the 'sovereign experiment of a nascent state'. The LTTE enacted the attributes of statehood – such as the formation of a government and control over a territory – through institutional 'mimicry'. The four-way typology may be fruitful when analysing this enactment of statehood. The remedial position was useful for articulating the Tamil aspiration to independence before a national and international audience when asserting sovereignty. It allowed Tamil separatist militants to adopt a variety of roles – such as the representation of a nation struggling for liberation from oppression or one that is a victim of oppression (particularly in performances by diaspora actors before international audiences, after 2009). The narrative that fits the second role entails severe adjustments to the first, as described by Klem: 'Victim reports by selected individuals who had suffered the government's final military campaign became a vital discursive currency, while adulated leaders and martyrs seeped out of the plot'.

Kosovo, Crimea, and eastern Ukraine

In 2007 Marti Ahtisaari, the UN secretary-general's special envoy on Kosovo's future status, had concluded that status negotiations between Serbia and Kosovo were not leading anywhere. This stalemate, he believed, would force the international community to take a bold step by supporting the option of independence for Kosovo under international supervision. Ahtisaari linked this thesis, which conflicted with the continuity position, but was in line with the effectivist and remedial positions, with a *sui generis* argumentation. Owing to 'unique' circumstances, Kosovo's independence would not set any precedent for other conflicts.

In his contribution, Janis Grzybowski sheds light on how the International Court of Justice (ICJ) treated the status of Kosovo in its advisory opinion of 2010 (Chapter 10). To the question of whether the UDI by the Provisional Institutions of Self-Government of Kosovo (PISG) in 2008 was in accordance with international law, the court answered that the 'adoption of that declaration did not violate any applicable rule of international law'. The ICJ did not engage with the arguments for or against a remedial right to secession, or with the description of the case of Kosovo as '*sui generis*'. Nor did it say whether its recognition by other states was or was not a breach of international law. According to the ICJ, the UDI was issued not by the PISG in the capacity of a legal institution empowered to do so by the UN interim administration, but by representatives of the people of Kosovo, outside the framework of that administration. Grzybowski points out that the ICJ still implied that there was 'a "people of Kosovo", distinct from that of Serbia'. In his view, the eschewal of numerous questions relating to legal obstacles to state creation, together with the positive reference to a people of Kosovo, hinted at the existence of a Kosovar state but 'as potential fact outside the law'. This assumption meant that the ICJ became a 'reluctant, limited, and indirect' co-producer of a claim to statehood.

The ICJ's answer to the question of the legality of Kosovo's UDI is not characteristic of any of the four positions included in the typology. Its reference to a people of Kosovo was not embedded in an endorsement of an external right to self-determination, as would have been the case in an argumentation in accord with the choice position. Nor did it share or oppose arguments in accord with any of the three other positions, even though the UDI itself was issued in line with the effectivist and remedial positions as interpreted by the main Western countries. From the application of the four-way typology to Grzybowski's analysis we may conclude that it is possible to assume the existence of a state without having to choose between these four positions – but then only, to use his expression, of a state 'in the shadows'.

Júlia Miklasová looks at the impact of the recognition of Kosovo, and of the ICJ's advisory opinion on Russia's justification of its recognition of both Crimea's independence in 2014 and, eight years later, of that of four Ukrainian regions as independent states – acts of recognition that were followed, each time, by their incorporation into the Russian Federation (Chapter 4). She mentions Russia's support for a remedial right to secession in international law during the ICJ proceedings on Kosovo, but then in order to undermine Kosovo's claims to independence. According to Russia's statement before the ICJ in 2009, Kosovo had no remedial right to secession, as there was no oppression by Serbia. By contrast, in 2022 Putin claimed that almost four million people in the Donbas were facing a Ukrainian policy of genocide, which would justify Russia's recognition of its people's republics. Miklasová further refers to Putin's earlier allegation, in 2014, that Crimea's secession from Ukraine received the 'stunning' support of its population in its referendum on joining Russia as a federal subject, in contrast to Kosovo, where no such referendum had taken place. This, according to Putin, meant that the secession of Crimea was more in line with the principle of national self-determination than that of Kosovo. This argument may be seen as being in accordance with the choice position. Miklasová also refers to a further Russian assertion, which was that its procedure for admitting new subjects into the Russian Federation did not contradict its respect for the 1991 *uti possidetis* border *status quo* for the post-Soviet space overall. Russia's recognition of new states referred to specific states, such as Ukraine, where (it claimed) the right of new republics to secede overrode the previously established international boundaries – which meant that Russia was not denying its previous acceptance of the continuity position. This shows how Russia pursued its persuasive strategy through a combination of three different positions.

According to Miklasová, the *sui generis* argumentation of governments in favour of Kosovo's UDI had an eroding impact on legal opinions on statehood generally. The unwillingness of the ICJ to distinguish clearly between admissible and inadmissible secession also facilitated the drawing of wrong inferences in other cases of secession. This generated a more permissive environment regarding the right to secession, allowing Russia to reorient its recognition policies in order to pursue subversive policies elsewhere. Miklasová concludes that it would be wrong, however, to state that there is any real ambiguity regarding the legal status of the Russian annexations in Ukraine. Still the shortcomings mentioned above have allowed Russia 'to project the air of lawfulness or at least ambiguity of its acts vis-à-vis the relevant international or domestic audiences'.

Western Sahara and Palestine

The dispute on the status of the Western Sahara is rooted in a thwarted process of decolonization from Spain, as indicated by Irene Fernández-Molina in her contribution to this volume (Chapter 6). Occupation by Morocco was superimposed on the legal status of a non-self-governing territory. This links the realization of the right to national self-determination for the Sahrawis firmly to the continuity position, in the context of the decolonization process. Morocco, by contrast, opposes such an application of the continuity position when asserting that this territory was once among its pre-colonial possessions.

The international community is divided on the question of the future of the Western Sahara and Palestine, but there is still widespread support for the view that their people's right to national self-determination is rooted in what is conceptualized in the present chapter as the continuity position. This interpretation expands the applicability of international humanitarian law and strengthens the legal status of both entities before international courts. Fernández-Molina analyzes the involvement of international courts in constructing the statehood of the Western Sahara as part of the lawfare being waged by the conflicting parties. The capacity of the Sahrawi Arab Democratic Republic (SADR) to wage such a legal struggle before the courts and to dispel some fundamental ambiguities in its best interests does not, however, eliminate its vulnerability as a contested state.

This is also the case for Palestine. As expounded by Grzybowksi (Chapter 10), the International Criminal Court (ICC), despite its attempt to 'functionally restrict the question of statehood for the purpose of establishing and circumscribing the ICC's jurisdiction' in investigating international crimes committed on the territory of Palestine, 'invoked a Palestinian state in ways that point beyond the specific purposes of international criminal law', without fully endorsing statehood.

The prominence of the continuity position in disputes on the status of the Western Sahara and Palestine does not rule out the presence of remedial arguments. Third parties, furthermore, defend an effectivist position to give a new direction to their policies on these two disputes when dealing with the *fait accompli* policies of Morocco and Israel, the respective occupying powers. The United States, Spain, and France, all three closely involved in the search for a settlement of the status of the Western Sahara, have fundamentally changed their position in line with the effectivist stance. Confronted with the lack of a feasible prospect of conflict resolution in line with the continuity position, they now favour autonomous status within Morocco as a workable solution for the Western Sahara, in contrast to their former non-recognition policies regarding Moroccan occupation (Africanews 2022).

As for the Israeli–Palestinian conflict, the relocation of the US embassy from Tel Aviv to Jerusalem in 2018, following the American recognition of this latter city as the Israeli capital a year before, was justified by the same effectivist position, even though the United States declared that this relocation did not affect its commitment to a two-state solution in which borders would have to be negotiated. The American recognition of Israel's annexation of the Golan Heights in 2019 can also be viewed in this context.

Conclusion

The international debates on the status of the contested states of Taiwan, Nagorno-Karabakh, Abkhazia and Tamil Eelam are dominated by interpretations of the continuity position that deny the statehood of these entities. The annihilation of the state structures of Nagorno-Karabakh and Tamil Eelam through the use of force also finds a normative justification in the continuity position, as a means of last resort. In the conflicts on the status of the Western Sahara and Palestine, by contrast, the dominant interpretation of the continuity position favours their entitlement to independent statehood – without, however, granting them full recognition immediately, or making them less vulnerable to military attack.

Arguments in line with the continuity position feature most prominently in this volume. The remedial position is very much present too, however, mostly in combination with others, as for instance in the disputes on the statehood of Kosovo or the annexation of Ukrainian territories by Russia. The choice position is marginal, reflecting its weakness in international law. In some of the conflicts that show no sign of being resolved, third parties justify a change of their (non-)recognition policies using arguments characteristic of the effectivist position. This is most salient in the case of Kosovo, but is also relevant to the conflicts on the future of the Western Sahara and Palestine.

In statehood disputes, states pursue persuasive strategies that are based on either a single position or a combination. The authors of this volume likewise adopt mixed positions, especially when taking a stance on a particular dispute on statehood or expressing their concern about the adverse consequences of particular recognition or non-recognition policies. One author, for instance, formulates a fundamental criticism of the continuity position that dominates international law; her own approach is based on a combination of the choice and remedial positions.

The contributors to this volume have divergent opinions on the degree and significance of the ambiguity of the contested statehood they observe in the cases they are discussing, although they converge in their finding that this ambiguity increases the vulnerability both of a contested state and of its population. One argument goes that such ambiguity does not allow for an unequivocal stance in legal disputes on contested statehood, at least not in the case the author is dealing with. Another goes that, while ambiguity is indeed a major issue in such disputes, it is still possible to take a clear stance on the legal status of contested states. According to a third view, ambiguity is a weapon that can be used in argumentative strategies to either weaken or strengthen the status of a contested state. Some contested states themselves make use, successfully, of existing ambiguities, for instance by taking the judicial route. A fourth will focus rather on the fact that the ambiguity of contested statehood is open to abuse by third parties who see it as a means to undermine the policies of their adversaries or to make their own policies more acceptable. A fifth argument states that the vulnerability of contested states results not only from the ambiguity inherent in their nature but also from the interpretation of law itself. Ambiguity is thus itself a term open to different interpretations – including in the study of contested statehood in war and law.

Acknowledgements

My thanks go to Catherine Woollard for her comments on this chapter and to Veronica Kelly for her language corrections.

References

Africanews (2022). Spain Changes Tune on Western Sahara. *Africanews*, www.africanews.com/2022/03/19/spain-changes-tune-on-western-sahara//.

Chan, P.C.W. (2009). The Legal Status of Taiwan and the Legality of the Use of Force in a Cross-Taiwan Strait Conflict. *Chinese Journal of International Law*, 8 (2), 455–492.

Coppieters, B. (2018). Four Positions on the Recognition of States in and after the Soviet Union, with Special Reference to Abkhazia. *Europe-Asia Studies*, 70 (6), 991–1014, https://doi.org/10.1080/09668136.2018.1487682.

Corten, O. (2021). *The Law Against War: The Prohibition on the Use of Force in Contemporary International Law*. London: Bloomsbury Publishing.

Samarasinghe, S.W.R. de A. (1990). Introduction. In: R.R. Premdas, S.W.R. de A. Samarasinghe, and A.B. Anderson (eds), *Secessionist Movements in Comparative Perspective*. London: Pinter, 1–9.

Silva, K.M. de (1990). Secessionist Movements in Comparative Perspective. In: R.R. Premdas, S.W.R. de A. Samarasinghe, and A.B. Anderson (eds), *Secessionist Movements in Comparative Perspective*. London: Pinter, 32–47.

Vidmar, J. (2013). Unilateral Declarations of Independence in International Law. In: D. French (ed.), *Statehood and Self-Determination: Reconciling Tradition and Modernity in International Law*, Cambridge: Cambridge University Press, 60–78.

Wellman, C. (2010). The Morality of Secession. In: D.H. Doyle (ed.), *Secession as an International Phenomenon*. Athens: University of Georgia Press, 19–36.

12

Speculative Legalities and the Ambiguities of Contested States

Rebecca Bryant

Introduction

In June 2024, Simon Aykut, head of the Afik Group of property investors and a citizen of Portugal, Israel, and Turkey, was arrested in the Republic of Cyprus (RoC) and detained pending trial for sale of Greek Cypriot properties in the island's north. Within weeks, the RoC also detained four more EU citizens – two German and two Hungarian – on charges of marketing or selling land in the unrecognized Turkish Republic of Northern Cyprus (TRNC). Reports in October 2024 were that the RoC had issued another 38 arrest warrants for foreign investors in the TRNC. In response, the Turkish Cypriot Union of Property Developers formed the Protection of Rights Initiative (Hakların Korunması İniyisatifi), issuing a statement that read in part, 'Our aim is peace. We want development within peace. It is to the benefit of the people of Cyprus for us to develop while protecting the rights of property owners in both North and South. Preventing this puts the people at odds and impedes a solution to the Cyprus problem' (Postasi 2024).

For more than three decades, lawfare has been one of the main ways in which Cypriots, caught in a longstanding and unresolved conflict, advance political claims (Bryant 2009; Bryant and Hatay 2009; Hatay 2024). As the Introduction (Grzybowski et al, this volume) and other chapters in this volume note, international law favours recognized states, and we see this in various judgments regarding the Cyprus dispute made by the European Court of Justice (ECJ) and the European Court of Human Rights (ECtHR). In these cases, the ECtHR labels the TRNC Turkey's 'subordinate authority' and accepts only Turkey as a respondent. Turkey has been found responsible, inter alia, for preventing the return of Greek Cypriots to their properties; for impeding the search for missing persons; and for violating rights of free movement on an island that since 2004 is technically an EU territory.

Like other examples discussed in this collection, this unevenness of the legal playing field leaves Turkish Cypriots vulnerable, as when a 1994 ECJ decision forbade the export of fruit and other products produced in the north that bore a TRNC stamp. Nevertheless, Turkish Cypriots, like citizens of other contested states, have developed forms of constrained agency – what a co-author and I elsewhere call 'aporetic agency' (Bryant and Hatay 2020). As we describe it, this is agency disguised as its lack, 'agency that is able to have real effects on the world but at the same time *should not* have those effects'. It is the agency of the work-around, of getting by, for example embargoes that prevent sale of goods abroad or the lack of direct flights to the island's north. As the Introduction (Grzybowski et al, this volume) to this collection notes, '[A]ctors in the grey zone creatively use, emphasize, or work around contested statehood'.

One of the creative ways of using that grey zone that has been most examined in the literature on unrecognized states is how actors employ ambiguous legality to their economic advantage (Blakkisrud and Kolstø 2011; 2012; Kolstø 2000; 2006; Kolstø and Blakkisrud 2008). As Charles King states it most starkly, 'War is the engine of state building, but it is also good for business' (2001: 524). According to King and others, certain conflicts are longstanding and seemingly irresolvable or 'frozen' in large part because certain groups have material interests in maintaining the *status quo*. 'Diamonds in Angola, timber in Cambodia, and coca in Colombia have all become spoils of war that fuel conflict while discouraging settlement' (King 2001).

I would like to suggest, however, that constrained agency in the aporetic grey zone of contested statehood may offer more than economic benefit; it may offer an opportunity to shift the grounds of the conflict. If citizens of a recognized 'parent state' have the legal high ground, citizens of an unrecognized secessionist entity have the literal ground, and this enables them to engage in what Tanja Aalberts and I (in progress) refer to as 'speculative legalities'. By speculative legalities we mean the ways that citizens of contested states use their constrained agency to employ practices that attempt to shape the future of law.

In this brief discussion, I will first give two examples from the Cyprus case before looking at how these allow us to think differently about cases in this collection. I will then conclude by suggesting that the contested states literature needs greater attention to temporality, and especially legal temporalities. This can help us understand how citizens of contested states use the means at their disposal to attempt to influence future outcomes that are otherwise out of their control.

Speculative legalities

In 2004, Cypriots were offered the opportunity to resolve their longstanding political problem in the form of a UN-sponsored plan that would have reunited the island in a bicommunal, bizonal federation. However, when that plan was put to referendum on both sides of the Green Line, Greek Cypriots overwhelmingly rejected it – despite, or perhaps because of, Turkish Cypriots' acceptance of it. Initially, there was some hope amongst Turkish Cypriots that the international community would 'reward' them for their 'yes' vote, either through implementing direct flights or direct trade or both. When neither of those materialized and further negotiations failed, rumblings began in Turkey and in nationalist circles in Cyprus that it was time to abandon the pointless negotiations and 'develop' the island's north.

Until that moment, proposals to build on Greek-titled property or to try to bring mass tourism of the sort that drives the economy of the island's south had generally been shot down and seen as short-sighted, in that the temporality in which Turkish Cypriots lived was one of temporariness, a situation that was legally liminal and could always change. Moreover, starting in 1996, cases brought by Greek Cypriots in the ECtHR began to pay off. In that year, a displaced Greek Cypriot woman, Titina Loizidou, won a case regarding her property in the seaside town of Kyrenia. The ECtHR ordered Turkey to pay restitution for preventing her return and for loss of use over by then more than two decades. Although Turkey ignored the judgment for several years, the government finally decided in 2001 that it would have to pay the compensation as part of its EU accession bid. Thousands of new cases followed, though the ECtHR was able to put these on hold for some time as reunification negotiations that would have solved the property problem were ongoing.

In the wake of the 2004 failed referendum, the court was less sympathetic and in 2006 decided that Turkey might establish an Immovable Property Commission in Cyprus's north as a court of first resort, effectively sending the thousands of dossiers clogging the court's docket back to the island. It was at this moment that a construction boom began on Greek Cypriot property in the island's north, apparently with the assumption that in any future negotiated settlement Greek Cypriot owners would need to accept compensation and would not be taking their land back.

The next almost two decades have been filled with various uses of local and international courts as Greek Cypriots have tried to use their legal upper hand to stall an economy that could only ever be built on appropriated land. One landmark case was *Apostolides v Orams*, a case that the appellant, Meletis Apostolides, began after the 2003 easing of movement restrictions across the Green Line. Until that opening, there had been almost three decades in which both Greek and Turkish Cypriots were effectively unable to access the properties that they had left behind on the 'other side' with the island's *de facto* division in 1974. That opening had, in turn, been a response to the Loizidou case, which was based on loss of access to the property.

Following that opening, Cypriots could access their property, though they could not reclaim it, and Meletis Apostolides crossed the Green Line to find that a British couple had built a large villa in what had been his orchard. With that case, Apostolides could also bring his suit in a local court, since with the opening a bailiff could cross the checkpoints and deliver a summons to the Orams' door. The Nicosia District Court and later the Supreme Court ruled in favour of Apostolides, ordering the Orams to demolish the villa. However, he was unable to enforce the decision because of the island's division and so took his case to the High Court of Justice in the United Kingdom, seeking to seize the Orams' assets there. By that time, the RoC had become an EU member state and so could seek enforcement of its judgements in other EU member states. Although the High Court of Justice ruled in favour of the Orams, Apostolides appealed to the European Court of Justice (ECJ), which in 2009 ruled in Apostolides' favour. The Orams sought to appeal to the Supreme Court of the United Kingdom, but their request was denied. They abandoned the villa and, in a deal with the TRNC government, claimed that the local authorities prevented them from demolishing it.

As one might expect, this and other problems cooled the real estate market for quite some time. What kickstarted it about a decade later was the 2017 failure of renewed negotiations and the more active involvement of the Turkish government in 'developing' the island's north. For decades, Turkish big business had been reluctant to invest in the island; wealthy Turkish businessman Sakıp Sabancı reportedly said in the past that he would not sink his money there because 'there's no point in writing on ice'. In the past decade or so, however, Turkish capital has been flowing into the island in the form of large hotels, casinos, and shopping malls. There has been a proliferation of four-lane highways, massive hotels on formerly pristine beaches, enormous mosque complexes, a new airport that is a replica of the one in Ankara, and plans for opening up more land to development. Large Turkish corporations have been making multi-million-euro investments, building high-rises on beaches and luxurious housing developments that have left marks on the landscape and in some cases brought global enterprises to the island's north.

Moreover, Turkish Cypriot developers have gone out looking for new markets, starting outside the EU. One initial market was Norway, which is not an EU member state. The Ukraine war accelerated that market transformation, as both Russian and Ukrainian citizens sought safe havens and places to park capital. Today, one finds 'for sale' signs not only in

Russian but also in Farsi, Arabic, and Hebrew, as persons seeking a safe haven snatch up beachfront properties in a place where international law cannot touch them.

Given the ongoing political conflict on the island, these are more than economic investments; they are investments in creating a particular type of future. They are speculative investments that gamble with the legal force of normalization through creating new facts on the ground. In a brilliant article that dissects the legal force of the *status quo*, Nomi Stolzenberg asks how facts on the ground created in Israel have acquired a normative force, one that creates a new *status quo* that is difficult to dismantle. She remarks:

> When we say that facts on the ground 'cannot' be undone, we do not mean that they 'cannot' be undone in a literal sense. (Of course, they *can* be undone; all it takes is physical force, as the [2006] pullout from Gaza boldly demonstrated). Rather, 'cannot' is a normative term, referring to political and moral 'impossibilities.' This is both the core idea and the basic mystery of facts on the ground. (2010: 22)

It is this basic mystery that is at the core of the Turkish government's current involvement in Cyprus, creating a state of confidence for investments that has transformed north Cyprus from a relative backwater where property values were low in comparison to the rest of the Mediterranean into a site of luxury developments with soaring prices to match. It has even put an unrecognized state in a frozen conflict at the top of Forbes' list of best beachfront buys (Peddicord 2021).

The latter is quite an interesting development, given that property is one of the most highly charged issues of the still-unresolved Cyprus problem. Much of the land on which new high-rises are being built have disputed title deeds that Greek Cypriots still claim. This may be one reason that the main customers in Iskele, the particular part of the island that Forbes recommends, are Russians, Iranians, and Israelis. Entire estate agencies are devoted to selling property to people from these countries. Given their own experiences with political turmoil and the vagaries of property markets, it seems these buyers have confidence that no one is going to come and take their property away. As one real estate agent with whom I spoke told me: 'The title deeds just don't matter anymore. No one's afraid of losing their property'.

One can see this as a legitimation of the *status quo*, the situation that has existed on the island since the 1974 ceasefire. It is also, however, a way of creating a new *status quo*, a new situation of irreversibility. These developments gamble that despite UN resolutions against the declaration of sovereignty of the state in northern Cyprus, and despite the protests of the Greek Cypriot owners of these properties, there will be no serious intervention that will reverse these changes. While there are different ways of creating facts on the ground, construction is the most literal one, as it cements changes into the landscape.

Legal ambiguities of contested states

This analysis is in consonance with chapters in this collection, several of which deal with normalization of the *status quo*, the creation of what Stolzenberg (2010) calls a 'normative force'. While my examples so far have been from north Cyprus and so represent the secessionist side of the contested state spectrum, some of the clearest examples of speculative legalities come from chapters looking at the actions of 'parent states', those recognized entities from which the unrecognized state has attempted to break away. Megan Price, for instance, writes of the gamble that the Sri Lankan state took in initially portraying its army as 'saving' civilians trapped in the island's north and west (Chapter 3). By portraying their actions as a rescue operation, 'the Sri Lankan government sought to disengage the law by narrating its military action so as to render the principles of distinction and proportionality irrelevant'. When later investigations showed that the Sri Lankan army's bombardment had killed many civilians, the government attempted to portray those civilians as complicit. 'In the event the government successfully characterizes a portion of the civilians as "voluntary shields", then on their logic, those civilians would be responsible for their *own* deaths.'

We see in this case how recognized governments with the legal upper hand can still work to stretch that advantage, particularly by creating particular facts on the ground that they gamble can be legitimized through their own role as legitimate narrators of the conflict. We see similar processes at work in Júlia Miklasová's contribution (Chapter 4), where she analyzes the role of Kosovo's secession in Russian claims over Ukrainian territory. Miklasová argues that the Kosovo case allows Russia 'to project the air of lawfulness or at least ambiguity of its acts vis-à-vis the relevant international or domestic audiences'. A similar gamble was at work in Azerbaijan's recent war to reclaim Nagorno-Karabakh, as Sheila Paylan describes in Chapter 5. As Miklasová notes for the Ukraine case, 'form prevails over the substance'. As I have attempted to show through the TRNC example, however, the gamble or speculation in such acts is the idea that form creates its own substance, a new *status quo* or facts on the ground that will ultimately be normalized, even in law.

We see such normalization, and the practices that emerge around it, particularly well in cases where legal regimes – or claims to legal regimes – intersect or clash. Giulia Prelz Oltramonti and Gaëlle Le Pavic's chapter illustrates this particularly well, as they demonstrate how ceasefire lines become more and more like borders over time. In the case of the ceasefire line dividing Georgia from the breakaway state of Abkhazia, Prelz Oltramonti and Le Pavic (Chapter 7) note:

> Because of its provisions on the illegality of economic and administrative activities in Abkhazia, the law deepens the divide between Abkhazia (and the other occupied territory of South Ossetia) and the rest of Georgia. It implicitly recognizes a profound difference between one side and the other of the CfL [ceasefire line] and codifies provisions aimed at rendering everyday activities in Abkhazia illegal.

In other words, such codification renders ceasefire lines border-like, normalizing division. We see similar practices in other contested cases. In Cyprus, for instance, following the 2016 EU–Turkey deal on migration and the effective closure of Turkey's Aegean border, several thousand refugees and migrants attempted to enter Cyprus through the unrecognized north and make their way to the south, where they could claim asylum. The result has been that the recognized RoC has hardened the ceasefire line, installing high-tech surveillance and making crossings more difficult for non-citizens. All this happens despite the RoC claiming sovereignty over the island's north. The effect, then, is similar to what Prelz Otramonti and Le Pavic observe for Georgia: 'While Georgian authorities justify these measures on security grounds, the extensive controls inadvertently make the divide more prominent and border-like, despite the official Georgian rhetoric framing Abkhazia as an "autonomous region of Georgia"'.

Bart Klem (Chapter 8) frames such practices in performative terms, taking the example of the LTTE to argue that its main actors, the LTTE 'boys', generated a sense of both pride and wonder among their constituents, as they 'were now flying round acting like suit-clad diplomats, shaking hands with dignitaries – without getting found out'. Klem notes that international actors engaged in what he calls (following Liza Wedeen) 'as-if' politics: 'treating the LTTE for what it enacted itself to be, a state-in-the-making'. Moreover, he asserts, this theatre captivated both local and international audiences precisely because of its vulnerability: '[A] lot was at stake, and it was radically unclear how the plot would end … To stick with the theatrical idiom, the curtains could fall unexpectedly, and it was unclear who would still be standing when they did – or indeed who would survive the next act'.

What the theatre metaphor allows us to see is how protagonists in this drama set the geopolitical stage. What I have tried to argue in this short chapter is that looking only at the action, the theatre, is not sufficient. One must also look at agency and intent, in other words, what such geopolitical theatre is intended to produce. In other words, one must also look – as the protagonists in these dramas do – to the future. Klem acknowledges this when he notes: 'These institutions may lack an accepted legal basis, but they gain implied forms of recognition, and as such they project an anticipation of graduating into a legally valid and politically recognized entity in the future'. The idea of graduating into legal validity is what I referred to earlier as normalization, that 'basic mystery of facts on the ground', as Stolzenberg (2010) put it, that makes them appear irreversible, as though they will continue into the distant future.

In sum, this important collection breaks new ground in demonstrating the malleability of law and the ways in which the law itself can become a party to conflict. It does so by creating the conditions of ambiguity, vulnerability, and constrained agency that define life in contested states for their citizens. However, it also becomes a tool by which those citizens manage, struggle against, and get around the constraints that bind them. In this intervention, I have attempted to point out that such tactics are not only of the moment but have their own temporalities that are often lasting. Indeed, that may be the point, as constrained citizens create new facts on the ground that they speculate will change the political and legal grounds of conflict.

References

Blakkisrud, H. and Kolstø, P. (2011). From Secessionist Conflict Toward a Functioning State: Processes of State- and Nation-Building in Transnistria. *Post-Soviet Affairs*, 27 (2), 178–210.

Blakkisrud, H. and Kolstø, P. (2012). Dynamics of de Facto Statehood: The South Caucasian de Facto States Between Secession and Sovereignty. *Southeast European and Black Sea Studies*, 12 (2), 281–298.

Bryant, R. (2009). Of Lemons and Laws: Property and the (Trans)national Order in Cyprus. In: B. Rose Johnston and S. Slyomovics (eds), *Waging War and Making Peace: Reparations and Human Rights*. San Francisco: Left Coast Press.

Bryant, R. and Hatay, M. (2009). *Suing for Sovereignty: Property, Territory and EU's Cyprus Problem*. Global Political Trends Center Policy Brief. Istanbul: Global Political Trends Center.

Bryant, R. and Hatay, M. (2020). *Sovereignty Suspended: Building the So-Called State*. Philadelphia: University of Pennsylvania Press.

Hatay, M. (2024). *The Cyprus Property Issue and the Return of Lawfare*. Occasional Paper Series. Nicosia: PRIO Cyprus Centre.

King, C. (2001). The Benefits of Ethnic War: Understanding Eurasia's Unrecognized States. *World Politics*, 53 (July), 524–552.

Kolstø, P. (2000). *Political Construction Sites: Nation-Building in Russia and the Post-Soviet States*. Boulder: Westview.

Kolstø, P. (2006). The Sustainability and Future of Unrecognized Quasi-States. *Journal of Peace Research*, 43 (6), 723–740.

Kolstø, P. and Blakkisrud, H. (2008). Living with Non-Recognition: State- and Nation- Building in South Caucasian Quasi-States. *Europe-Asia Studies*, 60 (3), 483–509.

Peddicord, K. (2021). 5 Best Beachfront Buys. *Forbes Magazine*, 3 February, www.forbes.com/sites/kathleenpeddicord/2021/02/05/5-best-beachfront-buys-for-2021/.

Postasi, K. (2024). Hakların Korunması İnisiyatifi eylem düzenliyor: Bizim amacımız barıştır, barış içinde kalkınma istiyoruz [The Rights Protection Initiative organizes action: Our goal is peace, we want development in peace], 9 October, www.kibrispostasi.com/c35-KIBRIS_HABERLERI/n535959-haklarin-korunmasi-inisiyatifi-eylem-duzenliyor-bizim-amacimiz-baristir-baris-icinde-kalkinma-istiyoruz?fbclid=IwY2xjawF3AHRleHRuA2FlbQIxMQABHfbkoOkHaio2Cku4Vc6jx57WBVO4ybYTdtuK7tNnPTLBfEwBWeBAuJVAkw_aem_eyK5AFpHf4nfXT_oE7ay3Q.

Stolzenberg, N.M. (2010). 'Facts on the Ground.' In: G.S. Alexander and E.M. Peñalver (eds), *Property and Community,*. Oxford: Oxford University Press, 107–139.

13

The Melancholy Statehood

Martti Koskenniemi

The desire for sovereign statehood persists. It persists even if historical experience shows that the struggle for sovereignty is a terrain of blood and tears, that the goal is anything but guaranteed, and that, once it has been attained, it may well show itself disappointing. Statehood may sometimes appear the proud achievement of an industrious people. But it may as well mark the final consolidation of a local elite whose power has been made invulnerable by the status granted by its peers abroad. Or it may be simply a side-effect of some geopolitical rivalry. And yet, as the chapters in this volume show, the desire for statehood frames some of the most intractable crises across the globe, creating hybrids, grey areas, and vulnerabilities with elements of state power awkwardly scattered here and there. That the search for justice must be imagined as a struggle for statehood is surely one of the less fortunate implications of legal-political frame that divides the world into states with all the sovereign rights, powers and privileges that the status entails and not-states with none of the qualities that make for the full agency ('legal subjecthood') in the international world.

The formalism of the distinction states/not-states has, of course, its solid historical justification. The time when international thought was comfortable with all kinds of half-sovereign or semi-sovereign entities, protectorates, and areas of special status derived from feudalism or colonialism reflected a political order catering to the histories, interests, and ambitions of few European powers. The strict formalism of statehood imposed by modern international law was designed to put an end to all that. The view that recognition by existing (great) powers was 'constitutive' of the statehood of a candidate entity collapsed. In the twentieth century, access to statehood would no longer be controlled by assessments of status based on differences in religion or degrees of civilization. Every nation would be entitled to decide on its political future. Big or small, wealthy or poor, whatever your resources, history, system of faith, demographic composition, once you fulfilled the law-determined criteria of statehood – a fixed territory, a stable population, and a government capable of guaranteeing the implementation of your international obligations – if all that came together, then statehood and all the rights, powers, and privileges attached to that status would fall your way. These ideas were eventually reflected in the right to membership of the United Nations reserved to 'peace-loving states' that would enjoy 'sovereign equality' under Article 2:1 of the UN Charter.

There is no point to demonstrate, once again, the utter unreality of that presentation of things. Of course, the international system is terribly unequal. Of course, states have different degrees of influence, independence, resources, and abilities to turn their officially declared policies into reality. Of course, the veil of formal statehood protects governments that are often best understood as mafioso arrangements managing a protection racket among their population. Besides, many entities have had access to statehood even if doubts may be presented regarding their fulfilment of the formal criteria while others are deprived of statehood – think of Taiwan, for example – even as they easily meet them. Despite all the well-known sociological, moral, and legal problems with sovereignty, formal statehood still has exceptional weight as a means to rally populations, especially those feeling themselves in the past unjustly treated, for a collective effort towards a better future. 'Statehood or Death!' we hear from across the world.

While statehood may be nothing empirically real, nor is it a mere *fiction*, as one of the sharpest thinkers of modern statehood, Georg Jellinek, noted at the turn of the twentieth century. It is not fiction, but an *abstraction*, a way to frame and organize groups of human beings in a determinate hierarchy by attributing to them some common project, 'nation-building', 'self-determination'. Its meaning and attraction cannot be analyzed without attention to the quality of that project, the objectives and values it is meant to realize. In writing thus, Jellinek was canvassing a 'legal' concept of statehood as an ideal of life in common in contradistinction to a 'sociological' one that focused on the historical and empirical facts about territorial power. Yet he also accepted that facts had a normative force that led observers to interpret well-established systems of rule as also legally valid as such (Jellinek 1905: 49–51, 334).[1] Hence the effort by groups in search of a better life to create *de facto* situations to which the rest of the world – and especially their neighbours – would simply have to yield. Jellinek did recognize the tension that existed between the normative goals and the empirical power – the two sometimes, maybe often, pointing in different directions (Jellinek 1905: 336–345). The potential of contestation is intrinsic in statehood, its

---

[1] On the fiction-abstraction distinction, see Jellinek 1892: 16.

normative and factual side in more or less sharp tension with each other. In the struggle between a consolidated territorial power and a normative element contesting it, as the chapters in this volume show, international law has taken, almost without exception, the side of the already-existing state. It has a strong bias against secession. For groups whose leaders are not invited to the tables of heads of state or government, it has had only crumbs to offer.

The crumbs consist of some set of minority and human rights, a little local autonomy, maybe some type of indigenous status, and so on, all at the sufferance of the formal sovereign. Such compromises often leave both dissatisfied. Still, it is hard to dispute the wisdom, employed by the International Court of Justice (ICJ), to yield to existing hierarchical arrangements in order to avoid 'fratricidal struggles' (ICJ 1986: para. 20). The melancholy truth is that little assistance has been received from the traditional criteria – territory, population, government. Neither Jellinek nor later jurists were able to dispense with the wide interpretive margin such expressions allowed or discussed them without recourse to a plethora of exceptions and anomalies, often engrained as '*de facto*' arrangements with the result, as the Introduction (Grzybowski et al, this volume) laid it out and the case studies amply demonstrated, of ambiguity, vulnerability, and constrained agency.

A predominant theme in the chapters is setting aside the law's formal concern for status and instead examining the situations under a 'functional' lens. In fact, this had also been Jellinek's perspective as he reflected on the justification of modern statehood. Its point, according to him, was neither transcendental happiness nor monarchic glory, but the security and welfare of a population, situated among others in a world of ambitious rulers and limited resources (Jellinek 1905: 580–609). The turn to functionalism is very common in late modern law. Once the assumption that statehood as a matter of applying sharp criteria or black and white rules has been set aside as excessively formalistic, the way is open for a casuistic treatment of situations as they arise with the view to pragmatic compromises around the most important interests. In the example discussed by Ming-chin Monique Chu (Chapter 2, this volume), for instance, regarding the application of the laws on the use of force with regard to Taiwan, a *de facto* state, the concerns of geopolitics and of the potential effects of all-out war utterly overwhelm concerns of formal status. Such an attitude towards sovereignty as a function of 'global governance' has characterized international efforts to deal with Kosovo and Palestine, during many decades, and is quite strikingly adopted with regard to the Kurdish territory of Rojava that rules itself as an autonomous administration in northern Syria with the tacit, albeit reluctant, consent of the surrounding states. As Grzybowski shows in his chapter (Chapter 10, this volume), and Lagerwall in hers (Chapter 9, this volume), the attitudes of international courts, too, towards Kosovo, Palestine, and the many *de facto* regimes on Europe's fringes have been characterized by deference to the diplomatic efforts to avoid being stuck with clear-cut determinations of status and instead to look for reasonable adjustments.

Such pragmatism is quite in line with the managerialism underlying present-day legal practices. Why fuss over formal status when more concrete results may be attained by identifying the preferences of the actors in dispute and calculate some sort of optimal accommodation? The bright rationality of the approach coincides with the (Kelsenian) view of sovereignty as really nothing else than a bundle of rights, powers, and privileges that a state may have under prevailing law and that a government may either withhold or contract away in view of some countervailing benefits, as regularly done in international treaties. As a result, a 'contested state' such as Taiwan may well possess some powers, rights, or privileges that members of the European Union lack because they have transferred them to the union. And yet, if EU members are still considered as 'sovereign' (which for the most part they of course are), this seems to show that possessing the quality of sovereign statehood is not (or not only) a fact, but a conclusion based on a complex determination of a legal situation.

But functionalism also has its obvious dark side. Is jockeying between local actors, as well as Brussels and Washington in regard to the situation of Western Sahara, as discussed by Irene Fernández-Molina (Chapter 6, this volume), really so different from the nineteenth-century African scramble, with native communities reduced to playthings for larger geopolitical ambitions? And what about the manipulations of neighbouring actors using the grievances of a local population – Russian advances in Donetsk or Luhansk, say? No doubt, what has prevented functional practices from ever attaining the status of reigning *theory* of sovereignty has to do with the ease with which it can be used to uphold colonial-inflected practices and hierarchies. Ambiguity of status is, after all, just another way of saying that things are up for grabs for those who can.

Which is why, despite its reasonableness or even banality of functionalism, the chapters in this volume also show that it is frequently unhelpful. It is not likely that there ever was a moment when the claims made by Russia on Ukraine, the situation of Nagorno-Karabakh, or the struggle of the Tamil Tigers for independence could have been disposed by some apparently rational redistribution of the rights, powers, and privileges of sovereignty. The very conflicts began with the absence of the kind of moderate reasonableness required. Maybe it is present only in rare cases. The settlement of the Åland islands problem between Sweden and Finland through the League of Nations in the early 1920s might have been an example. But here the dispute was between countries with a common history, and with no blood spilled on either side. It would be hard to apply it as a persuasive precedent in any of the above-discussed cases. And although diplomats like to cite precedents, one wonders about their persuasiveness among distant communities with wholly different histories.

In performances of statehood more is at issue than fulfilling preset criteria or declared willingness to a reasonable adjustment – even if the massive lawfare conducted by the parties routinely follow the prescribed notions. What works, how positions develop, depends on the expectations of domestic and foreign audiences that cannot be written into any algorithm. Palestine or the Sahrawi Arab Democratic Republic may seem quite sufficiently 'like' states in order to be treated as such by the great majority of the states in the world. The operation of sympathies is here obvious – and one may not exclude the readiness of the great majority of UN members to deal a blow to Western high-handedness. Besides, in these cases, no little role has been played by the skilful political work by the representatives of the contested states.

The other cases of contested statehood discussed in the chapters in this volume tend to confirm a standard pattern. The discussion of the Tamil Tigers by Klem (Chapter 8, this volume) shows that establishment and conduct of regular administration may go quite far without, nevertheless, inspiring any massive international push towards recognition. The law's strong conservative bias – the 'normative power of facts' – works against separatism. As shown by Megan Price (Chapter 3, this volume), the Sri Lankan position utterly outweighed the power of Tamil nationalist claims. Much more room opens for lawfare in a situation such as discussed by Prelz Oltramonti and Le Pavic (Chapter 7, this volume), where a ceasefire line is interpreted by the protagonists in contrasting ways in the case of Abkhazia and Georgia. The law is here less an element in settling a dispute than an instrument for keeping alive the conflict while allowing ad hoc arrangement on the ground. A factual situation may indeed be indeterminate in the sense of allowing conflicting interpretations of its legal meaning.

Having read these chapters, one is left with the impression that, however ambiguous the status of a *de facto* regime, whatever the degree of its vulnerability and whatever type of agency its representatives may expect to attain is immensely more dependent on the political context surrounding the regime than on however well it may seem to perform in view of its diplomatic audience. And the context may vary greatly in scale. Is it a single state in existence, that is bursting at its seams? Is it a group of people, situated between old adversaries, pushing and pulling their liminal space as the vicissitudes of history and ambition dictate? Is it a territory long contested as part of some regional balance of power – or perhaps a tipping-point in the struggle between global block leaders? The law speaks of self-determination and identity, but these are constantly constructed in relationship to something that they are not, that something pressing upon groups of people in a way to make their situation seem quite literally one of life and death. If present law and policy have constructed themselves in contrast to a nineteenth-century world of formal 'great power primacy' so as to make room for identity and self-determination, one may wonder how far we have come when political identity remains at the mercy of some description of its place in a field of tension provided by others.

I do not make these points to disparage over the hopes of communities whose just desires are trampled upon by realpolitik – the primacy law gives to *uti possidetis* over secession, functional diplomacy, or simply the diktat by a 'Great Power' – but to focus on the way such contexts are constructed though standard debates on foreign policy and global governance. There is, as many of the chapters note, a constant process of lawfare going on between the opposing sides. Some of the authors even participate in it by judging on the appropriateness or *bona fides* of one party or another, marking their sympathies and antipathies accordingly. As is familiar from many other international themes, law, politics, and scholarship mix into each other. I have no grudge against that. But I wonder whether attention could be directed also to the background conditions of the debate. After all, arguments in lawfare tend to remain rather predictable and rarely succeed in convincing anyone not already committed. The use of Kosovo as precedent by Russia to support the secession of Donetsk and Luhansk, as discussed by Júlia Miklosová (Chapter 4, this volume), or the legal argumentation of Azerbaijan in the conflict over Nagorno-Karabakh as displayed by Sheila Paylan (Chapter 5, this volume) may indeed strike commentators as a particularly cynical use of a formalist vocabulary. But it is unclear whether the point of lawfare in these cases is at all designed to convince anyone. Instead, the intention may be rather to invoke Western hypocrisy and the obvious open-endedness of the language it has so often used in its favour. Or then the point might be the one celebrated long ago by Vattel, to show that, by paying lip-service to the formal standards, one insists in belonging to the group instead of being indicted as 'monsters, unworthy the name of men ... [or] enemies to the human race, in the same manner as, in civil society, professed assassins and incendiaries are guilty' (Vattel 2008 [1758]: III. 3, para. 34).[2] One feature of these discussions is their repetitiousness; everyone already knows the positions of the other, and knows that neither can win merely by the strength of what they claim. Suave institutional actors may – perhaps like the Sahrawi Arab Democratic Republic – play successfully in international institutions prima facie sympathetic to their cause (though, as we have seen, those efforts may be hampered by an ulterior move of some outside power for reasons quite unrelated to any of the official arguments).

---

[2] On the 'doctrine of pretext', see further Whitman 2021: 125–132.

What I mean is that, as the power of formal legal arguments diminishes and managerial pragmatism becomes the reigning style, might the aspiring communities themselves loosen the tyranny of those arguments – rules, principles, issues of status and standing – in favour of a more complex view of how to liberate themselves. I will end with a story. Some years ago, I travelled to a location where families of refugees and displaced persons had spent many years, in some cases decades. One activist pointed to me two small boys playing football, saying that 'if you asked them, where their home is, they would immediately give you the name of a village where their parents came from, although they have never been there. All their life plans concentrate on returning to that place'. The contention of 'returning' to a place one has never even seen stuck with me. A physical return in years or even decades did not seem realistic then, nor is it any more now that I write this. I felt sorry about the parents who had had to leave, but equally sorry for the boys whose future had been hijacked by the memories and the pain of the parents. Whatever struggle there may be ahead for them, its conditions and likely outcomes had already been dictated by a melancholy vocabulary of statehood, self-determination, and diplomatic possibility that offered little grounds for optimism and closed down or made invisible alternatives that might offer them an escape from ambiguity, vulnerability, and contested agency.

References

ICJ (1986). *Burkina Faso-Mali Boundary,* Reports 1986.
Jellinek, G. (1892). *System der subjektiven öffentlichen Rechte*. Freiburg: Siebeck.
Jellinek, G. (1905). *Allgemeine Staatslehre*. 2nd edn. Berlin: Häring.
Vattel, E. de. (2008 [1758]). *The Law of Nations*, edited with an Introduction by B. Kapossy and R. Whatmore. Philadelphia: Liberty Fund.
Whitman, J.Q. (2021). *The Verdict of Battle. The Law of Victory and the Making of Modern War*. Cambridge, MA: Harvard University Press.

Index

A

Abbott, Tony 77
Abkhaz-Georgian Conflict 241–242, 262
  Abkhazia and Russia 91–92, 160
  background to 151–159
  the borderland 161–166
  the ceasefire lines 159–163
Abraham Accords 143
African Union 133, 136, 141
agency 145, 238
  and ambiguity 2–3
  constrained agency 12–14, 249–256
Ahtisaari, Martti 86
Akande. D. 116, 117, 118
Algeria 1, 131, 141
Aliyev, Ilham 117, 118, 119
al Qaeda 66
ambiguity 25, 43, 95, 98, 130–136
  and agency 2–3
  ambiguities and volatility 129–130
  ambiguity dimension 96
  of contested states 4–7, 247, 249–256
  Kosovo's ambiguity of status 83
  Taiwan's ambiguity of status 45
Amirthalingam, Appapillai 180–181
anti-access/area-denial (A2/AD) 44, 55, 56
Apostolides v Orams 251, 252
armed conflicts 10, 129, 157–158, 161
  classification of 3, 133
  Kosovo 86–87
  laws of 5, 63, 69–71, 74, 135
  Nagorno-Karabakh Conflict 106–107, 114–119
  Sri Lanka 66–67, 70–74, 182
  Western Sahara 133, 140–142
  see also force, use of
Armenia 119
  Armenians of Nagorno-Karabakh 106–107, 111
  and ECtHR 201–203
  interpretations of UN resolutions 108
  people forced to leave 117–118
  see also Nagorno-Karabakh Conflict
arms trade 38, 50, 55

Azerbaijan 1, 8, 9, 14, 241
  (il)legality of the use of force by 114–119
  background to conflict 105–107
  and ECtHR 202
  interpretations of legal instruments 110–111
  military assault by 107, 241
  Nagorno-Karabakh Republic dissolution 106

B

Baker Plans 134
Bandaranaike, Srimavo 180
Bangladesh 6, 7
Bartelson, J. 49
Biden, Joe 56
blockade by Azerbaijan 107, 110
Bogollogama, Rohitha 67
borders 11, 153–159, 161–163, 166
  administrative boundary line (ABL) 152
  customs checkpoint 182
  and everyday life 165, 167
  former borders of USSR 91
Bryant, Rebecca 15, 188
Bucha, massacres in 71
buffer zones 107, 140
Bush, George
  and al Qaeda 66
  terrorism and Sri Lanka 68, 76

C

Canadian government 75
Caroline Criteria 68
Cassese, Antonio 31
ceasefire agreements (CfAs) 3, 14, 107, 129, 254
  Abkhaz-Georgian conflict 151–156, 156–158
  ceasefire violations 67, 140
  managing the ceasefire line 167, 255
  Minsk II ceasefire agreement 94
  navigating the CfL 163–166
  Norwegian-brokered 66
Celebici case 70

Chechen Republic 9, 87, 160
Chelvanayakam, S.J.V 180
China 6, 8, 30, 36, 46, 218
 China's use of force 42
 Chinese Civil War in 1949 27
 containment policy towards China 56
 economic power 54, 56, 58
 geopolitical importance of 51, 55, 59
 military capability 27, 44, 55–58
 One-China policy 29, 36, 39, 47, 239–240
 sovereignty and territorial integrity 31
 as Taiwan's parent state 43
Chiragov and Others vs Armenia 109
choice theory 236, 238, 247
Chu, Ming-Chin Monique 14, 239, 240, 260
civilians 10, 63, 256
 civilian casualties 71, 72, 76, 78
 as human shields 74
 protection of 135
 targeting of civilians 144
civil war 43, 75, 77, 106, 117, 179, 218
colonialism 6, 174, 242
 and continuity position 237
 former Spanish colony 131, 132
 and Russia 156
 and self-determination 236
 and sovereignty 175
 and Sri Lanka 180, 186
combatants 3, 10, 11, 133, 144
 legal symmetry of 65–66
contested states 27, 33, 98, 213–214
 ambiguity of 4–7
 contested statehood 129–130
 dimensions of 1–4, 45
 and the ECtHR 197–204, 204–209
 four normative positions 235–239
 grey zones of 12–14, 250
 and international audience 212
 legal ambiguities 254–256
 photographers of 195–197
 and right of self-defence 38
 and vulnerability 8–12, 247
 see also ambiguity; recognition
continuity position 237, 239, 241, 246
 of Georgia 242
 interpretations of the 247
Coppieters, Bruno 15, 90
Corell, Hans 135, 137
Corten, O. 30, 34
COVID-19 pandemic 49
Crane, David 72–76
Crawford, J. 8, 212, 215
crime, transnational 10, 48, 49, 222
Crimea 83, 96, 243–245
 Crimea's secession 93–94, 246
Cyprus, property in
 see Turkish Republic of Northern Cyprus (TRNC)

D

decolonization 70, 180, 237
 following World War II 154
 ideology of decolonization 112
 and self-determination 111, 145
 from Spain 245
 and Western Sahara 129–133, 136
de facto regimes 145, 240, 252
 concept of 173–176
 de facto administrator 133, 214
 de facto independence 130
 de facto recognition 45–48
de jure 45, 46–48
 Ukrainian territory 97
democracy 27, 48, 175
de Silva, Desmond 72–76
diplomacy 3, 26, 46, 47, 261
 between Algeria and Morocco 140, 143
 diplomatic relations 27, 34, 131
displaced people 10–11, 70, 72, 107, 158, 264
 of entire population 241
 of the Kosovo Albanian population 85
dissolution of a region 105, 120, 237
 Soviet Union 91, 111, 153
documents 160, 161, 163, 165
 passports 14, 48, 156, 160, 165, 166
Donbas 7, 9, 94, 204, 212
Donetsk 1, 15, 83, 94
 and ECtHR 203–204
Dörr, O. 52
Doshi, R. 55
double standards, accusations of 91, 93, 97, 99
dramaturgical approach 176
 see also performative perspective
Dutch nationals killed on flight 203

E

East Jerusalem 225
economy/trade 4, 26, 137, 159, 162, 250
 economic relations 34, 47, 54, 57, 145
 merchants 13
 of natural resources 136
 and Taiwan 48, 50
Ediger, M.L. 54
effective control 109–110, 131
effectivist position 238, 244, 246
elections 27, 49, 177, 181, 187
electricity delivery 159, 163–164
elites 45, 258
embassies/consulates 26, 47, 142, 225
emphasis on results 76, 77
Enguri/Ingur River 14, 152, 154, 158, 161
 and movement across 160
 security zone 157
Ethiopia-Eritrea Claims Commission 117
ethnic groups 120, 121, 165, 180
 and continuity position 237
 distinct ethnic groups 52, 120

ethnic Armenians 106–107, 110, 118, 201
ethnic Chinese 59
ethnic cleansing 85, 112, 118, 237
ethnic Russians 114
and passports 165
Tamils of Sri Lanka 179–180
Eurasian international law 155
European Court of Human Rights (ECtHR) 15, 91, 214
and contested states 197–204, 204–209
and Donetsk and Luhansk 203–204
and Nagorno-Karabakh 201–203
Nagorno-Karabakh Conflict 109–110
and Northern Cyprus 205–209
and Transnistria 200–201, 207–209
European Union 133, 139
ambiguity of 145
EU-Morocco trade agreements 138, 139
and Sahrawi lawfare 137–140

F

Falk, R. 86
Feigenbaum, Evan 68, 69
Fernández-Molina, Irene 14, 245, 261
force, use of 3, 5, 9, 26, 29, 31, 215
by Azerbaijan 114–119
as means of last resort 247
by third states 6–7
forced disappearances 72
France 143, 157, 246, 247
French, David 2
Frowein, J.A. 52
functionalism 217–218, 226, 260
and colonialism 261

G

Gandhi, Rajiv 69, 183
Gaza 1, 37, 70, 221, 225
Geldenhuys, D. 45
Geneva Convention 10, 66, 133, 135, 221
breaches of the 70
and human shields 74
genocide/atrocities 107, 237
alleged genocide 93, 94, 96, 245
Bucha massacre 71
by Pakistani Forces 7
Sri Lanka 70–76, 186
geopolitical factors 43, 51, 121, 255
Georgia 39, 92
Georgia-Russia war 89, 157, 160
occupied territories law 162
see also Abkhaz-Georgian Conflict
Gessen, Masha 87
Ghali, Brahim 140
globalization 48
Goffman, E. 176
great-power politics 54–59, 69, 258, 262
Greek Cypriots' property 249–253

Grzybowski, Janis 15, 244, 245, 260
Guerguerat 140

H

Hague Convention 135
Harris, P. 57
Hatay, M. 188
Henderson, Christian 14, 51, 239, 240
High Court of Justice (UK) 252
historical contexts 113, 121, 154, 172, 237
historic Azerbaijani land 118
Russian and Crimea 94
hostage rescue narrative 72
humanitarian crisis 44, 85, 86, 160
starvation 107
human rights 3, 35, 108, 112, 214
and distinctive peoples 52
and ethnic identity 121
and Tamil nationalist politics 185, 186
violations by Azerbaijan 117–118
violations in Kosovo 88, 237
violations in Moldova 201
violations in Nagorno-Karabakh 203
violations of 6, 187, 204
see also European Court of Human Rights
human shields 73–76
Hurd, Ian 64, 66

I

Ichkeria 9
Ilascu case 200, 207–208
independence 6, 236, 237
declarations of 5, 26, 83, 93, 132, 220
stable regimes 52
India 7, 69, 70, 182, 183, 185
inequality 259
information technology 51
International Committee of the Red Cross 134
International Court of Justice 31, 37, 69, 70, 113, 260
interpretations by 213
and Kosovo 83–91, 217–221, 244
and Lachin corridor 110–111
and Palestine 221–226
International Criminal Court (ICC) 70, 214, 246
and Palestine 221–225
international humanitarian law (IHL) 10, 11, 106, 109, 130, 134, 144, 246
international law
and ambiguous states 4–7
applicable to resource activities 137
of blockade 37
and contested states 66–70, 70–76
destabilization of 99
enabling violence 10, 63–64, 77, 105, 241, 243

267

and ethics of secession 235
Eurasian international law 155
and international politics 64–70
interpretations of 109–111, 159
and Kosovo 88–91
and legitimation of state violence 63–64
and Nagorno-Karabakh 111–116
political performative interventions 187
and post-Soviet borders creation 153–159
principles of 89, 112, 166
Russian recognition practices 91–96
serving national agendas 120
and threat of force against Taiwan 51–59
tools and language of 84
vulnerability in law 8
see also sovereignty; statehood
international organizations, membership of 5, 26, 46
international peace and security 29, 237
and internal disputes 53, 238
threat from China 54, 240
international relations 4, 12, 28, 30, 37, 54, 198
and critical legalism 64–70
perspectives 43
scholarship 136
Israel 1, 37, 143, 246
illegal annexation 226
Israeli assault 70
occupation by 221–222, 225

J

Japan 6, 56, 57
Jellinek, George 259–260
Jerusalem 223, 225, 246
jus ad bellum 8, 64, 65–70, 115, 239
and Taiwan 27, 39, 40
jus cogens 33, 97
jus in bello 10, 65, 70–76, 133

K

Kabylie 143
Kennedy, David 65
Ker-Lindsay, J. 86, 90
Kittrie, O.F. 137, 144
Klem, Bart 14, 243, 255, 262
Knoll-Tudor, B. 115–116
Köhler, Horst 141
Korean War 53, 152
Koskenniemi, Martti 15, 111, 112
Kosovo 6, 15, 214, 243–245, 260
background to the case 85–88
declaration of independence 83, 85–91, 218–220
ICJ Advisory Opinion on 84, 88–91, 97, 217–221
impact of the recognition of 244
under international administration 86–87

people of 220, 226
and Russia's recognition practice 91–96
Krasner, S.D. 45, 132
Kurdish territory of Rojava 260

L

Lachin corridor 110–111, 202
Lagerwall, Anne 15, 260
Lai, William 44
lawfare 136–140, 137, 138, 249, 263
lawfare (legal activism) and warfare 130
legal activism
see lawfare
Le Pavic, Gaëlle 14, 241–242, 254, 255, 262
Liberation Tigers of Tamil Eelam (LTTE) 14, 63
contested state of Tamil Eelam 66–70
fighting and justifications 70–77
and international law 66–70
nationalist aspirations 179–118
performing after defeat 184–189
separatism experimentation 187–189
sovereign experiment 181–184
Tamil diaspora 183, 185, 187
Tamil Eelam 9, 15, 66–70, 77, 182, 186, 187, 242–243
Tamil victimhood 185, 187, 188
terrorist credentials 67, 77
used civilians as human shields 71–72
Loizidou case 199–200, 206, 251, 252
Luhansk 1, 83, 94

M

Malaysian Airlines Flight 17 203–204
managerial pragmatism 264
Manchukuo 6
Mauritania 131, 135
McKinley, J.M. 57
Mearsheimer, J.J. 55, 58
Medvedev, Dmitry 89, 157
'might is right' approach 120
migration crisis 143
Miklasová, Júlia 14, 161, 244–245, 254, 263
Milanovic, M. 89, 94
mimicry, institutional 177, 188, 189, 243
Mingrelians 165
missing people 72, 134, 250
Moldovan Republic of Transnistria 15, 91
and ECtHR 200–201, 207–209
Montevideo Convention on the Rights and Duties of States (1933) 4, 5, 26
Morocco 70, 145, 245
de facto control of Western Sahara 131
and the EU 137–139
human rights violations by 136
military action by 140–144
sovereignty recognised by US 69
and United Nations 135

violation of the ceasefire 142
and the Western Sahara 129–136
Mullaitivu 63, 71
Muslim community 68

N

Nagorno-Karabakh Conflict 1, 8–9, 15
  (mis) application of international law 111–114
  (mis) interpretation of judgement 109–111
  background to 105–107
  and the continuity position 241
  and ECtHR 201–203
  forced dissolution 119–120
  Lachlin corridor and ICJ 110–111
  leaders of 10
  UNSC resolutions 107–109
  use of force by Azerbaijan 114–119
Namibia 213
natural resources 137, 138, 250
Netherlands and plane disaster 203
non-governmental organizations (NGOs) 137
non-intervention tenet 5, 42, 52, 239
normalization 183, 253, 254, 256
North Atlantic Treaty Organization 85, 92, 218
  bombing against Serbia 87
  bombing of Yugoslavia 96
  membership prevented by Russia 92
Norwegian-facilitated ceasefire 182
nuclear weapons 31, 44, 54, 58

O

occupation 9, 37, 237
  conduct of occupying powers 11
  and decolonization 130–131
  by Israel 221–222, 225
  under lasting occupations 11
  Nagorno-Karabakh Conflict 116–119
  reclaiming territory 115
  by Russia 162
  and the UN 108, 135–136
Oltramonti, Giulia Prelz 14, 241–242, 254, 255, 262
oppression 6, 243, 245
Organization of African Unity (OUA) 132, 133
OSCE Minsk Group 107, 108, 115
Oslo Accords 225

P

Pacific Ocean 54, 57
Pakistan 6, 7
Palestine 6, 11, 213, 214, 245–246, 260
  illegal annexation 222
  membership in the United Nations 225
  Palestinian strategies 137
  and UNGA/ICJ/ICC 221–226

parent states 9, 27, 37, 212
  and the contested element 30
  recognition by the parent state 236
  use of armed force by 8
Paylan, Sheila 241, 254, 263
peacekeeping force 69, 152, 157
Pelosi, Nancy 44
people 38
  and borders 153, 159–160, 166
  in crossfire 8–13
  definition of a 'people' 220, 240
  and minority safeguards 53, 131, 180
  rights of 31, 32, 111, 121, 138
  security/welfare of 27, 259, 260
  and self-determination 6, 31, 53, 140
  vulnerability of 3, 189
  see also displaced people; refugees
performative perspective 172–173, 226, 243, 255
  expectations of audiences 262
  institutional performances 176, 177
  of sovereignty 177–179
  of Tamil nationalism 179–181, 184–189
Peters, A. 90
photographers of contested states 195–197
Polisario Front
  see Sahrawi Arab Democratic Republic
power 11, 55, 65
Prescott, J.R.V. 39
Price, Megan 14, 242–243, 254, 262
prisoners of war 10, 133, 134
property 158, 249, 251–252
proportionality 71, 72, 73, 74, 241
puppet states 6, 113, 204
Putin, Vladimir 83, 93, 160, 245

R

Rajapaksa family 67, 71, 75, 76, 184
Rambouillet accords 86
Randelzhofer, A. 52
ratione personae 14, 25, 27, 29, 33
  see also force, use of
real estate market 251–253
realities on the ground 4, 151, 167
recognition 25, 38, 46, 131, 215
  and international law 4–6
  international recognition 120, 130
  of Kosovo 87
  of Moroccan sovereignty 129
  of Nagorno-Karabakh 111
  of Palestine 225
  of Taiwan 27, 239
  that should be denied 198–204
referendums 84, 114, 131, 143, 145, 238, 251
  Crimea 94, 245
  Donetsk referendum 203
  Tamil nationalism 179, 186

refugees 13, 44, 107, 110, 158, 264
  EU-Turkey deal on migration 255
  status of refugees 10
remedial position 6, 15, 89, 220, 237, 240, 244, 247
repatriation 49
Republic of China (ROC)
  see Taiwan
rights 3, 6, 26, 52, 120
  equal rights 113
  to property 199, 201–203, 206, 251–252
  rights of free movement 250
  see also human rights
Rome Statute 222, 223, 224
Roth, B.R. 30
Russia 6, 14, 42, 71
  and Abkhaz-Georgian conflict 155–162, 242
  borders in post-Soviet regions 153–159
  and Chechen Republic 9, 52
  and ECtHR 203–204, 209
  illegal use of force 97, 98
  Malaysian Airlines Flight 17 203
  and Nagorno-Karabakh conflict 106–107, 111, 114
  Russian Federation 84, 87, 95
  Russia's contradictory position 156
  Russo-Georgian War 157, 159, 160
  sanctions imposed on Russia 165
  and Transnistria 200–201
  Ukraine: abduction of children 203
  Ukraine: invasion/annexation 1, 83–84, 244–245, 254, 263
  Ukraine: justifications of 87–89, 94–96
  Ukraine: pro-Russian Ukrainians 220
  Ukraine: recognition practices 91–96
  Ukraine: three-step integration scheme 84

S

Sahrawi Arab Democratic Republic 14, 70, 245
  armed struggle 140–144
  background of 129–136
  as a contested state 144–146
  and lawfare 136–140
  Polisario-held territory 69
  refugee camps 131
  Sahrawi people 130, 133
  Sahrawis 'state of war' narrative 142, 245
Samaraweera, Mangala 67
same-sex marriage 49
sanctions 34, 57, 165
Sarkozy, Nicolas 157
Savendra, Silva, 75
Scott, Shirley 64, 65
secession 6, 52, 67, 90, 91, 95, 260
  delegitimized movements 111
  ethics of secession 235, 238
  manufactured secessions 83–84, 92–96, 98
  remedial 15, 89, 92, 96, 237, 240, 244
  secessionist conflicts 151–153
  secessions of Ukrainian territories 83, 94, 96
self-defence 3, 8, 114
  right of self-defence 35–39, 239
  right to reclaim territories 115, 116
self-determination 6, 7, 89, 111, 154, 215
  denial of self-determination 11
  the ethnic Armenian population 114
  external self-determination 220, 244
  right to 129, 130, 132, 139, 221, 240, 246
semiconductors 50–51, 51, 56, 59
separatism 11, 117, 175
  creating the separatist entities 91
  post-Soviet separatism 91
  separatism experimentation 187–189
  separatist movements and *de facto* states 172
Serbia 9, 83–86, 217–219, 243
Shahramanyan, S. 119
Shaw, Martin 35
Silvestre, Rodríguez 115–116
Sinhalese 180, 181, 183, 184, 242
South Korea 56, 57
South Ossetia 91, 92, 94, 161
sovereignty 8, 42, 43, 238
  and Azerbaijan 105, 108
  concept of 2, 3, 5, 8, 45, 173–176
  and dissolution of Soviet Union 111
  four-component sovereignty 45
  Kelsenian view of 261
  and minorities 121
  over natural resources 137
  and self-determination in conflict 120
  sovereign experimentation 188
  sovereign performance 182
Spain 93, 131, 143, 246
  administration of Western Sahara 132, 145
speculative legalities 251–254
  and constrained agency 249–256
Sri Lanka 14, 15, 242–243, 254
  and international law 66–70
  legitimization of violence 63–64, 76–77
  use of force by government 70–77
  before the war 179–181
  see also Liberation Tigers of Tamil Eelam (LTTE)
Stalin, Joseph 106, 155
statehood 3, 212–217
  criteria of statehood 2, 26, 259
  'grey zone' of statehood 130
  legal character of 90, 215
  militancy becoming state-like 177
  performances of statehood 262
  state agency 12–14
  state-building 4, 155, 189, 215, 258
  state dissolution 105–106
  see also ambiguity; contested states

states-in-exile 129, 131, 144, 145
status quo 115, 116, 250, 260
Stolzenberg, Nomi 253, 254, 256
Sudan 143
sui generis arguments 88, 90, 94, 98, 220, 244, 245
Sukhumi 160
Syria 260

T

Taiwan 14, 28, 29, 239–241
  ambiguous status of 40, 43, 240
  bilateral agreements 47
  as a contested state 37–39, 43–51
  derecognition by US 38
  geopolitical importance of 50, 51
  recognition of 46
  right to collective self-defence 52
  right to self-determination 53
  semiconductor industry 50
  Strait tensions 8, 27, 30, 44, 57
  Taiwan Policy Act 2022 56
  Taiwan Relations Act 42
  Taiwan's military 56
  Taiwan's national security policy 36
  Taiwan's population 44
  threat of force against 33–35, 42–45, 51–59, 239
  transition to democracy 48–49
Tamil nationalist militancy in Sri Lanka *see* Liberation Tigers of Tamil Eelam (LTTE)
territorial integrity 87, 91, 105
  and Morocco 153, 154
  Nagorno-Karabakh conflict 3, 111–113, 117, 241
  principle of 8, 213, 215, 235, 259
  and Taiwan 28, 32, 52, 67
terrorism 1, 10, 36, 49
  al Qaeda 66
  LTTE as terrorists 67–68, 68, 76, 184, 212
  war on terror 14, 68, 76, 243
third parties 10, 32, 39, 40, 42, 55, 212, 239
Thottam, Jyoti 76
Tindouf 131
Transnistria 15, 91, 200–201, 207–209
Trump, Donald 141
  China and containment policy 55
  and a global US retreat 56
  sovereignty of W.Sahara 69, 129, 143
Tsagourias, Nicholas 33
Turkey 7, 9, 107, 160, 255
Turkish Republic of Northern Cyprus (TRNC) 15, 188
  and ECtHR 199–200, 205–209
  foreign investors in 249
  Loizidou case 199–200
  property in 251–253
Tzanakopoulos, A. 116, 117, 118

U

Ukraine 14, 42, 244–245, 254
  Crimea 83, 93–94, 96, 243–246
  Donbas 7, 9, 94, 204, 212
  Donetsk 1, 15, 83, 94, 203–204
  invasion/annexation of 1, 83, 84, 94, 95, 209
  Luhansk 1, 83
  massacres/atrocities in 71
  and pro-Russia Ukrainians 114, 220
  Russia's justification of actions 87–89, 92–94
  separatist/secession 95–97, 98
  status of Ukrainian territories 96–98
  Zaporizhzhia and Kherson Regions 83
unique case argument 50, 88, 95, 114
United Nations
  1970 Declaration of Friendly Relations 31
  China/Taiwan and use of force 28–32
  membership of 27, 28, 46, 221, 222
  and Nagorno-Karabakh conflict 107–109
  non-intervention tenet 42
  Observer Mission in Georgia 157
  'peacefully resolve disputes' 53, 69
  peacekeeping mission 144
  and self-defence 115, 116, 131
  self-defence and third parties 35–37
  and self-determination 6, 213
  and Sri Lanka 186, 187, 188
  and Sri Lankan massacre 71–72, 75
  and use of force 8
  Western Sahara conflict 133–135, 141, 144, 145
  see also International Court of Justice
United States 30, 42, 54, 57, 75, 218, 225
  1955 Formosan Resolution 38
  defence need for semiconductors 56
  and global role retreat 55
  and Jerusalem embassy 246
  and LTTE 69
  military strategy 55, 56, 57, 74, 76
  and Moroccan sovereignty 140, 142–143
  N. Pelosi 44
  President Biden 56
  President Bush 66, 68, 76
  President Trump 55, 56, 69, 129, 141, 143
  and Taiwan 44, 239
  and threats from China 43, 51, 55, 58, 59
  use of armed forces by the president 38
  war on terror 67–68, 76, 243
'unlawful combatants' 66
uti possidetis principle 263
  borders in Karabagh 112
  and the continuity position 237
  and Russia 154–156
  Russia and secession 91, 95

V

values, shared 47
Vattel, E. 263
Vidmar, J. 86, 96

Vienna Convention 28, 33, 35, 119, 224
volatility 14, 44
  and warfare in Western Sahara 140–144
  in Western Sahara 129
voluntary human shields 74
vulnerability 2, 14
  and contested states 3–4
  and individuals 10, 242, 243, 247
  in law and war 8–12
  LTTE 'by law' 77, 78, 243, 255
  of Polisaro Front 133, 144, 145
  and Taiwan 26, 40, 43, 51, 239

W

Wall advisory opinion 37
war crimes 106, 119, 187
  in Gaza 70
warfare 129–130
war on terror 68, 76, 243
Wellman, Christopher Heath 236
Western hypocrisy 263
Western Sahara Conflict 70
  consent of the people 11, 139, 140, 145
  decolonization of 129–130, 245–246
  and ICJ 213
  occupied territory 136
  US and Moroccan sovereignty 69, 129, 143
  as a war zone 142
  Western Sahara's waters 137, 138
  see also Sahrawi Arab Democratic Republic
Western universalism 155
Westphalian principle 42, 45, 132
  and domestic sovereignty 48–50
Wu, Joseph 46

X

Xenides-Arestis 206
Xi, Jinping 58

Y

Yerevan 9, 118
Yugoslavia 6, 70, 85, 96, 217
  breakup of 88

Z

Zaporizhzhia and Kherson Regions 83

www.ingramcontent.com/pod-product-compliance
Lightning Source LLC
Chambersburg PA
CBHW051531020426
42333CB00016B/1880